# First World War

## and Army of Occupation

# War Diary

## France, Belgium and Germany

47 DIVISION
140 Infantry Brigade
London Regiment 15th (County of London) Battalion
(P.W.O. Civil Service Rifles)
and London Regiment 17th (County of London) Battalion
(Poplar and Stepney Rifles)
17 March 1915 - 5 May 1919

WO95/2732/1

The Naval & Military Press Ltd
www.nmarchive.com
**Published in association with The National Archives**

Published by

The Naval & Military Press Ltd

Unit 10 Ridgewood Industrial Park,
Uckfield, East Sussex,
TN22 5QE England
Tel: +44 (0) 1825 749494

www.naval-military-press.com
www.nmarchive.com

*This diary has been reprinted in facsimile from the original. Any imperfections are inevitably reproduced and the quality may fall short of modern type and cartographic standards.*

# Contents

| Document type | Place/Title | Date From | Date To |
|---|---|---|---|
| Heading | WO95/2732 47 Div Mar' 15-May' 19 1/15 London R. | | |
| Heading | 47th Division 140th Infy Bde 1-15th London Regiment Mar 1915-May 1919. | | |
| Heading | 140th Inf. Bde. 47th Division. Battn disembarked Havre from England 18.3.15. War Diary 1/15th London Regt. March & April (17.3.15-30.4.15) 1915. | | |
| Heading | War Diary of 15th. Battn London Regt. (P.W.O. Civil Service Rifles) from 17th March 1915. Vol I. | | |
| War Diary | | 17/03/1915 | 30/04/1915 |
| Heading | 104th Inf. Bde. 47th Division. War Diary 1/15th London Regt. May 1915. | | |
| Heading | War Diary of 15th Battn London Regiment. (Prince of Water Own Civil Service Rifles) from 1st to 31st May 1915. Volume II. | | |
| War Diary | Abeuvriere | 01/05/1915 | 06/05/1915 |
| War Diary | Tuning Fork (Festubert) | 07/05/1915 | 10/05/1915 |
| War Diary | Festubert | 11/05/1915 | 01/06/1915 |
| Heading | 140th Inf. Bde. 47th Division. War Diary 1/15th London Regt. June 1915. | | |
| Heading | War Diary of 15th Battn London Regt. (Prince of Water Own Civil Service Rifles) from 1st to 30th June 1915. Volume III. | | |
| War Diary | Bethune | 01/06/1915 | 01/06/1915 |
| War Diary | Sailly La Bourse | 02/06/1915 | 07/06/1915 |
| War Diary | Les Brebis | 08/06/1915 | 10/06/1915 |
| War Diary | Grenay | 11/06/1915 | 17/06/1915 |
| War Diary | Mazingarbe & Le Philosophe | 18/06/1915 | 21/06/1915 |
| War Diary | Fosse No.7 | 22/06/1915 | 26/06/1915 |
| War Diary | Le Philosophe & Mazingabbe | 27/06/1915 | 27/06/1915 |
| War Diary | Le Philosophe | 28/06/1915 | 28/06/1915 |
| War Diary | Noeux Les Mines | 29/06/1915 | 30/06/1915 |
| Heading | 140th Bde. 47th Division. War Diary 1/15th Battalion London Regiment. July 1915 | | |
| War Diary | Noeux-Les-Mines. | 01/07/1915 | 01/07/1915 |
| War Diary | Mazingarbe | 02/07/1915 | 31/07/1915 |
| Heading | 140th Bde. 47th Division. War Diary 1/15th Battalion London Regiment August 1915. | | |
| Heading | War Diary of 15th Batt. London Regt (Civil Service Rifles) for August 1915. | | |
| War Diary | | 01/08/1915 | 31/08/1915 |
| Heading | 140th Bde. 47th Division. War Diary 1/15th Battalion London Regiment September and October 1915. | | |
| Heading | War Diary for September 1915 of 15th Batt. London Regt (P.W.O. Civil Service Rifles) | | |
| Heading | | 01/09/1915 | 30/09/1915 |
| Heading | War Diary of 15th Batt London Regt (P.W.O. Civil Service Rifles) for October 1915. | | |
| War Diary | | 01/10/1915 | 31/10/1915 |
| Heading | 1/15' Battalion London Regiment (P.W.O. Civil Service Rifles.) War Diary. -October, 1917. Vol 28. | | |

| | | | |
|---|---|---|---|
| War Diary | Front Line | 01/10/1917 | 03/10/1917 |
| War Diary | Aubrey Camp near Roclincourt | 04/10/1917 | 09/10/1917 |
| War Diary | Support | 10/10/1917 | 17/10/1917 |
| War Diary | Front Line | 18/10/1917 | 31/10/1917 |
| Heading | 1/15' Battn. London Regt. (P.W.D. Civil Service Rifles) War Diary. -November, 1917. Vol 29. | | |
| War Diary | Aubrey Camp | 01/11/1917 | 04/11/1917 |
| War Diary | Front Line | 05/11/1917 | 08/11/1917 |
| War Diary | Roundhay Camp | 09/11/1917 | 17/11/1917 |
| War Diary | Ecoivres | 18/11/1917 | 20/11/1917 |
| War Diary | Hermaville | 21/11/1917 | 21/11/1917 |
| War Diary | Wanquetin | 22/11/1917 | 22/11/1917 |
| War Diary | Gouy En Artois. | 23/11/1917 | 23/11/1917 |
| War Diary | Courcelles Le Comte | 24/11/1917 | 24/11/1917 |
| War Diary | Beaulencourt | 25/11/1917 | 26/11/1917 |
| War Diary | Doignies | 27/11/1917 | 30/11/1917 |
| Operation(al) Order(s) | Civil Service Rifles. Order No. 63. | 04/11/1917 | 04/11/1917 |
| Operation(al) Order(s) | Civil Service Rifles. Order No 89. | 17/11/1917 | 17/11/1917 |
| Operation(al) Order(s) | Civil Service Rifles. Order No 86. | | |
| Operation(al) Order(s) | Civil Service Rifles. Order No. 90. | 20/11/1917 | 20/11/1917 |
| Operation(al) Order(s) | Civil Service Rifles. Order No. 91. | 22/11/1917 | 22/11/1917 |
| Operation(al) Order(s) | Civil Service Rifles. Order No. 92. | 22/11/1917 | 22/11/1917 |
| Operation(al) Order(s) | Civil Service Rifles. Order No. 93 | 23/11/1917 | 23/11/1917 |
| Miscellaneous | Civil Service Rifles. | 01/11/1917 | 01/11/1917 |
| Heading | 1/15th Bn London Regt (P.W.O. Civil Service Rifles) War Diary. -December, 1917. Vol 30. | | |
| War Diary | Bourlon Wood. | 01/12/1917 | 01/12/1917 |
| War Diary | Havrincourt Wood. | 02/12/1917 | 03/12/1917 |
| War Diary | Graincourt | 04/12/1917 | 06/12/1917 |
| War Diary | Havrincourt Wood | 07/12/1917 | 07/12/1917 |
| War Diary | Bertincourt | 08/12/1917 | 15/12/1917 |
| War Diary | Front Line | 16/12/1917 | 21/12/1917 |
| War Diary | Morlancourt | 22/12/1917 | 29/12/1917 |
| War Diary | Mericourt | 30/12/1917 | 31/12/1917 |
| Miscellaneous | 140 Infantry Brigade | 13/12/1917 | 13/12/1917 |
| Miscellaneous | 1/15th Bn London Regiment Report on Operations December 4th 5th and 6th 1917 around Graincourt | 04/12/1917 | 04/12/1917 |
| Miscellaneous | Civil Service Rifles. Narrative of Operations covering period from 28th November 1917 to night of 1/2nd December, 1917 | 28/11/1917 | 28/11/1917 |
| Heading | War Diary. of 1/15" Bn. London Regt. (P.W.O. Civil Service Rifles.) from 1st January 1918 to 31st January 1918. Vol 31. | | |
| War Diary | Mericourt | 01/01/1918 | 10/01/1918 |
| War Diary | Bertincourt | 11/01/1918 | 11/01/1918 |
| War Diary | Ribecourt | 12/01/1918 | 12/01/1918 |
| War Diary | In Support. | 12/01/1918 | 24/01/1918 |
| War Diary | Front Line | 16/01/1918 | 24/01/1918 |
| War Diary | Bertincourt | 25/01/1918 | 31/01/1918 |
| Miscellaneous | Civil Service Rifles. Entraining Orders. | 09/01/1918 | 09/01/1918 |
| Operation(al) Order(s) | Civil Service Rifles. Order No. 100. | 23/01/1918 | 23/01/1918 |
| Operation(al) Order(s) | Civil Service Rifles Order No.99 | 15/01/1918 | 15/01/1918 |
| Operation(al) Order(s) | 1/15 Bn London Regiment. Order No. 97. | 12/01/1918 | 12/01/1918 |
| Heading | 140th Inf. Bde. 47th Division. War Diary 1/15th London Regt. November 1915. | | |
| War Diary | A 2 Section | 01/11/1915 | 07/11/1915 |

| | | | |
|---|---|---|---|
| War Diary | A 1 Section. | 08/11/1915 | 13/11/1915 |
| War Diary | Mazingarbe | 14/11/1915 | 14/11/1915 |
| War Diary | Lillers | 15/11/1915 | 30/11/1915 |
| Heading | 140th Inf. Bde. 47th Division. War Diary 1/15th London Regt. December 1915. | | |
| Heading | War Diary of 15th Battalion London Regiment (Prince of Wales Own Civil Service Rifles) Territorial Force for December 1915. | | |
| War Diary | Lillers | 01/12/1915 | 31/12/1915 |
| Heading | Jan 1916 | | |
| Heading | War Diary of the 15th Bn London Regiment (Prince of Wales Own Civil Service Rifles) from 1st to 31st January 1916. Vol VII. | | |
| War Diary | Sub-Section D2 | 01/01/1916 | 01/01/1916 |
| War Diary | Vermelles | 02/01/1916 | 02/01/1916 |
| War Diary | Houchin | 03/01/1916 | 03/01/1916 |
| War Diary | Les Brebis | 04/01/1916 | 04/01/1916 |
| War Diary | Sub Section C Maroc Sector. | 05/01/1916 | 07/01/1916 |
| War Diary | Les Brebis | 08/01/1916 | 31/01/1916 |
| Heading | Feb 1916. | | |
| Heading | War Diary of the 15th Bn London Regiment (P.W.O. Civil Service Rifles) for the month of February 1916. Vol VIII. | | |
| War Diary | Maroc. | 01/02/1916 | 01/02/1916 |
| War Diary | Bracquemont | 02/02/1916 | 29/02/1916 |
| Heading | March 1916 | | |
| Heading | 1/15 London Regt. Vol IX. | | |
| Heading | War Diary of the 15th Battn. London Regt. (P.W.O. Civil Service Rifles) for the month of March 1916. | | |
| War Diary | | 21/03/1916 | 21/03/1916 |
| War Diary | Ablain St Nazaire | 21/03/1916 | 26/03/1916 |
| War Diary | Verdrel | 26/03/1916 | 26/03/1916 |
| War Diary | Fresnicourt | 27/03/1916 | 31/03/1916 |
| War Diary | Erny St Julian | 01/03/1916 | 03/03/1916 |
| War Diary | Coyecques | 04/03/1916 | 08/03/1916 |
| War Diary | Nedon | 09/03/1916 | 09/03/1916 |
| War Diary | Divion | 10/03/1916 | 12/03/1916 |
| War Diary | Bouvigny Wood | 13/03/1916 | 13/03/1916 |
| War Diary | Ablain St Nazaire | 14/03/1916 | 21/03/1916 |
| Heading | April 1916 | | |
| Heading | 1/15 London Regt Vol 10 April 1916. | | |
| War Diary | Fresnicourt | 01/04/1916 | 01/04/1916 |
| War Diary | Bouvigny | 02/04/1916 | 02/04/1916 |
| War Diary | Huts | 03/04/1916 | 06/04/1916 |
| War Diary | Villers Au Bois. | 07/04/1916 | 07/04/1916 |
| War Diary | Souchez Centre | 08/04/1916 | 13/04/1916 |
| War Diary | Maisnil Bouche | 14/04/1916 | 19/04/1916 |
| War Diary | Villers Au Bois | 20/04/1916 | 24/04/1916 |
| War Diary | Souchez Left | 25/04/1916 | 30/04/1916 |
| Heading | May 1916 | | |
| War Diary | | 01/05/1916 | 01/05/1916 |
| War Diary | Fresnicourt | 02/05/1916 | 07/05/1916 |
| War Diary | Bouvigny Huts | 08/05/1916 | 13/05/1916 |
| War Diary | Ablain St Nazaire | 14/05/1916 | 20/05/1916 |
| War Diary | Camblain L'Abbe | 21/05/1916 | 31/05/1916 |

| | | | |
|---|---|---|---|
| Miscellaneous | 15th Battalion London Regiment (P.W.O. Civil Service Rifles) Operation Orders. | 14/05/1916 | 14/05/1916 |
| Heading | June 1916 | | |
| Heading | War Diary of 15th Battn. London Regiment (P.W.O. Civil Service Rifles) for June 1916. Vol 12. | | |
| War Diary | Calonne Ricquoart | 01/06/1916 | 11/06/1916 |
| War Diary | Hersin | 12/06/1916 | 13/06/1916 |
| War Diary | Souchez II | 14/06/1916 | 17/06/1916 |
| War Diary | Noulette Wood. | 18/06/1916 | 24/06/1916 |
| War Diary | Bouvigny | 25/06/1916 | 25/06/1916 |
| War Diary | Boyeffles | 26/06/1916 | 30/06/1916 |
| Heading | 140th Brigade. 47th Division. 1/15th Battalion London Regiment (P.W.O. Civil Service Rifles) July 1916. | | |
| War Diary | Souchez | 01/07/1916 | 04/07/1916 |
| War Diary | Ablain St Nazaire | 05/07/1916 | 07/07/1916 |
| War Diary | Bouvigny Huts | 08/07/1916 | 15/07/1916 |
| War Diary | Berthonval | 15/07/1916 | 21/07/1916 |
| War Diary | Camblain L'Abbe | 22/07/1916 | 25/07/1916 |
| War Diary | Houdain | 26/07/1916 | 26/07/1916 |
| War Diary | Valhuon | 27/07/1916 | 29/07/1916 |
| War Diary | Croisette | 30/07/1916 | 31/07/1916 |
| Heading | 15th Bn. London Regiment. Operation Order No. 5. | 03/07/1916 | 03/07/1916 |
| Heading | 140th Brigade. 47th Division. 1/15th Battalion London Regiment August 1916. | | |
| Heading | War Diary of the 15th Battn. London Regiment From 1st August to 31st August, 1916. Volume. I. | | |
| War Diary | Croissette | 01/08/1916 | 01/08/1916 |
| War Diary | Fortel | 02/08/1916 | 04/08/1916 |
| War Diary | Conteville | 05/08/1916 | 05/08/1916 |
| War Diary | Drucat | 06/08/1916 | 20/08/1916 |
| War Diary | Villers-Sous-Ailly | 21/08/1916 | 21/08/1916 |
| War Diary | Naours | 22/08/1916 | 22/08/1916 |
| War Diary | Mirvaux | 23/08/1916 | 23/08/1916 |
| War Diary | Franvillers | 24/08/1916 | 12/09/1916 |
| War Diary | Becourt Wood | 13/09/1916 | 14/09/1916 |
| Heading | War Diary of the 1/15th Battalion London Regiment (P.W.O. Civil Service Rifles) from 1st September-30th September 1916 Vol 15. | | |
| War Diary | High Wood | 15/09/1916 | 20/09/1916 |
| War Diary | Bottom Wood | 20/09/1916 | 20/09/1916 |
| War Diary | Albert | 21/09/1916 | 21/09/1916 |
| War Diary | Henencourt Wood | 22/09/1916 | 29/09/1916 |
| War Diary | Albert | 30/09/1916 | 30/09/1916 |
| Heading | War Diary of the 1/15th Battalion London Rgt. from 1st October 1916 to 31st October 1916. Vol 16. | | |
| War Diary | Albert | 01/10/1916 | 01/10/1916 |
| War Diary | Mametz | 02/10/1916 | 04/10/1916 |
| War Diary | Eaucourt L'Abbe | 05/10/1916 | 09/10/1916 |
| War Diary | Mametz | 10/10/1916 | 10/10/1916 |
| War Diary | Albert | 11/10/1916 | 13/10/1916 |
| War Diary | Villers | 14/10/1916 | 16/10/1916 |
| War Diary | Boeschepe | 17/10/1916 | 18/10/1916 |
| War Diary | Ypres Salient | 19/10/1916 | 29/10/1916 |
| War Diary | Ouderdom | 30/10/1916 | 31/10/1916 |
| Map | | | |

| | | | |
|---|---|---|---|
| Heading | War Diary. 1/15th Battalion London Regiment. 1st to 30th November 1916. Vol 17. | | |
| War Diary | Ottawa Camp Nr Ouderdom | 01/11/1916 | 07/11/1916 |
| War Diary | Halifax Camp nr. Vlamertinghe | 08/11/1916 | 12/11/1916 |
| War Diary | Front Line Hill 60 Sector | 13/11/1916 | 18/11/1916 |
| War Diary | Support Railway Dugouts | 19/11/1916 | 23/11/1916 |
| War Diary | Front Line Hill 60 Sector. | 24/11/1916 | 27/11/1916 |
| War Diary | Ottawa Camp Ouderdom. | 28/11/1916 | 30/11/1916 |
| Miscellaneous | H.Q. 47th Division. | 11/11/1916 | 11/11/1916 |
| Miscellaneous | | 17/12/1916 | 17/12/1916 |
| Miscellaneous | Raids. | 24/11/1916 | 24/11/1916 |
| Miscellaneous | | | |
| Miscellaneous | 1/15th Battn. London Regiment Scheme for proposed Raid on Enemy Trenches in Hill 60 sector. | 24/11/1916 | 24/11/1916 |
| Miscellaneous | H.Q. 47th Division. | 24/11/1916 | 24/11/1916 |
| Miscellaneous | G/240/35. | 25/11/1916 | 25/11/1916 |
| Miscellaneous | 142nd Inf Bde | 25/11/1916 | 25/11/1916 |
| Miscellaneous | | | |
| Miscellaneous | G.E.O. | 25/11/1916 | 25/11/1916 |
| Miscellaneous | H.Q. 140th Inf. Bde | | |
| War Diary | Ottawa Camp | 01/12/1916 | 08/12/1916 |
| War Diary | Swan Chateau near Ypres | 09/12/1916 | 29/12/1916 |
| War Diary | Ottawa Camp | 30/12/1916 | 31/12/1916 |
| Miscellaneous | X Corps. | | |
| Miscellaneous | H.Q. 47 Lon Div. | 19/12/1916 | 19/12/1916 |
| Miscellaneous | Headquarters 47 Lon Div. | 20/12/1916 | 20/12/1916 |
| Miscellaneous | Raids. | 20/12/1916 | 20/12/1916 |
| Miscellaneous | Xth Corps. | 21/12/1916 | 21/12/1916 |
| Miscellaneous | 23rd Division. 41st Division. | 21/12/1916 | 21/12/1916 |
| Miscellaneous | A Form. Messages And Signals. | | |
| Miscellaneous | 47 Div. | 23/12/1916 | 23/12/1916 |
| Miscellaneous | A Form. Messages And Signals. | | |
| Miscellaneous | Proposed Scheme for Artillery. Co-Operation on night of 21/22nd December 1916. | 21/12/1916 | 21/12/1916 |
| Miscellaneous | 1/15th Battalion London Regiment (P.W.O. Civil Service Rifles.) | 22/12/1916 | 22/12/1916 |
| Miscellaneous | Notes. | | |
| Miscellaneous | Operation Orders by Lt-Colonel W.F.K. Newson, Commanding, 1/15th Battalion London Regt. | 22/12/1916 | 22/12/1916 |
| Miscellaneous | Special Code for use in connection with Operation on night of 22/23rd December, 1916 only. | 22/12/1916 | 22/12/1916 |
| Miscellaneous | 1/15th Battalion London Regiment. | 23/12/1916 | 23/12/1916 |
| Miscellaneous | 1/15th Battalion London Regiment. (P.W.O. Civil Service Rifles) | | |
| Miscellaneous | Notes. | | |
| Miscellaneous | Proposed Scheme for Artillery. Co-Operation on night of 22/23 Dec. 1916. | 22/12/1916 | 22/12/1916 |
| Miscellaneous | Special Code for use in connection with Operation on night of 22/23rd December 1916 only. | 22/12/1916 | 22/12/1916 |
| Miscellaneous | H.Q. 47th Division | 23/12/1916 | 23/12/1916 |
| Miscellaneous | Report on Raiding Operations tonight. | 23/12/1916 | 23/12/1916 |
| Miscellaneous | Report on Raiding Operations to-Night. | 23/12/1916 | 23/12/1916 |
| Miscellaneous | Reference 140th Brigade Operation Order A.A./29/11/S. | 23/12/1916 | 23/12/1916 |
| Miscellaneous | Refer. 140 Bgde Operation Order S.S./29/11/8. | 23/12/1916 | 23/12/1916 |
| Miscellaneous | G.E.O. | 24/12/1916 | 24/12/1916 |

| | | | |
|---|---|---|---|
| Miscellaneous | 47th Div Arty | 24/12/1916 | 24/12/1916 |
| Miscellaneous | Xth Corps. | 25/12/1916 | 25/12/1916 |
| Miscellaneous | Xth Corps. | 26/12/1916 | 26/12/1916 |
| Miscellaneous | 1/15th Battalion London Regiment (P.W.O. Civil Service Rifles.) Scheme for proposed Raid on Enemy Trenches. | | |
| Miscellaneous | Notes. | | |
| Miscellaneous | 1/15th Battn. London Regiment. Proposed Scheme for Raid on Enemy Trenches in Canal Sub-Sector December 1916. | 16/12/1916 | 16/12/1916 |
| Miscellaneous | | 16/12/1916 | 16/12/1916 |
| Heading | 1916. War Diary 1/15 Batt. London Regt (P.W.O. Civil Service Rifles) December. Vol 18 | | |
| Heading | War Diary of the 1/15th Battalion London Regt from 1/1/1917 to 31/1/1917. Vol 19. | | |
| War Diary | Ottawa Camp near Ouderdom | 01/01/1917 | 08/01/1917 |
| War Diary | Hill 60 Ypres. | 09/01/1917 | 12/01/1917 |
| War Diary | Railway dugouts, near Zillibeke | 13/01/1917 | 17/01/1917 |
| War Diary | Hill 60 Ypres | 18/01/1917 | 21/01/1917 |
| War Diary | Halifax Camp near Vlamertinge | 22/01/1917 | 25/01/1917 |
| War Diary | Ottawa Camp near Ouderdom | 26/01/1917 | 31/01/1917 |
| Heading | 1/15" Battalion London Regt. War Diary February 1917. Vol 20. | | |
| War Diary | Ottawa Camp. | 01/02/1917 | 03/02/1917 |
| War Diary | Front Line | 04/02/1917 | 06/02/1917 |
| War Diary | Support Positions | 08/02/1917 | 12/02/1917 |
| War Diary | Front Line. | 13/02/1917 | 16/02/1917 |
| War Diary | Support Positions | 17/02/1917 | 19/02/1917 |
| War Diary | Ottawa Camp | 20/02/1917 | 28/02/1917 |
| Heading | 1/15th Battalion London Regiment (P.W.O. Civil Service Rifles) War Diary. March 1917. Vol 21. | | |
| War Diary | Ottawa Camp | 01/03/1917 | 21/03/1917 |
| War Diary | Front Line | 22/03/1917 | 29/03/1917 |
| War Diary | Swan Chateau | 30/03/1917 | 31/03/1917 |
| Heading | 1/15 Battalion London Regiment (P.W.O. Civil Service Rifles) War Diary April 1917. Vol 22. | | |
| War Diary | Canal Sub-Sector. | 01/04/1917 | 01/04/1917 |
| War Diary | Ypres. | 02/04/1917 | 11/04/1917 |
| War Diary | Devonshire Camp. | 12/04/1917 | 12/04/1917 |
| War Diary | Busseboom. | 12/04/1917 | 15/04/1917 |
| War Diary | Devonshire Camp. | 16/04/1917 | 20/04/1917 |
| War Diary | Spoil Bank Section, Ypres. | 21/04/1917 | 25/04/1917 |
| War Diary | Dominion Camp. Nr. Busseboom. | 26/04/1917 | 30/04/1917 |
| Heading | 1/15 Battalion London Regiment War Diary May, 1917. Vol 23 | | |
| War Diary | Dominion Camp | 01/05/1917 | 02/05/1917 |
| War Diary | Busseboom | 03/05/1917 | 07/05/1917 |
| War Diary | Swan Chateau | 08/05/1917 | 10/05/1917 |
| War Diary | Dickebusch | 11/05/1917 | 12/05/1917 |
| War Diary | Watou | 13/05/1917 | 13/05/1917 |
| War Diary | Sercus | 14/05/1917 | 14/05/1917 |
| War Diary | Moringhem | 15/05/1917 | 30/05/1917 |
| War Diary | Busseboom | 31/05/1917 | 31/05/1917 |
| Heading | 1/15 Batt London Regt. Civil Service Rifles. War Diary June 1917. Vol 24. | | |
| War Diary | Ebblinghem | 16/06/1917 | 27/06/1917 |

| | | | |
|---|---|---|---|
| War Diary | Meteren | 28/06/1917 | 28/06/1917 |
| War Diary | Voormezeele | 29/06/1917 | 29/06/1917 |
| War Diary | O.G.1 | 30/06/1917 | 30/06/1917 |
| War Diary | Dominion Lines, near Ouderdom. | 01/06/1917 | 02/06/1917 |
| War Diary | Swan Chateau. | 03/06/1917 | 05/06/1917 |
| War Diary | West Terrace | 06/06/1917 | 06/06/1917 |
| War Diary | Front Line. | 07/06/1917 | 07/06/1917 |
| War Diary | Ecluse Trench | 08/06/1917 | 08/06/1917 |
| War Diary | Front Line. | 10/06/1917 | 12/06/1917 |
| War Diary | Chippewa Camp | 13/06/1917 | 14/06/1917 |
| War Diary | Caestre | 15/06/1917 | 15/06/1917 |
| Miscellaneous | 1/15th Battalion London Regiment. | 07/06/1917 | 07/06/1917 |
| Miscellaneous | Record of Operations. | | |
| Map | A. | | |
| Heading | 1/15th Batt., London Regt. (Civil Service Rifles) War Diary. July 1917. Vol 25. | | |
| War Diary | Spoil Bank. | 01/07/1917 | 03/07/1917 |
| War Diary | Murrumbidgee Camp, La Clytte. | 04/07/1917 | 08/07/1917 |
| War Diary | Bois Confluent | 09/07/1917 | 14/07/1917 |
| War Diary | Front Line. | 15/07/1917 | 24/07/1917 |
| War Diary | Carnarvon Camp. | 25/07/1917 | 30/07/1917 |
| War Diary | Tatinghem | 31/07/1917 | 31/07/1917 |
| Operation(al) Order(s) | 140th Infantry Brigade. Operation Order No. 184. | 12/07/1917 | 12/07/1917 |
| Operation(al) Order(s) | 1/15th Battalion London Regiment. Order No. 74. | 17/07/1917 | 17/07/1917 |
| Heading | War Diary. 1/15th Batt. London Regt (P.W.O. Civil Service Rifles) August, 1917. Vol 26. | | |
| War Diary | Tatinghem. | 01/08/1917 | 10/08/1917 |
| War Diary | Moringhem. | 11/08/1917 | 14/08/1917 |
| War Diary | Tatinghem. | 15/08/1917 | 23/08/1917 |
| War Diary | Vancouver Camp. | 24/08/1917 | 31/08/1917 |
| Operation(al) Order(s) | Civil Service Rifles Operation Order No. 73. | 10/08/1917 | 10/08/1917 |
| Operation(al) Order(s) | Civil Service Rifles. Order No. 74. | 14/08/1917 | 14/08/1917 |
| Operation(al) Order(s) | Civil Service Rifles. Order No. 75. | | |
| Heading | 1/15 Batt. London Regt.-Civil Service Rifles War Diary September, 1917.-Vol 27. | | |
| War Diary | Vancouver Camp | 01/09/1917 | 06/09/1917 |
| War Diary | Chateau Segard. | 07/09/1917 | 08/09/1917 |
| War Diary | In Support | 09/09/1917 | 15/09/1917 |
| War Diary | Chateau Segard | 16/09/1917 | 17/09/1917 |
| War Diary | Steenvoorde | 18/09/1917 | 19/09/1917 |
| War Diary | Eecke | 20/09/1917 | 21/09/1917 |
| War Diary | Frevent Capelle | 22/09/1917 | 23/09/1917 |
| War Diary | Aubrey Camp | 24/09/1917 | 24/09/1917 |
| War Diary | Front Line | 25/09/1917 | 30/09/1917 |
| Operation(al) Order(s) | Civil Service Rifles. Order No.76. | 07/09/1917 | 07/09/1917 |
| Operation(al) Order(s) | Civil Service Rifles Order No. 77. | 08/09/1917 | 08/09/1917 |
| Miscellaneous | | | |
| Operation(al) Order(s) | Civil Service Rifles Order No. 78. | 13/09/1917 | 13/09/1917 |
| Miscellaneous | Action of 6th Battalion London Regt. Appendix I. | | |
| Operation(al) Order(s) | 1/15th Battn London Regiment Order No 60. | 03/06/1917 | 03/06/1917 |
| Operation(al) Order(s) | Civil Service Rifles. Order No. 79. | 23/09/1917 | 23/09/1917 |
| Operation(al) Order(s) | Civil Service Rifles. Order No. 80. | 24/09/1917 | 24/09/1917 |
| Heading | Missing Oct'17-Jan'18. | | |
| Heading | War Diary of 1/15th Battalion London Regiment (P.W.O. Civil Service Rifles. February 1918. Vol 32. | | |
| War Diary | Bertincourt. | 01/02/1918 | 02/02/1918 |

| | | | |
|---|---|---|---|
| War Diary | Flesquieres. | 02/02/1918 | 14/02/1918 |
| War Diary | Bertincourt. | 16/02/1918 | 21/02/1918 |
| War Diary | Manancourt. | 23/02/1918 | 28/02/1918 |
| Operation(al) Order(s) | Civil Service Rifles Order No 101. | 02/02/1918 | 02/02/1918 |
| Operation(al) Order(s) | Civil Service Rifles Order No.102 | 13/02/1917 | 13/02/1917 |
| Operation(al) Order(s) | Civil Service Rifles Order No 103. | 20/02/1918 | 20/02/1918 |
| Heading | 47th Division 140th Infantry Brigade Civil Service Rifles. War Diary 1/15th Battalion London Regiment March 1918. | | |
| Heading | Civil Service Rifles. War Diary March, 1918. 1/15 London Rgt Vol 33 | | |
| War Diary | Manancourt | 01/03/1918 | 18/03/1918 |
| War Diary | Etricourt | 19/03/1918 | 19/03/1918 |
| War Diary | Beaucamp Ridge | 19/03/1918 | 22/03/1918 |
| War Diary | Dessart Ridge | 23/03/1918 | 24/03/1918 |
| War Diary | Bazentin Le Petit | 24/03/1918 | 25/03/1918 |
| War Diary | Bouzincourt | 26/03/1918 | 26/03/1918 |
| War Diary | Couvencourt | 26/03/1918 | 26/03/1918 |
| War Diary | Clairfaye Farm | 26/03/1918 | 27/03/1918 |
| War Diary | Toutencourt | 27/03/1918 | 27/03/1918 |
| War Diary | Warloy | 28/03/1918 | 29/03/1918 |
| War Diary | Martinsart | 29/03/1918 | 31/03/1918 |
| Heading | 140th Brigade. 47th Division. War Diary 1/15th. Battalion (Civil Service Rifles) The London Regiment April 1918 Operation Order. | | |
| Heading | Civil Service Rifles. War Diary April 1918. 1/15 London Rgt Vol 34 | | |
| War Diary | Martinsart Senlis | 01/04/1918 | 04/04/1918 |
| War Diary | Bouzincourt. | 04/04/1918 | 07/04/1918 |
| War Diary | Senlis | 07/04/1918 | 08/04/1918 |
| War Diary | Hedauville | 08/04/1918 | 08/04/1918 |
| War Diary | Gezaincourt. | 09/04/1918 | 10/04/1918 |
| War Diary | Domart | 11/04/1918 | 11/04/1918 |
| War Diary | Canchy | 12/04/1918 | 29/04/1918 |
| War Diary | Warloy | 29/04/1918 | 30/04/1918 |
| Operation(al) Order(s) | Civil Service Rifles Operation Order No 1 by Lt Col Sadrave D.S.O. Cmodg. | 01/04/1918 | 01/04/1918 |
| Operation(al) Order(s) | Civil Service Rifles Order No 104. | 19/03/1918 | 19/03/1918 |
| Operation(al) Order(s) | Civil Service Rifles Order No.106 | 04/04/1918 | 04/04/1918 |
| Operation(al) Order(s) | Civil Service Rifles Order No.108 | 11/04/1918 | 11/04/1918 |
| Operation(al) Order(s) | Civil Service Rifles Order No.109 | | |
| War Diary | Warloy | 01/05/1918 | 01/05/1918 |
| War Diary | Line | 02/05/1918 | 06/05/1918 |
| War Diary | In Support. | 07/05/1918 | 10/05/1918 |
| War Diary | Line | 11/05/1918 | 15/05/1918 |
| War Diary | Warloy | 16/05/1918 | 17/05/1918 |
| War Diary | Bois La Haut | 18/05/1918 | 24/05/1918 |
| War Diary | Baizieux | 25/05/1918 | 25/05/1918 |
| War Diary | Lavieville Defences | 26/05/1918 | 31/05/1918 |
| Operation(al) Order(s) | Civil Service Rifles. Order No.112 App I. | 05/05/1918 | 05/05/1918 |
| Operation(al) Order(s) | Civil Service Rifles. Order No.113. App II. | 10/05/1918 | 10/05/1918 |
| Operation(al) Order(s) | Civil Service Rifles. Order No.114. App III. | 14/05/1918 | 14/05/1918 |
| Operation(al) Order(s) | Civil Service Rifles. Order No. 115. App IV. | 24/05/1918 | 24/05/1918 |
| Operation(al) Order(s) | Civil Service Rifles. Order No. 116. App V. | 26/05/1918 | 26/05/1918 |
| Heading | War Diary. 15th Battn. London Regt. (P.W.O. Civil Service Rifle.) June 1918. Vol 36. | | |

| | | | |
|---|---|---|---|
| War Diary | Franvillers | 01/06/1918 | 01/06/1918 |
| War Diary | Line | 02/06/1918 | 06/06/1918 |
| War Diary | In Support | 07/06/1918 | 09/06/1918 |
| War Diary | Line | 10/06/1918 | 14/06/1918 |
| War Diary | In Support | 15/06/1918 | 16/06/1918 |
| War Diary | Line | 17/06/1918 | 19/06/1918 |
| War Diary | Mollien Au Bois | 20/06/1918 | 20/06/1918 |
| War Diary | Guignemicourt | 21/06/1918 | 30/06/1918 |
| Operation(al) Order(s) | Civil Service Rifles Operation Order No.126. | 21/06/1918 | 21/06/1918 |
| Operation(al) Order(s) | Civil Service Rifles. Order No. 120. | 06/06/1918 | 06/06/1918 |
| Operation(al) Order(s) | Civil Service Rifles Order No. 121. | 09/06/1918 | 09/06/1918 |
| Operation(al) Order(s) | 1/Civil Service Rifles Order No.123 | 16/06/1918 | 16/06/1918 |
| Operation(al) Order(s) | Civil Service Rifles Order No. 122. | 14/06/1918 | 14/06/1918 |
| Operation(al) Order(s) | 1/Civil Service Rifles Order No.124. | 18/06/1918 | 18/06/1918 |
| Operation(al) Order(s) | 1/Civil Service Rifles Order No 125. | 19/06/1918 | 19/06/1918 |
| Operation(al) Order(s) | Civil Service Rifles. Order No. 117. App VI. | 29/05/1918 | 29/05/1918 |
| Operation(al) Order(s) | Order No. 118. App VII. | 05/05/1918 | 05/05/1918 |
| Miscellaneous | Draw 16 Tents | | |
| Operation(al) Order(s) | Civil Service Rifles Order No. 119. App VII. | 31/05/1918 | 31/05/1918 |
| Heading | July 1918. | | |
| War Diary | Guignemicourt | 01/07/1918 | 11/07/1918 |
| War Diary | Warloy | 12/07/1918 | 13/07/1918 |
| War Diary | Senlis-Henencourt Road | 17/07/1918 | 18/07/1918 |
| War Diary | Senlis-Millencourt Road | 19/07/1918 | 20/07/1918 |
| War Diary | Line | 21/07/1918 | 24/07/1918 |
| War Diary | Warloy | 14/07/1918 | 15/07/1918 |
| War Diary | Senlis-Henencourt Road | 16/07/1918 | 16/07/1918 |
| War Diary | Line | 24/07/1918 | 24/07/1918 |
| War Diary | Contay | 25/07/1918 | 28/07/1918 |
| War Diary | In Support | 29/07/1918 | 30/07/1918 |
| War Diary | Henencourt-Senlis Rd (Forward-Reserve Bde). | 31/07/1918 | 31/07/1918 |
| Operation(al) Order(s) | Civil Service Rifles Order No. 131 | 24/07/1918 | 24/07/1918 |
| Miscellaneous | | | |
| Operation(al) Order(s) | 1/Civil Service Rifles, Order No.127. | 11/07/1918 | 11/07/1918 |
| Operation(al) Order(s) | Civil Service Rifles. Order No. 128. | 15/07/1918 | 15/07/1918 |
| Operation(al) Order(s) | Civil Service Rifles Order No.132. | 28/07/1918 | 28/07/1918 |
| Operation(al) Order(s) | Civil Service Rifles. Order No.129. | 18/07/1918 | 18/07/1918 |
| Operation(al) Order(s) | Civil Service Rifles. Order No.130. | 20/07/1918 | 20/07/1918 |
| Miscellaneous | Warning Order. | 20/07/1918 | 20/07/1918 |
| Operation(al) Order(s) | Civil Service Rifles Order No 133. | 30/07/1917 | 30/07/1917 |
| Heading | 140th Bde. 47th Div. 15th Battalion, London Regiment, August 1918. | | |
| Miscellaneous | 140 Infantry Brigade. | 02/08/1918 | 02/08/1918 |
| Miscellaneous | E 26/101 | 18/09/1918 | 18/09/1918 |
| War Diary | In Support | 01/08/1918 | 03/08/1918 |
| War Diary | Warloy | 04/08/1918 | 05/08/1918 |
| War Diary | Line | 06/08/1918 | 09/08/1918 |
| War Diary | In Support | 10/08/1918 | 11/08/1918 |
| War Diary | In Baizieux | 12/08/1918 | 13/08/1918 |
| War Diary | Old British Line | 14/08/1918 | 16/08/1918 |
| War Diary | Front Line | 17/08/1918 | 20/08/1918 |
| War Diary | In Reserve | 21/08/1918 | 31/08/1918 |
| Miscellaneous | Reference Sheet 62D. NE. | | |
| Miscellaneous | | 01/09/1918 | 01/09/1918 |
| Miscellaneous | | | |
| Miscellaneous | | 07/09/1918 | 07/09/1918 |

| | | | |
|---|---|---|---|
| War Diary | | 01/09/1918 | 07/09/1918 |
| War Diary | Heilly | 08/09/1918 | 09/09/1918 |
| War Diary | Chocques | 10/09/1918 | 12/09/1918 |
| War Diary | Auchel | 13/09/1918 | 27/09/1918 |
| War Diary | Foufflin-Ricametz | 28/09/1918 | 30/09/1918 |
| Heading | War Diary., of 1/15th Battalion London Regiment (P.W.O. Civil Service Rifles. from 1st October, 1918 to 31st October, 1918. Vol 40. | | |
| War Diary | Foufflin-Ricametz | 01/10/1918 | 02/10/1918 |
| War Diary | Lestrem | 03/10/1918 | 03/10/1918 |
| War Diary | In Reserve | 04/10/1918 | 05/10/1918 |
| War Diary | In Support | 06/10/1918 | 09/10/1918 |
| War Diary | In Reserve | 10/10/1918 | 14/10/1918 |
| War Diary | Estaires | 15/10/1918 | 15/10/1918 |
| War Diary | St Venant | 16/10/1918 | 16/10/1918 |
| War Diary | Fontes | 17/10/1918 | 26/10/1918 |
| War Diary | Lomme | 27/10/1918 | 28/10/1918 |
| War Diary | Hellemmes | 29/10/1918 | 30/10/1918 |
| War Diary | Chereng | 31/10/1918 | 31/10/1918 |
| Operation(al) Order(s) | 1/Civil Service Rifles. Order No.164. | 13/10/1918 | 13/10/1918 |
| Miscellaneous | A Form Messages And Signals. | | |
| Operation(al) Order(s) | Civil Service Rifles. Order No. 166. | 16/10/1918 | 16/10/1918 |
| Operation(al) Order(s) | 1/Civil Service Rifles. Order No. 167. | 24/10/1918 | 24/10/1918 |
| Operation(al) Order(s) | 1/Civil Service Rifles. Order No. 168. | 29/10/1918 | 29/10/1918 |
| Operation(al) Order(s) | 1/Civil Service Rifles. Order No. 169. | 30/10/1918 | 30/10/1918 |
| Heading | 1/15th Battn. London Regt. (P.W.O. Civil Service Rifles.) War Diary November, 1918 Vol 41 | | |
| War Diary | Front Line | 01/11/1918 | 03/11/1918 |
| War Diary | Reserve | 05/11/1918 | 09/11/1918 |
| War Diary | Froyennes | 10/11/1918 | 10/11/1918 |
| War Diary | Barberie | 11/11/1918 | 11/11/1918 |
| War Diary | Tournai | 12/11/1918 | 13/11/1918 |
| War Diary | Pipaix | 14/11/1918 | 18/11/1918 |
| War Diary | Tournai | 19/11/1918 | 19/11/1918 |
| War Diary | Willems | 20/11/1918 | 26/11/1918 |
| War Diary | Habourdin | 27/11/1918 | 27/11/1918 |
| War Diary | Bethune | 28/11/1918 | 28/11/1918 |
| War Diary | Ferfay | 29/11/1918 | 30/11/1918 |
| Operation(al) Order(s) | 1/Civil Service Rifles. Order No. 170. | 03/11/1918 | 03/11/1918 |
| Operation(al) Order(s) | 1/Civil Service Rifles Order No. 171. | 10/11/1918 | 10/11/1918 |
| Operation(al) Order(s) | 1/Civil Service Rifles Order No. 172. | 11/11/1918 | 11/11/1918 |
| Operation(al) Order(s) | 1/Civil Service Rifles. Order No. 173. | 12/11/1918 | 12/11/1918 |
| Operation(al) Order(s) | 1/Civil Service Rifles Order No.174. | 17/11/1918 | 17/11/1918 |
| Operation(al) Order(s) | 1/Civil Service Rifles Order No.175 | 18/11/1918 | 18/11/1918 |
| Operation(al) Order(s) | 1st Civil Service Rifles. Order No. 176. | 25/11/1918 | 25/11/1918 |
| Operation(al) Order(s) | 1st Civil Service Rifles. Order No. 177 | 26/11/1918 | 26/11/1918 |
| Operation(al) Order(s) | 1st Civil Service Rifles. Order No. 178 | 27/11/1918 | 27/11/1918 |
| Heading | War Diary of 1/15th Battalion, London Regiment (P.W.O. Civil Service Rifles.) from 1/12/18 to 31/12/18. Vol 42. | | |
| War Diary | Ferfay | 01/12/1918 | 31/12/1918 |
| War Diary | Ferfay Pas-De-Calais | 31/01/1919 | 31/01/1919 |
| War Diary | Ferfay Pas-De-Calais | 28/02/1919 | 28/02/1919 |
| War Diary | Ferfay Pas-De-Calais | 31/03/1919 | 31/03/1919 |
| War Diary | Ferfay | 05/05/1919 | 05/05/1919 |

WO 95/2732

(1)

47 Div

Mar '15 - May '19

1/15 London R.

47TH DIVISION
140TH INFY BDE

1-15TH LONDON REGIMENT

MAR 1915- MAY 1919

140th Inf. Bde.

47th Division.

Battn disembarked Havre from England 18.3.15.

WAR DIARY

1/15th L O N D O N Regt.

M A R C H & A P R I L
(17.3.15 – 30.4.15)
1 9 1 5

Confidential

# WAR DIARY

of

15th Battn London Regt.
(P.W.O. Civil Service Rifles)

from 17th March 1915

~~to 30th April 1915~~

Vol I.

(Capt F. W. PARISH
Kept by) Adjutant
Civil Service Rifles

17th March

Battalion Strength 30 Officers 1046 Other Ranks under the command Col. A. M. RENNY left WATFORD in two trains in the early morning for SOUTHAMPTON. The Battalion embarked in the following steamers:– BALMORAL, CITY OF CHESTER, JUPITER and MUNICH. The boats sailed between the hours of 7.30 PM and 8.30 PM

J.W.P.

18th March.

HAVRE was reached in the early morning. At 9 A.M. Battalion disembarked and marched to No. 6 Rest Camp. HAVRE, where they went under canvas together with the 6th, 7th and 8th Battalions who formed with us the 4th London Infantry Brigade.

J.W.P.

19th March

Battalion entrained at 6 P.M.

J.W.P.

20th March.

Detrained at BERGUETTE at 4 P.M. and marched to CAUCHY A LA TOUR arriving at 10 P.M. where the Battalion was billeted.

J.W.P.

21st March

Settled down in billets.

J.W.P.

22nd March

Battalion as part of the Division was inspected by C in C Field Marshal Sir JOHN FRENCH who was accompanied by Genl Sir DOUGLAS HAIG and Genl MUNRO.

J.W.P.

23rd March to 6th April

Battalion remained at CAUCHY A LA TOUR and carried out daily Battalion and Company training. Machine Guns fired a course at LABEUVRIÈRE and grenade and bomb throwers from each Company were trained under Battalion bomb Officer. Trench digging also practised.

J.W.P.

7th April

Battalion marched to BETHUNE via AUCHEL MARLES LEZ MINES, LABEUVRIÈRE and ANNEZIN, and billeted in the COLLEGE DE JEUNES FILLES. One man died in hospital as result of Spinal Cerebro meningitis, and One officer and thirty men arrived from Base as first reinforcement, our numbers having been reduced by men going home to take up Commissions, and by sickness.

J.G.P.

8th April to 12th April.

Battalion attached to 4th (Guards) Brigade and were sent in to the trenches by Companies for a tour of 24 hours. Remainder of the Battalion employed in digging communication trenches and fatigue work. On 8th April two men wounded, on 12th April one man.

J.G.P.

13th April.

Battalion took over from 1st Bn HERTS Regt section of the line B1 at GIVENCHY. Reliefs were carried out without incident. Village of GIVENCHY was shelled at night without causing any casualties.

J.G.P.

14th April.

Village was again shelled in the morning, also the advanced and communication trenches with high explosive shells for about 10 minutes in the afternoon. No casualties.

J.G.P.

15th April.

Heavy mist all the morning. In the afternoon we were relieved by the 1st Bn HERTS Regt and marched back to the same billets at BETHUNE. Three men wounded one of whom died 17th April. J.G.P.

16th April to 18th April.

Battalion rested in BETHUNE

J.W.P.

19th April.

Battalion took over Section B2 from 2nd Bn. Grenadier Guards.

J.W.P.

20th April

Nothing of importance occurred except GIVENCHY village shelled during afternoon. One man killed in early morning in the advanced trenches.

J.W.P.

21st April

Battalion relieved by 8th Bn London Regt (Post Office Rifles). During the relief a certain amount of shelling of trenches took place. No casualties. Battalion took over billets at LE PREOL.

J.W.P.

22nd April

Battalion again took over Section B1 and relieved 3rd Bn Coldstream Guards.

J.W.P.

23rd April –

GIVENCHY village heavily shelled during morning. Battalion relieved during the afternoon by 1st Bn Herts Regt and returned to billets at LE PREOL

J.W.P.

24th April

Battalion moved from LE PREOL to LABEUVRIÈRE by way of BEUVRY, BETHUNE CHOCQUES. Billeted at LABEUVRIÈRE with Post Office Rifles

J.W.P.

25th April to 30th April.

Battalion carried out daily training whilst billeted at LABEUVRIERE. Machine Gun Section were attached to 6th London Infy. Brigade in the trenches on 28th April.

J.W.P.

140th Inf. Bde.

47th Division.

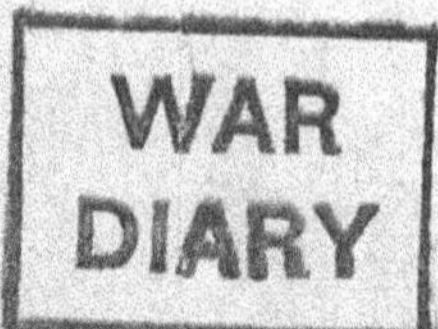


1/15th L O N D O N Regt.

M A Y 1915

Instructions regarding War Diaries and Intelligence Summaries are contained in F. S. Regs., Part II. and the Staff Manual respectively. Title pages will be prepared in manuscript.

# WAR DIARY

*or*

~~INTELLIGENCE SUMMARY.~~

*(Erase heading not required.)*

Army Form C. 2118.

| Place | Date | Hour | Summary of Events and Information | Remarks and references to Appendices |
|---|---|---|---|---|
| | | | Confidential<br>War Diary<br>of<br>15th Battn London Regiment<br>(Prince of Wales' Own Civil Service Rifles)<br>from 1st to 31st May 1915.<br>Volume II<br><br>Kept by Capt F. W. Parish<br>Adjutant,<br>Civil Service Rifles. | |

1577 Wt. W10791/1773 500,000 1/15 D. D. & L. A.D.S.S./Forms/C. 2118.

Army Form C. 2118.

Instructions regarding War Diaries and Intelligence Summaries are contained in F. S. Regs., Part II. and the Staff Manual respectively. Title pages will be prepared in manuscript.

# WAR DIARY

*or*

~~INTELLIGENCE SUMMARY.~~

*(Erase heading not required.)*

| Place | Date | Hour | Summary of Events and Information | Remarks and references to Appendices |
|---|---|---|---|---|
| LABEUVRIERE | May 1 | | Company training carried out. J.G.P. | |
| " | 2 Sunday | | Church Parade in field adjoining LABEUVRIERE Chateau. J.G.P. | |
| " | 3 | | Attack practice carried out at LE VERTBOIS FERME. | |
| | 4 | | J.G.P. | |
| " | 5th | 11.30AM. | Left LABEUVRIERE marching via ANNEZIN, BETHUNE, ESSARS] to GORRE, and occupied billets [at ESSARS and GORRE] vacated by 18th Bn London Regt. Headquarters, A and C Companies at GORRE – remainder of Battalion at ESSARS. J.G.P. | |
| | 6 | 3PM. | Headquarters, A and C Companies move to MARAIS (THE TUNING FORK) – one mile eastwards – remainder of Battalion moves to GORRE J.G.P. | |

1577 Wt W10791/1773 500,000 1/15 D. D. & L. A.D.S.S./Forms/C. 2118.

Army Form C. 2118.

Instructions regarding War Diaries and Intelligence Summaries are contained in F. S. Regs., Part II. and the Staff Manual respectively. Title pages will be prepared in manuscript.

# WAR DIARY
*or*
~~INTELLIGENCE SUMMARY.~~
*(Erase heading not required.)*

| Place | Date | Hour | Summary of Events and Information | Remarks and references to Appendices |
|---|---|---|---|---|
| TUNING FORK (FESTUBERT) | May 7 | | Arrangements for attack on following day cancelled at 11 P.M. J.W.T. | |
| " | 8 | | Arrangements made for attack on 9th inst. J.W.T. | |
| " | 9 | | Battalion occupied Intermediate line of breastworks at 3 A.M. German lines heavily bombarded at 5 A.M. by all British batteries. Enemy replied a little. J.W.T. 1 wounded. | |
| " | 10 | 2 P.M. | Battalion vacated breastworks. J.W.T. | |
| | | 8 P.M. | Battalion relieved 6th Battalion in C1 Section FESTUBERT. A and C Companies in front line, B Company supports at 'WELSH CHAPEL'. D Company in billets between front line and Intermediate line. J.W.T. | |

1577 Wt. W10791/1773 500,000 1/15 D. D. & L. A.D.S.S./Forms/C. 2118.

Army Form C. 2118.

Instructions regarding War Diaries and Intelligence Summaries are contained in F. S. Regs., Part II. and the Staff Manual respectively. Title pages will be prepared in manuscript.

# WAR DIARY
*or*
~~INTELLIGENCE SUMMARY.~~
*(Erase heading not required.)*

| Place | Date | Hour | Summary of Events and Information | Remarks and references to Appendices |
|---|---|---|---|---|
| FESTUBERT | MAY 11 | | Heavy bombardment by our artillery at 1 A.M. No reply by enemy. Fairly quiet throughout day. J.W.P. 1 man killed, 1 man wounded. | |
| " | 12 | | A and C Companies relieved by B and D Companies at night. J.W.P. 1 man killed. 1 man wounded | |
| " | 13 | | Artillery bombardment of enemy's lines J.W.P. 2 wounded | |
| " | 14 | | Fairly quiet day. J.W.P. 2nd Lieut B Scott wounded. | |
| " | 15 | | B and D Companies relieved by A and C. J.W.P. 1 wounded | |

1577 Wt. W10791/1773 500,000 1/15 D. D. & L. A.D.S.S./Forms/C. 2118.

Army Form C. 2118.

Instructions regarding War Diaries and Intelligence Summaries are contained in F. S. Regs., Part II. and the Staff Manual respectively. Title pages will be prepared in manuscript.

# WAR DIARY

*or*

~~INTELLIGENCE SUMMARY.~~

*(Erase heading not required.)*

| Place | Date | Hour | Summary of Events and Information | Remarks and references to Appendices |
|---|---|---|---|---|
| FESTUBERT | MAY 16 | | [Heavy fighting all day. Canadians on our left charged and took some trenches.] Battalion ordered to hold its own ground. Enemy shelled trenches severely. J.W.P. | |
| | | | 1 killed 9 wounded (1 subsequently died). | |
| " | 17 | | Rain - operations seriously interfered with accordingly. Enemy still shelling our trenches. J.W.P. | |
| | | | 2 killed. 4 wounded. | |

1577 Wt. W10791/1773 500,000 1/15 D. D. & L. A.D.S.S./Forms/C. 2118.

Instructions regarding War Diaries and Intelligence Summaries are contained in F. S. Regs., Part II. and the Staff Manual respectively. Title pages will be prepared in manuscript.

# WAR DIARY
*or*
~~INTELLIGENCE SUMMARY.~~
*(Erase heading not required.)*

Army Form C. 2118.

| Place | Date | Hour | Summary of Events and Information | Remarks and references to Appendices |
|---|---|---|---|---|
| | MAY | | | |
| FESTUBERT | 18 | | Working party of 6th Bn. London Regt. working in front of our advanced breastwork discovered by enemy in early morning. Party shelled causing very heavy casualties to the party – also several wounded of this Battalion. Shelled throughout the day. J.C.P. | |
| | | | 1 killed. Capt. W.F.K. Newson – wounded 6 other ranks – wounded. | |
| | 19 | | Advance on our left continued – more prisoners taken. Regimental First Line Transport lines shelled. Two horses killed. J.C.P. | |
| | | | 2 wounded. | |

Army Form C. 2118.

# WAR DIARY
*or*
~~INTELLIGENCE SUMMARY.~~
*(Erase heading not required.)*

Instructions regarding War Diaries and Intelligence Summaries are contained in F. S. Regs., Part II. and the Staff Manual respectively. Title pages will be prepared in manuscript.

| Place | Date | Hour | Summary of Events and Information | Remarks and references to Appendices |
|---|---|---|---|---|
| FESTUBERT | MAY 20 | | Battalion relieved at night by 6th Bn. London. Heavily shelled whilst relief being carried out. Moved to billets at TUNING FORK. J.W.P. 6 wounded. | |
| " | 21 | | Resting in billets J.W.P. | |
| " | 22 | | Enemy shelling vigorously J.W.P. 4 wounded. | |
| " | 23 | | French batteries of artillery brought up in our rear shelled the enemy heavily during afternoon. J.W.P. | |
| " | 24 | | Fatigue party carrying trench mortar bombs up to advanced trench at 2 AM heavily shelled. J.W.P. 3 killed 5 wounded | |

1577 Wt. W10791/1773 500,000 1/15 D. D. & L. A.D.S.S./Forms/C. 2118.

Instructions regarding War Diaries and Intelligence Summaries are contained in F. S. Regs., Part II. and the Staff Manual respectively. Title pages will be prepared in manuscript.

# WAR DIARY
or
~~INTELLIGENCE SUMMARY.~~
(Erase heading not required.)

Army Form C. 2118.

| Place | Date | Hour | Summary of Events and Information | Remarks and references to Appendices |
|---|---|---|---|---|
| FESTUBERT | MAY 25 | | 142nd Brigade on our Right successfully attacked at GIVENCHY. Covered their advance by fire on enemy communication trenches. Maxims hard at work but no real target. Sent 8 Bombers to help 8th Bn London Regt take J1 and J3. Trenches heavily shelled. Started a communication trench from end of YELLOW ROAD to J1. Night very bright and exposed to heavy shell fire and machine guns, but were able to dig enough to give cover to men crawling. J.B.P.<br>Officers: 1 KILLED 3 wounded<br>Other ranks 7 " 10 " | |
| " | 26 | 7P.M. | Received orders to occupy J7. J6 + to take over from 8th Battn. London Regt K3, J3. B Co under Maj WARRENDER ordered to occupy J7. J6, and they established themselves and dug in during the night. We were unmolested owing to the Germans taking up positions in rear and digging themselves in. Their parties could easily be heard. J.B.P.<br>Casualties - NIL | |

Instructions regarding War Diaries and Intelligence Summaries are contained in F. S. Regs., Part II. and the Staff Manual respectively. Title pages will be prepared in manuscript.

# WAR DIARY
*or*
# ~~INTELLIGENCE SUMMARY.~~
*(Erase heading not required.)*

Army Form C. 2118.

| Place | Date | Hour | Summary of Events and Information | Remarks and references to Appendices |
|---|---|---|---|---|
| FESTUBERT | MAY 27 | | Spent the day in making J6, J7 bullet proof and rebuilding K3, J3 and generally clearing up trench. Evacuating English and German wounded and burying the dead. Fairly heavily shelled during the day, especially in the afternoon. Minenwerfer on the S bend which appeared to be near I12 extremely busy but fortunately J7 seemed to be out of their range. The Germans brought up a 'fizz bang' to what appeared to be CHAPELLE ST ROCH, while a good many of the heavy shells which came over appeared to come from the direction of the railway triangle south of Canal. | |
| | | | 1 Officer wounded<br>2 Other Ranks killed<br>3 " " wounded<br>J.B.P. | |

Army Form C. 2118.

Instructions regarding War Diaries and Intelligence Summaries are contained in F. S. Regs., Part II. and the Staff Manual respectively. Title pages will be prepared in manuscript.

# WAR DIARY
*or*
# INTELLIGENCE SUMMARY.
*(Erase heading not required.)*

| Place | Date | Hour | Summary of Events and Information | Remarks and references to Appendices |
|---|---|---|---|---|
| FESTUBERT | MAY 28 | | New Battalion Headquarters were established at end of YELLOW ROAD, in the old breastworks. They appeared to be exceptionally close to the front line. In this kind of warfare the whole Battalion is up in the forward trenches which has its advantage of Battalion Headquarters being able to keep in touch with Companies, even when the telephone wires were broken which was continually happening. The Germans loosed a good many heavy shells on WILLOW ROAD (which was our old route to the trenches) which had little effect as all fatigues came down YELLOW ROAD. The German shells seemed to enfilade our trenches which makes one feel that the majority of their heavy guns were on the South side of the Canal. They seem to have brought up 6 'fiz bangs' which they continually let off together on the new communication trench to J1. A large number of their heavy shells were 'blind'. J.L.P. | |
| | | | 3 Other Ranks wounded. | |

1577 Wt. W10791/1773 500,000 1/15 D. D. & L. A.D.S.S./Forms/C. 2118.

Army Form C. 2118.

# WAR DIARY
*or*
# ~~INTELLIGENCE SUMMARY.~~
*(Erase heading not required.)*

Instructions regarding War Diaries and Intelligence Summaries are contained in F. S. Regs., Part II. and the Staff Manual respectively. Title pages will be prepared in manuscript.

| Place | Date | Hour | Summary of Events and Information | Remarks and references to Appendices |
|---|---|---|---|---|
| FESTUBERT | MAY 29 | | The amount of shelling this day made us think that at last the Germans were going to counter attack. The necessity of deep digging and building up parapet in J6. J7. was ~~[illegible]~~ fully shown as the German shells did little harm to the men. J.L.P. One wounded (Other Ranks) | |
| FESTUBERT | 30 | | More shelling - especially during the afternoon. Since 26th May 25,000 sandbags have been filled and used for the breastworks - the majority in J6. J7. The last supplies of sandbags seem to have been very white. Had they been ~~[illegible]~~ more varied in colour the top of the parapet would not have been so apparent. New trench started two nights previously - running North from between J6. J4 towards the Canadians was finished being cut. Men greatly handicapped by the amount of water which was reached at 2'6" level. J.L.P. Other Ranks. Killed - 2 Wounded - 4 | |

1577 Wt. W10791/1773 500,000 1/15 D. D. & L. A.D.S.S./Forms/C. 2118.

Army Form C. 2118.

# WAR DIARY

*or*

~~INTELLIGENCE SUMMARY.~~

*(Erase heading not required.)*

Instructions regarding War Diaries and Intelligence Summaries are contained in F. S. Regs., Part II. and the Staff Manual respectively. Title pages will be prepared in manuscript.

| Place | Date | Hour | Summary of Events and Information | Remarks and references to Appendices |
|---|---|---|---|---|
| FESTUBERT | May 31 | | A quieter day. Battalion relieved by 1st Grenadier Guards during the night. Marched back to BETHUNE, where it was billeted at the COLLEGE DES JEUNES FILLES, and HOSPITAL MATERNITÉ. The last companies arrived at billets at 3.30 A.M. | |
| | JUNE 1 | | J. G. P. | |
| | | | 12 Sheets. | |
| | | | J. G. Parish. Capt & Adjt. | |
| | | | June 1st 1915 — 15th London Regt (Civil Service Rifles) | |
| | | | | Cas for month K 1 + 19. W 6 + 61. |

1577 Wt. W10791/1773 500,000 1/15 D. D. & L. A.D.S.S./Forms/C. 2118.

140th Inf. Bde.

47th Division.

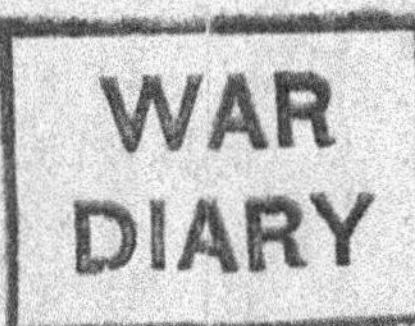


1/15th L O N D O N Regt.

J U N E 1 9 1 5

Instructions regarding War Diaries and Intelligence Summaries are contained in F. S. Regs., Part II. and the Staff Manual respectively. Title pages will be prepared in manuscript.

# WAR DIARY
*or*
~~INTELLIGENCE SUMMARY.~~
*(Erase heading not required.)*

Army Form C. 2118.

| Place | Date | Hour | Summary of Events and Information | Remarks and references to Appendices |
|---|---|---|---|---|
| | | | Confidential.<br>War Diary<br>of<br>15th Battn London Regt.<br>(Prince of Wales' Own Civil Service Rifles)<br>from 1st to 30th June 1915.<br>Volume III.<br>Kept by Capt. F W PARISH<br>Adjutant,<br>Civil Service Rifles | |

1577 Wt. W10791/1773 500,000 1/15 D. D. & L. A.D.S.S./Forms/C. 2118.

Instructions regarding War Diaries and Intelligence Summaries are contained in F. S. Regs., Part II. and the Staff Manual respectively. Title pages will be prepared in manuscript.

# WAR DIARY
*or*
# ~~INTELLIGENCE SUMMARY.~~
*(Erase heading not required.)*

Army Form C. 2118.

| Place | Date | Hour | Summary of Events and Information | Remarks and references to Appendices |
|---|---|---|---|---|
| BETHUNE | JUNE 1st | 3AM. | ~~Early this morning~~ The Battalion arrived in BETHUNE having marched from the trenches at FESTUBERT after relief by the 1st Bn Grenadier Guards. The relief was carried out without incident. | |
| | | 8P.M. | Battalion moves again and takes over billets of Black Watch, 1st Brigade 1st Division at SAILLY LABOURSE. J.B.P. | |
| SAILLY LABOURSE | 2-6 | | Battalion resting, sending up working parties into LE RUTOIRE J.B.P. | |
| do | 7th | | Battalion attached to 142nd Infantry Brigade and moves into billets at LES BREBIS J.B.P. | |
| LES BREBIS | 8-9 | | Battalion remains at LES BREBIS providing working parties each night in the GRENAY (W) Section of the line J.B.P. | |
| do | 10 | | The Battalion moves up and relieves the 22nd Battn London Regt in W 2 Section. The relief was carried out without event. J.B.P. | |

1577 Wt. W10791/1773 500,000 1/15 D. D. & L. A.D.S.S./Forms/C. 2118.

Instructions regarding War Diaries and Intelligence Summaries are contained in F. S. Regs., Part II. and the Staff Manual respectively. Title pages will be prepared in manuscript.

# WAR DIARY
*or*
# ~~INTELLIGENCE SUMMARY.~~

(*Erase heading not required.*)

Army Form C. 2118.

| Place | Date | Hour | Summary of Events and Information | Remarks and references to Appendices |
|---|---|---|---|---|
| GRENAY | JUNE 11-12 | | Quiet days except for occasional artillery fire which was generally directed against FOSSE No 5 which the enemy evidently think is an artillery observation post and they also seem to be aware of the position of Battalion Headquarters in the 'crater' but not one of the shells fired seem to have reached the crater although they have done damage elsewhere. J.B.P. | |
| -do- | 13th | | Unusually heavy amount of high ~~explosive~~ velocity shells and some howitzers were directed at the Company in reserve and the small wood which is held by the Battalion at the top of the dump known as the Spinney. J.B.P.<br>Casualties: Other ranks - 4 wounded. | |
| -do- | 14th | | In connection with the attack of the 4th Corps which is being launched to-morrow parties were sent out with bombs to some houses in between our own and the German lines. The enemy evidently thought that an attack was coming and for half an hour we were subjected to extremely heavy rifle fire. The trenches are evidently strongly held here. The German guns also replied, mostly on the roads behind us presumably expecting | |

Instructions regarding War Diaries and Intelligence Summaries are contained in F. S. Regs., Part II. and the Staff Manual respectively. Title pages will be prepared in manuscript.

# WAR DIARY
*or*
# ~~INTELLIGENCE SUMMARY.~~
*(Erase heading not required.)*

Army Form C. 2118.

| Place | Date | Hour | Summary of Events and Information | Remarks and references to Appendices |
|---|---|---|---|---|
| GRENAY | JUNE 14th | | reinforcements to be brought up J.b.P. | |
| | | | Casualties. Other ranks : 1 wounded | |
| -do- | 15th | | The real attack of 4th Corps took place this day. Frequent bursts of rifle fire were directed against the enemy's trenches at selected points. At night time our patrols discovered a strong German patrol in the houses we had visited the day before. The French artillery were communicated with and fired but with what damage we were unable to ascertain J.b.P. | |
| | | | Casualties. Other ranks. 2 wounded. | |
| -do- | 16th | | Subjected to a great deal of heavy artillery fire most of which was directed at dummy trenches built half a mile behind our front line. J.b.P. | |
| | | | Casualties NIL. | |
| -do- | 17th | | German guns shelling BULLY GRENAY. Battalion relieved in the evening by the 22nd Bn. London Regt and takes over billets from the 17th Bn. London Regt in LE PHILOSOPHE and MAZINGARBE J.b.P. | |
| | | | Casualties. NIL | |

1577 Wt. W10791/1773 500,000 1/15 D. D. & L. A.D.S.S./Forms/C. 2118.

Army Form C. 2118.

Instructions regarding War Diaries and Intelligence Summaries are contained in F. S. Regs., Part II. and the Staff Manual respectively. Title pages will be prepared in manuscript.

# WAR DIARY
*or*
~~INTELLIGENCE SUMMARY.~~
*(Erase heading not required.)*

| Place | Date | Hour | Summary of Events and Information | Remarks and references to Appendices |
|---|---|---|---|---|
| MAZINGARBE & LE PHILOSOPHE | JUNE 18-20 | | Battalion at rest and was subjected at odd times to shelling which was directed at a battery of 4.7 guns at LE PHILOSOPHE. On the 19th June the Battalion was ordered to be ready to move at a moments notice. J.B.P. | |
| -do- | 21st | | Battalion moves up and relieves the 7th Bn. London Regt in X 2 Section - FOSSE No 7 de BETHUNE. Relief effected without event. J.B.P. Casualties: Other Ranks. 1 wounded. | |
| FOSSE No 7 | 22nd | | Quiet day. One shell burst in the front trench wounding five men. J.B.P. Casualties: Other Ranks 5 wounded. | |
| -do- | 23rd | | Reserve Company at FOSSE No 7 subjected to some 5.9 shells. J.B.P. Casualties: Other Ranks 2 wounded. | |
| -do- | 24th | | Very quiet day. J.B.P. Casualties: NIL | |

1577 Wt. W10791/1773 500,000 1/15 D. D. & L. A.D.S.S./Forms/C. 2118.

Instructions regarding War Diaries and Intelligence Summaries are contained in F. S. Regs., Part II. and the Staff Manual respectively. Title pages will be prepared in manuscript.

# WAR DIARY
*or*
# ~~INTELLIGENCE SUMMARY.~~
*(Erase heading not required.)*

Army Form C. 2118.

| Place | Date | Hour | Summary of Events and Information | Remarks and references to Appendices |
|---|---|---|---|---|
| FOSSE No 7 | JUNE 25th | | Quiet day. A good deal of rain which made the trenches almost impassable. Water was in some places over two feet deep. A lot of work was performed in these trenches and on this day we occupied a new front line which we made by connecting up two saps. J.B.P. Casualties NIL | |
| – | 26th | | The new trench can now be considered bullet-proof and it is well traversed everywhere. We were relieved during the evening by the 7th Bn London Regt and returned to the old billets at LE PHILOSOPHE and MAZINGARBE. Reliefs were carried out without event. J.B.P. Casualties : NIL | |
| LE PHILOSOPHE & MAZINGARBE | 27th | | Quiet day with certain amount of rain. J.B.P. Casualties : NIL | |

1577 Wt. W10791/1773 500,000 1/15 D. D. & L. A.D.S.S./Forms/C. 2118.

Instructions regarding War Diaries and Intelligence Summaries are contained in F. S. Regs., Part II. and the Staff Manual respectively. Title pages will be prepared in manuscript.

# WAR DIARY
*or*
# ~~INTELLIGENCE SUMMARY.~~
*(Erase heading not required.)*

Army Form C. 2118.

| Place | Date | Hour | Summary of Events and Information | Remarks and references to Appendices |
|---|---|---|---|---|
| LE PHILOSOPHE | JUNE 28th | | Battalion Headquarters were subjected to a heavy bombardment in which four civilians were killed and five wounded (whom we had taken in for safety). We also had ~~[illegible]~~ eleven wounded. Curious coincidence that each of the Battalion Headquarters in LE PHILOSOPHE had been bombarded in the same way, evidently some spies about who had given our position away. It was at first thought that fire was directed at the 4.7" battery which was only 200 yards in front but evidently they were carefully ranging on the house and did a lot of damage. In the evening the Battalion moved into billets at NOEUX LES MINES, the whole Brigade having been relieved by the 142nd Infantry Brigade. | |
| | | | J.b.P. Casualties: Officers 1 wounded; Other Ranks 10 wounded | |
| NOEUX LES MINES | 29th 30th | | Resting at NOEUX LES MINES. | |
| | | | J.b.P. | |

1577 Wt. W10791/1773 500,000 1/15 D. D. & L. A.D.S.S./Forms/C. 2118.

140th Bde.
47th Division.

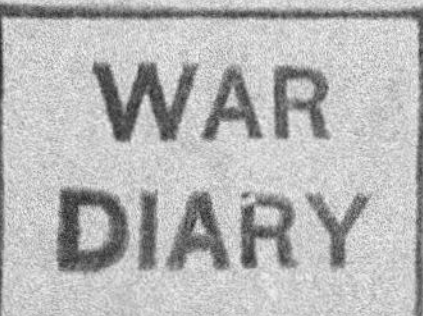


1/15th Battalion LONDON Regiment.

JULY 1915

1

# WAR Diary
## of
## 15th Batt London Regt
## (P.W.O. Civil Service Rifles)

July 1st 1915

July 1st NOEUX-LES-MINES. The Battalion receives orders during the morning to return to MAZINGARBE. Our week of rest is thus cut short as we returned into the shelled area again. This morning the mine line was shelled (about 6 8" falling into the dump) this is the first time this has happened since last November.

July 2nd MAZINGARBE J.W.P. working party of 250 on second line. J.W.P.

July 3rd MAZINGARBE. Battalion engaged on making dug outs behind their billets

J.G.P.

July 4th MAZINGARBE. First time [illegible] billets shelled during the afternoon no casualties

J.G.P.

July 5th MAZINGARBE. Quiet day J.G.P.

July 6th MAZINGARBE. The Brigade relieves the 141st Inf Bdge in the W section. The Battalion relieved the 15th Batt London Regt in the W2 section which we had previously held when attached to the 142nd Inf Bdge The 7th Batt were on our right and next to the French. on our left the 6th Batt. London Regt. J.C.P.

July 7th A quiet day except for shelling of the reserve company who where in dug outs made of mine props. So one half this company was moved during the night into some houses as the cellars seem to be safer. J.C.P. Casualties 2 wounded

July 8th A quiet day but the Germans for the first time shelled the ration waggons (no damage to them) at 10 pm - unusual as their artillary here are generally very quiet at night. Casualties 2 wounded.
J.C.P.

July 9th A quiet day. The French artillary who up to now had supported us were relieved by our own Divisional artillary
Casualties nil. J.C.P.

July 10th a very quiet day. Casualties nil.
J.C.P.

July 11th a quiet day except for one sniper who continually annoyed anybody crossing the mine yard. The Germans send a lot of blind shells today. Casualties nil. J.C.P.

July 12th + 13th Quiet days no casualties
J.C.P.

July 14th The French very busy but are again very quiet J.G.P. No casualties

July 15th to July 19th all very quiet days 3 men slightly wounded. J.G.P.

July 20th 2 companies 8th Seaforth Highlanders & some officers of the 12th [illegible] arrive for instruction for 48 hours. For the 1st 24 hours they were mixed up with our men along the front line, they seemed disappointed as they did not jump over the parapet ~~and~~ what they thought an attack ought to take place every day. One man killed in the mine yard. J.G.P

July 21st The Germans shelled our front trenches rather heavily but they did no damage except to parapet. One man wounded. J.G.P

July 22nd The houses ~~[illegible]~~ in which the reserve ½ Coy were kept, were heavily shelled but the cellars were not penetrated except in one house next the Regimental aid post. The Brigade was relieved by the 22nd Brigade after we had been in for 16 days. We returned to MAZINGARBE

J.G.P

MAZINGARBE.

July 23rd A big working party all night.

J.G.P

July 24th A quiet day for the Battalion but we suffered heavily at a bomb school at NOEUX-LES-MINES where owing to some accident 1 Sgt + 3 men were killed and one officer + 3 other ranks wounded.

J.W.T.

July 25th to July 29th The Battalion rested but provided working parties each night.

July 30th The 140th Inf Bdge relieved the 141st Inf Bdg in X section. We relieved the 19th Batt + had the 8th Batt on our right we being in X 2 section.

July 31st A quiet day - one man slightly wounded.

J.W.T.

140th Bde.
47th Division.

1/15th Battalion LONDON Regiment

AUGUST 1915

WAR DIARY

of

15th Batt London Regt
(Civil Service Rifles)

for

August 1915

kept by

Capt & Adj J. G. Parish

1st Still in X2 a quiet day, big working parties come up each night & billpoding on new front line. JBP

2nd Another quiet day, QUALITY STREET where Batt Headquarters and the reserve company are billeted was shelled a certain amount but we had no casualties.

3rd Battalion relieved during the afternoon by the 11th A & S Highlanders. The relief drew no fire which seemed to show that as the Germans work so hard all night that they sleep during the afternoon, as on more than one occasion the relieving unit disliking the standing water in the trenches, got out & walked over the open in full view of the German front line & within 800 yards. On relief the Battalion moved to LE PHILOSOPHE which we left for LABEUVRIERE at 11 pm. marching via NOYELLES VERMELLES – SAILLY-LABOURSE VAUDRICOURT & GOSNAY. We reached billets at 5AM, the men came in very well & only one man fell out & he had been ill for some days. JBP

4th to 25th The Battalion remained at rest at LABOUVRIERE where after a few days rest a programme of training was carried out, beside the ordinary company & battalion training extra bombers machine gunners signallers etc were trained & at the end of the rest all specialists through out the Battalion were duplicated. JWP

26th The Battalion paraded at 2pm and moved up to the trenches taking over W2 section from the 12th H.L.I. The day was hot & an hours halt was made at HOUCHIN where the men had tea. A very trying march as the day was exceptionally hot. JWP

27th A quiet day excepting for aerial Torpedoes which did a lot of damage to an RE working party killing 8 out of a party of 10. JWP

28th Aerial Torpedoes very busy we had some 50 land within 100 yards of Battalion Headquarters which were in a sort of crater and up to this date thought to be safe from shell fire. but these Torpedoes appear to fall at an angle of 80° when they are fired from 400 yards range. Their explosions are very powerful & big pit props were displaced & thrown a distance of over 50 yards. JWP

29th A quieter day. no casualties JWP

30th Aerial torpedoes again bothered us a lot but we escaped with only 2 casualties from them. The heavy artillery 15" was turned on but evidently the position, although smoke could be seen as the aerial torpedoes were fired, was difficult to locate. The afternoon was quite except for some heavy shells which landed also in the mine yard & appeared to come from the direction of HOLLOCK. Again we found a covering party to dig the new forward trench.

31st We bombarded the double crassier all the morning & except for one aerial torpedo at 8.10 AM there was no reply.

J.W. Tanns Capt & Adj

15th Batt London Regt

140th Bde.
47th Division.

1/15th Battalion LONDON Regiment

SEPTEMBER
and
OCTOBER

1 9 1 5

WAR DIARY

for

September 1915

of

15th Batt. London Regt
(P.W.O. Civil Service Rifles)

kept by Capt & Adjt J. L. Parish[?]
15th Batt London Regt

1st We again shelled the Double Crassiers & there was practically no reply. A very wet night. We found the usual covering party for the new trench. JWP

2nd Bombardment continues to which the Germans replied with their heavies & aerial torpedoes again; they did a good deal of damage to our trenches & the mine yard. Very wet night. JWP

3rd A wet night the Batt. was relieved during the evening by the 22nd Batt. A quiet day opposite us but the French seemed to be bombarding very hard. After relief the battalion was on a working party and at 2.30 AM 4th motor buses being provided we proceeded to HAILLICOURT. JWP

5th Nothing to report JWP

6th " " " JWP

7th Battalion proceeds to LES BREBIS by motor buses, where it worked until 2 AM on the new line in front of W 2. JWP

8th Battalion working party all night on W 2 JWP.

9th Continued the work returned to HOUCHIN by motor bus at 2.30 AM

10th to 16th The Battalion remained at rest at HOUCHIN, men cleaned themselves & drill of all sorts took place during the morning. games in the afternoons. J.W.P.

17th Battalion proceeded to LES BREBIS by motor bus & formed a working party

18th Battalion employed in carrying gas cylinders into the new gas trench & placing them in position. It required a good deal of organization but the men did well & it was successfully carried out without incident. J.W.P.

19th again employed carrying cylinders also & placing them in position. The Batt. then returned to HALLICOURT by motor buses J.W.P.

20th Battalion rested J.W.P.

21st Battalion returns to LES BREBIS by motor buses J.W.P.

23rd Battalion relieves 22nd Batt in new trench: & takes over the front in W.2 which was previously held by one company. A very wet night. & the artillery very active the whole time J.W.P.

24th more rain & the trenches awful a bad look out for tomorrow's attack. During the night we were relieved by the 6th & 7th Batt. & returned to a new trench near N Maroc Church. J.W.P.

25th The Battalion was in Brigade reserve & moved up to our now old front line as soon as the 6th & 7th Batts had carried out their successful attack. We supplied a party of 25 men to carry over bombs, they had a bad time crossing & only 4 were neither killed or wounded: immediately they left our front trench they came under a heavy fire from the right. A most striking event of the attack was the absolute silence of the German guns as our first 4 lines went over. There was also not enough wire cut the Germans had machine guns concentrated on all places where it was cut & our men lost heavily at these points. The gas seemed to do no actual damage & not a single dead German killed by gas was found opposite us: though without doubt it frightened many: the prisoners who were brought in certainly did not appear to be in any way affected & except for a very few oxygen respirators the only thing they had was a wad of cotton wool. JWP

26th A noisy early morning & the Brigade stood to arms most of the day as the Germans were expected to counter attack & although we were heavily shelled nothing more happened. JWP

27th The Battalion now holds the front from the DOUBLE CRASSIER to our old front line at the QUARRIES, which is the natural pivot of the whole advance. The trench is very shallow less than 3' in a lot of places. We were lucky not to have that part [illegible] of the trench shelled JWP

28th Another wet day. they shelled [illegible] with gas shells upset a lot of the men; we were unexperienced & tried to stay in a cellar when our lad knocked the house down on the top of us; our smoke helmets were useless & we were eventually driven into the street & then the fresh air soon revived us - Cocaine placed into our eyes proved a great relief. During the night 28th we relieved the 6th Batt London Regt in the captured German 2nd & front lines. Relief very slow.

29th A quiet day except for some shelling during the morning. Our left is now on the BETHUNE - LOOS Road & on our right are the 8th Batt London Regt whose left is on the DOUBLE CRASSIER. The nights are busy with wiring & burying dead, the former seemed the most important & we badly required help for the latter work - JWP

4.

30th A very wet day. We were relieved that night by the French who only took over our front line. When we left there were still a large number of dead to bury & rifles etc to be salvaged. After relief we spent the night until 5 a.m. near the LOOS ROAD redoubt & moved into Quality STREET for a 6 hours rest before moving on to VERQUIN.

JWP

WAR DIARY

of

15th Batt London Regt

(P.W.O. Civil Service Rifles)

for

October 1915

Kept by

Capt & Adjt J. H. Parish

15th Batt London Regt

4

1st We left QUALITY STREET at NOON & marched to VERQUIN via MAZINGARBE FOSSE NO 2 de NOEUX across country to HOUCHIN & on to VAUDRICOURT and then to VERQUIN. a long tiring march but the men stayed well, the billets seem to be better than those we previously had.
2nd to 5th The Battalion after cleaning up did some route marches & drill JWP
6th The Battalion moved to NOEUX-LES-MINES. very wet muddy march JWP
7th Route march & practising of rapid deployment into artillery formations JWP
8th In the afternoon the brigade was inspected by General Sir H Rawlinson, we then left for MAZINGARBE. JWP
9th The Battalion was lent to the 2nd Brigade & we spent the night in the old British front line just in front of LE ROUTOIRE
10th Rested.
11th & 12th The Battalion supplied big working parties ~~each night~~, digging communication trenches up to our new front line
13th The Batt moved up at night to the old British front line trenches near Quality Street, after being there an hour we were moved to the trenches

we had occupied on the night of the 9th

13th The Bombardment of HULLUCH & LOOS seemed very heavy. The German replied on our trench a certain amount we had some casualties. In the evening we moved forward at 5.30pm into the old German front line near LONE TREE & then at midnight the 13th/14th received orders to take over front line trenches from the 8th Berks & London Scottish, the communication trenches were full of wires but the relief was carried out without loss — during the morning of the 14th we took over more trenches to our left & relieved the Black Watch. A quiet day on the whole. J.W.P.

15th Hard at work improving the trenches. A quiet day J.W.P.

16th We were heavily shelled in the afternoon and a good deal of damage was done to our front line. J.W.P.

17th We were relieved by the 6th Batt & moved back to the old German front line where we were during the 18th & 19th. We found working & carrying parties each night.

20th relieved the 6th Batt in the front line

21st & 22nd Quiet days on the whole but we & the trenches suffered from rain. A curious mist every morning which suddenly lifted very quickly & on 2 occasions burying parties were fired upon, they being in full view of the German lines while 2 mins before it was impossible to see 20 yards. JLP

23rd relieved by 19th Battn & go back to old British front line. JLP

24th 25th & 26th stayed in our British line which we had occupied on night of the 9th Oct. Rained hard all day & each night we found working parties of 300 men. JLP

27th returned to MAZINGARBE, & we supplied a company for the King's inspection.

28th 29 30th. Rested & cleaned ourselves at MAZINGARBE.

31st relieved the 19th Battn in the Chalk Pit section. The Germans very offensive & shelled us at odd times during the night.

JLP

K/66

R

Vol 28

1/15th Battalion London Regiment
(P.W.O. CIVIL SERVICE RIFLES.)

# WAR DIARY. –

# October, 1917. –

Instructions regarding War Diaries and Intelligence Summaries are contained in F. S. Regs., Part II. and the Staff Manual respectively. Title pages will be prepared in manuscript.

# WAR DIARY

~~or~~

~~INTELLIGENCE SUMMARY.~~

(*Erase heading not required.*)

Army Form C. 2118.

| Place | Date | Hour | Summary of Events and Information | Remarks and references to Appendices |
|---|---|---|---|---|
| | Oct. | | | |
| FRONT LINE | 1. | | In Front Line trenches, GAVRELLE, Casualties, Nil. | |
| | 2. | | " " " " " " " | |
| | 3. | | (Relieved about 11.0 a.m. by 1/18th Battalion London Regiment and moved back to AUBREY Camp (Casualties, 1 O.R. wounded. | |
| AUBREY CAMP near ROCLINCOURT | 4. | | At AUBREY Camp. Casualties, nil. | |
| | 5. | | " " " " " | |
| | 6. | | " " " " " | |
| | 7. | | " " " " " | |
| | 8. | | " " " " " | |
| | 9. | | " " " " " | |
| SUPPORT | 10. | | Relieved 22nd Battalion London Regiment in Support, Casualties, nil. | |
| | 11. | | In Support. Casualties, nil. | |
| | 12. | | " " " " | |
| | 13. | | " " " " | |
| | 14. | | " " " " | |
| | 15. | | " " " " | |
| | 16. | | " " " 1 O.R. wounded. | |
| | 17. | | " " " nil. | |
| FRONT LINE | 18. | | Relieved 1/7th Battalion London Regiment in Front Line. Casualties, Nil. | |
| | 19. | | In Front Line. Casualties, nil. | |
| | 20. | | " " " " " | |
| | 21. | | " " " " 2 O.R. wounded. | |

Army Form C. 2118.

Instructions regarding War Diaries and Intelligence Summaries are contained in F. S. Regs., Part II. and the Staff Manual respectively. Title pages will be prepared in manuscript.

# WAR DIARY
*or*
# INTELLIGENCE SUMMARY.
*(Erase heading not required.)*

| Place | Date | Hour | Summary of Events and Information | Remarks and references to Appendices |
|---|---|---|---|---|
| FRONT LINE | 22. | | In Front Line. Casualties, 1 O.R. wounded. | |
| | 23. | | " " " " nil. | |
| | 24. | | " " " " 1 O.R. killed, 1 O.R. wounded. | |
| | 25. | | " " " " nil. | |
| | 26. | | Relieved by 1/20th London Regiment and moved to AUBREY Camp. Casualties. nil. | |
| | 27. | | At AUBREY Camp. Casualties, nil. | |
| | 28. | | " " " " " | |
| | 29. | | " " " " " | |
| | 30. | | " " " " " | |
| | 31. | | " " " " " | |

Harold Marshall
Major,
Cdg., 1/15th Battalion London Regiment,
(P.W.O. CIVIL SERVICE RIFLES.)

T2134. Wt. W708—776. 500000. 4/15. Sir J. C. & S.

1/15' Battn. London Regt. (P.W.O. Civil Service Rifles)

WAR DIARY. –

NOVEMBER, 1917. –

Army Form C. 2118.

Instructions regarding War Diaries and Intelligence Summaries are contained in F. S. Regs., Part II. and the Staff Manual respectively. Title pages will be prepared in manuscript.

# WAR DIARY
*or*
# INTELLIGENCE SUMMARY.
*(Erase heading not required.)*

| Place | Date | Hour | Summary of Events and Information | Remarks and references to Appendices |
|---|---|---|---|---|
| AUBREY CAMP | 1/11/17 | | Platoon and Company training and small working parties. – Casualties Nil. | |
| " | 2/11/17 | | Platoon and Company training and small working parties – Casualties Nil | |
| " | 3/11/17. | | Baths and small working parties. – Casualties Nil | |
| " | 4/11/17 | | Church parades. – Casualties Nil. | |
| FRONT LINE | 5/11/17 | | Relieved composite Battalion of 23rd and 24th London in front line R1. sector immediately | Order No. 85 attached |
| " | | | S. of GAVRELLE. – Casualties 2 O.R. wounded | |
| " | 6/11/17 | | A quiet day. Casualties Nil | |
| " | 7/11/17 | | Work on trench improvements. – Casualties Nil | |
| " | 8/11/17 | | A Quiet day. – Casualties Nil | |
| ROUNDHAY CAMP | 9/11/17 | | Relieved by 7th Battalion London Regiment and moved to Brigade Reserve at | Order No. 86 |
| " | | | ROUNDHAY CAMP on ARRAS - BAILLEUL ROAD. – Casualties Nil. | attached |
| " | 10/11/17 | | Working parties under R.E. in forward area. – Casualties Nil. | |
| " | 11/11/17. | | Baths and working parties. Casualties 2 O.R. wounded by explosion of a bomb | |
| " | | | which was struck by a pick on the cable burying party near NAVAL TRENCH. | |
| " | 12/11/17. | | At ROUNDHAY Camp, Casualties Nil | |
| | 13/11/17. | | At ROUNDHAY Camp Casualties Nil | |

A6945 Wt. W11422/M1160 350,000 12/16 D. D. & L. Forms/C./2118/14.

Instructions regarding War Diaries and Intelligence Summaries are contained in F. S. Regs., Part II. and the Staff Manual respectively. Title pages will be prepared in manuscript.

# WAR DIARY
*or*
# INTELLIGENCE SUMMARY.
(*Erase heading not required.*)

Army Form C. 2118.

| Place | Date | Hour | Summary of Events and Information | Remarks and references to Appendices |
|---|---|---|---|---|
| ROUNDHAY CAMP | 14/11/17 | | At Roundhay Camp. Casualties Nil | |
| " | 15/11/17 | | do do. | |
| " | 16/11/17 | | do. do. | |
| " | 17/11/17 | | do. do | |
| ECOIVRES | 18/11/17 | | Relieved by 13th East Yorks Regiment and moved to ECOIVRES. – Casualties Nil | O.O. 89 attached |
| " | 19/11/17 | | At ECOIVRES Casualties Nil | |
| " | 20/11/17 | | do. do. | |
| HERMAVILLE | 21/11/17 | | Moved to billets at HERMAVILLE. – Casualties Nil | O.O. 90 attached |
| WANQUETIN | 22/11/17 | | Moved to huts at WANQUETIN. – Casualties Nil | O.O. 91 attached |
| GOUY en ARTOIS. | 23/11/17 | | Moved to billets at GOUY-EN-ARTOIS. – Casualties Nil | O.O. 92 attached |
| COURCELLES LE COMTE | 24/11/17 | | Moved to COURCELLES le COMTE and billetted in huts. – Casualties Nil | O.O. 93 attached |
| BEAULENCOURT | 25/11/17 | | Moved to BEAULENCOURT and billetted in huts – Casualties Nil | |
| " | 26/11/17 | | At BEAULENCOURT, Casualties Nil | |
| DOIGNIES | 27/11/17 | | Moved to bivouac camp at DOIGNIES. – Casualties Nil | |
| | 28/11/17 | | At 10. am moved to HINDENBURG LINE arriving about 12.30 pm. – Relieved 4th Cavalry Battalion in ~~right~~ of BOURLON WOOD area. Relief complete 1.30 am 29.11.17 – Casualties 4. O.R. Killed in Action 17. O.R. Wounded | (See narrative attached) |

A6945 Wt. W11422/M1160 350,000 12/16 D. D. & L. Forms/C/2118/14.

Army Form C. 2118.

Instructions regarding War Diaries and Intelligence Summaries are contained in F. S. Regs., Part II. and the Staff Manual respectively. Title pages will be prepared in manuscript.

# WAR DIARY
*or*
# INTELLIGENCE SUMMARY.
*(Erase heading not required.)*

| Place | Date | Hour | Summary of Events and Information | Remarks and references to Appendices |
|---|---|---|---|---|
| | 28/11/17 | | in action; 2 OR. Missing.- | |
| | 29/11/17 | | In BOURLON WOOD. - Casualties Killed in Action 6. O.R.; Wounded in Action 2/Lt. T. WOODS, 52 O.R; Missing, 2. OR. - | See Narrative of Operations attached |
| | 30/11/17 | | In BOURLON WOOD. - Casualties. Killed in Action 2/Lt C.V. Marchant, 2/Lt G.E. Tatum 39 OR.; Wounded in Action. Capt P. Davenport, MC. (Gas) Capt P. Dallon, Capt D.C. McArdle (Remained) (Gas): Lt & QM. W.G. Hodge (Gas) Lieut. H.A. Berry, 2/Lt W.E. Hale: 2/Lt B.A. Ditter (Gas) 2/Lt R.W. Telling (Gas) 122 OR.; Missing 40 OR. | - do. - |

Harold Marshall
Major
Cdg/15 Bn London Regt
(P.W.O. Civil Service Rifles)

A6945 Wt. W11422/M1160 350,000 12/16 D. D. & L. Forms/C./2118/14.

War Diary

SECRET. **CIVIL SERVICE RIFLES.** COPY NO. 2

ORDER NO. [illegible]

[illegible] November, 191[illegible]

Ref. Map, France,
Sheet [illegible], 1/20000

1. The Battalion will relieve 22nd and 24th Battalions in [illegible] Sub-sector as follows:-

   A.Coy. will relieve D.Coy. 22nd Batt. (Right front).
   D.Coy. " " B. " " " (Left front).
   B. " " " C. " 24th Batt. (Support).
   C. " " " A. " " " (Reserve).

2. Battalion will parade in column of route on main road outside the camp ready to move at [illegible] a.m. Order of march will be C., A., B., H.Q. & D.Coy. Route to be followed is via [illegible], [illegible], [illegible] to [illegible]. Guides will be met at [illegible] of [illegible] and [illegible] ROAD at 10.0 a.m. A distance of 200 yards will be maintained between companies on the march.

3. Advance parties of 1 officer and 1 senior N.C.O. per Coy. will report to 24th Batt. H.Q. at 9.0 a.m. to take over trench stores, etc. The R.S.M. will take over stores for Batt. H.Q. Gas N.C.O.s will accompany the advance parties.

4. Copies of receipts for trench stores, maps, aeroplane photos, etc. will be forwarded to Batt. H.Q. by [illegible] p.m.

5. All works, schemes and water guards will be taken over.

6. Lewis Gun limbers will leave at 7.45 a.m. [illegible] Mess cart, medical [illegible] will leave at the same time.

7. Code word for relief complete will be Coy. Commander's name.

[signature]

Capt. and Adjutant,
CIVIL SERVICE RIFLES.

Copy No. 1 CO.
2 War Diary.
3 File.
4 O.C. A.Coy.
5 " B.
6 " C.
7 " D.
8 L.G.O.
9 Signals.
10 Q.M. & T.O.
11 Medical Officer.
12 24th Batt.
13 140th Infy. Bde.

Secret

Copy No 3

## CIVIL SERVICE RIFLES

## ORDER No 89. –

Ref. Map France Sheet 57B N.W. 1/20,000

17th November 1917

1. Battalion will be relieved by "5" East Yorks Battn and will move into Corps Reserve at ECOIVRES. –
2. On relief Companies will march independently to [illegible] JUNCTION behind the ROUNDWAY BATHS, where they will entrain for ECOIVRES.
3. The C.Q.M.S. of each Company and one man per platoon will report to Capt P. Fallow at the Transport Lines at 2.30 p.m. for billeting.
4. Receipts will be taken for all trench stores, aeroplane photos, [illegible] etc, and will be handed in to Headquarters on arrival at ECOIVRES. –
5. Transport will move by road. –
6. [illegible] and [illegible] will be ready for collection by Transport Officer by 8.0 a.m.
7. All [illegible] and mess [illegible] will be dumped at the Guard Room by 8.0 a.m. Blankets will be carried by the men.
8. Lewis Gun limbers will be loaded at 3.0 p.m. [illegible]
9. Code word for relief complete will be Company Commanders name.
10. Only breakfast rations and haversack rations will be sent to Companies this afternoon.

[signature: Davenport]
Capt & Adjutant
Civil Service Rifles

Copy No [illegible]

[illegible distribution list]

SECRET. Copy No. 3

[illegible]

[illegible] 16

Ref. Map.
France 1/10000 51C N.W.

1. Battalion will be relieved by 7th Battalion tomorrow and will move into Reserve at ROUNDHAY CAMP H7c.

A. Coy will be relieved by A. Coy 7th
B. " " " " " B " 7th
C. " " " " " D " 7th
D. " " " " " C " 7th

2. One guide per platoon will report to Lt. G.R. Mellitt(?) at Bn. H.Q. at 9.30 a.m. They will then proceed to junction of TONY ALLEY and [illegible] ROAD where incoming platoons will be met at 10.30 a.m.

3. All trench stores, aeroplane photos and programmes of work will be handed over and receipts forwarded to Orderly Room on arrival at ROUNDHAY CAMP.

4. O.C. D. Coy will detail one officer and 30 O.R. for work on RED LINE under C.R.E. They will meet a guide at Bn. H.Q. ROUNDHAY at 1.0 p.m. tomorrow.

5. All packs of Lewis Gunners will be dumped at Ration Dump by 6.0 p.m. tonight to be taken back by ration limbers.

6. Lewis Gun limbers and limber for [illegible], medical stores and mess things will be at junction of TONY ALLEY and TONY TRACK at 12.30 p.m.

7. Billeting party of one senior N.C.O. per Coy will report to 2/Lt. Gurney(?) at Bn. H.Q. at 8.0 a.m.

8. Code word for relief complete will be Coy Commander's name.

[illegible signature]
Capt. & Adjt.
[illegible]

Copy No. 1 C.O.
2 File
3 War Diary
4 O.C. A. Coy
5 " B. "
6 " C. "
7 " D. "
8 Signals
9 L.G.O.
10 Works
11 T.O. & Q.M.
12 H.Q. [illegible]
13 7th [illegible]

SECRET.                                                    COPY NO. 3.

CIVIL SERVICE RIFLES.

ORDER NO. 90.

20th November, 1917.

Reference Map :- LENS No.11, 1/100,000.

1. BATTALION will move to billets in HERMAVILLE to-morrow.

2. Battalion will parade in column of route at 9.45 a.m. in the main road outside Battalion Headquarters facing W. Order of march will be :- A. B. H.Q. C. D. Transport.

3. Billeting parties consisting of C.Q.M.S. of each Company and one man per platoon will report to Captain FALLON outside the Orderly Room at 7.30 a.m.

4. Cookers and water carts will be ready for collection by Transport Officer at 8.45 a.m.

5. Blankets will be rolled in bundles of 10 and dumped outside Guard Tent at 8.0 a.m. Valises and mess boxes will be at same place at 8.30 a.m.

6. Certificates that billets have been left clean will be handed in on parade.

Davenport.

Capt. and Adjutant,
CIVIL SERVICE RIFLES.

Copy No.1 C.O.
2 File.
3 War Diary.
4 O.C. A Coy.
5 O.C. B Coy.
6 O.C. C Coy.
7 O.C. D Coy.
8 Signals.
9 L.G.O.
10 Works Officer.
11 T.O. & Q.M.
12 140th Infantry Brigade.

SECRET

ORDER No. [illegible]

22nd Nov. 19[illegible]

Infantry Sheffield [illegible] LENS. [illegible]

1. Battalion will move to the WANQUETIN SIMENCOURT area this morning.

2. Battalion will parade in column of route on the main road facing [illegible] Q.M. Stores ready to move at 10.00 a.m.

3. Order of march will be:-

C. H.Q. D. B. A.

4. Blankets, valises, and mess boxes will be dumped at Q.M. Stores by 9.0 a.m.

5. Billeting parties will report to Capt. FALLON at the [illegible] at 8.30 a.m. and proceed by cycle. they will report to Town Major at WANQUETIN at 9.0 a.m.

6. Cookers and water carts will be collected by T.O. at 9.30 a.m.

R. Davenport

Capt. & Adjutant,
CIVIL SERVICE RIFLES.

Copy No. 1 C.O.
2 [illegible]
3 War Diary
4 O.C. A Coy
5 O.C. B Coy
6 O.C. C Coy
7 O.C. HQ Coy
8 Signals
9 [illegible]
10 R.S.M.
11 T.O.
12 [illegible]

Secret

Copy No. 3

# Civil Service Rifles

## Order No. 93

Reference Map LENS No. 11 1/100000

23rd November 1917

1. Battalion will move to COURCELLES le COMTE area tomorrow

2. Battalion will parade in column of route in RUE D'ARRAS facing S.E. ready to move at 9.15 a.m. — Head of column will be at junction of RUE D'ARRAS and RUE TRAVERSIN. —

3. Order of march will be:—

   Band. B. C., H.Q., A., D.. Coys.

4. Packs clearly marked will be dumped at Q.M. Stores at 7.45 a.m. to be carried by lorry, — Blankets in bundles of ten and valises will be at the same place at same time. — Mess boxes to be at Q.M. Stores at 8.30 a.m. — Mess Cart will call & collect them at that time

5. Certificates that billets have been left clean will be handed in on parade. —

6. Cookers and water carts will be collected by Transport Officer at 8.30 a.m.

Davenport.
Capt & Adjutant
Civil Service Rifles

Copy No. 1 C.O.
" " 2 2/ic
" " 3 War Diary
" " 4 O.C. A Coy
" " 5 " B "
" " 6 " C "
" " 7 " D "
" " 8 Signals
" " 9 L.G.O.
" " 10. ~~[illegible]~~ Q.M.
" " 11. 30 ~~[illegible]~~
" " 12. 140 Infy Bde

## Civil Service Rifles

Narrative of [illegible] 25th November [illegible] of 1[illegible]

[illegible] HERMIES [illegible]

The Battalion took over that portion of the front held by the 2nd [illegible] Cadets [illegible] Brigade [illegible] on the night of the 23rd [illegible]. Two Companies were in the front line, B Company under [illegible] from E.16.a [illegible] to E.18.b [illegible] and D Company under [illegible] on the right from E.[illegible] to E.7.c.[illegible]. C Company under [illegible] was in support in the SUNKEN ROAD at [illegible]. A Company under [illegible] was in reserve in the vicinity of Battalion Headquarters which were at [illegible]. The Battalion moved up from the [illegible] LINE [illegible] K.[illegible] [illegible] 12 [illegible] and [illegible] by platoons at 100 yards interval. [illegible] of the Battalion reached [illegible] STATION [illegible] the enemy barraged the ground between this point and Battalion Headquarters with H.E. and gas shells. Gas masks were put on and the Battalion pushed on through the barrage. D and B Companies had no casualties but C Company lost 18 men and A Company [illegible] men. The relief was reported complete about 1.30 a.m. on the [illegible] [illegible] through the [illegible] enemy commenced to bombard the front line positions, the [illegible] and Battalion Headquarters. [illegible] were suffered during the day. [illegible] the [illegible] the night was fairly quiet and advantage was taken of this to improve the position and to patrol the Battalion front. Two patrols were sent out from each of the front line Companies towards the [illegible] Village [illegible] nothing exceptional was reported. Our artillery carried out a practice barrage at 5.0 a.m. on the [illegible] and the enemy [illegible] retaliation for about an hour. [illegible] quiet then until about [illegible] [illegible] [illegible] whole front. [illegible] [illegible]

[illegible]

[illegible]

[illegible]

[illegible]

the front of the [illegible]

standing [illegible]

suffering casualties [illegible] the [illegible]

continued [illegible]

north, the [illegible]

Company "C" [illegible]

[illegible] position [illegible]

[illegible]

[illegible] the [illegible]

position [illegible]

of B Company, [illegible]

[illegible]

enemy [illegible]

the enemy [illegible]

front. [illegible]

by B Company and [illegible]

[illegible]

position [illegible] about [illegible]

[illegible]

[illegible]

[illegible]

[illegible]

[illegible]

[illegible]

[illegible]

[illegible]

[illegible]

[illegible]

Shortly after this A Company [illegible] to a line from [illegible] touch with B Company on the right and on the left with the 9th Battalion. [illegible] previously [illegible]. The next day was uneventful and the Battalion was relieved by the 21st Battalion on the night of the [illegible] December, and moved back to hutted camp at [illegible] WOOD [illegible].

Harold Marshall

Major,

Commanding 1/15th Battn. London Regt.

(P.W.O. Civil Service Rifles)

Compiled from Reports of Officers in the absence of Col E Segrave DSO (gassed)

1/15th Bn London Regt (P.W.O. Civil Service Rifles)

WAR DIARY. -

DECEMBER. 1917. -

Instructions regarding War Diaries and Intelligence Summaries are contained in F. S. Regs., Part II. and the Staff Manual respectively. Title pages will be prepared in manuscript.

# WAR DIARY
*or*
# INTELLIGENCE SUMMARY.
*(Erase heading not required.)*

Army Form C. 2118.

| Place | Date | Hour | Summary of Events and Information | Remarks and references to Appendices |
|---|---|---|---|---|
| | December 1917. | | | |
| BOURLON WOOD. | 1 | | Relieved by 21st Bn London Regiment and marched to camp at HAVRINCOURT. – Casualties 4 O.R Killed 2/Lt G.M. MARGRETT, 10 O.R. Wounded. | |
| HAVRINCOURT WOOD. | 2. | | At HAVRINCOURT WOOD Casualties Nil. | |
| | 3. | | do. do. | |
| GRAINCOURT | 4. | | Took up position Right and Left of GRAINCOURT, – Casualties Nil. – | See Narrative attached. |
| | 5. | | See Narrative attached. – Casualties 3, O.R Killed 1. OR Wounded. | do |
| | 6. | | Marched to HAVRINCOURT WOOD. – Casualties. – Major H.F.M. WARNE, Capt L.L. BURTT, Lieut W.A.S. HOUSLOP, 2/Lts S.P. POTTS, A.E. KING, Missing; 5. O.R. Killed; 2/Lt W.B. LACY, 63. O.R. Wounded; 42 O.R. Missing. – | do |
| HAVRINCOURT WOOD | 7 | | At HAVRINCOURT WOOD. – Casualties Nil. – | |
| BERTINCOURT | 8 | | Marched to billets in BERTINCOURT. – Casualties Nil | |
| " | 9 | | At BERTINCOURT, Casualties Nil. | |
| " | 10 | | do. Casualties 1. O.R wounded by aeroplane bomb. | |
| " | 11 | | do. Casualties Nil. | |
| " | 12. | | do. do. | |
| " | 13. | | do. do | |

T2134. Wt. W708–776. 500000. 4/15. Sir J. C. & S.

Instructions regarding War Diaries and Intelligence Summaries are contained in F. S. Regs., Part II. and the Staff Manual respectively. Title pages will be prepared in manuscript.

# WAR DIARY
*or*
# INTELLIGENCE SUMMARY.
*(Erase heading not required.)*

Army Form C. 2118.

| Place | Date December | Hour | Summary of Events and Information | Remarks and references to Appendices |
|---|---|---|---|---|
| | 1917 | | | |
| BERTINCOURT | 14 | | At BERTINCOURT, Casualties Nil. | |
| " | 15. | | Relieved 20th Bn London Regiment in Front Line. Casualties Nil | |
| FRONT LINE | 16 | | In Front Line. - Casualties 3. O.R. wounded. | |
| " | 17 | | do. Casualties Nil | |
| " | 18 | | do do | |
| " | 19 | | do. do. | |
| " | 20 | | do. do. | |
| " | 21 | | Relieved by 10th Sherwood Foresters and marched to billets in BERTINCOURT. - Casualties 1. O.R. killed 3. O.R. wounded | |
| MORLANCOURT | 22 | | Entrained at ETRICOURT. - Detrained at MERICOURT and marched to billets in MORLANCOURT. - Casualties Nil. | |
| " | 23 | | At MORLANCOURT, Casualties Nil | |
| " | 24 | | do. do. | |
| " | 25 | | do. do. | |
| " | 26 | | do. do | |
| " | 27 | | do do. | |

Army Form C. 2118.

Instructions regarding War Diaries and Intelligence Summaries are contained in F. S. Regs., Part II. and the Staff Manual respectively. Title pages will be prepared in manuscript.

# WAR DIARY
*or*
# INTELLIGENCE SUMMARY.
*(Erase heading not required.)*

| Place | Date December 1917. | Hour | Summary of Events and Information | Remarks and references to Appendices |
|---|---|---|---|---|
| MORLANCOURT | 28 | | At MORLANCOURT, Casualties nil. | |
| " | 29 | | Marched to billets in MERICOURT. Casualties nil | |
| MERICOURT | 30 | | At MERICOURT, Casualties nil | |
| " | 31 | | do do. | |

E Segrave
Lt Colonel
Cdg 1/15 Bn London Regiment
(P.W.O. Civil Service Rifles)

T2134. Wt. W708-776. 500000. 4/15. Sir J. C. & S.

140 Infantry Brigade

Herewith Narrative of the operations in BOURLON WOOD. —

Harold Marshall
Major
Cg/15 Bn London Regiment
(P.W.O. Civil Service Rifles)

13th December 1917

1/15th Bn London Regiment

Report on Operations December 4th 5th and 6th 1917

around GRAINCOURT

On December 4 orders were received for the Battalion to move from HAVRINCOURT in the afternoon and take up a position Right and Left of GRAINCOURT.-

This was done after dusk. A and B. Coys on the Left of the village under Lieut L.C. MORRIS, MC. on the road from about K.5. a. 9.7. to E 28. d. 8.4 and our Left was in touch with the 2nd Division

With 4. MG. of 140 Coy

C and D Companies took up a position on the right of the village in some old trenches and gun pits N. of the road at about K. 6. a. 9.4 to L. 1. a. 1.1. and connected up with the 59th Division on the right :- Capt L.L. BURTT in command.

In this position were also placed 4 guns of the 142 MG. Coy. under Lt. CHAMBERS.

The village was not occupied but posts were established in the SUNKEN ROADS NE of the village and withdrawn at dawn.

During the night I went over the whole of the dispositions through the front line and in front of the village and arranged with Lieut. CHAMBERS for the gun positions covering the front of the village and with him and an officer of the Sherwood Foresters for cross fire at the junction of our Right with the 59th.

Lewis Guns were disposed on the Left also for Cross fire and a night gun was put at about E 29. c. 8. 9. -

The troops from the old front line passed through us as arranged. The whole front line was patrolled until dawn.

On the morning of the 5th about 10.0 am a small number of the enemy were seen advancing cautiously down the slope and as their numbers increased the Artillery were notified and did some excellent shooting - the enemy bolting at once. - Later on they appeared and in considerable numbers, forming up in rear of the Sugar Refineries and also lining the BAPAUME - CAMBRAI ROAD - some filtered through into ANNEUX. -

Targets were frequently indicated to the Artillery and engaged with good effect. - The enemy losses at this period must have been very severe and some good results were obtained on the Right by M.G. L.G. and Rifle fire on many parties of the enemy approaching that portion of our Line from ANNEUX. Fire was also opened on small parties making for the village and in all cases during daylight the enemy was dispersed.

Towards dusk, however, a few of the enemy had penetrated to the cemetery and were engaged by M.G. fire but nothing could be done to hold the front of the village (other than by cross fire)

During the night our patrols were very active and frequent engagements took place with success to us in every case. We captured one light M.G. and one prisoner. the remainder of that party being killed except one wounded who got away.

Our Runners were in several cases involved and did some good fighting accounting for seven enemy between them.

Owing to the area of the village and the many means of getting in and out by the enemy it was impossible to control the situation except to keep patrolling and fighting where he could be found and in this on the left a platoon of the R.W.F. who were consolidating with us responded to my request and joined in to push out some enemy who were attempting to get through on the road at about K.5 A 6.1. and his advance in that direction was stopped. The R.W.F. entered into the spirit of the operations with great zeal but had to withdraw at daylight.—

It was impossible to stop the filtering through the village on the South and by dawn 40 or 50 enemy had got through and took up a position about the old gun pits.— These were engaged by Lewis Gun and Rifle fire from the Strong Point K 11 A 3.7. and many casualties were inflicted by Riflemen as well as L.G.— The garrison was R.W.F.

At dusk on the evening of the 5th Major H.F.M. WARNE took over Command of the Right Front and arrangements were made to post a Lewis Gun before dawn on the road about K 6 C.3.2. He also took confirming orders that on withdrawal the garrison on the right were to occupy the right strong post.— He reported that everything was in order and that both companies had already reconnoitred the route.

Rations were sent through from B. H.Q. the last party leaving H.Q. about 6.0 am 6th inst (having to make two journeys) this party arrived at the front line safely but no runners were received from the front line after about that time.—

Two Platoons of the R.W.F. engaged on consolidation work on the right and left about 4.0 am

About 4.30 am 6th inst 2/Lt AYLMORE took a Lewis Gun and team to the point abovementioned with instructions from Major WARNE to deal with enemy on South side of village as far as possible but not to become too much involved but to withdraw to the post in K.17. 6.5.6.

The Lewis Gun was in position about 5.0 am and an enemy patrol soon after tried to rush it but were dispersed with the loss of several wounded and killed and one wounded prisoner was taken by the team.

After daylight two patrols tried to envelope the gun but without success. They were driven off with a number of casualties but with a loss to our team of one killed and one wounded who was brought out.—

As other parties of the enemy were on the move for a further attack the gun was withdrawn but before doing so 2/Lt AYLMORE sent his runner to Major WARNE to acquaint him of the situation. Whilst this gun was in the Strong Post an enemy attack developed on the Right of the Strong Post and our gun was posted on the Sunken Road away from the Post and with the garrison and M.G and L.G fire the attack was beaten off with very heavy losses.

As to the doings of the right garrison on the 6th please refer to written statements sent to Brigade on 8th inst from 2/Lt AYLMORE. Sgt COOKE and Sergeant MANTHORPE. no copies of which have been kept.

Orders were sent out for withdrawal at 5.30 pm on 6th inst but it had commenced before the runner could get through. The whole garrison had however a warning order that if after the night of the 5/6th it was impossible to hold on that they were to withdraw to the post before indicated as might be ordered by the senior officer present.

The garrison of the right sector had apparently a very good time with splendid targets of masses of the enemy crossing diagonally N.W to S.E. and entered into the defence with great spirit (Ammunition had been sent to whole line the previous night by the R.W.F. working party.)

The enemy attack developed beyond our right where apparently not much resistance was offered and it was discovered that the troops on our right had withdrawn and the enemy was closing round our right rear and at the same time round our left rear from the village. – The garrison turned about and the order was given by 2/Lt KING and 2/Lt LACY to cut their way out. A Lewis Gun on each flank did splendid work in crumpling up the enveloping troops inflicting such punishment that the riflemen's task was made easier. Both guns got clear and during the withdrawal again got into action and effectively dealt with bodies of the enemy who tried to bar the way and on this occasion with only two good men on each gun they were invaluable. – Both guns were brought out to the Rest Camp by the same men.

After various bouts of fighting on the way the post arranged for was reached the troops being in good heart and much pleased with the days work.

2/Lt LACY was brought in wounded. 2/Lt KING was last seen in rear of our troops binding up his sergeant who was unable to walk.

As to the other officers Major WARNE, Capt L.L. BURTT, 2/Lt POTTS Lieut HOUSLOP it is difficult to say what happened and they were not seen during the withdrawal. I think some or all were probably cut off. –

As to O.R the S.Bs and some wounded including Lieut CHAMBERS were in the trench and probably taken prisoners. probably 12 – 15.

On the left during the 6th nothing much happened except M.G. fire and communication was kept up throughout by making a wide detour and the use of some gallant runners who were tireless and unafraid of M.G fire. The left garrison withdrew according to orders at 5.30 pm.

The Regimental Aid Post was evacuated by the M.O and staff at 6.0 pm all the wounded having been sent down.

Battalion H.Q. arrived at HAVRINCOURT about 11.0 pm

2/Lt AYLMORE collected our people in the Strong Post and sent them back to camp also the 1 x 2nd Machine Gunners to their

H.Q. He also saw all wounded evacuated.— No wounded were left out within 300 to 400 yards of the post and search was made along the line of withdrawal to that extent.—

The operations coming after recent heavy fighting and gassing was trying to the men added to which the cold was intense so much so that the water in M.G. sockets in silent guns out in shell holes froze frequently and the guns had to be changed whilst being thawed out. When however the enemy appeared on the 5th and the patrol fighting started that morning all ranks responded with a will and showed a magnificent spirit

—Sgd HAROLD MARSHALL
Cdg 1/15 London Regt

Addendum.

On the morning of the 6' GRAINCOURT was occupied by a considerable number of the enemy.— On the guns being turned on they bolted out.— Two or three hours after they returned and the guns settled down and did some very fine shooting on the village generally and on the position of M.Gs on the West especially.

NOTE. The Battalion Strength - Left was 5 off 113. OR.
on right 6. off. 112 O.R.
H.Q. 3 off 25. O.R.

## Civil Service Rifles.

Narrative of Operations covering period from 28th November 1917 to night of 1st/2nd December, 1917.

Reference Map [illegible]

The Battalion took over that portion of the front held by the [illegible] Monmouthshire [illegible] and the [illegible] the frontage being from [illegible] on the night of the 27th/28th [illegible]. Two Companies were in the front line, B Company under [illegible] from [illegible] and D Company under [illegible] being on the right from [illegible]. C Company under [illegible] Company under [illegible] was in reserve [illegible] of Battalion [illegible] the Battalion [illegible] was [illegible] and [illegible] by [illegible] the [illegible] of the Battalion [illegible] the enemy [illegible] between the [illegible] and Battalion Headquarters [illegible] was [illegible] and the Battalion [illegible] through the [illegible] and B Companies [illegible] C Company [illegible] 18 men and [illegible] Company [illegible] men. The relief was reported complete about [illegible] on the 28th. During the 29th the enemy commenced to bombard the front line positions, the [illegible] and Battalion Headquarters. Many casualties were suffered during the day. [illegible] the exception of [illegible] shelling the night was fairly quiet, and advantage was taken of this to [illegible] the position and to patrol the Battalion front. [illegible] patrols were pushed out from each of the front line [illegible] nothing exceptional was reported. The artillery carried out a practice barrage at [illegible] and the enemy retaliation [illegible] about 8.50 a.m. [illegible] the barrage [illegible] along the [illegible] front line [illegible]

[illegible]

[illegible] the infantry

halted [illegible]

[illegible]

[illegible] Company, which [illegible]

[illegible] platoon [illegible]

[illegible] the platoon [illegible]

reinforcing the right of [illegible] Company, and the second

platoon under [illegible] reinforcing the right

of B Company. [illegible] platoon under

[illegible] of the [illegible] that the

enemy [illegible]

the enemy [illegible] of the [illegible]

front. [illegible] fire [illegible]

by B Company and the left platoon of D Company.

At [illegible] it was found a [illegible] of one

platoon [illegible] was about [illegible]

[illegible] A Company and the

[illegible] including [illegible] officers

[illegible]

about [illegible] with the right flank on

the [illegible]

[illegible]

[illegible] machine gun [illegible]

machine gun [illegible]

[illegible] the [illegible] and [illegible] that

[illegible] was established [illegible]

Shortly after dusk A Company [illegible] to a line from [illegible] touch with B Company on the right and [illegible] with the 8th Battalion [illegible] Company [illegible] The night [illegible] and the [illegible] Battalion was relieved by the [illegible] Battalion on the night of the [illegible] and moved back to [illegible] about [illegible]

Harold Marshall

Major

Commanding 16th Batt. London Regt.

([illegible] Rifles)

Compiled from Report of Company Officers in the absence of Col E Legrave D.S.O. (gassed)

Vol 31

# WAR DIARY.

of

1/15th Bn. LONDON REGT. (P.W.O. CIVIL SERVICE RIFLES.)

from 1st January 1918 to 31st January 1918.

Instructions regarding War Diaries and Intelligence Summaries are contained in F. S. Regs., Part II. and the Staff Manual respectively. Title pages will be prepared in manuscript.

Army Form C. 2118.

# WAR DIARY
*or*
# INTELLIGENCE SUMMARY.
*(Erase heading not required.)*

| Place | Date | Hour | Summary of Events and Information | Remarks and references to Appendices |
|---|---|---|---|---|
| | 1918 | | | |
| MERICOURT | Jan. | | | |
| | 1 | | At MERICOURT. - Casualties nil. | |
| | 2 | | do. do. | |
| | 3 | | do. do. | |
| | 4 | | do. do. | |
| | 5 | | do. do. | |
| | 6 | | do. do. | |
| | 7 | | do. do. | |
| | 8 | | do. do. | |
| | 9 | | do. do. | |
| | 10 | | Entrained at MERICOURT. D etrained at ETRICOURT and marched to billets in BERTINCOURT. Casualties nil. | Entraining orders attached. |
| BERTINCOURT | 11 | | At BERTINCOURT. - Casualties nil. | |
| RIBECOURT | 12 | | Moved to Support positions in RIBECOURT relieving 24th Bn.London Regt. - Casualties nil. | Order No.97 attached. |
| IN | 13 | | In Support. - Casualties nil. | |
| | 14 | | do. do. | |
| SUPPORT | 15 | | ~~Relieved 8th Bn. London Regt. in Front Line.~~ In Support. - Casualties nil. | Order No.99 attached. |
| FRONT LINE. | 16 | | In Front Line. - Casualtie s nil. Relieved 8th Battn London Regt. | |
| | 17 | | do. do. nil. | |
| | 18 | | do. Casualties 1 O.R. wounded. | |
| | 19 | | do. do. nil. | |
| | 20 | | do. do. nil. | |
| | 21 | | do. do. 2 O.R. wounded. | |
| | 22 | | do. do. nil. | |
| | 23 | | do. do. nil. | |
| | 24 | | Relieved by 19th Bn. London Regt. and moved to billets in BERTINCOURT Casualties 1 O.R. wounded. | Order No. 100 attached. |
| BERTINCOURT | 25 | | At BERTINCOURT. - Casualties nil. | |
| | 26 | | do. do. | |
| | 27 | | do. do. | |
| | 28 | | do. do. | |

A5834 Wt. W4973 M687 750,000 8/16 D. D. & L. Ltd. Forms/C.2118/13.

Instructions regarding War Diaries and Intelligence Summaries are contained in F. S. Regs., Part II. and the Staff Manual respectively. Title pages will be prepared in manuscript.

# WAR DIARY
*or*
# INTELLIGENCE SUMMARY.

*(Erase heading not required.)*

Army Form C. 2118.

| Place | Date | Hour | Summary of Events and Information | Remarks and references to Appendices |
|---|---|---|---|---|
| BERTINCOURT | 29 | | At BERTINCOURT. - Casualties nil. | |
| | 30 | | do. do. | |
| | 31 | | do. do. | |

Elgrave [illegible]

Major,
Cdg., 1/15th Bn. London Regt.
(P.W.O. CIVIL SERVICE RIFLES.)

B/42*

A5834 Wt. W4973 M687 750,000 8/16 D. D. & L. Ltd. Forms/C.2118/13.

War Diary

# CIVIL SERVICE RIFLES.

## ENTRAINING ORDERS.

9th January, 1918.

1 A party for loading both "omnibus trains" consisting of 30 O.R., H.Q. Coy, 1 Officer and 40 O.R., A Coy and 1 Officer, 30 O.R. B Coy will be at MERICOURT Station at 7 a.m. On completion of loading duties they will entrain in the second omnibus train, which leaves at 12 noon. Reveille for this party 5.15 a.m.; Breakfast 6 a.m. Lieut. Eccles will be in charge of this party and will report to R.T.O., MERICOURT. Remainder of A and B Coys. will be at the Station at 11.30 a.m. and will also travel in the second omnibus train.

2. H.Q. (less 30 O.R.), C and D Coys. will assemble outside MERICOURT Station at 9.30 a.m and will travel by first omnibus train leaving at 10 a.m.

3. On arrival at detraining station an unloading party consisting of 1 Officer and 50 O.R. from each of C and D Coys. will remain at the station and unload both "omnibus" trains. 2/Lt. Aylmore will be in charge of this party.

4. One blanket per man will be carried on the man. Greatcoats will be carried in packs (weather permitting), but may be put on in the train. Haversack rations (including bully beef) will be carried on the man. Water bottles will be filled before 9 a.m.

Reveille 6 a.m. Breakfast 7.15 a.m. Sick parade 7 a.m.

5. Transport.

By 1st omnibus train (to be at station by 7.30 a.m)

Lewis Gun Limbers

A and B Coy Cookers.

Mess Cart

Medical Cart

By 2nd omnibus train (to be at station by 9.10 a.m).

2 Tool Carts

C and D Coy. Cookers.

2 Water Carts.

6 Officers' kits and mess boxes will be stacked at Batt. Canteen by 8 a.m. Officers kits at RIBEMONT will be stacked at Q.M. Stores. Remainder of blankets in bundles of 10 tightly rolled and tied at each end

will be stacked, A, B and C Coys in A Coy billet, H.Q. and D Coy at Battn. canteen by 8 a.m. Palliasses of A, B and C Coys will be taken to Q.M. Stores, H.Q. and D Coy to PICCADILLY CIRCUS (Refilling Point) by 7.30 a.m. Palliasses will be emptied at these places and the straw stacked separately.

A Whiteley 2/Lt. and A/Adjutant
Civil Service Rifles

War Diary

SECRET | CIVIL SERVICE RIFLES | COPY No. 11

ORDER No. 100.

23rd January, 1918

1 The Regiment will be relieved by the 19th London tomorrow night and will proceed to BERTINCOURT to billets now occupied by 19th London.

2 All work defence schemes, trench maps etc. will be handed over and receipts forwarded to Bn H.Q. by 2 p.m., 24th.

3 The unused portion of the iron ration now at Coy H.Q. and camp kettles will be handed over to relieving Coys.

4 Report of relief complete will be sent to Bn H.Q. by wire by giving Coy Commanders name.

5. Two guides per Coy and H.Q. Coy will meet relieving Battalion at junction of STATION AVENUE and TRESCAULT ROAD L25c22 at 6 p.m. under command of 2/Lt Stevenson. Guides will assemble at Reserve Billet H.Q. in RIBECOURT by 5.15 p.m.

6 Order of march of relieving Coys: C D A HQ B.
Coys will relieve their opposite "letter" Coys.

7. Advance parties of 19th London will be at Coy H.Q. about noon tomorrow to take over gum boots and other trench stores.

8. Transport for Lewis Guns and panniers, mess boxes, medical stores &c will be at junction of STATION AVENUE with FLESQUIERES-RIBECOURT ROAD at 8.30 p.m.

9 Hot cocoa will be available from one of the Regimental Field Kitchens at the Entraining Station and supper on arrival in billets.

10. H.Q., C and D Coys' packs will be taken away by transport tonight. B Coy will have packs outside Reserve Coy. H.Q. under proper charge and will load them on transport which will be there at 8.30 p.m. 24th inst. A Coy will also load their packs at the same spot on conclusion of relief.

11 Coys will move to Entraining Station independently immediately on conclusion of relief.

12 Entraining orders will be issued later.

A W Whiteley
Capt and Adjt
Civil Service Rifles

Usual distribution

~~[illegible]~~ War Diary

SECRET — CIVIL SERVICE RIFLES — COPY No 8

## ORDER No. 99

15th Jan 1918

1 The Battalion will relieve 5th London in the trenches tomorrow 16th after dusk:—

A Coy. Left front relieving A Coy 5th
B " Right " " C " "
C " Support " " D " "
D " remaining in RIBECOURT.

2 Coy. officers will meet guides of 5th at 9.30 a.m. tomorrow 16th at ~~[illegible]~~ Left Bn. H.Q. in STATION AVENUE. One officer per Coy. should remain with the Coy.

3 The 2 front Coys. will be disposed as follows:— 1 platoon consisting of 4 Lewis Gun posts made up of half Lewis Gunners and half Riflemen in BEET TRENCH; The remaining platoon in KAISER TRENCH will relieve the front line platoon every 24 hours.

4 Hour for guides on relief will be notified later. Relief to be carried out over the top, not via communication trenches.

A Whiteley 2/Lt. A/Adjutant
Civil Service Rifles

Usual Distribution

War Diary

# 1/15th Bn London Regiment.

## ORDER No 97.

Reference Map.
[illegible] [illegible], 1/10,000

12th January 1918.

1. Battalion will relieve the 24th London (Right Brigade Support Battalion) at RIBECOURT today.
Companies will relieve the same letter companies of the 24th.

2. The Battalion will probably move to TRESCAULT by Light Railway. – Orders as to time will be issued later. –
100 yards distance will be kept between companies on march from detraining point. –

3. Two guides per Company will be met at junction of STATION AVENUE and TRESCAULT–RIBECOURT Road (Q 25. c. 25. 55) at 8.0 pm.
Order of march: –
H.Q. A, B, C, D Company.

4. All Trench Maps, Defence Schemes, Aeroplane photographs, Works Programmes and Trench Stores will be taken over and copies sent to Battalion H.Q. by 12 noon tomorrow 13th inst. –

5. Relief complete will be notified to Battalion H.Q. by Company Commander's [illegible]. –

6. There is to be as little movement as possible in RIBECOURT during daylight.

7. Box respirators will be worn slung by troops in BERTINCOURT ([illegible] Zone). They will be worn in the alert position when E. of METZ. – Notice boards have been erected to show the exact points.

8. Three pairs of socks will be taken over. Socks will be changed daily and clean pairs will be sent up with the rations every evening starting on Monday 14th. – The usual daily certificate as to changing of socks and rubbing of feet will be rendered daily by 10.0 am. –

Acknowledge.

A W Hitchcock Capt & Adjutant
(Civil Service Rifles)

Usual Distribution

140th Inf. Bde.

47th Division.

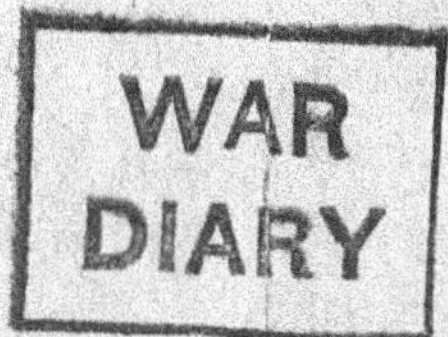


1/15th L O N D O N Regt.

NOVEMBER 1 9 1 5

Instructions regarding War Diaries and Intelligence Summaries are contained in F. S. Regs., Part II. and the Staff Manual respectively. Title pages will be prepared in manuscript.

# WAR DIARY
or
~~INTELLIGENCE SUMMARY.~~
(Erase heading not required.)

Army Form C. 2118.

| Place | Date | Hour | Summary of Events and Information | Remarks and references to Appendices |
|---|---|---|---|---|
| A 2 Section | 1st Nov | | Very wet. Germans shelled us heavily during the morning. Trenches in bad condition + owing to weather + bombardment there are frequent falls of earth. CASUALTIES 2 Killed 3 wounded. | WRh |
| | 2nd Nov | | Still raining. Intermittent shelling during the day. CASUALTIES 2 Killed 3 wounded. | WRh |
| | 3rd Nov | | Line reorganised on basis of 2 Battalions in front line. We took over the new A 2 Sector from CHALK PITS to GRENAY-BONIFONTAINE ROAD. These trenches were in a better state of repair, but the water in places was 12 to 15 inches deep. CASUALTIES. 4 wounded | WRh |
| | 4th Nov | | Quiet day except for intermittent shelling. Weather improving WRh CASUALTIES 4 wounded | |
| | 5th Nov | | Relieved by 8th BATTN after a quiet day + moved back to Old German front line around LOOS ROAD REDOUBT WRh CASUALTIES 8 wounded | |
| | 6th Nov | | Quiet day + fine. The Lord Mayor of London inspected the Battalion as it stood by platoons in the trench. He was no doubt impressed by the appearance of the men who had been 5 days in front line trenches in very wet weather + no supply of water for washing or shaving purposes. WRh | |
| | 7th Nov | | A quiet day WRh CASUALTIES 1 Killed 2 wounded | |
| A 1 Section | 8th Nov | | A quiet day. Relieved the 7th BATTN. in A1 Sector. WRh CASUALTIES 3 wounded | |
| | 9th Nov | | Intermittent shelling. Rain at night. WRh CASUALTIES 3 Killed 9 wounded | |

1577 Wt. W10791/1773 500,000 1/15 D. D. & L. A.D.S.S./Forms/C. 2118.

2

Army Form C. 2118.

# WAR DIARY
*or*
~~INTELLIGENCE SUMMARY.~~
*(Erase heading not required.)*

Instructions regarding War Diaries and Intelligence Summaries are contained in F. S. Regs., Part II. and the Staff Manual respectively. Title pages will be prepared in manuscript.

| Place | Date | Hour | Summary of Events and Information | Remarks and references to Appendices |
|---|---|---|---|---|
| A1 Section | 10th Nov | | Considerable shelling during the day. Very wet, windy + cold. The damage to trenches caused by weather + bombardment is so bad that it is almost impossible to keep pace with the work of repairs. In places the trenches are quite impassable by day. WKH<br>CASUALTIES 3 Killed 13 wounded | |
| | 11 Nov | | A quieter day. Relieved by 8th BATTN at night + moved to support line WKH<br>CASUALTIES 2 Killed 6 wounded | |
| | 12 Nov | | Very wet + cold. Trenches in bad condition. Working parties of 200 found WKH<br>CASUALTIES 1 wounded. | |
| | 13 Nov | | The weather is still very bad. A quiet time. Working parties of 150 found. WKH | |
| Mazingarbe | 14 Nov | | A quiet day + much finer. Relieved by 1st BATTN CAMERON HIGHLANDERS + marched to MAZINGARBE where we stayed the night. WKH | |
| Lillers | 15th Nov | | Marched to NOEUX LES MINES – passing a cinema camera on the way – where we entrained for LILLERS. WKH | |
| | 16th Nov<br>}<br>30th Nov | | Resting in CORPS RESERVE – we are promised a real rest + after 2 days cleaning up are to parade each day from 10 am to 1 pm for platoon, company, and battalion drill, bayonet fighting + rifle exercises. Many details found for courses. Bombing. Trench Mortar. Machine Gun – Leave also considerably increased 30 N.C.Os or men per week. WKH | |

140th Inf. Bde.

47th Division.

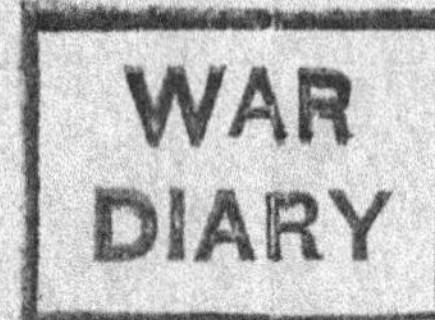


1/15th L O N D O N Regt.

DECEMBER 1915

47th Div

Instructions regarding War Diaries and Intelligence Summaries are contained in F. S. Regs., Part II. and the Staff Manual respectively. Title pages will be prepared in manuscript.

# WAR DIARY
*or*
# INTELLIGENCE SUMMARY.
*(Erase heading not required.)*

Army Form C. 2118.

| Place | Date | Hour | Summary of Events and Information | Remarks and references to Appendices |
|---|---|---|---|---|
| | | | War Diary<br>of<br>15th Battalion London Regiment<br>(Prince of Wales' Own Civil Service Rifles)<br>Territorial Force<br>for<br>December 1915.<br>kept by<br>MAJOR W. F. K. NEWSON.<br>Vol VI | 121/7957 |

1577 Wt. W10791/1773 500,000 1/15 D. D. & L. A.D.S.S./Forms/C. 2118.

Army Form C. 2118.

Instructions regarding War Diaries and Intelligence Summaries are contained in F. S. Regs., Part II. and the Staff Manual respectively. Title pages will be prepared in manuscript.

# WAR DIARY

*or*

~~INTELLIGENCE SUMMARY.~~

*(Erase heading not required.)*

| Place | Date | Hour | Summary of Events and Information | Remarks and references to Appendices |
|---|---|---|---|---|
| LILLERS | 1 Dec | | In accordance with orders received the previous night DIVISION moved for a 2 days TREK. 140th INFANTRY BRIGADE – ADVANCE GUARD – 15th BATTALION and some of DIVISIONAL MOUNTED TROOPS – VANGUARD. Reveillé 4 am & moved off at 6 am, a very wet and dark morning. Marched via St HILAIRE & passed AIRE on the WEST. The roads were good & the weather cleared about 10.30. We arrived at Rendezvous about 2 pm. & immediately took up an outpost line to cover the rest of the DIVISION billetted in the villages near. The line was inspected by G.O.C. the DIVISION who expressed satisfaction with the disposition – & the G.O.C. 4th CORPS also saw 2 companies in the line. At 7 pm. the line was withdrawn & the Battalion occupied billets at ROQUETOIRE for the night. [initials] | |
| | 2 Dec | | Rear Guard. Reveillé 5 & March at 7.30 am. The start was slow & tedious, but afterwards the pace improved, & the battalion reached its billets at LILLERS about 3 pm. after passing the G.O.C. 4th Corps on route who expressed himself as satisfied with the appearance of the BATTALION. Only 6 men fell out on the march during the 2 days. The distance covered approximates 34 miles. [initials] | |

1577 Wt. W10791/1773 500,000 1/15 D. D. & L. A.D.S.S./Forms/C. 2118.

Army Form C. 2118.

Instructions regarding War Diaries and Intelligence Summaries are contained in F. S. Regs., Part II. and the Staff Manual respectively. Title pages will be prepared in manuscript.

# WAR DIARY

*or*

~~INTELLIGENCE SUMMARY.~~

*(Erase heading not required.)*

| Place | Date | Hour | Summary of Events and Information | Remarks and references to Appendices |
|---|---|---|---|---|
| Lillers | 3 Dec. | | No parades. Resting + cleaning WKn | |
| | 4 Dec – 14 Dec | | Training recommenced + continued till 14th December. During this period all men not trained as Grenadiers threw bombs – Entertainments were very good The Follies gave a show three night – the battalion also arranged a concert which was quite successful. WKn | |
| | 15 Dec | | Reveille at 5 am. + battalion moved to Railway Station at 8.30 to entrain for Noeux les MINES – where we arrived about 10.20 am + marched to LABOURSE where we billetted WKn | |
| | 16 Dec – 18 | | In reserve WKn | |
| | 19 Dec | | Reveille 4 am + moved at 6.15. Battalion took over subsection C 2 from 19th Battn – having the 6th Battn in C 1. Casualties Killed 1 wounded 1. WKn | |
| | 20 | | ESSEX TRENCH attacked at dawn we had to withdraw about 18 yards. At night we attacked to recover the lost ground but owing to the bright moonlight the movement was seen too soon to enable us to effect a surprise, our men however pushed on well + three entered the GERMAN TRENCHES but they could not be properly supported + after nearly three hours fighting we took up and consolid[ated] | |

1577 Wt. W10791/1773 500,000 1/15 D. D. & L. A.D.S.S./Forms/C. 2118.

Instructions regarding War Diaries and Intelligence Summaries are contained in F. S. Regs., Part II. and the Staff Manual respectively. Title pages will be prepared in manuscript.

# WAR DIARY
*or*
~~INTELLIGENCE SUMMARY.~~
*(Erase heading not required.)*

Army Form C. 2118.

| Place | Date | Hour | Summary of Events and Information | Remarks and references to Appendices |
|---|---|---|---|---|
| | | | the morning position. The Grenadiers - 2 sections - from 7th and 8th Battalion moved up + rendered great help in the enterprise. Casualties 2nd Lt A M THOMPSON Killed Lt G. C. GRIMSDALE wounded. Other ranks Killed 9 wounded 57 missing 3 | |
| | 21 | ~~21~~ | Col SHARMAN-CRAWFORD of Royal Irish Rifles attached for instruction A quiet day till evening, when 2nd DIVISION launched a gas attack the artillery on both sides immediately commenced a vigorous bombardment Casualties Killed 2 wounded 8 | |
| | 22 | | Quiet day wet and dull. Wounded 3 missing 1 | |
| | 23 | | Relieved by POST OFFICE RIFLES + moved into Brigade Reserve at NOYELLES LES VERMELLES. Orders received to move at 5 am. on 24th to support lines | |
| | 24 | | Reveillé 3 am. + moved at 5 to CURLEY CRESCENT + MINE ~~[illegible]~~ buildings near. Heavily shelled in early morning but afterwards quieter. Wounded 3 | |
| | 25 | | Remained in trenches till 8. pm. A quiet day. G. O. C. DIVISION went round the lines. Returned to NOYELLES LES VERMELLES. | |
| | 26 | | Remained at NOYELLES LES VERMELLES. | |

1577 Wt. W10791/1773 500,000 1/15 D. D. & L. A.D.S.S./Forms/C. 2118.

Instructions regarding War Diaries and Intelligence Summaries are contained in F. S. Regs., Part II. and the Staff Manual respectively. Title pages will be prepared in manuscript.

# WAR DIARY
*or*
# ~~INTELLIGENCE SUMMARY.~~
*(Erase heading not required.)*

Army Form C. 2118.

| Place | Date | Hour | Summary of Events and Information | Remarks and references to Appendices |
|---|---|---|---|---|
| | 27 Dec & 30. | | Brigade relieved by 142nd. Brigade. Battalion moved to LABOURSE and rested. Baths arranged, clothing issued, + clothes + equipment cleaned | WM |
| | 31. | | Relieved 19th. Battalion London Regiment in D2. During relief support + communication trenches were shelled but without effect. The Germans celebrated the New Year - 11pm. our time - by considerable musketry + machine gun fire, + some rifle grenades. WM | |

1577 Wt. W10791/1773 500,000 1/15 D. D. & L. A.D.S.S./Forms/C. 2118.

JAN
1916

Army Form C. 2118.

Instructions regarding War Diaries and Intelligence Summaries are contained in F. S. Regs., Part II. and the Staff Manual respectively. Title pages will be prepared in manuscript.

# WAR DIARY
or
# INTELLIGENCE SUMMARY.

(*Erase heading not required.*)

| Place | Date | Hour | Summary of Events and Information | Remarks and references to Appendices |
|---|---|---|---|---|
| | | | 41<br>War Diary<br>of the<br>15th Bn London Regiment<br>(Prince of Wales' Own Civil Service Rifles)<br>from<br>1st to 31st January 1916.<br>Vol VII<br>Kept by<br>Major W. F. K. Newson | |

1577 Wt. W10791/1773 500,000 1/15 D. D. & L. A.D.S.S./Forms/C. 2118.

Instructions regarding War Diaries and Intelligence Summaries are contained in F. S. Regs., Part II. and the Staff Manual respectively. Title pages will be prepared in manuscript.

# WAR DIARY

*or*

# ~~INTELLIGENCE SUMMARY.~~

*(Erase heading not required.)*

Army Form C. 2118

| Place | Date | Hour | Summary of Events and Information | Remarks and references to Appendices |
|---|---|---|---|---|
| Sub-section D2 | 1 Jan | | Battalion holding sub section D2. HOHENZOLLERN. 3 companies in line 1 in support. Enemy exploded mine about 6.10 a.m. apparently prematurely as considerable damage was done to their own trenches otherwise a quiet day. Officers of the Cavalry Division reconnoitred prior to taking over. Casualties Killed 2. | |
| VERMELLES | 2nd Jan | | Relieved by 8th Battalion (Post Office Rifles) and moved to VERMELLES in support. Casualties wounded 1 | |
| HOUCHIN | 3 Jan | | Relieved by Cavalry Division & marched to HOUCHIN. A fine day. | |
| LES BREBIS | 4th " | | Marched at 3 p.m. for LES BREBIS where we arrived about 6.15 p.m. | |
| Sub-section C [illegible] | 5th " | | Moved to sub section C of MAROC sector where we relieved 66th Regiment of Infantry, FRENCH ARMY. This was the ground captured by the 141st INFANTRY BRIGADE on 25th September 1915 and on the completion of the relief the following order was published by GENERAL SIR GEORGE LEFEVRE commanding the 18th FRENCH DIVISION. "At the moment of handing over the command of the 47th (LONDON) DIVISION to "MAJOR GENERAL C BARTER C.V.O., C.B. chief of this Division I wish to inform this "General Officer of my great admiration for the manner in which everyone of his Division have been working during the relief operations and for the "superb attitude of his troops in every circumstance." | |

Instructions regarding War Diaries and Intelligence Summaries are contained in F. S. Regs., Part II. and the Staff Manual respectively. Title pages will be prepared in manuscript.

# WAR DIARY
*or*
# INTELLIGENCE SUMMARY.
*(Erase heading not required.)*

Army Form C. 2118.

| Place | Date | Hour | Summary of Events and Information | Remarks and references to Appendices |
|---|---|---|---|---|
| | | | "The 18th French Division leaves the LOOS sector with regret but knows "that it cannot be in better hands than in those of the 47th British Division "who conquered it. | |
| | | | "I personally am proud to have had this Division under my "orders. I owe this favor to the confidence with which the British High "Authorities have had the kindness to honour me." | |
| | 6th | | Quiet day. Weather has improved and been comparatively a sunny day. | |
| | 7th | | Fine day & Quiet. | |
| LES BREBIS | 8th | | Quiet day. Relieved at night by 19th BATTALION and moved to LES BREBIS in DIVISIONAL RESERVE | |
| | 9th | | Battalion resting & cleaning | |
| | 10th & 11 | | Battalion in reserve. 200 men found for fatigue parties. | |
| | 12th | | Battalion moved at 4.30 pm to left section LOOS SECTOR and relieved 19th Battalion | |
| | 13th | | Quiet day. | |
| | 14th | | Fine day. Intermittent shelling in morning but no serious result. | |
| | 15th | | Section visited by Officers of 7th Batt. CAMERON HIGHLANDERS also by G. O. C. 140th BRIGADE | |

1577 Wt. W10791/1773 500,000 1/15 D. D. & L. A.D.S.S./Forms/C. 2118.

Instructions regarding War Diaries and Intelligence Summaries are contained in F. S. Regs., Part II. and the Staff Manual respectively. Title pages will be prepared in manuscript.

# WAR DIARY
*or*
~~INTELLIGENCE SUMMARY.~~
*(Erase heading not required.)*

Army Form C. 2118.

| Place | Date | Hour | Summary of Events and Information | Remarks and references to Appendices |
|---|---|---|---|---|
| | 15th | | Relieved in evening & moved back in support to O.G.1 (ie Old German Front line) Casualties Killed one wounded one | |
| | 16th | | Fine day. Quiet. Fatigue parties formed for improving communication trenches. One Officer attached to ARTILLERY to observe and visit battery to see the system under which that arm works & cooperates with Infantry. Casualties Wounded four | |
| | 17th | | Fine day. Commanding Officer visited artillery | |
| | 18th | | Battalion moved to LEFT sub section LOOS sector and relieved 6th Battn. 2 Platoons of 7th LEINSTERS attached for instruction | |
| | 19th | | Fine day. Some shelling in morning otherwise quiet. Enemy rifle grenades were annoying but as soon as we replied to them they ceased. Casualties Killed one wounded 3. Three men of LEINSTERS also wounded. | |
| | 20 | | Fine day. Some shelling in morning but not at all effective. Relieved by 22nd BATTALION in evening & moved to LES BREBIS. The discipline and general conduct of the attached troops during the 48 hours they were with the battalion left much to be desired. They were dirty in their habits and did not seem to realize that orders when issued were to be at once complied with. Casualties wounded one. | |

1577 Wt. W10791/1773 500,000 1/15 D. D. & L. A.D.S.S./Forms/C. 2118.

Army Form C. 2118.

Instructions regarding War Diaries and Intelligence Summaries are contained in F. S. Regs., Part I and the Staff Manual respectively. Title pages will be prepared in manuscript.

# DIARY
or
# INTELLIGENCE SUMMARY.
(*Erase heading not required.*)

| Place | Date | Hour | Summary of Events and Information | Remarks and references to Appendices |
|---|---|---|---|---|
| LES BREBIS | 21 to 24 | | In Divisional Reserve. Found working parties by day, + men were given opportunities of obtaining baths + clean clothing WTKn | |
| | 24* | | Relieved 20th LONDON REGT in centre sub section, MAROC SECTOR Relief complete 9.15 pm. WTKn | |
| | 25 | | Some shelling otherwise a quiet day. WTKn | |
| | 26 | | Considerable artillery activity, + some bombing on Southern Crassier. Casualties Wounded 5. WTKn | |
| | 27 | | Heavy shelling throughout the day on front line, support and reserve trenches. At 6 pm. information was received that 15th DIVISION immediately NORTH of us was being attacked. Our artillery fired on Night lines, + all companies stood to arms, by 7 pm. normal conditions prevailed again Casualties. wounded. 3. WTKn | |
| | 28 | | Continual shelling of trenches. Gas shells used on MAROC. Casualties Killed 1 wounded 2 suffering from shell shock 2. WTKn | |
| | 29 | | Enemy attempted to cut wire opposite 15th DIVISION + also South of the CRASSIER A quieter day. Casualties Wounded 2 suffering from shell shock 1. | |
| | 30 | | A foggy day. Enemy much quieter. Trenches previously blown in repaired. Casualties 5 wounded WTKn | |

1577 Wt. W10791/1773 500,000 1/15 D. D. & L. A.D.S.S./Forms/C. 2118.

Instructions regarding War Diaries and Intelligence Summaries are contained in F. S. Regs., Part II. and the Staff Manual respectively. Title pages will be prepared in manuscript.

# WAR DIARY

*or*

~~INTELLIGENCE SUMMARY.~~

*(Erase heading not required.)*

Army Form C. 2118.

| Place | Date | Hour | Summary of Events and Information | Remarks and references to Appendices |
|---|---|---|---|---|
| | 31st | | Considerable artillery activity on both sides. Enemy used minenwerfer + fired 5 times in 24 hours. German barricades on all roads bombarded by our artillery with considerable effect. Casualties Wounded 4. TMK | |

1577 Wt. W10791/1773 500,000 1/15 D. D. & L. A.D.S.S./Forms/C. 2118.

FEB
1916

Instructions regarding War Diaries and Intelligence Summaries are contained in F. S. Regs., Part II. and the Staff Manual respectively. Title pages will be prepared in manuscript.

# WAR DIARY

*or*

~~INTELLIGENCE SUMMARY.~~

*(Erase heading not required.)*

Army Form C. 2118.

47

| Place | Date | Hour | Summary of Events and Information | Remarks and references to Appendices |
| --- | --- | --- | --- | --- |
| | | | War Diary<br>of the<br>15th Bn London Regiment<br>(P.W.O. Civil Service Rifles)<br>for the<br>month of February 1916.<br><br>Vol VIII<br><br>Kept by<br>Major W. F. K. NEWSON | |

1577 Wt. W10791/1773 500,000 1/15 D. D. & L. A.D.S.S./Forms/C. 2118.

Instructions regarding War Diaries and Intelligence Summaries are contained in F. S. Regs., Part II. and the Staff Manual respectively. Title pages will be prepared in manuscript.

# WAR DIARY

*or*

~~INTELLIGENCE SUMMARY.~~

*(Erase heading not required.)*

Army Form C. 2118.

| Place | Date | Hour | Summary of Events and Information | Remarks and references to Appendices |
|---|---|---|---|---|
| MAROC. | Feb. 1st | | A quiet day. Admiral Hon: Cecil Colville visited the battalion. Aeroplane activity + bombs dropped near reserve billets. Relieved by 22nd Battalion. Casualties Killed 2 wounded 5. [illegible] | |
| BRACQUEMONT | 2nd | | Battalion in DIVISIONAL RESERVE. [illegible] | |
| | 3 | | do Commanding Officer assumed command of 140th Infantry Brigade. Fatigue parties found chiefly road repair [illegible] | |
| | 4th | | as on 3rd. [illegible] | |
| | 5th | | Battalion moved to position of Brigade Reserve in ~~Left sub section~~ LOOS sector, relieving the 19th BATTN. [illegible] | |
| | 6th | | Quiet day. Found the usual working parties. Killed one. [illegible] | |
| | 7 | | as on 6th. Casualties. Wounded 2 [illegible] | |
| | 8 | | as on 7th. Heavy artillery bombardment some miles to the South. Casualties wounded 2 [illegible] | |
| | 9th | | Moved to Left sub section LOOS SECTOR. + relieved 6th Battn. Casualties. Killed 2 wounded 1 [illegible] | |
| | 10th | | Except for activity with rifle grenades a quiet day. Casualties Killed one. [illegible] | |
| | 11th | | Considerable activity with rifle grenades. Catapult erected in evening. Casualties Killed 3 wounded 3. [illegible] | |

1577 Wt. W10791/1773 500,000 1/15 D. D. & L. A.D.S.S./Forms/C. 2118.

Instructions regarding War Diaries and Intelligence Summaries are contained in F. S. Regs., Part II. and the Staff Manual respectively. Title pages will be prepared in manuscript.

# WAR DIARY
*or*
~~INTELLIGENCE SUMMARY.~~
*(Erase heading not required.)*

Army Form C. 2118.

| Place | Date | Hour | Summary of Events and Information | Remarks and references to Appendices |
|---|---|---|---|---|
| | 12 Feb | | A quiet day. Company on LOOS CRASSIER shot 3 Germans at Dawn + in the evening enemy trenches were effectually bombed with rifle grenades and catapult. [initials] | |
| | 13 | | A quiet day. [initials] | |
| | 14 | | Mine exploded opposite centre sub section _ 7th BATTN. All support + reserve troops stood to arms ready for eventualities _ but the 7th BATTN entirely held their own, + quite prevent enemy securing any advantage from the surprise. Their machine guns opened fire before debris had ceased to fall. considerable enemy bombardment of support trenches from 6.50 am till 8 am. Relieved at night by 2nd R. Munster Fusiliers + moved to LES BREBIS. Casualties wounded 5 [initials] | |
| | 15th | | Moved to NOEUX at 1.30 pm. + entrained for LILLERS. Battalion occupy same area as formerly. [initials] | |
| | 16th 28th | | Division in reserve. Resting. Company + battalion training. Inspection by General MONRO commanding 1st Army of Brigade. + Inspection of Battalion by Brigadier [initials] | |
| | 29th | | Battalion moved to 1st army training area. [initials] | |

1577 Wt. W10791/1773 500,000 1/15 D. D. & L. A.D.S.S./Forms/C. 2118.

MARCH
1916

140. 47

1/15 London Regt.

Vol ~~XIII~~ IX

Army Form C. 2118.

# WAR DIARY

*or*

~~INTELLIGENCE SUMMARY.~~

*(Erase heading not required.)*

Instructions regarding War Diaries and Intelligence Summaries are contained in F. S. Regs., Part II. and the Staff Manual respectively. Title pages will be prepared in manuscript.

| Place | Date | Hour | Summary of Events and Information | Remarks and references to Appendices |
|---|---|---|---|---|
| | | | War Diary<br>of the 15th Battn. London Regt.<br>(P.W.O. Civil Service Rifles)<br>for the month of March 1916<br><br>Kept by<br>Major W.F.K. Newson. | |

1577 Wt. W10791/1773 500,000 1/15 D. D. & L. A.D.S.S./Forms/C. 2118.

Instructions regarding War Diaries and Intelligence Summaries are contained in F. S. Regs., Part II. and the Staff Manual respectively. Title pages will be prepared in manuscript.

# WAR DIARY
*or*
~~INTELLIGENCE SUMMARY.~~
*(Erase heading not required.)*

Army Form C. 2118.

| Place | Date | Hour | Summary of Events and Information | Remarks and references to Appendices |
|---|---|---|---|---|
| | March | | | |
| | 21 | | the other two companies & Lewis Gun Detachment to CARENCY, & ~~took over~~ became the SUPPORT BATTALION of the French Brigade. WHw | |
| ABLAIN ST NAZAIRE | 21-26 | | A quiet time. Battalion furnished working parties at night WHw | |
| VERDREL | 26 | | Relieved by 22nd BATTN and moved to VERDREL WHw | |
| FRESNICOURT | 27th | | Moved to FRESNICOURT, & took over billets from 17th BATTALION. WHw | |
| | 28-31 | | DIVISIONAL RESERVE. BATHS. Musketry, training, & instruction of N.C.Os. & young officers carried out. & from time to time working parties found both by day & night. Some cases of measles, resulting in B Coy. 1 platoon each from A & D. & Headquarters being isolated. WHw | |

Instructions regarding War Diaries and Intelligence Summaries are contained in F. S. Regs., Part II. and the Staff Manual respectively. Title pages will be prepared in manuscript.

# WAR DIARY
or
~~INTELLIGENCE SUMMARY.~~
(Erase heading not required.)

Army Form C. 2118.

| Place | Date | Hour | Summary of Events and Information | Remarks and references to Appendices |
|---|---|---|---|---|
| | MARCH | | | |
| ERNY ST JULIAN | 1-3 | | Battalion and Brigade training in Manoeuvre Area. Weather cold + considerable falls of snow WMH | |
| COYECQUES | 4th | | Battalion moved to COYECQUES WMH | |
| | 5th-8th | | Training continued. Weather cold. Snow fell every day. WMH | |
| NEDON | 9th | | Moved to NEDON. Start from ERNY ST JULIAN delayed owing to difficulties of 141st Brigade Transport WMH | |
| DIVION | 10th | | Moved to DIVION. WMH | |
| | 11-12. | | At DIVION. Resting and cleaning up. WMH | |
| BOUVIGNY WOOD | 13 | | Moved to BOUVIGNY WOOD and billetted in huts. WMH | |
| ABLAIN ST NAZAIRE | 14 | | Relieved 9th YORKS in support trenches on NOTREDAME de LORETTE SPUR. Relief complete 8 pm. WMH | |
| | 15-21st | | Held this position for six days. Enemy artillery were active during this time searching for one of our batteries. Headquarters were heavily shelled on two occasions. At night battalion found working parties to improve trenches. On 16th we had some casualties Wounded other ranks 4 of whom one subsequently died WMH | |
| | 21st | | Relieved by 24th BATTN. + moved to VILLERS AU BOIS. Headquarters + 2 companies | |

1577 Wt. W10791/1773 500,000 1/15 D. D. & L. A.D.S.S./Forms/C. 2118.

APRIL
1916

47
―
1160

1/15 London Regt

Vol 10

April
1916

Instructions regarding War Diaries and Intelligence Summaries are contained in F. S. Regs., Part II. and the Staff Manual respectively. Title pages will be prepared in manuscript.

# WAR DIARY
*or*
~~INTELLIGENCE SUMMARY.~~
*(Erase heading not required.)*

Army Form C. 2118.

| Place | Date | Hour | Summary of Events and Information | Remarks and references to Appendices |
|---|---|---|---|---|
| FRESNICOURT | 1 apl. | | In Reserve. Battalion training + working parties at night WH | |
| BOUVIGNY HUTS | 2 | | Moved to SUPPORT position in BOUVIGNY WOOD. Battalion in huts WH | |
| | 3 | | Battalion finds night working parties 250 strong. An outbreak of measles put 125 in isolation. 3 wounded on working party to LEFT SUBSECTION. WH | |
| | 4-6 | | Battalion in support, + continues to find working parties WH | |
| VILLIERS AU BOIS | 7 | | Moved to VILLIERS AU BOIS + CARENCY WH | |
| SOUCHEZ CENTRE | 8 | | Relieved 19th Battn in CENTRE SUBSECTION. Relief complete 11.20 p.m. WH | |
| | 9 | | Considerable activity with TRENCHMORTARS by both sides. LEFT COMPANY shelled. Considerable amount of work carried out improving trenches. Wounded 6. WH | |
| | 10 | | Heavy bombardment of PIMPLE. Garrison reduced as much as possible. Considerable retaliation but quite ineffective except to break down part of support lines. Casualties 1 wounded. WH | |
| | 11 | | Quiet day. The line was visited by Brig. General commanding. Casualties 6 wounded. WH | |
| | 12 | | Heavy enemy bombardment in afternoon. Casualties 2 wounded. WH | |
| | 13 | | Quiet day. Some bombing at night, but not effective. Casualties 1 wounded. WH | |
| MAISNIL BOUCHE | 14 | | Quiet day. Relieved by 24th BATTALION. Relief complete 11 p.m. + moved to MAISNIL BOUCHE. Casualties. 1 Killed 4 wounded. WH | |

1577 Wt. W10791/1773 500,000 1/15 D. D. & L. A.D.S.S./Forms/C. 2118.

Army Form C. 2118.

# WAR DIARY
*or*
~~INTELLIGENCE SUMMARY.~~
*(Erase heading not required.)*

Instructions regarding War Diaries and Intelligence Summaries are contained in F. S. Regs., Part II. and the Staff Manual respectively. Title pages will be prepared in manuscript.

| Place | Date | Hour | Summary of Events and Information | Remarks and references to Appendices |
|---|---|---|---|---|
| MAISNIL BOUCHE | 15th to 19 | | Battalion in Reserve. Musketry & Grenade training carried out, also Battalion Drill. The G.O.C. DIVISION inspected battalion & expressed his satisfaction of what he saw & also of our work both in & out of trenches. WHA | |
| Villers au Bois | 20th to 24th | | Moved to Villers au BOIS to support position. Company training was carried on here & considerable progress was made WHA | |
| SOUCHEZ LEFT | 25. | | Moved into LEFT SUB SECTION & relieved 17th BATTN. WHA | |
| | 26th | | Relief complete 1.15 am. Enemy exploded a mine at 3.30 am some distance SOUTH but immediately put up a very heavy barrage along ZOUAVE VALLEY & our support lines. All communication was soon broken. Afterwards things were quiet till 7 pm when enemy exploded another mine, which was followed by another heavy barrage fire. Later there was some bombing & machine gun fire. Casualties 3 wounded WHA | WHA |
| | 27th | | Some artillery activity in early morning, otherwise a quiet day. Casualties 8 wounded | WHA |
| | 28th | | A quiet day. Owing to enemy activity in strengthening & improving their front line. Brigade ordered new line of wire to be put out & this was commenced. Casualties 1 wounded | WHA |
| | 29th | | Generally a quiet day. At 6.55 pm enemy exploded mine opposite left of CENTRE SUBSECTION, & this was followed by the usual artillery barrage. 6th BATTALION | |

1577 Wt. W10791/1773 500,000 1/15 D. D. & L. A.D.S.S./Forms/C. 2118.

Instructions regarding War Diaries and Intelligence Summaries are contained in F. S. Regs., Part II. and the Staff Manual respectively. Title pages will be prepared in manuscript.

# WAR DIARY
*or*
~~INTELLIGENCE SUMMARY.~~
*(Erase heading not required.)*

Army Form C. 2118.

| Place | Date | Hour | Summary of Events and Information | Remarks and references to Appendices |
|---|---|---|---|---|
| SOUCHEZ LEFT | 29 | | lost somewhat heavily + 2 sections of GRENADIERS. 1 LEWIS GUN TEAM were sent across to their support + further supplies of grenades were carried over afterwards the night was quiet + the position on the new crater consolidated. The putting out of new wire was also carried on. Casualties 2 killed 10 wounded | WM |
| | 30th | | Intermittent shelling in morning + afterwards some activity with Minnenwerfer between 5 + 6.30pm. Working party on new wire were interrupted + suffered some loss from Rifle grenades. 23rd BATTN came up to relieve. Casualties 1 Killed 7 wounded | WM |

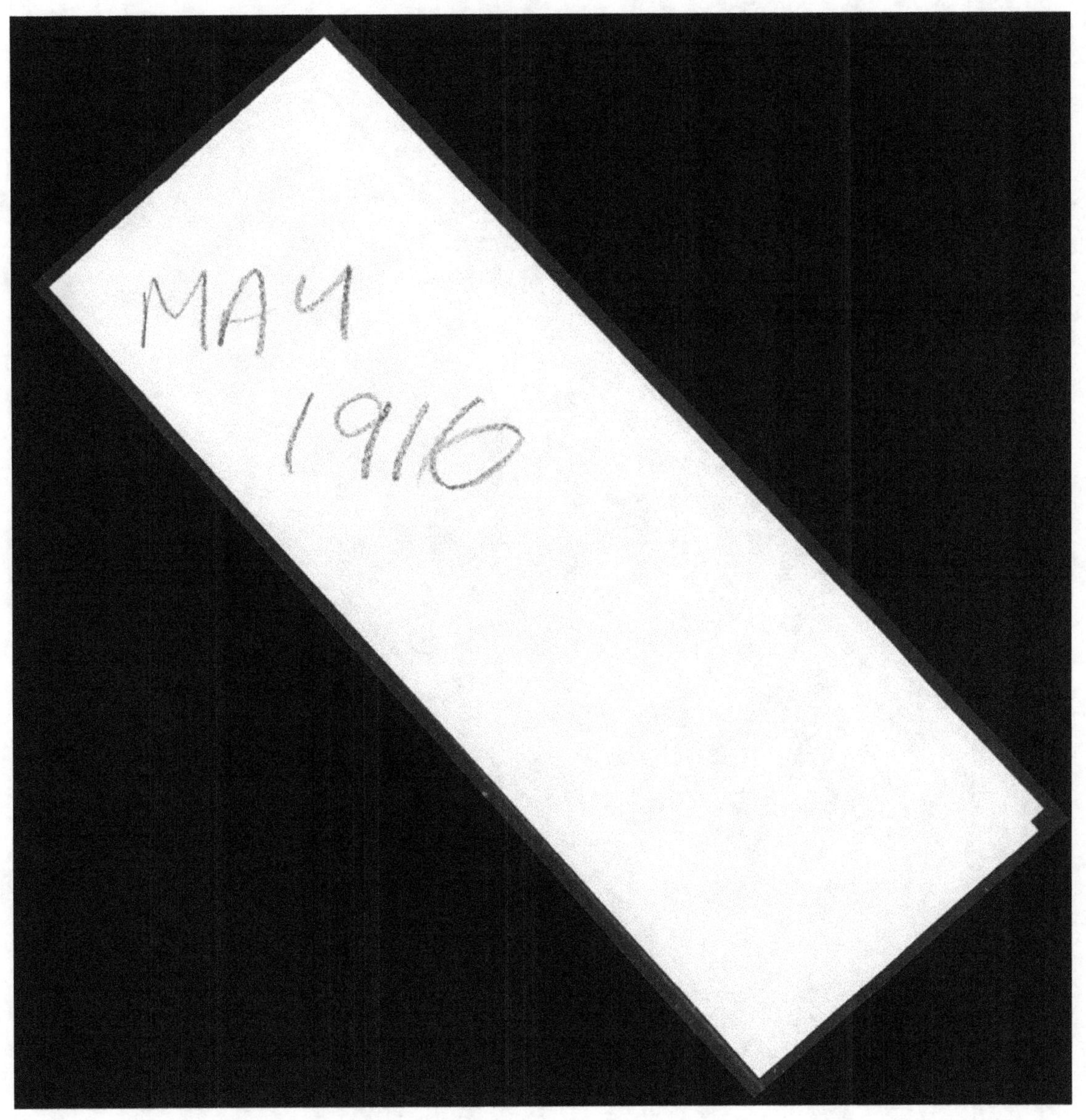
MAY
1916

Instructions regarding War Diaries and Intelligence Summaries are contained in F. S. Regs., Part II. and the Staff Manual respectively. Title pages will be prepared in manuscript.

# WAR DIARY

*or*

~~INTELLIGENCE SUMMARY.~~

*(Erase heading not required.)*

May 1916

15 London Regt 41

Vol XI

Army Form C. 2118.

140

| Place | Date | Hour | Summary of Events and Information | Remarks and references to Appendices |
|---|---|---|---|---|
| | 1 May | 2 am | Relieved by 23rd BATTN. LONDON REGT. Relief complete + marched to VILLERS AU BOIS arriving there about 4 am. Battalion rested + moved on to FRESNICOURT at 2 pm. Casualties Killed 3 wounded 6 WHA | |
| FRESNICOURT | 2nd May | | Corpl. TICKLE and DRUMMER HOGWOOD awarded the military medal for conspicuous gallantry at HOHENZOLLERN on 1st January 1916. Casualty killed one WHA | |
| | 2nd-7th | | Battalion remained at FRESNICOURT finding working parties of 200 each night + during the day training was carried out by companies + specialist sections. All ranks bathed + had clean clothes issued. WHA | |
| BOUVIGNY HUTS | 8th | | Moved to BOUVIGNY HUTS + relieved 6th BATTALION LONDON REGT. WHA | |
| | 9-13th | | Remained at BOUVIGNY HUTS. working parties each night of 100 men. Casualties 13th Killed one WHA | |
| ABLAIN ST NAZAIRE | 14th | | Relieved 6th BATTN LONDON REGT on LORETTE SPUR. Relief complete 10.20 pm WHA | |
| | 15th | | A quiet day. at 8.30 pm we sprang some mines on VIMY RIDGE. A very heavy bombardment at once ensued which lasted an hour. Afterwards the night was quiet. WHA | |
| | 16th | | Artillery were active all day, + some shells fell in ABLAIN ST NAZAIRE. About 9.45 a 10.15 pm aeroplanes were reported flying low, + dropped some bombs near CARENCY Battery. WHA | |

1577 Wt. W10791/1773 500,000 1/15 D. D. & L. A.D.S.S./Forms/C. 2118.

Army Form C. 2118.

Instructions regarding War Diaries and Intelligence Summaries are contained in F. S. Regs., Part II. and the Staff Manual respectively. Title pages will be prepared in manuscript.

# WAR DIARY
*or*
~~INTELLIGENCE SUMMARY.~~
*(Erase heading not required.)*

| Place | Date | Hour | Summary of Events and Information | Remarks and references to Appendices |
|---|---|---|---|---|
| | 17 May | | Quiet day [initials] | |
| | 18 " | | Relieved by 12 DURHAM LIGHT INFANTRY. Relief complete 11 pm + moved to BOUVIGNY HUTS. | [initials] |
| | 19 " | | Remained at BOUVIGNY HUTS [initials] | |
| | 20th | | Relieved at 5 pm. by 1st BATTN WORCESTER REGT. + moved to CAMBLAN L'ABBE where battalion was well billetted in huts [initials] | |
| CAMBLAN L'ABBE | 21st | | Church parade in morning, shortly after 3 pm. heavy bombardment was heard. | |
| | | 4.15pm | Ordered to move to VILLERS AU BOIS + report arrival | |
| | | 6.15pm | arrived VILLERS AU BOIS + reported | |
| | | 6.40pm. | ordered to move to MAISTRE LINE defences across CABARET ROAD | |
| | | 7.50pm | Headquarters details arrived MAISTRE LINE + met orderly with instructions that BATTALION was to occupy position SOUTH of CABARET ROAD only + an officer was to report at BRIGADE HEADQUARTERS. | |
| | | 8.20pm. | BATTALION in position + MAJOR NEWSON sent forward to Brigade. subsequently the battalion moved forward by companies in the following order B, C, 2 Lewis guns + 2 sections of Grenadiers, Headquarters, D Company + remaining details A Company was detailed to pick up rations + follow on. | |

1577 Wt. W10791/1773 500,000 1/15 D. D. & L. A.D.S.S./Forms/C. 2118.

Army Form C. 2118.

# WAR DIARY
*or*
~~INTELLIGENCE SUMMARY.~~
*(Erase heading not required.)*

Instructions regarding War Diaries and Intelligence Summaries are contained in F. S. Regs., Part II. and the Staff Manual respectively. Title pages will be prepared in manuscript.

| Place | Date | Hour | Summary of Events and Information | Remarks and references to Appendices |
|---|---|---|---|---|
| | | 10-15pm | CAPT FARQUHAR with B Company reported to Brigade Hdqrs at CABARET ROUGE. 200 extra rounds of ammunition per rifleman + extra bombs were issued, + this company was sent forward with MAJOR NEWSON to report to the Officer Commanding the 8th BATTN LONDON REGT in left sub sector BERTHONVAL Section. During the move from MAISTRE LINE to CABARET ROUGE the area was heavily shelled with lachrymatory shells, owing to these the progress made was very slow. | |
| | | 11pm | B Company moved off + CAPT GAZE with C Company + details reported. Instructions were given for extra ammunition to be drawn + arrangements made for guides. MW | |
| | 22nd | 1 am | B Company reported to Hdqrs 8th Battn + were informed that our resistance + support lines had been lost. A counter attack was being organised in which 1 Company of the 18th Battn, 25 Bombers + details of 8th Battn + B Coy 15th Battn were to take part + that the whole would move forward at 2 am. it having been arranged that the 6th + 7th Battalions would cooperate on the right. | |
| | | 1-30 am | Captn Gaze with C Company + details reported. | |

Instructions regarding War Diaries and Intelligence Summaries are contained in F. S. Regs., Part II. and the Staff Manual respectively. Title pages will be prepared in manuscript.

# WAR DIARY

*or*

~~INTELLIGENCE SUMMARY.~~

*(Erase heading not required.)*

Army Form C. 2118.

| Place | Date | Hour | Summary of Events and Information | Remarks and references to Appendices |
|---|---|---|---|---|
| | May 22nd | 2.10 am | B Company moved forward attacking in two lines 2 platoons in each line | |
| | | 2.15 am | Lt Col Warrender cmdg 15th Battn 1 company - D - and details arrived at the same time a very heavy musketry + machine gun fire was opened by the enemy supported by strong artillery barrage fire. | |
| | | 2.27 am | Capt HOBBS commanding company of 18th BATTN LONDON REGT reported + asked for reinforcements - 2 platoons of C Company under 2nd LIEUT F OSBORNE were sent forward, + though unable to get in touch with the company of the 18th BATTN were able to get into + secure GRANBY STREET as a defensive flank. | |
| | | 2.45 am | Two platoons of D Company under Captn ROBERTS were sent forward on the left to support B Company, but only got in touch with some small scattered parties, he was however able to get into the support line trench between ERSATZ ALLEY and GRANBY STREET and made good his position here. | |
| | | 4 am | The line was generally speaking quiet | |
| | | 4.30 am | Col MAXWELL CMDG 8th BATTN. wounded left handing over to O.C. 15th BATTN LONDON REGT. | |

1577 Wt. W10791/1773 500,000 1/15 D. D. & L. A.D.S.S./Forms/C. 2118.

Instructions regarding War Diaries and Intelligence Summaries are contained in F. S. Regs., Part II. and the Staff Manual respectively. Title pages will be prepared in manuscript.

# WAR DIARY
*or*
~~INTELLIGENCE SUMMARY.~~
*(Erase heading not required.)*

Army Form C. 2118.

| Place | Date | Hour | Summary of Events and Information | Remarks and references to Appendices |
|---|---|---|---|---|
| | | | D + C Companies worked hard on the lines held by them, as soon as possible a sketch shewing the position was sent back to the BRIGADE. During the afternoon there was an intense bombardment lasting an hour from 4.50 pm. to 5.50 pm over the ZOUAVE VALLEY. + this was followed by another between 9 + 11 pm. when the 24th BATTN LONDON REGT was coming in to relieve us. Casualties. 2 officers Capt. H B Farquhar + Lt B. Scott wounded + missing. 8 other ranks missing. 9 killed. 73 wounded | |
| | 23 | 1.15 am | Relief complete + moved back to CAMBLAIN L'ABBE where battalion arrived between 4 + 5 am. | |
| | 24 | | At CAMBLAIN L'ABBE | |
| | 25th | | Marched at 8 am. to CALONNE RICQUOART where Battn arrived 12-45 pm | |
| | 26th | | Leave re opened, + commanding officer started. Battalion training + cleaning up | |
| | 27th | | Battalion had baths at FOSSE 6 + clean clothes issued. Casualties 1 died of wounds | |
| | 28th | | Church parade. Brigadier General commanding attended | |
| | 29/30 | | Company + Battalion training, refitting + cleaning clothes + equipment. | |
| | 31st | | Brigade inspected by Brigadier General commanding. He expressed his entire satisfaction with the appearance + steadiness of the battalion | |

8245

SECRET Copy No 11

15TH BATTALION LONDON REGIMENT (P.W.O.CIVIL SERVICE RIFLES)

## OPERATION ORDERS.

(Ref.-Sheets No. 36 B & C 1/40,000)

IN THE FIELD, 14th May,1916.

1. The 15th Battalion will relieve the 6th Battalion London Regiment in the LORETTE trenches on the evening of Sunday,14th inst

2. The Battalion will be ready to move off at 7.40 p.m. by platoons at two minutes interval in the following order:-

Headquarters
"B" Company
"A" "
Bombers
"C" Company
"D" "
Lewis Det.

Companies will occupy the same positions as when last in these trenches, viz.-

| | |
|---|---|
| LEFT | "B" Company |
| CENTRE | "A" " |
| RIGHT | "C" " |
| LOCAL RESERVE | "D" " |

3. GUIDES. Guides will be met as follows at the old Brigade Headquarters in ABLAIN ST NAZARRE at 8.30 p.m.

| | |
|---|---|
| Headquarters | 1 |
| "B" Company | 4 |
| "A" " | 4 |
| Bombers | 1 |
| "C" Company | 4 |
| RIGHT HALF, "D" Co. | 2 |
| Lewis Guns. | 4. |

(20)

Two Guides for the LEFT HALF of "D" Company will be met at the barricade R33c3.5. at 8.30 p.m.

The Lewis Gun limbers will leave in sufficient time to enable them to reach ABLAIN ST NAZARRE via GOUY SERVINS by 8.30 p.m., where the teams will meet them, unload the limbers, pick up guides and proceed to the positions allocated to them.

4. RELIEF COMPLETE: O.C. Companies, Lewis Det. & Grenadier Platoon will send the usual message to Battalion Headquarters when the relief is complete.

F. Wood(?)
2/Lt. & Actg.Adjutant
15th Battalion London Regiment
(P.W.O.CIVIL SERVICE RIFLES)

Copy No. 1 War Diary
2 Brigade H.Q's
3 Bde.M.G.Coy.
4 "A" Company
5 "B" "
6 "C" "
7 "D" "
8 H.Q's
9 Bombing Officer
10 Lewis Gun Officer
11 6th Battalion
12 15th Battalion

JUNE
1916

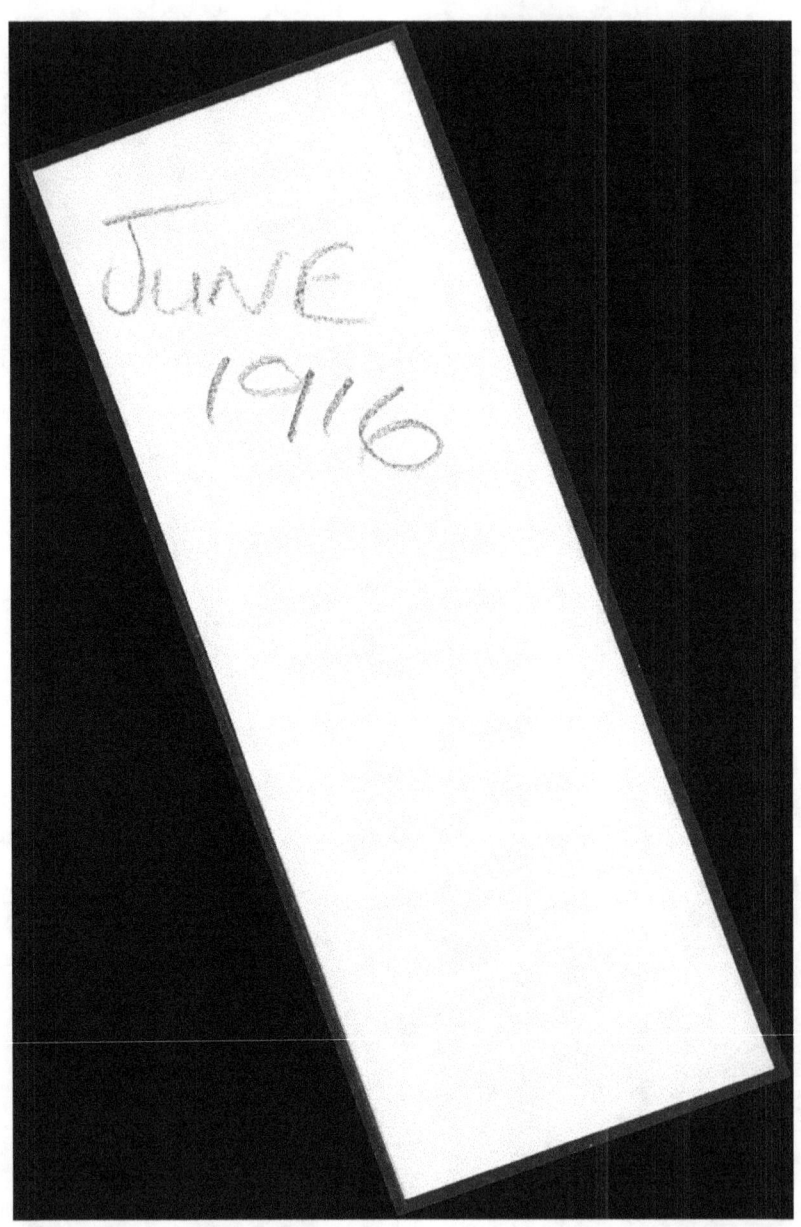

Instructions regarding War Diaries and Intelligence Summaries are contained in F. S. Regs., Part II. and the Staff Manual respectively. Title pages will be prepared in manuscript.

# WAR DIARY
*or*
# INTELLIGENCE SUMMARY.
*(Erase heading not required.)*

Army Form C. 2118. 447

| Place | Date | Hour | Summary of Events and Information | Remarks and references to Appendices |
|---|---|---|---|---|
| | | | Vol 12 | |
| | | | War Diary<br>of<br>15th Battn. London Regiment<br>(P.W.O. Civil Service Rifles)<br>for<br>June 1916. | |
| | | | Kept by<br>Major W. F. K. Newson. | |

1577 Wt. W10791/1773 500,000 1/15 D. D. & L. A.D.S.S./Forms/C. 2118.

Army Form C. 2118.

Instructions regarding War Diaries and Intelligence Summaries are contained in F. S. Regs., Part II. and the Staff Manual respectively. Title pages will be prepared in manuscript.

# WAR DIARY
*or*
~~INTELLIGENCE SUMMARY.~~
*(Erase heading not required.)*

| Place | Date | Hour | Summary of Events and Information | Remarks and references to Appendices |
|---|---|---|---|---|
| | June | | | |
| CALONNE RICQUOART | 1 | | Battalion, Company + Specialist training. [initials] | |
| | 2 | | Distribution of awards + Brigade Inspection by G.O.C. 1st Army. Lt Genl. Sir C. MUNRO Sergts NOTTINGHAM and KNAPP receive the D.C.M. [initials] | |
| | 3 | | Training in morning. Regimental sports in afternoon. Brigadier General CUTHBERT attended + distributed prizes. 5 officers and 90 other ranks arrived. [initials] | |
| | 4 | | Church parade with 8th Battn. The following appeared in the Birthday Honor list:- Lt Col H.V. Warrender appointed to D.S.O. Pte W.H. Harris awarded the Military medal. Later in the day in 4th Corps routine orders it ~~also~~ was announced that ~~Temp~~ 2nd Lieut (temp. Captain) B. Barnes and 2nd Lt F. Osborne had been awarded the MILITARY CROSS and No 1070 Sergt. McKinley, No 3415 Lcpl. Hall M.W. No 1489 Lacpl BRESSEY S.H. + No 3207 Pte Flanagan L. the Military Medal. [initials] | |
| | 5th | | 5 Officers and 100 other ranks arrived. Battalion Route marched, returning to billets at 3.45 p.m. Re inoculation commenced. [initials] | |
| | 6th | | A wet day. Battalion re-armed with short rifles. Reinoculation continued [initials] | |
| | 7th | | Baths allotted to Battalion. Company training carried out. [initials] | |
| | 8th | | Practice alarm 5.30 a.m. Battalion moved at 8 am. to MARIST where an | |

1577 Wt. W10791/1773 500,000 1/15 D. D. & L. A.D.S.S./Forms/C. 2118.

Instructions regarding War Diaries and Intelligence Summaries are contained in F. S. Regs., Part II. and the Staff Manual respectively. Title pages will be prepared in manuscript.

# WAR DIARY
*or*
~~INTELLIGENCE SUMMARY.~~
*(Erase heading not required.)*

Army Form C. 2118.

| Place | Date | Hour | Summary of Events and Information | Remarks and references to Appendices |
|---|---|---|---|---|
| | | | outpost position was taken up. Brigadier General G. C. Cuthbert C.B., C.M.G. inspected the line in the afternoon. Owing to very heavy rain the line was withdrawn at 8.10 pm. + companies returned to billets independently. During the day information was received that Coy Sergt Major Harris had been awarded the MILITARY CROSS. Commanding Officer returned from leave. [initials] | |
| | 9th. | | A wet day. Company training carried on [initials] | |
| | 10th. | | Company training. In the evening the Battalion gave a concert at DIVION. This was most successful. The concert items were very good + the entertainment concluded with a revue which was very topical and very well played. [initials] | |
| | 11th. | | Church Parade. Battalion marched passed Lord Mayor of London who afterwards inspected a Company Cooker. He expressed his pleasure at what he had seen. [initials] | |
| HERSIN | 12th. | | Battalion moved to Hersin Fosse 10 [initials] | |
| | 13th. | | Battalion took over sub section SOUCHEZ II, relieving 10th West Riding Regt. [initials] | |

1577 Wt. W10791/1773 500,000 1/15 D. D. & L. A.D.S.S./Forms/C. 2118.

Instructions regarding War Diaries and Intelligence Summaries are contained in F. S. Regs., Part II. and the Staff Manual respectively. Title pages will be prepared in manuscript.

# WAR DIARY
*or*
~~INTELLIGENCE SUMMARY.~~
*(Erase heading not required.)*

Army Form C. 2118.

| Place | Date | Hour | Summary of Events and Information | Remarks and references to Appendices |
|---|---|---|---|---|
| SOUCHEZ II | 14th | | Relief complete 12.55 am. Very quiet. Wiring at night when party was fired on by Machine Guns. Casualties Killed one. WTHa | |
| | 15th | | Very quiet day. WTHa | |
| | 16th | | Very quiet day. Casualties. Wounded one WTHa | |
| | 17th | | Some trench mortar activity. Casualties Killed one. Relieved by 7th Battn London Regt. WTHa | |
| NOULETTE WOOD. | 18th | | Relief complete 12.15 am. Battalion moved to NOULETTE WOOD WTHa | |
| | 19th to 24th | | Battalion in BRIGADE RESERVE. Furnished large working parties at night. carrying material of all kinds and also digging Trench Mortar emplacements. WTHa | |
| BOUVIGNY | 25th | | Moved to BOUVIGNY BOYEFFLES Divisional Reserve WTHa | |
| BOYEFFLES | 26th to 30th | | Company training. Training of special company. and working parties furnished. Moved up to line and relieved 21st Battn London Regt in SOUCHEZ I sub section. WTHa | |

140th Brigade.
47th Division.

--------

1/15th BATTALION

LONDON REGIMENT (P.W.O. Civil Service Rifles)

J U L Y 1 9 1 6:

Instructions regarding War Diaries and Intelligence Summaries are contained in F. S. Regs., Part II, and the Staff Manual respectively. Title pages will be prepared in manuscript.

# WAR DIARY
*or*
# ~~INTELLIGENCE SUMMARY.~~
(*Erase heading not required.*)

Army Form C. 2118.

1/15th Battn London Regt

Vol 13

| Place | Date | Hour | Summary of Events and Information | Remarks and references to Appendices |
|---|---|---|---|---|
| SOUCHEZ | 1-7-16 | | Relief complete 12 55am. A quiet day. Wire cutting by our own artillery. Casualties Wounded 2 Other Ranks | W.G.J. |
| | 2 July | | Wire cutting by our artillery continued. Patrols out at night. A quiet day. Casualties NIL. | W.G.J. |
| | 3 " | | Our artillery active cutting wire and bombarding various strong points. Special Company completed final preparations for raid against enemy salient in S2.b. Casualties Wounded O.R. 10 Killed 1. | W.G.J. |
| | 4 " | | Raiding parties moved out at 1 15am, but owing to enemy vigilance could make little progress. At 1.45am intense box barrage opened by our Artillery and Trench Mortar Battery. Northern party were able to bomb 2 saps and enemy front line trench. Southern party was hung up by wire among undergrowth of BOIS en HACHE and eventually had to withdraw. Enemy retaliated with field guns. Minenwerfer and rifle grenades on both his and our front lines of trenches. Parties all back by 2.45am. and remainder of day quiet. Brigadier General Commanding visited Battalion Headquarters about mid-day. Battalion relieved by 7th Battalion London Regt. Casualties Officers Killed one, Wounded one Other Ranks wounded 7. | W.G.J. |
| ABLAIN ST NAZAIRE | 5 " | | Relief complete 1am moved to LORETTE SPUR. Quiet day. Some rain. Casualties NIL. | W.G.J. |
| | 6 " | | Some artillery activity otherwise quiet. Working party found at night. Casualties NIL. | W.G.J. |
| | 7 " | | Quiet day. Relieved by 17th Battn Lond Regt. Casualties NIL. | W.G.J. |

1577 Wt. W10791/1773 500,000 1/15 D. D. & L. A.D.S.S./Forms/C. 2118.

Army Form C. 2118.

Instructions regarding War Diaries and Intelligence Summaries are contained in F. S. Regs., Part II. and the Staff Manual respectively. Title pages will be prepared in manuscript.

# WAR DIARY
*or*
# ~~INTELLIGENCE SUMMARY.~~
*(Erase heading not required.)*

| Place | Date | Hour | Summary of Events and Information | Remarks and references to Appendices |
|---|---|---|---|---|
| BOUVIGNY HUTS | 8/7/16 | | Relief complete 1am ~~and~~ moved to BOUVIGNY HUTS. Casualties NIL. WD | |
| | 9th–15th | | At BOUVIGNY HUTS. Company training carried on and at night working parties were found working under R.E. Casualties NIL. WD | |
| BERTHONVAL | 15 | | Relieved by 23rd Batt. London Regt. and moved to subsection I of BERTHONVAL SECTOR where the Battalion relieved 23rd Battalion Royal Fusiliers 99th Inf. Bde. Casualties NIL. WD | |
| | 16 | | Relief complete 1.30am. Quiet day. Casualties NIL WD | |
| | 17 | | Quiet day. Brigadier General Viscount HAMPDEN visited the line. Casualties O.R. Wounded 1. WD | |
| | 18 | | Our Trench Mortars fired with effect on Enemy working party. Retaliation by enemy on Battalion on right. Casualties Other Ranks Wounded 3. WD | |
| | 19 | | Between 5 & 7 am. enemy howitzers put over about 40 H.E. shells into ZOUAVE VALLEY behind our lines without doing any damage. Day quiet. From 10pm to midnight our machine guns kept up intermittent fire on enemy lines and ground behind. Casualties Other Ranks Wd. 3. WD | |
| | 20 | | Between 6 & 8 am about 30 H.E. Shells dropped by enemy in ZOUAVE VALLEY. Day quiet. From 10pm to midnight our Machine Guns fired as on 19th. Casualties O.R. Wounded 2. WD | |
| | 21 | | Quiet day. Relieved by 7th Battn. Lond. Regt. Casualties Other Ranks Wounded 1 WD | |

1577 Wt. W10791/1773 500,000 1/15 D. D. & L. A.D.S.S./Forms/C. 2118.

Army Form C. 2118.

Instructions regarding War Diaries and Intelligence Summaries are contained in F. S. Regs., Part II. and the Staff Manual respectively. Title pages will be prepared in manuscript.

# WAR DIARY
*or*
~~INTELLIGENCE~~ ~~SUMMARY~~.
*(Erase heading not required.)*

| Place | Date | Hour | Summary of Events and Information | Remarks and references to Appendices |
|---|---|---|---|---|
| CAMBLAIN L'ABBE | 22/7/16 | | Relief complete 1 am. Battn moved to CAMBLAIN L'ABBE arriving at 4 30 am. Afternoon spent in inspections. Casualties NIL. | |
| | 23 | | Church Parade at 10-30 am. Brigadier General Viscount HAMPDEN attended Casualties NIL | |
| | 24 & 25 | | Spent in Company training Casualties NIL. | |
| HOUDAIN | 26 | | Brigade left BERTHONVAL SECTOR for HOUDAIN District. Battalion left CAMBLAIN L'ABBE 1 pm Brigade concentrated at GAUCHIN LE GAL 2 pm. Battalion arrived at HOUDAIN 4 pm Casualties NIL. | |
| VALHUON | 27 | | Brigade left HOUDAIN district for VALHUON district, N of St POL. Battalion marched from HOUDAIN 9 30 am. Brigade concentrated DIVION 10 am. Marched via OURTON & DIEVAL to VALHUON Arrived 2 pm. Casualties NIL. | |
| | 28 & 29 | | Company training at VALHUON. Casualties NIL. | |
| CROISETTE | 30 | | Brigade left VALHUON district for CROISETTE district. Battalion left VALHUON 11·35 am via ST POL Arrived CROISSETTE 3·30 pm. Very hot day, causing many men to fall out. Left 1st Army and came under 3rd Army 12 noon. Casualties NIL. | |
| | 31 | | At CROISETTE. Company training. Casualties NIL. | |

W Blake[?] Adjt.
15th Battn Lanc Fus[?]
1/8/1916

COPY No. 2

SECRET.

15th Bn. London Regiment.

OPERATION ORDER No. 5.



Reference Sheet 36c S.W.1/20000.
Secret Tracing 1/2500, Square S.

1. The Special Company will carry out a Raid on the enemy salient at S.2.b on the morning of 4th July.

2. The raiding force will be divided into two parties, NORTH PARTY and SOUTH PARTY.
NORTH PARTY will leave our front line at point S.2.b.2.4. Its objective will be TRENCH JUNCTION S.2.b.3.4.
SOUTH PARTY will leave our front line at point S.2.b.2½.0. X Its objective will be TRENCH JUNCTION S.2.b.4.2½.

3. Both parties will enter enemy trench simultaneously at ZERO.

4. The two parties will operate towards each other along the CHORD and FRONT LINE of the SALIENT.

5. The failure of either of the parties to penetrate into the enemy line will not involve the abandonment of the enterprise by the other party.

6. The operation will close at 20 minutes after ZERO or earlier, if complete.

7. When the operation is closed parties will return independently by the same route as on entering.

8. The signal for return will be the Battalion call blown by buglers in the FRONT LINE, and a series of alternate red and green rockets sent up at intervals of 15 seconds from the CRATER in COMPANY TRENCH. These rockets will serve as a guide for the returning parties. A bonfire will be lighted at junction of ARRAS ROAD and BAJOLLE LINE to serve as an additional guide.

9. An Artillery barrage on the lines already arranged will open automatically at ZERO, or earlier, on receipt of message "RATS" from Battalion H.Q.

10. Trench Mortars and Lewis guns will co-operate on the flanks.

11. The word "RETIRE" will not be used.

12. ZERO will be at 1.45 a.m.

(Sd) H.V.WARRENDER, Lt. Colonel,
Comdg. 15th Bn. London Regiment.

No distinguishing marks? Password? R.E.?

The following will be the CODE words:-
RATS = Barrage at once.
C.O. = Raid commencing.
DUD = Raid cancelled.



[signature]
Major,
Brigade Major,
140th Infantry Brigade.

| | | | | | |
|---|---|---|---|---|---|
| COPY No. | 1 | 47th Division. | Copy No. | 6 | 142nd B.M.G.Coy. |
| ,, | 2 | do. | ,, | 7 | 140 T.M.Battery. |
| ,, | 3 | Right Group. | ,, | 8 | 100th Btry. R.G.A. |
| ,, | 4 | 2/3rd Coy. R.E. | ,, | 9 | |
| ,, | 5 | 140th B.M.G.Coy. | ,, | 10 | |

140th Brigade.
47th Division.

---

1/15th BATTALION

LONDON REGIMENT

AUGUST 1 9 1 6

Vol 14

# War Diary

of the

15th Battn. London Regiment

from

1st August to 31st August, 1916.

Volume. I

Instructions regarding War Diaries and Intelligence Summaries are contained in F. S. Regs., Part II. and the Staff Manual respectively. Title pages will be prepared in manuscript.

# WAR DIARY

or

~~INTELLIGENCE SUMMARY.~~

*(Erase heading not required.)*

Army Form C. 2118.

(1)

| Place | Date | Hour | Summary of Events and Information | Remarks and references to Appendices |
|---|---|---|---|---|
| CROISSETTE | 1.8.16 | | Left CROISSETTE and marched to FORTEL - Casualties Nil | |
| FORTEL | 2.8.16 | | Company training at FORTEL - Casualties Nil. | |
| | 3.8.16 | | Company training at FORTEL - Casualties Nil | |
| | 4.8.16 | | Left FORTEL and marched via AUXI-LE-CHATEAU to CONTEVILLE - Casualties Nil. | |
| CONTEVILLE | 5.8.16 | | Left CONTEVILLE and marched via ST RIQUIER to DRUCAT - Casualties Nil. | |
| DRUCAT | 6.8.16 | | Company training at DRUCAT - Casualties Nil. | |
| | 7.8.16 | | Company training on ST. RIQUIER training area, near DRUCAT, Casualties Nil | |
| | 8.8.16 | | Battalion training on ST RIQUIER training area, near DRUCAT, Casualties Nil | |
| | 9.8.16 | | Battalion training on ST. RIQUIER training area, near DRUCAT, Casualties Nil | |
| | 10.8.16 | | Battalion training on ST RIQUIER training area, near DRUCAT, Casualties Nil | |
| | 11.8.16 | | Brigade training on ST RIQUIER training area, near DRUCAT. Casualties Nil | |
| | 12.8.16 | | Battalion training on ST RIQUIER training area, near DRUCAT, Casualties Nil | |
| | 13.8.16 | | At DRUCAT, Sunday, no training. - Casualties Nil. | |
| | 14.8.16 | | Brigade training on ST RIQUIER training area, near DRUCAT, Casualties Nil | |
| | 15.8.16 | | Battalion training on ST RIQUIER training area, near DRUCAT Casualties Nil | |
| | 16.8.16 | | Brigade Route march DRUCAT Casualties Nil<br>[illegible] Forêt de Crécy | |

H. Osborne 2nd Lt & Asst Adjt
1/15th Batt. London Regt

1577 Wt. W10791/1773 500,000 1/15 D. D. & L. A.D.S.S./Forms/C. 2118.

Instructions regarding War Diaries and Intelligence Summaries are contained in F. S. Regs., Part II. and the Staff Manual respectively. Title pages will be prepared in manuscript.

# WAR DIARY
~~or~~
## ~~INTELLIGENCE SUMMARY.~~
*(Erase heading not required.)*

Army Form C. 2118.

(2)

| Place | Date | Hour | Summary of Events and Information | Remarks and references to Appendices |
|---|---|---|---|---|
| | 17.8.16 | | Battalion Training on ST. RIQUIER training area, near DRUCAT, Casualties Nil H.O. | |
| | 18.8.16 | | Battalion Training on ST RIQUIER training area, near DRUCAT, Casualties Nil H.O. | |
| | 19.8.16 | | Very wet day. Brigade route march arranged, but abandoned. Casualties Nil H.O. | |
| | 20.8.16 | | Left DRUCAT and marched to VILLERS-SOUS-AILLY, carry out Brigade Outpost scheme H.O. | |
| | | | en route – Casualties Nil. – H.O. | |
| VILLERS-SOUS-AILLY | 21.8.16 | | Left VILLERS-SOUS-AILLY and marched to NAOURS. – Casualties Nil H.O. | |
| NAOURS | 22.8.16 | | Left NAOURS and marched to MIRVAUX, Casualties Nil H.O. | |
| MIRVAUX | 23.8.16 | | Left MIRVAUX and marched via BEAUCOURT to FRANVILLERS, Casualties Nil H.O. | |
| FRANVILLERS | 24.8.16 | | Company training at FRANVILLERS, Casualties Nil H.O. | |
| | 25.8.16 | | Company training at FRANVILLERS, Casualties Nil H.O. | |
| | 26.8.16 | | Company training at FRANVILLERS, Casualties Nil H.O. | |
| | 27.8.16 | | Sunday, no training, Casualties Nil H.O. | |
| | 28.8.16 | | Battalion training at FRANVILLERS, Casualties Nil H.O. | |
| | 29.8.16 | | Battalion training at FRANVILLERS, Casualties Nil H.O. | |
| | 30.8.16 | | Company training at FRANVILLERS, Casualties Nil H.O. | |
| | 31.8.16 | | Battalion training at FRANVILLERS, Casualties Nil. H.O. | |

H Osborne 2nd Lt & Asst Adjt
1/15th Batt. London Regt

1577 Wt. W10791/1773 500,000 1/15 D. D. & L. A.D.S.S./Forms/C. 2118.

Army Form C. 2118.

Instructions regarding War Diaries and Intelligence Summaries are contained in F. S. Regs., Part II. and the Staff Manual respectively. Title pages will be prepared in manuscript.

# WAR DIARY
*or*
~~INTELLIGENCE SUMMARY.~~
*(Erase heading not required.)*

| Place | Date | Hour | Summary of Events and Information | Remarks and references to Appendices |
|---|---|---|---|---|
| FRANVILLERS | 1.9.16 | | Training at FRANVILLERS Casualties Nil. | [illegible] |
| | 2.9.16 | | Training at FRANVILLERS. Casualties Nil. | [illegible] |
| | 3.9.16 | | At FRANVILLERS, Sunday, no training. Casualties Nil | [illegible] |
| | 4.9.16 | | Training at FRANVILLERS Casualties Nil. | [illegible] |
| | 5.9.16 | | Training at FRANVILLERS. Casualties Nil. | [illegible] |
| | 6.9.16 | | Training at FRANVILLERS Casualties Nil | [illegible] |
| | 7.9.16 | | Training at FRANVILLERS Casualties Nil | [illegible] |
| | 8.9.16 | | Training at FRANVILLERS Casualties Nil | [illegible] |
| | 9.9.16 | | Training at FRANVILLERS Casualties Nil. | [illegible] |
| | 10.9.16 | | At FRANVILLERS, Sunday, no training. Casualties Nil. | [illegible] |
| | 11.9.16 | | Training at FRANVILLERS Casualties Nil | [illegible] |
| | 12.9.16 | | Battalion left FRANVILLERS and moved in to reserve to Front Line Division. Relieved 2nd Royal Sussex at BECOURT WOOD Casualties Nil. | [illegible] |
| BECOURT WOOD | 13.9.16 | | Resting at BECOURT WOOD. Casualties Nil. | [illegible] |
| | 14.9.16 | | Relieved 2 Companies 21st London Regiment in HIGH WOOD at 6.0 p.m. Casualties Nil | [illegible] |

1577 Wt. W10791/1773 500,000 1/15 D. D. & L. A.D.S.S./Forms/C. 2118.

# WAR DIARY

of the

1/15th Battalion London Regiment (P.W.O. CIVIL SERVICE RIFLES)

from

1st September – 30th September

1916

Instructions regarding War Diaries and Intelligence Summaries are contained in F. S. Regs., Part II. and the Staff Manual respectively. Title pages will be prepared in manuscript.

# WAR DIARY
*or*
~~INTELLIGENCE SUMMARY.~~
*(Erase heading not required.)*

Army Form C. 2118.

| Place | Date | Hour | Summary of Events and Information | Remarks and references to Appendices |
|---|---|---|---|---|
| HIGH WOOD | 15.9.16 | | Battalion took part in HIGH WOOD in general attack by IV Army. 17th London Battalion attacked on left in HIGH WOOD, 7th London Regiment on right outside wood. ZERO 5.50 a.m. "A" Company on right immediately successful and pushed through to Support line. "B", "C" and "D" Companies were cut up by Machine Gun fire + were unsuccessful. 7th Battalion on right entirely successful. 17th on left entirely unsuccessful on account of machine gun fire. | Map showing site of operations annexed. [initials] |
| | | 11.00 a.m. | Enemy front line bombarded by Stokes Mortars. As a result of this and progress of Divisions on right and left, enemy surrendered and by 12 noon we were in possession of whole of HIGH WOOD + SWITCH LINE. Rest of day spent in consolidating new position in front of SWITCH LINE and in joining up with 17th Battalion on left and 7th Battalion on right. Meanwhile 6th London Regt. pushed through 7th on right + occupied E half of STARFISH and COUGH DROP. | |
| | | 6.0 p.m. | 21st London Regt attacked from HIGH WOOD on West half of STARFISH and COUGH DROP. Practically annihilated by Artillery + Machine Gun fire. | |

1577 Wt. W10791/1773 500,000 1/15 D. D. & L. A.D.S.S./Forms/C. 2118.

3

Instructions regarding War Diaries and Intelligence Summaries are contained in F. S. Regs., Part II. and the Staff Manual respectively. Title pages will be prepared in manuscript.

# WAR DIARY

*or*

# ~~INTELLIGENCE SUMMARY.~~

*(Erase heading not required.)*

Army Form C. 2118.

| Place | Date | Hour | Summary of Events and Information | Remarks and references to Appendices |
|---|---|---|---|---|
| HIGH WOOD | 15.9.16 | | Casualties - Officers Killed - Capt Roberts, Capt Gaze, Capt Davies, 2/Lt Hoole Missing :- 2/Lt Fletcher. Wounded :- 2/Lt Fallon, 2/Lt Townsend, 2/Lt Thomas, 2/Lt Richardson, 2/Lt Ray, 2/Lt Roberts, 2/Lt Hunslop, 2/Lt Barnes, 2/Lt Burtt. O.R's :- about 250 killed, wounded and missing. | MB |
| | 16.9.16 | | Morning quiet. Consolidation proceeded. | |
| | | 9.00 a.m | 23rd London Regt attacked from HIGH WOOD on West portion of STARFISH and COUGH DROP. Practically annihilated by shell & machine gun fire. Day quiet, except for intermittent shelling of HIGH WOOD and SWITCH LINE by heavy howitzers. | |
| | | 9.0 p.m | Battalion moved up to take over DROP ALLEY, leading from COUGH DROP to FLERS LINE, on information that FLERS LINE EAST of DROP ALLEY was held by 6th London Regiment. On arrival, found that 6th Battalion were NOT occupying FLERS LINE, but were in COUGH DROP. Battalion accordingly occupied WESTERN half of COUGH DROP and threw back defensive flank towards STARFISH LINE and PRUE TRENCH. Night quiet. Consolidation of COUGH DROP proceeded. | MB |

Map showing site of operation annexed MB

1577 Wt. W10791/1773 500,000 1/15 D. D. & L. A.D.S.S./Forms/C. 2118.

4

Army Form C. 2118.

# WAR DIARY
or
# ~~INTELLIGENCE SUMMARY.~~

(*Erase heading not required.*)

Instructions regarding War Diaries and Intelligence Summaries are contained in F. S. Regs., Part II. and the Staff Manual respectively. Title pages will be prepared in manuscript.

| Place | Date | Hour | Summary of Events and Information | Remarks and references to Appendices |
|---|---|---|---|---|
| HIGH WOOD | 17.9.16 | | COUGH DROP heavily shelled. Consolidation proceeded. 2/Lt E L Townsend died of wounds. WB | Map showing site of operations annexed WB |
| | 18.9.16 | | 6th, 8th and 15th London Regiments attacked FLERS LINE between DROP ALLEY and GOOSE ALLEY (left of New Zealand Division) At same time 15th London Regiment occupied DROP ALLEY and established block at its junction with FLERS LINE. ZERO 5.30 a m Attack successful but owing to loss of direction, troops in FLERS LINE and DROP ALLEY did not quite join up. Several unsuccessful attempts made during day to link up. | |
| | | 12 noon | 6th, 8th & 15th London Regts relieved in FLERS LINES by 8th OTAGO Battn. N Z. Division + moved back to DROP ALLEY and STARFISH. | |
| | | 6.0 pm | Combined bombing attack by New Zealanders along FLERS LINE and 15th London Regt up DROP ALLEY failed. Night fairly quiet WB | |
| | 19.9.16 | 6.0 am | Enemy bombed down DROP ALLEY but was easily driven back | |
| | | 7.0 pm | Enemy again bombed down DROP ALLEY, and owing to state of exhaustion of troops, it was not possible again to dislodge him. Casualties. 2/Lt B K Ware killed. WB | |
| | 20.9.16 | 3.0 a.m. | Relieved by 1st Battn. Black Watch + moved back to BOTTOM WOOD near MAMETZ WOOD. Total Casualties 15th to 20th: Officers 15 O. R's. 365 Killed, Wounded and Missing. WB | |

1577 Wt. W10791/1773 500,000 1/15 D. D. & L. A.D.S.S./Forms/C. 2118.

Army Form C. 2118.

Instructions regarding War Diaries and Intelligence Summaries are contained in F. S. Regs., Part II. and the Staff Manual respectively. Title pages will be prepared in manuscript.

# WAR DIARY
*or*
~~INTELLIGENCE SUMMARY.~~

*(Erase heading not required.)*

| Place | Date | Hour | Summary of Events and Information | Remarks and references to Appendices |
|---|---|---|---|---|
| BOTTOM WOOD | 20.9.16 | 5.30pm | Left BOTTOM WOOD and moved to ALBERT. Casualties Nil | [illegible] |
| ALBERT | 21.9.16 | | Left ALBERT and moved back to HENENCOURT WOOD. Casualties Nil. | [illegible] |
| HENENCOURT WOOD | 22.9.16 | | Training and Refitting at HENENCOURT WOOD. Draft of 1 Officer and 375 O.R. arrived. Casualties Nil | [illegible] |
| | 23.9.16 | | Training and Refitting at HENENCOURT WOOD. Casualties Nil | [illegible] |
| | 24.9.16 | | Training and Refitting at HENENCOURT WOOD. Casualties Nil | [illegible] |
| | 25.9.16 | | Training and Refitting at HENENCOURT WOOD. Casualties Nil | [illegible] |
| | 26.9.16 | | Training and Refitting at HENENCOURT WOOD. Casualties Nil | [illegible] |
| | 27.9.16 | | Training and Refitting at HENENCOURT WOOD Casualties Nil | [illegible] |
| | 28.9.16 | | Training and Refitting at HENENCOURT WOOD Casualties Nil. | [illegible] |
| | 29.9.16 | | Moved to ALBERT. Casualties Nil. | [illegible] |
| ALBERT | 30.9.16 | | Moved to the QUADRANGLE near MAMETZ WOOD in reserve to attack of 141st Brigade on EAUCOURT L'ABBE. Casualties Nil. | [illegible] |

[illegible] Lt & Adjt
1/15th Battn London Regt
1/10/16

1577 Wt. W10791/1773 500,000 1/15 D. D. & L. A.D.S.S./For[illegible]

# War Diary

of the

1/15th Battalion London Regt.

from

1st October 1916

to

31st October 1916.

Vol 16

/ 15th Battn: London Regt.
(P: W: O: Civil Service Rifles.)

# WAR DIARY
*or*
~~INTELLIGENCE SUMMARY.~~
*(Erase heading not required.)*

Army Form C. 2118.

Instructions regarding War Diaries and Intelligence Summaries are contained in F. S. Regs., Part II. and the Staff Manual respectively. Title pages will be prepared in manuscript.

| Place | Date 1916 | Hour | Summary of Events and Information | Remarks and references to Appendices |
|---|---|---|---|---|
| | OCTOBER | | | |
| ALBERT | 1 | | Left ALBERT and moved to the QUADRANGLE, MAMETZ WOOD in reserve to attack of 141st Bde. Casualties Nil | |
| MAMETZ | 2 | | At the QUADRANGLE, MAMETZ WOOD. Casualties Nil | |
| | 3 | | At the QUADRANGLE, MAMETZ WOOD. Casualties Nil | |
| | 4 | | Left QUADRANGLE at 5.0 p.m. and moved up to EAUCOURT L'ABBE relieving 17th Battalion London Regiment in the FLERS LINE Casualties Nil | |
| EAUCOURT L'ABBE | 5 | | At EAUCOURT L'ABBE in the FLERS line. Casualties 1 wounded | |
| | 6 | | At EAUCOURT L'ABBE in the FLERS line. Casualties 1 killed 3 wounded | |
| | 7 | | At EAUCOURT L'ABBE. Attack on the WARLENCOURT LINE by 140th Bde at 1.30 p.m. * Attack unsuccessful. Battalion badly cut up. The remnants of the Battalion under Capt. G.G.Bates dig themselves in in an advanced position on the right of the Brigade front astride the EAUCOURT L'ABBE - LE BARQUE road. Casualties:-<br>Officers. Killed 1 Wounded 4 Missing 1<br>O. R's. Killed 22 Wounded 257 Missing 65 approx.<br><br>* Complete account of operations will be forwarded as an Appendix. | * See note below entry for 7/10/16 |
| | 8 | | At EAUCOURT L'ABBE Casualties 7 wounded | |
| | 9 | | Relieved in the front line at EAUCOURT L'ABBE by 7th Battalion Seaforth Highlanders and moved back to the horse lines at MAMETZ WOOD. Casualties 2 wounded | |

5724

A5834 Wt. W4973/M687 750,000 8/16 D. D. & L. Ltd. Forms/C.2118/13.

1/15th Battn: London Regt
(P.W.O. Civil Service Rifles)

Army Form C. 2118.

Instructions regarding War Diaries and Intelligence Summaries are contained in F. S. Regs., Part II. and the Staff Manual respectively. Title pages will be prepared in manuscript.

# WAR DIARY
or
~~INTELLIGENCE SUMMARY.~~

*(Erase heading not required.)*

| Place | Date 1916 | Hour | Summary of Events and Information | Remarks and references to Appendices |
|---|---|---|---|---|
| | OCTOBER | | | |
| MAMETZ | 10 | | Left the horse lines, MAMETZ WOOD and moved back to ALBERT. Casualties Nil | [illegible] |
| ALBERT | 11 | | At ALBERT Casualties Nil | [illegible] |
| | 12 | | At ALBERT Casualties Nil | [illegible] |
| | 13 | | Left ALBERT at 4.0 p.m. and entrained for LONGRE-LES-CORPS SAINTS, near ABBEVILLE. Casualties Nil | [illegible] |
| VILLERS | 14 | | Detrained at LONGRE-LES-CORPS-SAINTS and marched to VILLERS SOUS AILLY Casualties Nil | [illegible] |
| | 15 | | At VILLERS SOUS AILLY Casualties Nil | [illegible] |
| | 16 | | Left VILLERS SOUS AILLY and entrained at 5.30 p.m. at LONGRE-LES-CORPS-SAINTS for the Northern area. Casualties Nil | [illegible] |
| BOESCHEPE | 17 | | Detrained 1.0 a.m. at CAESTRE near HAZEBROUCK and marched to BOESCHEPE. Casualties Nil | [illegible] |
| | 18 | | At BOESCHEPE Casualties Nil | [illegible] |
| YPRES SALIENT | 19 | | Moved into support to the front line, BLUFF SECTOR, YPRES SALIENT, relieving 16th Battalion Australian Infantry. Casualties Nil | [illegible] |
| | 20 | | In support, BLUFF SECTOR. Casualties Nil | [illegible] |
| | 21 | | In support, BLUFF SECTOR. Casualties Nil | [illegible] |
| | 22 | | In support, BLUFF SECTOR. Casualties 1 killed | [illegible] |
| | 23 | | In support, BLUFF SECTOR. Casualties 1 killed 1 wounded | [illegible] |

A5834 Wt. W4973/M687 750,000 8/16 D. D. & L. Ltd. Forms/C.2118/13.

1/15th Battn: London Regt.
(P.W.O. Civil Service Rifles)

Army Form C. 2118.

# WAR DIARY

*or*

# ~~INTELLIGENCE SUMMARY~~.

*(Erase heading not required.)*

Instructions regarding War Diaries and Intelligence Summaries are contained in F. S. Regs., Part II. and the Staff Manual respectively. Title pages will be prepared in manuscript.

| Place | Date 1916 | Hour | Summary of Events and Information | Remarks and references to Appendices |
|---|---|---|---|---|
| | OCTOBER | | | |
| YPRES SALIENT | 24 | | Relieved 8th Battalion London Regiment in left Sub Section BLUFF SECTOR, YPRES SALIENT. Casualties Nil | |
| | 25 | | In the front line, left Sub Section, BLUFF SECTOR. Casualties 2 killed, 6 wounded. | |
| | 26 | | In the front line, left Sub Section, BLUFF SECTOR. Casualties 2 wounded. | |
| | 27 | | In the front line, left Sub Section. BLUFF SECTOR. Casualties 1 wounded. | |
| | 28 | | In the front line, left Sub Section, BLUFF SECTOR. Casualties 1 killed, 1 wounded. | |
| | 29 | | Relieved in left Sub Section, BLUFF SECTOR, by 17th Battalion London Regiment. Casualties Nil | |
| OUDERDOM | 30 | | Arrived at OTTAWA CAMP, near OUDERDOM, 2.0 a.m. Casualties Nil | |
| | 31 | | At OTTAWA CAMP. Casualties Nil | |

[illegible] 2nd Lt. & Adjt.
1/15th Battn London Regt.
3/11/1916.

A5834 Wt. W4973/M687 750,000 8/16 D. D. & L. Ltd. Forms/C.2118/13.

# W A R   D I A R Y,

## 1/15th BATTALION LONDON REGIMENT,

1st to 30th November 1916.

-----------

Army Form C. 2118.

Instructions regarding War Diaries and Intelligence Summaries are contained in F. S. Regs., Part II. and the Staff Manual respectively. Title pages will be prepared in manuscript.

# WAR DIARY
*or*
# INTELLIGENCE SUMMARY.
*(Erase heading not required.)*

| Place | Date | Hour | Summary of Events and Information | Remarks and references to Appendices |
|---|---|---|---|---|
| | Novr. | | | |
| OTTAWA CAMP nr OUDERDOM | 1st | | Company Training at OTTAWA CAMP, OUDERDOM. Casualties Nil. | WGI |
| | 2nd | | Inspection by G.O.C. 2nd Army at BUSSEBOOM. " " | WGI |
| | 3rd | | Company Training at OTTAWA CAMP. " " | WGI |
| | 4th | | Company Training at OTTAWA CAMP. " " | WGI |
| | 5th | | Sunday. No training. " " | WGI |
| | 6th | | Company Training at OTTAWA CAMP. " " | WGI |
| | 7th | | Company Training at OTTAWA CAMP. " " | WGI |
| HALIFAX CAMP nr. VLAMERTINGHE | 8th | | Moved to HALIFAX CAMP, near VLAMERTINGHE in support to Front Line. Casualties Nil. | WGI |
| | 9th | | In reserve at HALIFAX CAMP. Company Training. " " | WGI |
| | 10th | | In reserve at HALIFAX CAMP. Company Training. " " | WGI |
| | 11th | | In reserve at HALIFAX CAMP. Company Training. " " | WGI |
| | 12th | | Sunday. In reserve at HALIFAX CAMP. No Training. " " | WGI |
| FRONT LINE HILL 60 SECTOR | 13th | | Relieved 6th Battn. London Regt. in Left Sub Section, Hill 60 Sector. Relief complete 9.0 p.m. Casualties Nil. | WGI WGI |
| | 14th | | In Front Line trenches. Heavy Minenwerfer fire in afternoon. Casualties - Killed 2 O.R's. | WGI |

T2134. Wt. W708—776. 500000. 4/15. Sir J. C. & S.

Instructions regarding War Diaries and Intelligence Summaries are contained in F. S. Regs., Part II. and the Staff Manual respectively. Title pages will be prepared in manuscript.

# WAR DIARY
*or*
# INTELLIGENCE SUMMARY.
*(Erase heading not required.)*

Army Form C. 2118.

| Place | Date | Hour | Summary of Events and Information | Remarks and references to Appendices |
|---|---|---|---|---|
| | Novr. | | | |
| FRONT LINE HILL 60 SECTOR. | 15th | | In Front Line trenches. Heavy Minenwerfer fire in afternoon. Casualties 1 Officer wounded (shell shock) 7 O.R's killed, 1 wounded. | |
| | 16th | | In Front Line trenches. Casualties - 4 wounded. | |
| | 17th | | In Front Line trenches. Casualties - 1 O.R. killed, 1 wounded. | |
| | 18th | | In Front Line trenches. Relieved by 6th Battn. London Regiment and moved back to Support in RAILWAY DUGOUTS. Relief complete 9.30 p.m. Casualties Nil. | |
| SUPPORT RAILWAY DUGOUTS | 19th | | In Support at RAILWAY DUGOUTS. Casualties Nil. | |
| | 20th | | In Support at RAILWAY DUGOUTS. Casualties Nil. | |
| | 21st | | In support at RAILWAY DUGOUTS. Casualties Nil. | |
| | 22nd | | In Support at RAILWAY DUGOUTS. Casualties Nil. | |
| | 23rd | | In Support at RAILWAY DUGOUTS. Relieved 6th Battalion London Regiment in FRONT LINE. Relief complete 9.0 p.m. Casualties Nil. | |
| FRONT LINE HILL 60 SECTOR. | 24th | | In FRONT LINE. Casualties 2 O.R's wounded. | |
| | 25th | | In FRONT LINE. Casualties 3 O.R's wounded. | |
| | 26th | | In FRONT LINE. Casualties Nil. | |
| | 27th | | In FRONT LINE. Casualties Nil. | |

T2134. Wt. W708—776. 500000. 4/15. Sir J. C. & S.

Army Form C. 2118.

Instructions regarding War Diaries and Intelligence Summaries are contained in F. S. Regs., Part II. and the Staff Manual respectively. Title pages will be prepared in manuscript.

# WAR DIARY
*or*
# INTELLIGENCE SUMMARY.
*(Erase heading not required.)*

| Place | Date | Hour | Summary of Events and Information | Remarks and references to Appendices |
|---|---|---|---|---|
| | Novr. | | | |
| OTTAWA CAMP OUDERDOM. | 28th | | In front line. Relieved by 17th Battalion London Regiment. Relief complete 9.40 p.m. | |
| | | | Moved back into Divisional Reserve, OTTAWA CAMP, OUDERDOM. Casualties Nil. | |
| | 29th | | At OTTAWA CAMP. Casualties Nil. | |
| | 30th | | At OTTAWA CAMP. Casualties Nil. | |

[signature] Capt & Adjt
1/15 London Regt.
1/12/1916.

Secret.

90/10

Raid file

G/240/27
11/4/16

H.Q.
47th Division.

Your G/240/10/6 of today.
Owing to the fact that I shall be handing over the command of the Brigade tomorrow morning to Lt Colonel Mildren and shall not be returning before the 21st or 22nd I think it as well to put my views on paper with reference to the proposed raid & general policy leading up to the same.
I propose that 2 officers & 50 men of the 15th Bn should carry out the raid from the vicinity of Berry & Glasgow Posts on the enemy's front line due South of these Posts. No definite scheme can be decided upon until accurate information is received as to the manner in which this line is held and the state of the wire.
From now onwards the Artillery & T.M.s should systematically cut wire along the front from I 29 d 2.5 to the Right of the sector and on the night of the raid barrage should be placed on the enemy's support & communication trenches from I 29 d 1.3 to I 29 d. 3. 4 (approximately) ten minutes before the raiding party is timed to enter the enemy trench in the vicinity of I 29 d. 7. 4.
This procedure on the part of the

Artillery should take the enemy's attention off that part of the trench to be raided and he will probably place his barrage on our front line & No Man's Land to the South West of 'The Snout'.

Between now & the 25th inst – the date proposed for the raid – the raiding party will carry out ~~[illegible]~~ nightly reconnaissances of the trenches East of 'The Snout' & acquire a thorough knowledge of the ground between them and Square Wood.

An alternative scheme to the above would be to raid the trenches in the neighbourhood of the Verbrandenmolen Road. This on paper would be a more straightforward & simpler affair but with the knowledge the enemy now has regarding our raids & the commanding positions he occupies on Hill 60 & the Caterpillar I am of opinion that its success would be doubtful. Also he would be more prepared owing to the wire cutting previously carried out by our T.M's.

In any case it is most important that damaged trenches & wire should be kept under fire from Lewis Guns at night & so prevent repair.

Up to the present it cannot be said that our retaliation of the Enemy's trench mortars has been as effective as it ought to be. and if the bursts of Artillery & Trench Mortar fire which have been arranged for do not have the desired result I am strongly of the opinion that the addition of the Heavies should prove beneficial.

In order to get on with the work in this sector it is of vital importance that the Enemy's Minenwerfer activities should be put an end to. ~~and~~ I am informed that in other parts of the line retaliation by bursts of 5 or 10 minutes fire from Div' Arty and Heavies have had the desired result, and I think it probable that, at any rate, until the sector is provided with sufficient 2" T.Ms in position it will be necessary to resort to this procedure.

Hampden Brig Genl
Comd 140th Inf Bde

10.Nov.1916.

17 XII 16

My dear [illegible]

Speaking of it as the raid —

Chief Commander is very strongly opposed to any raid carried out without heavy preliminary bombardment — he was [illegible] the time when the question was first to have [illegible] up [illegible] then the 23 [illegible] had [illegible] latter [illegible] carried out raid [illegible] bombardment — former without preliminary latter successful former unsuccessful although the raiders got into the enemy [illegible] they did not succeed in their objective of securing identifications —

We must therefore arrange to carry out the raid under [illegible] of heavy artillery bombardment of at least 15 minutes then fire barrage —

[illegible] the word [illegible] [illegible]
informed his division that the plan to
be based on an Artillery bombardment
to flatten out enemy front line wire etc.
and bombing parts M; etc in front line
that the barrage should creep lently forward
[illegible] follow close up to barrage — they
[illegible] about 15 minutes clean up objective and
under cover of our big barrage [illegible] and then
come out —

I will send Turner round to [illegible]
amended plan with you —

Yours sincerely

[illegible]

P.S.

Enemy been strangely quiet these last
2 days.

Secret.

## R A I D S.

| Corps. | Division. | Brigade. | Unit. | Date. | Nature. | Front. | Strength. | Extra arms (ammn.) required. | Remarks. |
|---|---|---|---|---|---|---|---|---|---|
| Xth | 47th | 140th | 15th Lon.Regt. | 26 Nov. | Enter front line for purpose of securing prisoners for identification | I.29.d.60.55 to I.29.d.80.45 | 2 Officers 50 O.R. | | Scheme has been already forwarded. |

(sd.) HAMPDEN, Brig. General,
Comdg.140th Infantry Brigade.
24th November, 1916.

## RAIDS.

| Corps. | Division. | Brigade. | Unit. | Date. | Nature. | Front. | Strength. | Extra amm. required. | Remarks. |
|---|---|---|---|---|---|---|---|---|---|
| X" | 47" | 140" | 15th London R. | 26. Nov. | Enemy front line for purpose of securing prisoners for identification | I.29d.60.55 to I.29d.80.45 | 2 officers 50 O.R. | | Scheme has been already forwarded |

Hampden Brig Genl
Comm. 140th Inf Bde
24. Nov. 1916

4. METHODS. (continued) only sufficiently long to dispose of the garrison and secure prisoners, and will then return by the same route. The rear party will be divided into two sections, and will remain outside the wire, ready to assist the leading party and prevent their being attacked from the flanks or rear across the open. They will carry wire-cutters and will improve the gaps in the enemy's wire as far as possible, to facilitate the return of the parties in the trench. If the raiding party should be discovered before they reach the enemy wire, they will retire on to GLASGOW POST

5. RETURN. To guide the parties back, a rocket station will be established in X trench at I 29 b 03. Rockets of one colour will be sent up at ¼ minute intervals commencing 3 minutes after ZERO. A dummy Rocket Station will be established at I. 29 b 7.7. Rockets of a different colour will be sent up from it at ¼ minute intervals to distract attention from X trench Station.

6. RE-ORGANISATION. The parties will re-form in ZILLEBEKE SWITCH after the raid.

7. EQUIPMENT. The Raiding party will go out in loose order, with rifle and bayonets fixed. Faces and hands will be blacked, and bayonets dulled. Each bomber will carry 4 bombs and each of the other men 2 bombs. A proportion of the party will carry electric torches.

8. ARTILLERY and T.M. COOPERATION. At ZERO a box barrage will be opened by the artillery on and behind the enemy front line in Square I. 29 c. It is hoped that this will have the effect of distracting the

90/10

1/15th Battn. London Regiment

SCHEME

for proposed Raid on Enemy Trenches
in HILL 60 Sector.

1. OBJECTIVE:- Enemy Front Line trenches from about I 29 d 60.55 to I 29 d 80.45

2. FORCE Two Officers, fifty other ranks.

3. OBJECT. To enter enemy's front line, inflict as many casualties as possible, and secure one or more prisoners for identification purposes.

4. METHODS. Patrols will go out at dusk and lay a lead wire from gaps in enemy's wire to GLASGOW POST. At ZERO minus minutes the raiding force in two parties at 50 yards distance will advance from GLASGOW POST against the enemy front line, endeavouring to reach his wire without being discovered. The advance will be timed so as to arrive at that point at ZERO. Immediately the wire is reached, the leading party will cross it by existing gaps and by the aid of blankets and will rush the enemy trench. The leading party will be organised into two halves, with bombers on the flanks. The right half of the party will work to the right and the left half to the left. In the event of the trench being found to be unoccupied at the point of entry, the parties will work along in opposite directions until the enemy is encountered. They will remain

Secret.

H.Q.
47th Division.

Herewith scheme for Raid by 15th London R.

Hampden Brig Genl
Comm 140th Inf Bde

23 Nov. 1916.

BM/126B.

G/240/35.

SECRET.

140th Inf Bde
47th Div Arty

1. Your proposals for the raid on the night of the ~~28/29th~~ 26/27th are generally approved. The Divisional Commander however considers a fuller use could be made of Artillery to cover the raiding party during it's stay in the hostile trenches and during it's withdrawal, without in any way prematurely disclosing the exact locality of the raid.

2. The following amendments are therefore suggested :-

A. From Zero plus 3, when the Stokes commence firing on the SNOUT, to Zero plus 12, a 8" Howitzer will also open fire at the same objective. The Divisional Artillery will at the same time place a box barrage round the party, and bring the SNOUT and any likely Machine Gun positions on the left of the raiding party under a steady rate of fire.

B. Zero plus 12 to Zero plus 30. As in A. except an intense rate of fire is required to cover withdrawal of party.

C. Zero plus 30 to Zero plus 50. A steady rate of fire as in B., which will gradually slacken according to enemy's retaliation.

D. Wire will be cut tomorrow at selected points along the Right Sector of the Divisional front, and a dummy artillery raid will be carried out, at a point selected by Brigadier General Commanding Right Sector.

3. Detailed artillery arrangements to be worked out between G.O.C. 140th Brigade and Artillery Group Commander.

4. Acknowledge by wire.

A. Thorne

Lt.Colonel,
General Staff,
47th (London) Division.

G/240/35.

25th November 1916.

Cancelled - but forwarded for information.

SECRET.

142nd Inf Bde

A raid is being carried out by the 140th Brigade in the vicinity of the SNOUT tomorrow night at a time to be notified later.

The Divisional Commander wishes you to co-operate in the following manner :-

(i) Cutting wire at selected points tomorrow during the day.

(ii) A short concentration of artillery fire at Zero hour to simulate a raid at one of the selected points where wire has been cut.

2. Acknowledge by wire.

A.S. Turner

Lt.Colonel,
General Staff,
47th (London) Division.

G/240/35/2.

25th November 1916.

Not sent

8 ARTILLERY & T.M. COOPERATION. (continued) attention of enemy artillery, minenwerfer and M.G.s in that direction, ensuring a safe return for the raiders. At ZERO + 3 minutes STOKES MORTARS will open rapid fire on the SNOUT, to keep down the fire of any M.G.s which by that time may have located the point attacked.

NOTES.

1. Gaps in enemy wire will be marked by patrols and on the night of the raid patrols will go out beforehand and lay lead wires back from them to GLASGOW POST.

2. The time of starting out of the parties will be determined by actual practice over the ground. Ample time will be allowed to permit of the party arriving at the wire at ZERO.

3. Each Party will have a definite signal for return – two or more blasts on a whistle. A pass word will be arranged. A few easy German phrases will be learnt. The word "Retire" will not be used.

4. All identity discs, badges and papers which might give information will be left behind.

5. An aid post will be established in ZILLEBEKE SWITCH.

H.V. Warrender Lt Col
Cdg 1/15th Lon. Regt

G.S.O.,

What will the strength of the covering party be? — is the party to cover retirement —

Where will they be — will not Glasgow post be likely to be subjected to enemy Artillery retaliation? — & wd. it not be best to occupy another but adjacent position? —

I think Artillery in R. group shd open fire at Zero + 3 & that we should cut wire systematically in this sector at one of selected places all day previous to attract attention to Right Sector —

Please speak with C.R.A.'s programme when it comes in —

[illegible] 25.XI.16

H.Q. 140th Inf. Bde

My dear General.

I am sending you proposals from O.C. 15th London R. re raid.

He, & the two officers undertaking the operation do not wish to have any artillery preparation nor is it desired that the guns should fire on the 'Snout'.

I saw O.C. Left Group today who informs me that the guns in Maple Copse are probably unable, owing to the ridge in front of them, to fire on enemy trenches East of the 'Snout'. He is looking into this tomorrow & will let me know. Even if they can it is doubtful how much good they would do as the raiders, if successful, should get away before enemy supports could come into action. The other guns of Left Group cannot safely fire on front line of 'Snout' unless we evacuate the crater.

I am afraid there would be considerable difficulty in discovering after the raid whether all the party had left the trench & in letting the artillery know. Of course if this could be achieved artillery fire would be useful in covering the retirement.

Also
the possibility of having to collect wounded men from in front of Enemy's wire has to be considered.

Yrs sincerely

Hampden

Instructions regarding War Diaries and Intelligence Summaries are contained in F. S. Regs., Part II. and the Staff Manual respectively. Title pages will be prepared in manuscript.

# WAR DIARY
*or*
# INTELLIGENCE SUMMARY.
*(Erase heading not required.)*

Army Form C. 2118.

| Place | Date | Hour | Summary of Events and Information | Remarks and references to Appendices |
|---|---|---|---|---|
| OTTAWA CAMP | Dec. 1st to 7th | | At OTTAWA CAMP, Casualties Nil | |
| | 8th | | Moved to Support position in Canal Sub Sector and relieved 22nd Battalion London Regt., Casualties Nil | |
| SWAN CHATEAU near. YPRES | 9th to 17th | | In support. Furnished working parties daily. Raiding party under 2/Lt. C. F. Grove organised and trained. Casualties 9th December to 15th December, Nil. Casualties 15th December 1 O.R. wounded. Casualties 16th to 17th December Nil. | |
| | 18th | | Relieved 6th Battalion London Regiment in centre section CANAL SUB SECTOR. Relief complete 8.20 p.m. Casualties Nil. | |
| | 19th | | In front line Casualties Nil. | |
| | 20th | | In front line Casualties 4 O.R. wounded, 3 Shell Shock, 1 O.R. Killed. | |
| | 21st | | In front line Casualties, Nil. | |
| | 22nd | | In front line. Raiding party carried out Raid in accordance with special scheme, operation orders and report annexed. Enemy retaliation on our front line slight. Casualties 2 O.R. killed, 8 O.R. wounded. | |
| | 23rd | | In front line. Fighting patrol went out at 7.30 p.m. and attacked enemy working party with bombs. They were, however, unable to secure a prisoner. Casualties, 1 O.R. wounded. | |
| | 24th | | In front line. Took over front of left section and relieved 8th Batt. Relief complete 8.30. p.m. Casualties 1 O.R. killed. | |
| | 25th | | In front line. A very quiet day. Casualties, Nil. | |
| | 26th | | In front line. Killed 1. O.R. wounded 2 O.R. | |
| | 27th | | In front line. Casualties, Nil. | |
| | 28th | | In front line. Relieved by 17th Batt. London Regt. Relief complete 8.30 p.m. Casualties Nil. Marched to YPRES and entrained. | |
| | 29th | | At OTTAWA CAMP resting, Casualties, Nil. | |

A5834 Wt. W4973/M687 750,000 8/16 D. D. & L. Ltd. Forms/C.2118/13.

Army Form C. 2118.

Instructions regarding War Diaries and Intelligence Summaries are contained in F. S. Regs., Part II. and the Staff Manual respectively. Title pages will be prepared in manuscript.

# WAR DIARY
*or*
# INTELLIGENCE SUMMARY.

*(Erase heading not required.)*

| Place | Date | Hour | Summary of Events and Information | Remarks and references to Appendices |
|---|---|---|---|---|
| OTTAWA CAMP | Dec. 30th | | Training, Casualties, Nil. | |
| | 31st | | Sunday, Casualties, Nil. | |

A5834 Wt. W4973/M687 750,000 8/16 D. D. & L. Ltd. Forms/C.2118/13.

X Corps.

Dec. 17

Dear Turner

The Corps Commander would like to see the plans of the raid which General Gwynne proposes to carry out on 20th as he likes to know what is going to happen before he gives authority for such operations to be carried out.

Yours sincerely

A.R. Cameron

HEADQUARTERS
GENERAL STAFF
No. G/240/10/8
Date 19/12/16
47th (LONDON) DIVISION

Secret

H.Q.
47 Lon Div.

~~Dr~~ Could you please obtain ~~thirty~~ one dozen ~~Full~~ Life size dummy figures for use in the forthcoming raid.

22/12/16
[illegible]

Hampden
Br General
Commanding Bde

SS/29/11/2

18/12/16

I have asked Corps for 12 dummy heads. Urgent.

[illegible]

**Secret.**

Headquarters
47 Lon Div.

Herewith scheme (original and 2 copies) for raid to be carried out by the 15th Lon Regt on 21st inst.

22nd

Also special form completed and artillery programme.

SS/29/11/3

20/12/16

Hampden
Brigadier General
Cmdg 140th Inf Bde.

Secret.

Headquarters
47 Lon Div.

Ref my SS/29/11/3 - 20/12/16 -
Zero will be at 6 P.M.

SS/29/11/4
20/12/16

Hampden
Brig General
Comg 140 Inf Bde

# Raids.

| Corps. | Division | Brigade. | Unit | Date | Nature | Front | Strength | Extra arms required. | Remarks. |
|---|---|---|---|---|---|---|---|---|---|
| XIth | 47th | 140th | 15th Bn. London Regt. | ~~21st~~ 22 December | Enter front line for purpose of securing prisoners for indentification and obtaining information regarding of two earth high mound at I. 34. d. 14. 39 | I. 34. d. 17. 46 to I. 34. d. 08. 32 including enemy Sap No. 2 and dug-outs South East of Sap No. 2. | 2 Officers 50 O.R. | | Scheme forwarded herewith. |

Hampden

Brigadier General,

Comdg. 140th Infantry Brigade.

SECRET.

Xth Corps.

With reference to your G/58/17/7 of the 14th December, herewith scheme for the Raid in the CANAL Sub-sector which will be carried out on the evening of the 22nd December.

Zero hour will be 6 p.m.

G/~~235~~ 240/10/8 Major General,

21st Decr.1916. Commanding 47th (London) Division.

SECRET.

23rd Division.

41st Division.

===============

A Raid will take place in the CANAL Sub-sector at 6 p.m. on the 22nd December.

The point of entry will be at I.34.d.2.4.

G/240/10/8

21st Decr.1916.

Major General,

Commanding 47th (London) Division.

ARMY
YD 22.XII.16.G –
TELEGRAPHS

Sm 79R [illegible]
Harlow
Elf Priority
Elf John 1.45P 6.34P

Bm/L11 22
Raiders entered German lines AAA
Some enemy reported killed AAA
think no prisoners

343
6.47P

Elf 9
6.45P

"A" Form.

Army Form C.2121 (in pads of 100).

# MESSAGES AND SIGNALS.

No. of Message ..........

Prefix .......... Code .......... m. | Words | Charge | This message is on a/c of: .......... Service. | Recd. at .......... m.

Office of Origin and Service Instructions.

Sent At .......... m. To .......... By ..........

(Signature of "Franking Officer.")

Date .......... From .......... By ..........

TO: 10 Corps | 23 Div | 41 Div
BP 20 | PAPER | VISITOR

| Sender's Number. | Day of Month. | In reply to Number. | AAA |
|---|---|---|---|
| * GT. 48. | 22 | | |

Following reports received from CHIMNEY AAA Timed 6-45 pm begins Raiders entered enemys lines some enemy killed believed no prisoners Ends AAA Timed 7-40 pm begins Raid successful Identification obtained Ends AAA Addressed SHAW Repeated ARTHUR GEORGE PAPER PRIZE VISITOR

PRIORITY

From JOHN

Place

Time 8 pm

The above may be forwarded as now corrected.

(Z) ........ Censor.

St A Turner Lt Col

Signature of Addressor or person authorised to telegraph in his name.

* This line should be erased if not required.

750,000. W 2183-M509. H. W. & V., Ld. 6/16.

"A" Form.

Army Form C.2121
(in pads of 100).

# MESSAGES AND SIGNALS.

No. of Message..........

| Prefix ......Code ......m. | Words | Charge | This message is on a/c of: | Recd. at ..........m. |
|---|---|---|---|---|
| Office of Origin and Service Instructions. | Sent | | ..........Service. | Date .......... |
| | At..........m. | | | From .......... |
| | To .......... | | | |
| | By .......... | | (Signature of "Franking Officer.") | By .......... |

TO

| 10th Corps | 23rd Div | 41st Div | 47th DivArty |
|---|---|---|---|
| 141st Inf Bde | 142nd Inf Bde | E.P.SO. | |

| Sender's Number. | Day of Month. | In reply to Number. | AAA |
|---|---|---|---|
| * G.M.50 | 22 | | |

Raid in BLUFF Subsector this evening was successful AAA Many Germans kill d in their trenches AAA No prisoners could be brought back but identification of 416th Regt was obtained AAA Casualties among raiding party one officer and four other ranks slightly wounded AAA Addressed SHAW repeated ARTHUR GEORGE WISING VISITOR PAPER and PRIZE

From JOHN

Place

PRIORITY

Time 10 p.m.

The above may be forwarded as now corrected. (Z)

Censor. (Sd) R. S. McCLINTOCK Major G.S. Signature of Addressor or person authorised to telegraph in his name.

* This line should be erased if not required.

750,000. W 2135 M509. H. W & V., Ld. 6/16.

ARMY
YD 23.XII.15.G-
TELEGRAPHS

KCO 10.5 10.10 am

47 Div

GA.826. 23 aaa

The Corps Commander congratulates all ranks of the 15th London Regt on their successful raid last night

370
10-15 am

Tenth Corps
9.55 am

ARMY TELEGRAPHS
YC 23 XII.16. G–

[illegible] Kel to [illegible]

K.C. [illegible]

47th Div

GA827 22

Second Army [illegible] as follows [illegible] Army Commander [illegible] Corps [illegible] Congratulations to [illegible] [illegible] on the [illegible] of last nights raid by 47th Div which not [illegible] much damage on the enemy but established a very valuable identification

371
10 30 am

10th Corps
10.15 am

"A" Form. Army Form C.2121 (in pads of 100).

# MESSAGES AND SIGNALS.

No. of Message ..........

Prefix .......... Code .......... m. | Words | Charge

Office of Origin and Service Instructions.

Sent
At .......... m.
To ..........
By ..........

*This message is on a/c of:*

.......... *Service.*

(Signature of "Franking Officer.")

Recd. at .......... m.
Date ..........
From ..........
By ..........

TO E59 VISITING

| Sender's Number. | Day of Month. | In reply to Number. | AAA |
|---|---|---|---|
| * GT 59 | 22 | | |

Following from SHAW begins AAA Army Commander wishes to convey his congratulations to all concerned in the success of last nights raid by Frame which not only inflicted much damage on the enemy but established a very valuable identification AAA ends

From JOHN
Place
Time 12 noon

*The above may be forwarded as now corrected.* (Z) [illegible]

*Censor.* Signature of Addressor or person authorised to telegraph in his name.

* This line should be erased if not required.

750,000. W 2183 M529. H. W & V., Ld. 6/16.

PROPOSED SCHEME FOR ARTILLERY.

CO-OPERATION on night of 21/22nd December 1916.

1. Our front line to be cleared between points 100 yards North and 80 yards South of Hedge Row.

2. Infantry is to operate in enemy front line from I. 34 d. 16. 42. to I& 34 d. 08. 30 and is not to extend outside those points. No artillery fire between I. 34. d. 17. 59. and I. 34. c. 99. 17 except during the 2 minutes initial bombardment.

3. The Left Group will co-operate by carrying out bombardment or barrage on part of their front as arranged direct between Group Commanders.

4. The points of assault by the Infantry havebeen chosen by the G. O. C. 140th Infantry Brigade by reason of the weakness of the wire at those points. No special wire cutting for the operation is being carried out on those points but lanes are being cut at other points.

5. Programme of firing.

(a) From minus 2 minutes until ZERO 18 pdrs. on front line from I. 34. d. 16. 63 to I. 34. c. 95. 07.
From minus 2 minutes until Zero Belgians from I. 34 d. 50.63. to I. 34. d. 40. 25.
From minus 2 minutes until ZERO howitzers
one on I.34. c. 95. 15
" " I.34. d. 30. 67 Machine Gun
" " I.34. d. 16. 00 Machine Gun
" " I.34. d. 51. 21
" " I.34. d. 61. 34

Rate of fire.

Field guns - 3 rounds per gun per minute.
Howitzers - 2 rounds per gun per minute.

(b) From ZERO onwards, Box barrage formed by 18 pdrs from I. 34. c. 99. 17. through I. 34. d. 22. 16. to I. 34. d. 40. 25.
Belgians as before and 18 pdrs. from I. 34. d. 50. 63. through I. 34. d. 32. 68. to I. 34. d. 16. 64.
Howitzers as before except that 1 howitzer moves from I. 34. c. 95. 15 to I. 34. c. 95. 07.

Rate of Fire.

Field guns - 2 rounds per gun per minute
Howitzers - 1 round per gun per minute.

Box barrage will continue until ZERO plus 30 unless party returns earlier than that hour.

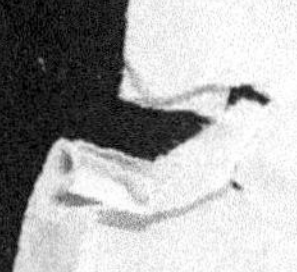

1/15th Battalion London Regiment
(P.W.O. CIVIL SERVICE RIFLES.)

6.0 p.m. 22nd Dec. 1916.

SCHEME for proposed Raid on Enemy Trenches.

OBJECTIVE. Enemy front line from about I 34. d. 17. 46 to I 34. d. 08. 32, including enemy sap No. 2 and dugouts South East of Sap No. 2.

Force. 2 officers and 50 O. R.

OBJECT. To enter enemy's front line, inflict as many casualties as possible, secure prisoners for identification and ascertain nature of and reason for high mound of new earth about I. 34. d. 14. 39.

METHOD. The force will be divided into the following parties:-

1st Party. 2 officers 32 O. R. actual raiders.
2nd Party. 1 N. C. O. and 6 men for Sap No. 2.
3rd Party. 1 N. C. O. and 10 men as rear party.

The force will move into No-mans-land and get into position within 50 yards of the objective at ZERO - 10. At ZERO the 1st and 2nd party will rush their objectives. The 3rd party moving in rear and remaining on enemy parapet to take charge of prisoners, will assist the raiders to vacate enemy's trench.

1st Party will be organised into 4 groups as follows:-
No.1 Group to block enemy trench at I. 34 d. 17. 46.
No.2 Group to block trench at I. 34 d. 08.32
No.3 Group to clear the dugout about I. 34 d. 15. 38.
No. 4 Group to clear enemy trenches and any other dugouts that may exist between the two blocks.

2nd Party will enter Sap No. 2 and deal with any garrison found there.

3rd Party will be accompanied by Tunnelling Engineers. They will improve existing gaps and prepare easy exits for No. 1 party.

CO-OPERATION OF OTHER UNITS.

(1) Artillery. At ZERO - 2 a bombardment will open on enemy front line. At ZERO the bombardment will lift and a "box barrage" be formed on the flanks of the raided area and on enemy's rear lines until ZERO plus 30.
(2) Stokes Mortars. At ZERO will bombard Western face of the SHRINE and enemy sap South East of MACK'S WALK.
(3) Machine Guns will bring cross fire to bear on ground behind area raided from vicinity of trenches I. 34 1 and I 34.5.
(4) Rifle Grenades. will fire from positions at end of MACK'S WALK and HEDGE ROW.

DEMONSTRATION. To deceive enemy a party with dummies will be posted in No-mans-land in old sap between I. 34 1 and I 34.2.

RETURN. To guide the force back, at ZERO plus 15 green rockets will be sent up at ½ minute intervals. To distract enemy, white rockets will be sent up from another point at similar intervals. Party to be clear of enemy trenches by ZERO plus 25.

REORGANISATION. On return to our lines the raiders will be sent down LOVERS LANE to report at CENTRE BATTALION NEW HEADQUARTERS, where the roll will be called.

## NOTES.

1. EQUIPMENT. The raiding party will go out in loose order, with rifle and bayonets fixed. Faces and hands will be blacked and bayonets dulled. Each bomber will carry 6 bombs, and each other man 2 bombs. A proportion of the party will carry electric torches and revolvers.

2. START. The time of starting out of the parties will be determined by actual practice over the ground. Ample time will be allowed, to permit of the party reaching their position at ZERO - 10.

3. RETURN. The signal for return will be single green rockets fired at ½ minute intervals commencing at ZERO plus 15.

4. IDENTIFICATION. All identity discs, badges and papers which might give information will be left behind.

5. AID POST. An aid post will be established at CENTRE BATTALION NEW HEADQUARTERS.

SECRET.                                                                 COPY NO 15.

OPERATION ORDERS BY LT-COLONEL W. F. K. NEWSON,

Commanding, 1/15th Battalion London Regt.

In the Field,
22/12/16.

Refce map
1/5000 CANAL SUBSECTOR.

Operations in accordance with attached S cheme already in the hands of Special party and other co-operating units will be carried out tonight.

1. INFORMATION. Enemy's wire is weak in front of objective and, from frequent reconnaisance, the line does not appear to be very strongly garrisoned.

2. INTENTION. It is intended to enter the enemy line, secure prisoners or identifications and inflict as many casualties as possible.

3. DISPOSITIONS. The Special Party will carry out instructions in accordande with scheme. By ZERO minus 20 that part of the front line held by B and D company will be cleared and the garrison ddisposed in WINE STREET - D Company to the N. E. Side of LOVERS LANE and B. Company to the S. W. side L. Gs will close to right and left flanks at same time. A. Company will close on E. MACK'S WALK with their left on I. 34 c. 95 - 50. At ZERO plus 2 D. Company and all Lewis Guns (front line) will move to their original places in the front line and be in position there by ZERO Plus 10. A. and B. companies will not return to the front line until ordered. O. C. A. Company will detail a party of 1 N. C. O. and 4 men to work dummy figures in disused trench in NO MANS LAND at about I 34 c. 90 - 40.

4. COMMUNICATION. 2nd Lt. A. WILSON will be in telephonic communication from front line to Major G. G. BATES at D. Company H. Q. In the event of the wires being cut 2/Lt. WILSON will keep communication by runners. After Zero plus 10 LOVERS LANE will be closed for up traffic (except authorised runners.)

5. SIGNALS. O. C. C. Company will arrange to have rockets fired as follows:-
Green rockets at ½ minute intervals from ZERO plus 15 till ZERO plus 30 from near SP 7 and similarly white rockets from about 400 yards South of SP7.

6. COMMAND. During the operations all troops forward of SUNKEN ROAD will be under the immediate command of MAJOR G. G. BATES who will be established at D. Company H. Q.

7. ZERO. Zero will be at 6.0 p.m.

-sgd- W. F. K. NEWSON,
Lt-Colonel,
Commanding, 1/15th Battalion London Regiment,
(P.W.O. CIVIL SERVICE RIFLES.)

SECRET.

SPECIAL CODE for use in connection with OPERATIONS on night of 22/23rd December, 1916 only.

---

| | |
|---|---|
| Raiders have entered German line | = ROSE |
| Raiders have not entered German line | = THORN |
| Raid successful | = NETTLE |
| German Prisoners | = TULIPS<br>One<br>Two<br>Three etc. |
| German killed | = BULBS |
| German wounded | = COWSLIPS. |
| Our killed | = Myrtle |
| " wounded | = LAUREL |
| " missing | = HOLLY |
| Stop firing | = DAISY |
| Continue firing | = PANSY |
| Machine Guns | = SNAP DRAGON |
| Reduce rate of fire | = VIOLET |
| Increase rate of fire | = PEONY |
| Lengthen range | = BEAN |
| Shorten range | = PLUM |
| Raiders returned | = APPLE |
| Troops in position | = MAY. |

[Handwritten signature] Lt
Adj Adjt
1/18 Batt

SECRET.

1/15th Battalion London Regiment.

In The Field,
23/12/16.

Reference 140th Brigade Operation Order .......

Sir,

I have the honour to report that the raid was carried out last night as ordered.

Action of raiders.

The artillery barrage and Stokes Mortar fire enabled the party to enter the e nemy trenches within a minute or so of ZERO. The point of entry was approximately 12 or 15 yards S. of high mound of new earth about I 34 d. 14. 39. The blocking parties at once moved to the left and right respectively. The left party proceeded 25 yards up the trench northwards where they found that the Artillery had knocked in the trench so successfully that a ready made block was formed. This party claimed to have killed 5 Germans. The enemy attempted to bomb them while they held the block but didnt reach them. The right party proceeded in a S. direction and about 20 yards from point of entry found a bend in the trench from which point it ran straight for 30 yards. They accordingly established themselves at this corner and met no opposition. They claim to have killed two Germans. The party detailed to locate and exp,lore Sap 2 found nothing beyond a series of shell holes. The fourth party, whose mission was to explore dugout indicated on previously captured German map, proceeded down the communication trench, which - 10 or 12 yards from point of entry - bears off in a southerly direction. They secured this trench for a distance of about 20 yards. Hostile bombs thrown had no effect, The trench where it bent was badly damaged, while the parallel trench immediately in rear of front line appears to be used as a drain. No sign of a dugout was found but party claim one killed.

Information

There being further time available front line was explored and a few dugouts (capacity two or three men ) were found. Into these, wounded had crawled and some had already died. No signal wires were seen. Several of the enmy were observed to be wearing their gas helmets "at the "ready" position. Pockets of the dead were searched but no papers were found. This party claim three killed.

Identifications. Several efforts were made to get a live Hun but they invariably resisted and had to be disposed of. A shoulder strap button and cap were secured however and would appear to conclusively establish identification of the troops opposed to us. These two articles have been sent to you already.

Enemy trench.

The length of trench occupied by us would appear to be about 50 yards. It was in good condition where not actually knocked in by our bombardment and was revetted and boarded; there were few traverses but trench was quite 8 ft deep.

No difficulty was found in withdrawing and the tapes proved an efficient guide.

Action of enemy.

At the outset the enemy used a considerable number of stick bombs. They burst noisily with result that it was at one moment reported that he had evacuated and was shelling his own front line. Beyond this resistance of garrison was not great. There was much hostile rifle fire throughout the operation but enemy M. Gs did not open fire to any great extent till 6.23 p.m. He started retaliation at 6.9 with L. H. V. on front line and rearwards with 5.9 T. M. shells. He did not seem to have located position of raid till after party were clear.

Cooperating units.

The preliminary bombardment by our artillery was in every respect entirely successful and their shooting contributed to a large measure to the results achieved by raiders.

The Stokes Mortars had their targets very well ranged and, I think, the small amount of M. G. fire was no doubt due to their effective bombardment of the points to be covered, Sap 3 in particular.

The M. G. Companies left gun jammed after firing two belts while the right gun fired continuously throughout.

The dummies utilised appear to have drawn enemy retaliation on right battalion.

Casualties.

Our casualties were in trench garrison - 1 slightly wounded, while nine of the party were wounded (none dangerously) and two are missing. Enquiries have been made in regard to the last mentioned. Cpl. Geary was known to have been wounded. He was helped out of enemy trench but, later, could not be found, and it was thought that he had returned safely to our lines. The man next him when hit states that he fell heavily and being badly wounded may have died on the way back. The missing man - Pearson - formed one of the S. "Pulling Out" party. Another of this party last saw Pearson half way over. He was then off to the right a little and was not seen again. He was thought to have taken cover temporarily and was expected to follow up. A wounded man I saw personally told me last night that Pearson was alright and no further search was made. This indeed was well nigh impossible as after operation No-mans land was well swept by M. G. fire and flooded with lights. (Later - The right company sent out a patrol to bring in tapes and saw no signs of the missing man).

I wish to call attention to the good work accomplished by the two officers in training and organising parties at short notice and the spirit and dash displayed by all ranks. I do not think this could be improved upon.

Recommendations.

Where all did so well it is difficult to draw distinctions but at the same time I would beg to bring to your notice the good work done by the two under named N. C. Os, both did excellent patrol work before the raid and acted admirably on the night itself. The first named secured an identification. The names are:-

1897 Cpl. Swain, J. H.
2511 L/S. Steele H. J.

I have the honour to be,
Sir,
Your obedient servant,

-sgd- W. F. K. NEWSON,
Lt-Colonel,
Commanding, 1/15th Batt. London Regt.
(P.W.O. CIVIL SERVICE RIFLES.)

G. O. C.,
140th Infantry Brigade.

*Secret*

1/15th Battalion London Regiment.
(P.W.O. Civil Service Rifles)

---

SCHEME for proposed Raid on Enemy Trenches.

OBJECTIVE. Enemy front line trench from About I.34.d.17.46 to I.34.d.08.32, including enemy Sap No. 2 and dugouts South East of Sap No. 2.

FORCE. 2 Officers and 50 O.R.

OBJECT. To enter enemy's front line, inflict as many casualties as possible, secure prisoners for identification and ascertain nature of and reason for high mound *of new earth* about I.34.d.14.39.

METHOD. The force will be divided into the following parties :-

1st Party. 2 Officers 32 O.R. actual raiders.
2nd Party. 1 N.C.O. and 6 men for Sap No. 2.
3rd Party. 1 N.C.O. and 10 men as rear party.

The force will move into No-mans-land and get into position within 50 yards of the objective at ZERO - 10. At ZERO the 1st and 2nd party will rush their objectives. The 3rd party moving in rear and remaining on enemy parapet to take charge of prisoners, will assist the raiders to vacate enemy's trench.

1st Party will be organised into 4 groups as follows :-
No. 1 Group to block enemy trench at I.34.d.17.46.
No. 2 Group to block trench at I.34.d.08.32.
No. 3 Group to clear the dugout about I.34.d.15.38.
No. 4 Group to clear enemy trenches and any other dugouts that may exist between the two blocks.

2nd Party will enter Sap No.2 and deal with any garrison found there

3rd Party will be accompanied by Tunnelling Engineers. They will improve existing gaps and prepare easy exits for No.1 party.

CO-OPERATION OF OTHER UNITS.

(1( Artillery. At ZERO - 2 a bombardment will open on enemy front line. At ZERO the bombardment will lift and a "box barrage" be formed on the flanks of the raided area and on enemy's rear lines.
(2) Stokes Mortars. at ZERO will bombard Western face of the SHRINE and enemy sap South East of MACK'S WALK.
(3) Machine guns will bring cross-fire to bear on ground behind area raided from vicinity of trenches I.34.1 and I.34.5.
(4) Rifle Grenades will fire from positions at end of MACK'S WALK and HEDGE ROW.

DEMONSTRATION. To deceive enemy a party with dummies will be posted in No-mans-land in old sap between I.34.1 and I.34.2.

RETURN. To guide the force back, at ZERO +15 green rockets will be sent up at ½ minute intervals. To distract enemy, white rockets will be sent up from another point at similar intervals. *Party to be clear of enemy trenches by Zero +25.*

REORGANISATION. On return to our lines the raiders will be sent down LOVERS LANE to report at CENTRE BATTALION NEW HEADQUARTERS, where the roll will be called

NOTES.

1. EQUIPMENT. The Raiding party will go out in loose order, with rifle and bayonets fixed. Faces and hands will be blacked and bayonets dulled. Each bomber will carry 6 bombs, and each other man 2 bombs. A proportion of the party will carry electric torches and revolvers.

2. START. The time of starting out of the parties will be determined by actual practise over the ground. Ample time will be allowed, to permit of the party reaching their position at ZERO -10.

3. RETURN. The signal for return will be single green rockets fired at ½ minute intervals commencing at ZERO + 15.

4. IDENTIFICATION. All identity discs badges and papers which might give information will be left behind.

5. AID POST. An aid post will be established at CENTRE BATTALION NEW HEADQUARTERS,

PROPOSED SCHEME FOR ARTILLERY.

CO-OPERATION on night of 21/22nd Dec. 1916.
22/23

1. Our front line is to be cleared between points 100 yards and North and 80 yards South of HEDGE ROW.

2. Infantry is to operate in enemy front line from I.34.d.16.42 to I.34.d.08.30, and is not to extend outside those points. No artillery fire between I.34.d.17.59 and I.34.c.99.17 except during the 2 minutes initial bombardment.

3. The Left Group will co-operate by carrying out bombardment or barrage on part of their front as arranged direct between Group Commanders.

4. The points of assault by the Infantry have been chosen by the G.O.C., 140th Infantry Brigade by reason of the weakness of the wire at those points. No special wire cutting for the operation is being carried out on those points but lanes are being cut at other points.

5. Programme of firing.

(a) From minus 2 minutes until ZERO 18-pdrs. on front line from I.34.d.16.63 to I.34.c.95.07.
From minus 2 minutes until ZERO Belgians from I.34.d.50.63 to I.34.d.40.25.
From minus 2 minutes until ZERO Howitzers
one on I.34.c.95.15. Machine Gun.
" " I.34.d.30.67. Machine Gun.
" " I.34.d.16.00.
" " I.34.d.31.21.
" " I.34.d.61.34.

Rate of fire.

Field Guns - 3 rounds per gun per minute.
Howitzers - 2 rounds per gun per minute.

(b) From ZERO onwards. Box barrage formed by 18-pdrs. from I.34.c.99.17 through I.34.d.22.16 to I.34.d.40.25
Belgians as before and 18-pdrs. from I.34.d.50.63 through I.34.d.32.68 to I.34.d.18.64.
Howitzers as before except that 1 howitzer moves from I.34.c.95.15 to I.34.c.95.07.

Rate of fire.

Field guns - 2 rounds per gun per minute.
Howitzers - 1 round per gun per minute.

Box barrage will continue until Zero+30 unless party returns to our lines earlier than that time

SECRET.



SPECIAL CODE for use in connection with OPERATIONS
on night of 22/23rd December 1916 only.

| | | |
|---|---|---|
| Raiders have entered German line | = | ROSE. |
| Raiders have not entered German line | = | THORN. |
| Raid successful | = | NETTLE. |
| Raid unsuccessful | = | STING. |
| German prisoners | = | TULIPS.<br>One<br>Two<br>Three etc. |
| German killed | = | BULBS. |
| German wounded | = | COWSLIPS. |
| Our killed | = | MYRTLE. |
| " wounded | = | LAUREL. |
| " missing | = | HOLLY. |
| Stop firing | = | DAISY. |
| Continue firing | = | PANSY. |
| Machine guns | = | SNAP DRAGON. |
| Reduce rate of fire | = | VIOLET. |
| Increase rate of fire | = | PEONY. |
| Lengthen range | = | BEAN. |
| Shorten range | = | PLUM. |
| Raiders returned | = | APPLE. |
| *Troops in position* | = | *MAY* |

*Ack. G.C.*

H. Q.
47th Division

Herewith report of O.C. 1/15th London Regt on last night's raid.
With reference to the recommendations he makes I propose to submit these in proper form.

Hampden Brig Genl
Comdg 140th Inf Bde

23. Dec. 1916.

HEADQUARTERS GENERAL STAFF
G/240/10/8
Date 23/12/16
47th (LONDON) DIVISION

BRIGADE OFFICE
No. BM/335/B
23 DEC. 1916
140th INFANTRY BRIGADE

Recd 7.40pm from Q

Headquarters

47th (London) Division.



## REPORT on Raiding Operations tonight.

The raiding party assembled outside our wire at 5.30 p.m. and entered the enemy trench without difficulty as soon as the barrage lifted. The shooting of the artillery was very accurate and effective throughout and there was no firing on the party as they went over. The enemy trench which consisted of a breastwork was considerably damaged and several dead and wounded Germans were lying in the trench. The raiding party accounted for some six of the enemy and estimate his casualties from actual observation at 12 killed and 10 wounded.

Attempts were made to bring back prisoners but they resisted with violence and were suitably dealt with.

The following identifications were brought back :-

(a) Shoulder strap bearing number 416 in red letters (forwarded herewith)
(b) Button from same individual with No.4 (forwarded)
(c) Cap (not yet submitted), also 2 rifles.

No deep dugouts were noticed - only splinter proof shelters.

The mound of newly thrown up earth was reconnoitred and appeared to be without any defensive or effective significance.

Our casualties amounted to 7 wounded (none serious)

The hostile artillery retaliation was not severe and was distributed over the front line and support trenches.

Theparty returned by 6.30 p.m.

A detailed report will be forwarded tomorrow.

Hampden
Brigadier General,

Comdg. 140th Infantry Brigade.

47th Div. No. G/240/10/8.

47th (London) Division.

REPORT on Raiding Operations to-night.

The Raiding Party assembled outside our wire at 5.30 p.m. and entered the enemy trench without difficulty as soon as the barrage lifted. The shooting of the artillery was very accurate and effective throughout and there was no firing on the party as they went over. The enemy trench which consisted of a breastwork was considerably damaged and several dead and wounded Germans were lying in the trench. The Raiding Party accounted for some six of the enemy and estimate his casualties from actual observation at 12 killed and 10 wounded.

Attempts were made to bring back prisoners but they resisted with violence and were suitably dealt with.

The following identifications were brought back :-

(a) Shoulder strap bearing number 416 in red letters (forwarded herewith).

(b) Button from same individual with No. 4 (forwarded).

(c) Cap (not yet submitted), also 2 rifles.

No deep dugouts were noticed - only splinter-proof shelters.

The mound of newly thrown up earth was reconnoitred and appeared to be without any defensive or effective significance.

Our casualties amounted to 7 wounded (none serious).

The hostile artillery retaliation was not severe and was distributed over the front line and support trenches.

The party returned by 6.30 p.m.

A detailed report will be forwarded to-morrow.

Sgd. HAMPDEN,
Brigadier General,
Commanding 140th Infantry Brigade.

B.M./309B
22nd December 1916.

2.

Xth Corps.

Forwarded. The raid appears to have been successful.

AGT.
Major General,
Commanding 47th (London) Division.

G/240/10/8
23rd December
1916.

Copy to 47th Div.Arty.for information.

SECRET. 1/15th Bn. London Regt.

In the Field.
23/12/16.

Reference 140th Brigade Operation Order
A.A./29/11/S.

Sir,

I have the honour to report that the raid was carried out last night as ordered.

Work of Raiders.

The artillery barrage and Stokes Mortar fire enabled the party to enter the enemy trenches within a minute or so of ZERO. The point of entry was approximately 12 or 15 yards South of high mound of new earth about I.34.d 14.39.

The blocking parties at once moved to the left and right respectively.

The left party proceeded 25 yards up the trench Northwards where they found that the Artillery had knocked in the trench so successfully that a ready made block was formed. This party claimed to have killed 5 Germans. The enemy attempted to bomb them while they held the block but didn't reach them. The right party proceeded in a Southerly direction and about 20 yards from point of entry found a bend in the trench from which point it ran straight for 30 yards. They accordingly established themselves at this corner and met no opposition. They claim to have killed 2 Germans.

The party detailed to locate and explore Sap 2 found nothing beyond a series of shell holes.

The 4th party, whose mission was to explore dugout indicated on previously captured German map, proceeded down the communication trench, which 10 or 12 yards from point of entry bears off in a Southerly direction. They secured this trench for a distance of about 20 yards.

Hostile bombs thrown had no effect.

The trench where it bent was badly damaged while the parallel trench immediately in rear of front line appears to be used as a drain. No sign of a dugout was found but party claim 1 killed.

There being further time available front line was explored and a few dugouts (capacity 2 to 3 men) were found. Into these, wounded had crawled and some had already died. No Signal wires were seen. Several of the enemy were observed to be wearing their gas helmets at the "ready" position. The pockets of the dead were searched but no papers were found.

This party claim 3 killed.

Identifications. Several efforts were made to get a live Hun but they invariably resisted and had to be disposed of. A shoulder strap, button and cap were secured however and would appear to establish conclusively the identification of the troops opposed to us. These two articles have been sent you already.

Enemy Trench.

The length of trench occupied by us would appear to be about 50 yards. It was in good condition where not actually knocked in by our bombardment and was revetted and boarded; there were few traverses but trench was quite 8 feet deep.

No difficulty was found in withdrawing and the tapes proved an efficient guide.

Action of enemy.

At the outset the enemy used a considerable number of stick bombs. They burst noisily with result that it was at one moment reported that he had evacuated and was shelling his own front line. Beyond this resistance of garrison was not great. There was much hostile rifle fire throughout the operation but enemy Machine Guns did not open fire to any great extent till 6.23 p.m.
He started retaliation at 6.9 p.m. with L.H.V. on front line and rearwards with 5.9 and T.M. shells. He did not seem to have located position of raid till after party were clear.

Co-operating units.

The preliminary bombardment by our artillery was in every respect entirely successful and their shooting contributed in large measure to the results achieved by the raiders.

The Stokes Mortars had their targets very well ranged and, I think, the small amount of hostile Machine Gun fire was no doubt due to their effective bombardment of the points to be covered, Sap 3 in particular.

The Machine Gun Company's left gun jambed after firing 2 belts while the right gun fired continuously throughout.

The Dummies utilised appear to have drawn enemy retaliation on right battalion.

Our casualties.

Our casualties were in trench garrison - 1 slightly wounded, while 9 of the party were wounded (none dangerously) and 2 are missing. Enquiries have been made in regard to the last mentioned. Cpl. GEARY was known to have been wounded. He was helped out of enemy trench but, later, couldn't be found and it was thought he had returned safely to our lines.

The man next him when hit states that he fell heavily and being badly wounded may have died on the way back.

The missing man - PEARSON - formed one of the S. "Pulling-out" party. Another of that party last saw PEARSON half way over. He was then off to the right a little and was not seen again. He was thought to have taken cover temporarily and was expected to follow up. A wounded man I saw personally told me last night that PEARSON was all right and no further search was made. This indeed was well nigh impossible as after operation NO MAN'S LAND was well swept by Machine Gun fire and flooded with lights.

(Later the Right Battalion sent out a patrol to bring in tapes and saw nothing of the missing men).

I wish to call attention to the good work accomplished by the two officers in training and organising parties at short notice and the spirit and dash displayed by all ranks. I do not think this could have be improved upon.

Recommendations. Where all did so well it is a difficult to draw distinctions, but at the same time I would beg to bring to your notice the good work done by the two undermentioned N.C.O's. Both did excellent patrol work before the raid and acted admirably on the night itself. The first named secured an identification. The names are :-

1897. Corporal SWAIN J.H.
2511. L/Sergeant. STEELE H.J.

I have the honour to be, Sir,

Your obedient servant,

G.O.C. (sgd) W.F.K.NEWSON. Lieut.Colonel.

140th Inf. Bde. Cmdg. 1/15th London Regt.

S E C R E T.

1/15th Bn. London Regt.

In the Field.
23/12/16.

Reference 140th Brigade Operation Order
A.A./29/11/S.

Sir,

I have the honour to report that the raid was carried out last night as ordered.

Work of Raiders.

The artillery barrage and Stokes Mortar fire enabled the party to enter the enemy trenches within a minute or so of ZERO. The point of entry was approximately 12 or 15 yards South of high mound of new earth about I.34.d 14.39.

The blocking parties at once moved to the left and right respectively.

The left party proceeded 25 yards up the trench Northwards where they found that the Artillery had knocked in the trench so successfully that a ready made block was formed. This party claimed to have killed 5 Germans. The enemy attempted to bomb them while they held the block but didn't reach them. The right party proceeded in a Southerly direction and about 20 yards from point of entry found a bend in the trench from which point it ran straight for 30 yards. They accordingly established themselves at this corner and met no opposition. They claim to have killed 2 Germans.

The party detailed to locate and explore Sap 2 found nothing beyond a series of shell holes.

The 4th party, whose mission was to explore dugout indicated on previously captured German map, proceeded down the communication trench, which 10 or 12 yards from point of entry bears off in a Southerly direction. They secured this trench for a distance of about 20 yards.

Hostile bombs thrown had no effect.

The trench where it bent was badly damaged while the parallel trench immediately in rear of front line appears to be used as a drain. No sign of a dugout was found but party claim 1 killed.

There being further time available front line was explored and a few dugouts (capacity 2 to 3 men) were found. Into these, wounded had crawled and some had already died. No Signal wires were seen. Several of the enemy were observed to be wearing their gas helmets at the "ready" position. The pockets of the dead were searched but no papers were found.

This party claim 3 killed.

Identifications. Several efforts were made to get a live Hun but they invariably resisted and had to be disposed of. A shoulder strap, button and cap were secured however and would appear to establish conclusively the identification of the troops opposed to us. These two articles have been sent you already.

| | |
|---|---|
| Enemy Trench. | The length of trench occupied by us would appear to be about 50 yards. It was in good condition where not actually knocked in by our bombardment and was revetted and boarded; there were few traverses but trench was quite 8 feet deep.<br><br>No difficulty was found in withdrawing and the tapes proved an efficient guide. |
| Action of enemy. | At the outset the enemy used a considerable number of stick bombs. They burst noisily with result that it was at one moment reported that he had evacuated and was shelling his own front line. Beyond this resistance of garrison was not great. There was much hostile rifle fire throughout the operation but enemy Machine Guns did not open fire to any great extent till 6.23 p.m. He started retaliation at 6.9 p.m. with L.H.V. on front line and rearwards with 5.9 and T.M. shells. He did not seem to have located position of raid till after party were clear. |
| Co-operating units. | The preliminary bombardment by our artillery was in every respect entirely successful and their shooting contributed in large measure to the results achieved by the raiders.<br><br>The Stokes Mortars had their targets very well ranged and, I think, the small amount of hostile Machine Gun fire was no doubt due to their effective bombardment of the points to be covered, Sap 3 in particular.<br><br>The Machine Gun Company's left gun jambed after firing 2 belts while the right gun fired continuously throughout.<br><br>The Dummies utilised appear to have drawn enemy retaliation on right battalion. |
| Our casualties. | Our casualties were in trench garrison - 1 slightly wounded, while 9 of the party were wounded (none dangerously) and 2 are missing. Enquiries have been made in regard to the last mentioned. Cpl. GEARY was known to have been wounded. He was helped out of enemy trench but, later, couldn't be found and it was thought he had returned safely to our lines.<br><br>The man next him when hit states that he fell heavily and being badly wounded may have died on the way back.<br><br>The missing man - PEARSON - formed one of the S. "Pulling-out" party. Another of that party last saw PEARSON half way over. He was then off to the right a little and was not seen again. He was thought to have taken cover temporarily and was expected to follow up. A wounded man I saw personally told me last night that PEARSON was all right and no further search was made. This indeed was well nigh impossible as after operation NO MAN'S LAND was well swept by Machine Gun fire and flooded with lights.<br><br>(Later the Right Battalion sent out a patrol to bring in tapes and saw nothing of the missing men). |

I wish to call attention to the good work accomplished by the two officers in training and organising parties at short notice and the spirit and dash displayed by all ranks. I do not think this could have be improved upon.

Recommendations. Where all did so well it is a difficult to draw distinctions, but at the same time I would beg to bring to your notice the good work done by the two undermentioned N.C.O's. Both did excellent patrol work before the raid and acted admirably on the night itself. The first named secured an identification. The names are :-

1897. Corporal SWAIN J.H.
2511. L/Sergeant. STEELE H.J.

I have the honour to be, Sir,

Your obedient servant,

(sgd) W.F.K.NEWSON. Lieut.Colonel.

Cmdg. 1/15th London Regt.

G.O.C.

140th Inf. Bde.

SECRET.

1/15 London Regt.

HEADQUARTERS
G/240/10/8
Date 23/12/16
(LONDON) DIVISION

To the ... Col
23/...

Refce 140 Bgde Operation
Order SS/29/16/S.

Sir,

I have the honour to report that the raid was carried out last night as ordered.

WORK OF RAIDERS

The Artillery barrage & Stokes Mortar fire enabled the party to enter the enemy trenches within 1½ minutes or so of ZERO. The point of entry was approximately 12 or 15 yds S. of high mound of new earth about T 34 d. 14. 39. The blocking parties at once moved to the left and right respectively. The left party proceeded 25 yards up the trench northwards where they found that the Arty. had knocked in the trench so successfully that a ready made block was formed. This party claimed to have killed 5 Germans The enemy attempted to bomb

(1)

them while they held the block but didn't reach them. The right party proceeded in a S. direction & about 20 yds. from point of entry found a bend in the trench from which point it ran straight for 30 yds. They accordingly established themselves at this corner and met no opposition. They claim to have killed 2 Germans. The party detailed to locate & explore Sap 2 found nothing beyond a series of shell holes. The 4th party, whose mission was to explore dug-out indicated on previously captured German map, proceeded down the commn. trench, which — 10 or 12 yds from point of entry — bears off in a Southerly direction. They secured this trench for a distance of about 20 yards. Hostile bombs thrown had no effect. The trench where it bent was badly damaged while the parallel trench immediately in rear of front line appears to be used as a drain. No sign of a dug-out was found

INFORMATION

but party claim 1 killed.
There being further time available front line was explored and a few dug-outs (capacity 2 to 3 men) were found into these, wounded had crawled and some had already died. No signal wires were seen. Several of the enemy were observed to be wearing their gas helmets at the "ready" position. The pockets of the dead were searched but no papers were found. This party claim 3 killed.

IDENTIFICATIONS Several efforts were made to get a live Hun but they invariably resisted and had to be disposed of. A shoulder strap button & cap were secured however and would appear to conclusively establish identification of the troops opposed to us. These 2 articles have been sent to you already.

The length of trench occupied by us would appear

(iii)

to be about 50 yards. It was in good condition where not actually knocked in by our bombardment and was revetted and boarded; there were few traverses but trench was quite 8 feet deep.

ENEMY TRENCH

No difficulty was found in withdrawing & the tapes proved an efficient guide.

At the outset the enemy used a considerable number of stick bombs. They burst noisily with result that it was at one moment reported that he had evacuated & was shelling his own front line. Beyond this resistance of garrison was not great. There was much hostile rifle fire throughout the operation but enemy MG'S did not open fire to any great extent till 6.23 pm. He started retaliation at 6.9 with LHV on front line and rearwards with 5.9 & TM shells. He did not seem to have located position of raid till after party were clear.

ACTION OF ENEMY

CO-OPERATING UNITS

The preliminary bombard[t]. by our artillery was in every respect entirely successful and their shooting contributed in large measure to the results achieved by raiders.

The Stokes mortars had their targets very well ranged and, I think, the small amount of hostile M.G. fire was no doubt due to their effective bombardment of the points to be covered, Sap 3 in particular.

The M.G. Coy's left gun jambed after firing 2 belts while the right gun fired continuously throughout.

The Dummies utilised appear to have drawn enemy retaliation on right battalion.

OUR CASUALTIES

Our Casualties were in trench garrison – 1 slightly wounded, while 9 of the party were wounded (none dangerously) and 2 are missing. Enquiries have been made in regard to the last-mentioned. Cpl Geary was known to have been

(V)

wounded. He was helped out of enemy trench but, later, couldn't be found & it was thought he had returned safely to our lines. The man next him when hit states that he fell heavily & being badly wounded may have died on the way back.
The missing man – Pearson – formed one of the S. "Pulling-out" party. Another of his party last saw Pearson half-way over. He was then off to the right a little & was not seen again. He was thought to have taken cover temporarily & was expected to follow up. A wounded man I saw personally told me last night that Pearson was all right & no further search was made. This indeed was well nigh impossible as after operation No man's land was well swept by M.G. fire & flooded with lights (Later the Rt. Coy sent out a patrol to bring in Lopes & saw no signs of the missing men).

(VI)

I wish to call attention to the good work accomplished by the 2 Officers in training & organising parties at short notice and the spirit & dash displayed by all ranks. I do not think this could have been improved upon.

RECOMMENDATIONS

Where all did so well it is difficult to draw distinctions but at the same time I would beg to bring to your notice the good work done by the 2 undernamed NCOS. Both did excellent patrol work before the raid and acted admirably on the night itself. The first-named secured an identification. The names are:–

1897 CPL. SWAIN J.H.
2511 L/SGT STEELE H.J.

I have the honour
to be, Sir,
Your obedient servant,

[signature]
Lt. Col.
Cmdg 1/15 LONDON

G.O.C.
140 Inf Bde

(viii)

G.S.O.,

1) Please speak – circulate to CRA & say that the Artillery cooperation was most creditable to all concerned

2) The arrangements for withdrawal & evacuation of wounded require looking into

3) We must also teach how to make prisoners come away with us

J.L.
24.XII.16

FILE COPY G/240/10/8.

47th Div Arty

The attached report received from the Commanding Officer of the party of the 15th Battalion which carried out the raid on the evening of the 22nd inst. is forwarded for your information.

2. The Divisional Commander understands that the Artillery co-operation was most creditable to all concerned and shows the good work of which the 47th Divisional Artillery is capable.

3. The Divisional Commander hopes that the same high standard will be maintained in future.

Sd. A.J. Turner Lt.Col.
General Staff,
47th (London) Division.

G/240/10/8.
24th December 1916.

S E C R E T .

Xth Corps.

Herewith copy of report received from the Commanding Officer 1/15th Battn. The London Regiment. on the raid carried out on the 22nd.December 1916.

G/240/10/8. Major General,

25th December 1916. Commanding 47th (London) Division.

SECRET.

Xth Corps.

Herewith copy of report received from the Commanding Officer 1/15th Bn. The London Regiment on the raid carried out on the 22nd December, 1916.

G/240/10/8.
25th Dec. 1916.

(sd) G.F.Gorringe, Major Genl.
Commanding 47th (London) Divn.

2.

Second Army.

Forwarded. The raid seems to have been well planned and carried out with dash and determination.

Kindly return.

2nd Lt. G.F. GROVE, 3/9th Manchester Rgt., attached 15th London Regt. was the officer in Command.

sgd J.L.A. Morland

Lieut. General,
Commanding Xth Corps.

26/12/16.

47th Div.
Kindly see Corps Comdrs remarks

1/15th Battalion London Regiment
(P.W.O. Civil Service Rifles)

## Scheme for proposed Raid on Enemy Trenches

Objective. Enemy front line trench from about I. 34. d. 17. 46 to I. 34. d. 08. 32, including enemy Sap No. 2 and dug-outs South East of Sap No. 2.

Force. 2 Officers and 50 O. R.

Object. To enter enemy's front line, inflict as many casualties as possible, secure prisoners for identification and ascertain nature of and reason for high mound about I. 34. d. 14. 39.

Method. The force will be divided into the following parties:-

1st Party. 2 Officers 32 O. R. actual raiders.
2nd Party. 1 N.C.O. and 6 men for Sap No. 2
3rd Party. 1 N.C.O. and 10 men as rear party.

The force will move into No Man's Land and get into position within 50 yards of the objective at ZERO-10. At ZERO the 1st and 2nd party will rush their objectives. The 3rd party, moving in rear and remaining on enemy parapet to take charge of prisoners, will assist the raiders to vacate enemy's trench.

1st Party will be organized into 4 groups as follows:-

No. 1 Group to block enemy trench at I.34.d.17.46.
No. 2 Group to block trench at I.34.d.08.32.
No. 3 Group to clear the dugout about I.34.d.15.38.
No. 4 Group to clear enemy [illegible] and any other dug outs that may exist between the two blocks.

2nd Party will enter Sap No 2 and deal with any garrison found there.

Method (continued) 3rd Party will be accompanied by ... Tunnelling Engineers. They will improve existing gaps and prepare easy exits for No. 1 Party.

Co-operation of other Units.

(1) Artillery. At ZERO-2 a bombardment will open on enemy front line. At ZERO the bombardment will lift and a "box barrage" be formed on the flanks of the raided area and on enemy's rear lines.

(2) Stokes Mortars at ZERO will bombard western face of the Shrine and enemy sap South East of MACKS WALK.

(3) Machine Guns will bring cross-fire to bear on ground behind area raided from vicinity of trenches I.34.1 and I.34.5.

(4). Rifle Grenades will fire from positions at end of MACKS WALK and HEDGE ROW.

Demonstration. To deceive enemy a party with dummies will be posted in No Man's Land in old sap between I.34.1 and I.34.2.

Return. To guide the force back, at ZERO+15 green rockets will be sent up at ½ minute intervals. To distract enemy, white rockets will be sent up from another point at similar intervals.

Reorganisation. On return to our lines the raiders will be sent down LOVERS LANE to report at CENTRE BATTALION NEW HEADQUARTERS, where the roll will be called.

W.H.K. Renwood [signature] Major

Commdg. 15th Battn. London Regt.
(P.W.O. Civil Service Rifles.)

## NOTES.

1. Equipment. The Raiding Party will go out in Loose order, with rifle and bayonets fixed. Faces and hands will be blacked, and bayonets dulled. Each bomber will carry 6 bombs, and each other man 2 bombs. A proportion of the party will carry electric torches and revolvers.

2. Start. The time of starting out of the parties will be determined by actual practice over the ground. Ample time will be allowed, to permit of the party reaching their position at ZERO – 10.

3. Return. The signal for return will be single green rockets fired at ½ minute intervals commencing at ZERO + 15.

4. Identification. All identity discs, badges and papers which might give information will be left behind.

5. Aid post. An aid post will be established at Centre Battalion new Headquarters.

W H Newson Major

Commdg. 15th Battn. London Regt.
(P.W.O. Civil Service Rifles.)

1/1 th Battn. London Regiment.

PROPOSED SCHEME for Raid on Enemy Trenches in CANAL SUB-SECTOR December 1916.

1. OBJECTIVE. Enemy front line trenches from about I.34.d.18.47 to I.34.d.10.35 including Machine Gun in Sap 2 and enemy dugouts S.E. of latter.

2. FORCE. 2 Officers and 50 Other Ranks.

3. OBJECT. To enter enemy's front line inflict as many casualties as possible and secure one or more prisoners for identification purposes.

4. METHODS. Two covering parties of 1 N.C.O. and 5 Other Ranks each will go out at ZERO less minutes to protect the flanks.

At ZERO less minutes the Raiding Force consisting of 2 Officers and 32 O.R. will advance against enemy front line endeavouring to reach his wire without being discovered.

The advance will be timed so as to arrive at that point at ZERO.

Immediately the wire is reached the force will cross it by the aid of blankets and will rush the enemy trench A party of 1 N.C.O. and 5 O.R. will remain on the enemy parapet to assist the Raiding Force to vacate the enemy lines at ZERO + 10

The Raiding Force will be organised into two sections A Right and a Left party ~~will work along enemy trench~~ with Bombers and bayonet men leading each party. The Left party will work along enemy trench to the left and establish a block at I.34.d.20.55. The Right party will establish a block to the right at point I.34.d.10.35. The enemy trench between these points will be cleared and searched thoroughly.

At ZERO + 10 the party will start the return journey to our own lines.

5. RETURN. To guide the party back a white tape will be laid across No-mans-land

6. REORGANISATION. The whole force will assemble after the Raid at new Centre Battalion Headquarters, LOVERS LANE.

7. ARTILLERY and T.M. CO-OPERATION. At ZERO + 5 the Artillery will bombard trenches opposite I.34.6

At ZERO + 10 Stokes Mortars will open rapid fire on SAP 3 and Western face of the SHRINE, and on front line I34 d.05.25 and the Artillery will bombard the trenches behind the point actually raided.

8. LEWIS GUNS. Will be disposed in our front line to cross-fire behind our Raiding Party in enemy's lines.

16. Dec. 1916.

My dear General.

I am sending the 15th Bn's scheme for a raid – the most suitable night would be the 20th or 21st –

The two officers who take part in the operation greatly desire that no artillery fire should be opened until the raiding party is due to leave the trench. They think that if a barrage is put up by us to protect them when in the enemy's trenches it will have the effect of immediately drawing the enemy's artillery fire on to No Man's Land & thereby rendering it difficult for them to return. They think they can get into enemy's trench & deal with the situation themselves and that the opening of our guns and stokes at zero + 10 will give them the signal to retire and cover their retirement;

It is proposed at zero + 5 to open

artillery fire an Enemy salient opposite I.34.6. with a view of taking attention off the real part of the raid.

There is a M.G. in the portion of Enemy trench proposed to raid and on the German map there is marked what is presumably a dugout "Rotenberg". The M.G. & the dugout are the objectives. The party propose to return the same way as they came. I have not discussed the scheme with Colonel Massy yet.

My front very quiet today but one of the few Minnies hit of the beyond Entrance to No. Tunnel & blew it in. It is opened again.

EV
Hampden

A/65

Vol 18

1916.

WAR DIARY

1/15th Batt. London Regt

(P.W.O. Civil Service Rifles)

DECEMBER

Vol 19

War Diary
of the
1/15th Battalion London Regt
from
1/1/1917
to
31/1/1917

Instructions regarding War Diaries and Intelligence Summaries are contained in F. S. Regs., Part II. and the Staff Manual respectively. Title pages will be prepared in manuscript.

# WAR DIARY
*or*
# INTELLIGENCE SUMMARY.
*(Erase heading not required.)*

Army Form C. 2118.

| Place | Date 1917 | Hour | Summary of Events and Information | Remarks and references to Appendices |
|---|---|---|---|---|
| | JAN. | | | |
| OTTAWA CAMP near Ouderdom | 1 - 7 | | In reserve at OTTAWA CAMP. Casualties NIL. | |
| do. | 8 | | Moved up to FRONT LINE, relieving 19th Battn. London Regt. in Left Section, HILL 60 Sub-sector, YPRES. Casualties NIL. | |
| HILL 60 YPRES. | 9 | | IN front line at HILL 60, YPRES, Casualties NIL. | |
| do. | 10 | | do. do. Casualties NIL. | |
| do. | 11 | | do. do. Casualties 1 O.R. killed, 4 O.R. wounded. | |
| do. | 12 | | do. do. Casualties 3 O.R. killed, 1 O.R. missing, 19 O.R. wounded. | |
| RAILWAY dugouts, near ZILLEBEKE | 13 | | do. Relieved by 6th Battn. London Regt. Moved back to Support position, Railway dugouts, near ZILLEBEKE Casualties NIL. | |
| | 14 | | In support at Railway dugouts. Casualties 10 O.R. wounded. | |
| do. | 15 | | do. do. Casualties NIL. | |
| do. | 16 | | do. do. Casualties 3 O.R. wounded. | |
| do. | 17 | | do. do. Casualties NIL. | |
| HILL 60 YPRES | 18 | | do. Moved up at night to Left Section HILL 60 Subsector, and relieved 6th Battn. London Regt. Casualties 1 O.R. killed, 7 O.R. wounded | |
| do. | 19 | | In front line at HILL 60 YPRES. Casualties NIL. | |
| do. | 20 | | do. do. Casualties NIL. | |
| do. | 21 | | do. do. Casualties NIL. | |
| HALIFAX CAMP near VLAMERTINGE | 22 | | do. Relieved at night by 6th Battn. London Regt. and moved back into Brigade reserve at HALIFAX CAMP near VLAMERTINGE. Casualties NIL. | |
| do. | 23 | | In reserve at HALIFAX CAMP, VLAMERTINGE. Casualties NIL. | |
| do. | 24 | | do. do. Casualties NIL. | |
| do. | 24 | | do. do. Casualties NIL. | |
| do. | 25 | | do. do. Casualties NIL. | |
| OTTAWA CAMP near OUDERDOM | 26 | | do. Relieved in afternoon by 20th Battn. London Regt. and moved back into Divisional reserve at OTTAWA CAMP near OUDERDOM. Casualties NIL. | |
| do. | 27 | | At OTTAWA CAMP, training. Casualties NIL. | |
| do. | 28 | | do. do. Casualties NIL. | |
| do. | 29 | | do. do. Casualties NIL. | |

[illegible] Capt & Adjt
1/15th Battn London Regt
1/2/1917

A5834 Wt. W4973/M687 750,000 8/16 D. D. & L. Ltd. Forms/C.2118/13.

Army Form C. 2118.

# WAR DIARY
*or*
# INTELLIGENCE SUMMARY.
*(Erase heading not required.)*

Instructions regarding War Diaries and Intelligence Summaries are contained in F. S. Regs., Part II, and the Staff Manual respectively. Title pages will be prepared in manuscript.

| Place | Date | Hour | Summary of Events and Information | Remarks and references to Appendices |
|---|---|---|---|---|
| | 1917 JAN. | | | |
| OTTAWA CAMP near OUDERDOM | 30 | | At OTTAWA CAMP, training, Casualties NIL. [initials] | |
| | 31 | | do. do. Casualties NIL. [initials] | |

W. [illegible] Capt. & Adjt
1/15th Batt. London Regt
1/2/1917

A5834 Wt. W4973/M687 750,000 8/16 D. D. & L. Ltd. Forms/C.2118/13.

1/15th Battalion London Regt.

War Diary

February 1917.

Army Form C. 2118.

Instructions regarding War Diaries and Intelligence Summaries are contained in F. S. Regs., Part II. and the Staff Manual respectively. Title pages will be prepared in manuscript.

# WAR DIARY
*or*
# INTELLIGENCE SUMMARY.

*(Erase heading not required.)*

| Place | Date | Hour | Summary of Events and Information | Remarks and references to Appendices |
|---|---|---|---|---|
| | FEB.1917. | | | |
| OTTAWA CAMP. | 1. | | In Divisional Reserve, Casualties Nil . | |
| do. | 2. | | In Divisional Reserve, Casualties Nil. | |
| do. | 3. | | Moved to Front Line, left section, Canal Subsector, and relieved 22nd Battalion London Regiment. Relief complete 9.30 p.m. Casualties, Nil. | |
| FRONT LINE | 4. | | In Front Line, Casualties, Nil. | |
| do. | 5. | | In Front Line, Casualties, 1.O. R. Killed. 12 O.R. Wounded. | |
| do. | 6. | | In Front Line, Casualties, 1.O.R. Killed. | |
| do. | 7. | | Relieved by 8th Battalion London Regiment, and moved back to Support Positions. Casualties, Nil. | |
| SUPPORT POSITIONS | 8. | | In Support, Casualties, Nil. | |
| do. | 9. | | In Support, Casualties, Nil. | |
| do. | 10. | | In Support, Casualties, 1 O.R. wounded. | |
| do. | 11. | | In Support, Casualties, Nil. | |
| do. | 12. | | Relived 8th Battalion London Regiment in Front Line trenches, left section, Canal Subsector, Casualties, Nil. | |
| FRONT LINE. | 13. | | In Front Line, Casualties, 1 Officer, wounded at duty. | |
| do. | 14. | | In Front Line, Casualties, 1 O.R. wounded (accidental) | |
| do. | 15. | | In Front Line, very quiet, Casualties 2.O, R. Wounded. | |
| do. | 16. | | In Front Line, enemy replied vigorously to our French Mortars in the afternoon. Relieved by 8th Battalion London Regiment and moved back to Support Positions, Casualties, 1 O.R. wounded. | |
| SUPPORT. POSITIONS | 17. | | In Support, Casualties, 1. O.R. wounded. | |
| | 18. | | In Support, Casualties, Nil. | |
| do. | 19. | | In Support, relieved by 19th Battalion London Regiment, and move back to Divisional Reserve at Ottawa Camp, Casualties, Nil. | |
| OTTAWA CAMP | 20. | | In Divisional Reserve. Baths and general cleaning of kits. Casualties, 1 O.R. wounded. | |
| do. | 21. | | In Divisional Reserve, Training. Casualties, Nil. | |
| do. | 22. | | Relieve 21st Battalion London Regiment as Works Battalion to the Division. | |

A5834 Wt. W4973/M687 750,000 8/16 D. D. & L. Ltd. Forms/C.2118/13.

Army Form C. 2118.

Instructions regarding War Diaries and Intelligence Summaries are contained in F. S. Regs., Part II. and the Staff Manual respectively. Title pages will be prepared in manuscript.

# WAR DIARY
*or*
# INTELLIGENCE SUMMARY.

*(Erase heading not required.)*

| Place | Date | Hour | Summary of Events and Information | Remarks and references to Appendices |
|---|---|---|---|---|
| | Feb.1917. | | | |
| | 22. | | Disposition od Companies:- A. Coy. Belgian Chateau, B. Coppernollehoek, C. Pacific Sidings, D. Coy. at Vancouver Camp, Headquarters at Ottawa Camp. Casualties, Nil aw. | |
| OTTAWA CAMP | 23. | | Casualties, Nil. aw. | |
| do. | 24. | | Casualties, Nil. aw. | |
| do. | 25. | | Casualties, Nil. aw. | |
| do. | 26. | | Casualties, Nil. aw. | |
| do. | 27. | | Casualties, Nil. aw. | |
| do. | 28. | | Casualties, Nil. aw. | |

H B Balyne [signature]

Major,
Commanding,1/15th Battalion London Regiment,
(P.W.O. CIVIL SERVICE RIFLES.)

A5834 Wt. W4973/M687 750,000 8/16 D. D. & L. Ltd. Forms/C.2118/13.

Vol 21

1/15th Battalion London Regiment
(P.W.O. Civil Service Rifles)

WAR DIARY.

MARCH 1917.

Instructions regarding War Diaries and Intelligence Summaries are contained in F. S. Regs., Part II. and the Staff Manual respectively. Title pages will be prepared in manuscript.

# WAR DIARY

~~or~~

## ~~INTELLIGENCE SUMMARY.~~

*(Erase heading not required.)*

Army Form C. 2118.

| Place | Date | Hour | Summary of Events and Information | Remarks and references to Appendices |
|---|---|---|---|---|
| | March 1917 | | | |
| OTTAWA CAMP | 1 | | Works Battalion. Disposition of Companies A. Coy. Belgian Chateau, B. Coy. Coppernollehoek, C. Coy. Atlantic Sidings, D. Coy. Vancouver Camp. Headquarters at Ottawa Camp. Casualties Nil. | |
| do. | 2 | | do. do. Casualties 1 wounded. | |
| do. | 3 | | do. do. Casualties Nil. | |
| do. | 4 | | do. do. Casualties 2 wounded. | |
| do. | 5 | | do. do. Casualties Nil. | |
| do. | 6 | | do. do. Casualties Nil. | |
| do. | 7 | | do. do. Casualties Nil. | |
| do. | 8 | | do. do. Casualties Nil. | |
| do. | 9 | | do. do. Casualties Nil. | |
| do. | 10 | | do. do. Casualties Nil. | |
| do. | 11 | | do. do. Casualties Nil. | |
| do. | 12 | | do. do. Casualties Nil. | |
| do. | 13 | | do. do. Casualties Nil. | |
| do. | 14 | | do. do. Casualties Nil. | |
| do. | 15 | | do. do. Casualties Nil. | |
| do. | 16 | | do. do. Casualties Nil. | |
| do. | 17 | | do. do. Casualties Nil. | |
| do. | 18 | | do. do. Casualties 1 wounded. | |
| do. | 19 | | do. do. Casualties Nil. | |
| do. | 20 | | Battalion reassembled at Ottawa Camp, Casualties Nil. | |
| do. | 21 | | Battalion relieved 22nd Battalion London Regiment in Front Line, Left Section, Canal Subsector, Casualties, Nil. | |
| FRONT LINE | 22 | | In front line, Casualties Nil. | |
| do. | 23. | | In front line, Casualties Nil. | |
| do. | 24 | | In front line. Hostile aeroplane brought down by Anti Aircraft and Machine Gun fire between enemy's front and support lines and wrecked by our Artillery fire. Casualties 2 wounded | |
| do. | 25 | | In front line, Casualties, 1 killed, 1 wounded. | |
| do. | 26 | | In front line, Casualties, Nil. | |
| do. | 27 | | In front line, Casualtbes 1 wounded. | |

Army Form C. 2118.

# WAR DIARY

or

~~INTELLIGENCE SUMMARY~~.

*(Erase heading not required.)*

Instructions regarding War Diaries and Intelligence Summaries are contained in F. S. Regs., Part II. and the Staff Manual respectively. Title pages will be prepared in manuscript.

| Place | Date | Hour | Summary of Events and Information | Remarks and references to Appendices |
|---|---|---|---|---|
| FRONT LINE | 28 | | In Front Line, Casualties, Nil. | |
| do. | 29 | | Relieved by 1/8th Battalion London Regiment and moved into Support. Casualties, Nil. | |
| SWAN, CHATEAU | 30 | | In Support, Casualties, 2 wounded. | |
| do | 31 | | In Support, Casualties, Nil. | |

H B Baeyon [?] Major
1/15 London Regt.

T2134. Wt. W708—776. 500000. 4/15. Sir J. C. & S.

E/104

Vol 22

1/15 Battalion London Regiment
(P.W.O. Civil Service Rifles)

WAR DIARY

April 1917.

Army Form C. 2118.

Instructions regarding War Diaries and Intelligence Summaries are contained in F. S. Regs., Part II. and the Staff Manual respectively. Title pages will be prepared in manuscript.

# WAR DIARY

*or*

~~INTELLIGENCE SUMMARY~~

*(Erase heading not required.)*

| Place | Date | Hour | Summary of Events and Information | Remarks and references to Appendices |
|---|---|---|---|---|
| CANAL SUB-SECTOR. YPRES. | 1. | | In Support at Swan Chateau. Casualties:Nil. | |
| | 2. | | do. do. Casualties:Nil. | |
| | 3. | | do. do. Casualties:Nil. | |
| | 4. | | do. do. Casualties:Nil. | |
| | 5. | | do. do. Casualties:Nil. | |
| | 6. | | do. do. Casualties:Nil. | |
| | 7. | | do. do. 18th Battalion London Regiment raided German lines between Hill 60 and Bluff. 15th Battalion London Regiment relieved 18th Batt.London Regiment in Left Section, Canal Sub-Sector at midnight. Casualties;Nil. | |
| | 8. | | In front line,Left Section,Canal Sub-Sector. Casualties :- Wounded 2/Lt.M.F.Jarvis. | |
| | 9. | | do. do. do. Enemy raided Battalion on left at 6-30 p.m. Casualties :- Killed. 1 O.R. Wounded 1 O.R. | |
| | 10. | | do. do. do. Casualties:- Killed 12 O.R.,Wounded. 17 O.R. | |
| | 11. | | do. do. do. Casualties:- Nil. | |
| DEVONSHIRE CAMP. BUSSEBOOM. | 12. | | do. do. do. Relieved by 21st Batt.London Regiment at 11-0 p.m. and moved back into Reserve at DEVONSHIRE CAMP, BUSSEBOOM. Casualties:- Killed.2 O.R. Wounded. 1 O.R. | |
| | 13. | | In reserve at Devonshire Camp. Casualties:- Wounded. 1 O.R. | |
| | 14. | | do. do. Casualties:- Nil. | |
| | 15. | | do. do. Casualties:- Nil. | |

A5834 Wt. W4973/M687 750,000 8/16 D. D. & L. Ltd. Forms/C.2118/13.

Army Form C. 2118.

Instructions regarding War Diaries and Intelligence Summaries are contained in F. S. Regs., Part II. and the Staff Manual respectively. Title pages will be prepared in manuscript.

# WAR DIARY
*or*
~~INTELLIGENCE~~ ~~SUMMARY~~.

*(Erase heading not required.)*

| Place | Date | Hour | Summary of Events and Information | Remarks and references to Appendices |
|---|---|---|---|---|
| DEVONSHIRE CAMP. | 16. | | In reserve at Devonshire Camp. Casualties:- Nil. | |
| | 17. | | do. do. Casualties:- Nil. | |
| | 18. | | do. do. Casualties:- Nil. | |
| | 19. | | do. do. Casualties:- Nil. | |
| | 20. | | do. do. Casualties:- Nil. | |
| SPOIL BANK SECTION, YPRES. | 21. | | Relieved 8th Battalion London Regt. in Spoil Bank Section, at midnight. Casualties:- Nil. | |
| | 22. | | In front line, Spoil Bank Section, Ypres. Casualties:- Nil. | |
| | 23. | | do. do. do. Casualties:- Nil. | |
| | 24. | | do. do. do. Casualties:- Nil. | |
| | 25. | | do. do. do. Enemy attempted raid at 4-30 a.m. Unsuccessful. Casualties:- Killed 1 O.R. Wounded. Capt. A. D. Oliver, attd. from 5th Batt. Manchester Regt.. (afterwards died of wds.) 6 O.R. | |
| DOMINION CAMP. Nr BUSSEBOOM. | 26. | | do. do. Relieved by 6th Batt. London Regiment at midnight and moved back into Reserve at DOMINION CAMP, near BUSSEBOOM. Casualties:- Nil. | |
| | 27. | | At Dominion Camp. Casualties:- Nil. | |
| | 28. | | do. Casualties:- Nil. | |
| | 29. | | do. Casualties:- Nil. | |
| | 30. | | do. Casualties:- Nil. | |

Harold Marshall Lt Col
Comm 1/15th Batt. London Regt

A5834 Wt. W4973/M687 750,000 8/16 D. D. & L. Ltd. Forms/C.2118/13.

F/94

Vol 23

1/15 BATTALION LONDON REGIMENT.

# WAR DIARY

MAY, 1917.

Army Form C. 2118.

Instructions regarding War Diaries and Intelligence Summaries are contained in F. S. Regs., Part II. and the Staff Manual respectively. Title pages will be prepared in manuscript.

# WAR DIARY
*or*
# INTELLIGENCE SUMMARY.
*(Erase heading not required.)*

| Place | Date | Hour | Summary of Events and Information | Remarks and references to Appendices |
|---|---|---|---|---|
| DOMINION CAMP BUSSEBOOM | May 1 | | at Dominion Camp Casualties, Nil | |
| | 2 | | do. do | |
| | 3 | | do do | |
| | 4 | | do. do. | |
| | 5 | | do. do | |
| | 6 | | do. do | |
| | 7 | | do. do | |
| SWAN CHATEAU | 8 | | Relieved 8th Battalion London Regiment at SWAN CHATEAU. Casualties Nil | |
| | 9 | | At Swan Chateau - Casualties 1 O.R. Wounded | |
| | 10 | | at Swan Chateau - Casualties 4 O.R. Killed 8 O.R. Wounded. | |
| DICKEBUSCH | 11 | | Relieved by 19th Battalion London Regt and moved to DICKEBUSCH. Casualties Nil. | |
| | 12 | | At DICKEBUSCH Casualties Nil | |
| WATOU | 13 | | Marched to WATOU - Casualties Nil. | |
| SERCUS | 14 | | Marched from WATOU to SERCUS - Casualties Nil | |
| MORINGHEM | 15 | | Marched from SERCUS to MORINGHEM Casualties Nil | |
| | 16 | | at Moringhem Training - Casualties Nil | |
| | 17 | | do. do do. | |
| | 18 | | do do do | |
| | 19 | | do. do do. | |
| | 20 | | do do do. | |
| | 21 | | do. do. do | |
| | 22 | | do. do do | |
| | 23 | | do do do | |
| | 24 | | do do do. | |
| | 25 | | do. do do | |

A5834 Wt. W4973/M687 750,000 8/16 D. D. & L. Ltd. Forms/C.2118/13.

Instructions regarding War Diaries and Intelligence Summaries are contained in F. S. Regs., Part II. and the Staff Manual respectively. Title pages will be prepared in manuscript.

# WAR DIARY
*or*
# INTELLIGENCE SUMMARY.
*(Erase heading not required.)*

Army Form C. 2118.

| Place | Date | Hour | Summary of Events and Information | Remarks and references to Appendices |
|---|---|---|---|---|
| | May | | | |
| MORINGHEM | 26 | | At MORINGHEM training. Casualties Nil | |
| | 27 | | do do. | |
| | 28 | | do do. | |
| | 29 | | do do. | |
| | 30 | | do do. | |
| BUSSEBOOM | 31 | | Entrained at ST. OMER for POPERINGHE, and marched to bivouac camp DOMINION CAMP, BUSSEBOOM. Casualties Nil | |

[illegible] Major for Lt Colonel
Cdg 1/15 Battalion London Regt
(PWO Civil Service Rifles)

21/100

Vol 24

1/15th Batt London Regt.
Civil Service Rifles. —

# War Diary

June. 1917.

Instructions regarding War Diaries and Intelligence Summaries are contained in F. S. Regs., Part II. and the Staff Manual respectively. Title pages will be prepared in manuscript.

# WAR DIARY
*or*
# INTELLIGENCE SUMMARY.
*(Erase heading not required.)*

Army Form C. 2118.

| Place | Date | Hour | Summary of Events and Information | Remarks and references to Appendices |
|---|---|---|---|---|
| | June. | | | |
| EBBLINGHEM | 16 | | Marched from Caestre to Ebblinghem. Casualties, Nil. | |
| | 17 | | At Ebblinghem, Casualties Nil. | |
| | 18 | | do. do. | |
| | 19 | | do. do. | |
| | 20 | | do. do. | |
| | 21 | | do. do. | |
| | 22 | | do. do. | |
| | 23 | | do. do. | |
| | 24 | | do. do. | |
| | 25 | | do. do. | |
| | 26 | | do. do. | |
| | 27 | | do. do. | |
| METEREN | 28 | | Marched from Ebblinghem to Meteren, Casualties, Nil. | |
| VOORMEEZ-EELE | 29 | | Marched from Meteren to Voormeezeele, Casualties, Nil. | |
| O.G.1 | 30 | | Relieved 10th Royal West Kents in O. G. 1. Casualties, Nil. | |

Harold Marshall

Lt-Colonel,
Commanding, 1/15th Batt. London Regiment,
(P.W.O. CIVIL SERVICE RIFLES.)

T2134. Wt. W708–776. 500000. 4/15. Sir J. C. & S.

Instructions regarding War Diaries and Intelligence Summaries are contained in F. S. Regs., Part II. and the Staff Manual respectively. Title pages will be prepared in manuscript.

# WAR DIARY
*or*
# INTELLIGENCE SUMMARY.
*(Erase heading not required.)*

Army Form C. 2118.

| Place | Date | Hour | Summary of Events and Information | Remarks and references to Appendices |
|---|---|---|---|---|
| | 1917 June, | | | |
| DOMINION Lines, near OUDERDOM. | 1 | | At Bivouac Camp, Dominion Lines, Casualties, Nil. | |
| | 2 | | do. do. do. do. | |
| SWAN CHATEAU. | 3 | | Relieved 17th Batt. London Regt., in Swan Chateau Area. Casualties, Nil. | |
| | 4 | | At Swan Chateau, Casualties, Nil. | |
| | 5 | | do. do. 2. O. R. Wounded. | |
| WEST TERRACE | 6 | | Moved into position for attack. Casualties, Nil | |
| FRONT LINE. | 7 | | Co-operated in attack by Second Army on the MESSINES-WYTSCHAETE Ridge. Narrative of operations attached. Relieved by 73rd Infantry Brigade after the attack and moved back to ECLUSE TRENCH. Casualties:- 2 Off. 26 O. R. Killed; 2 Off. died of wounds; Wounded 2 Off. 120 O. R.; 1 Off. and 9 O. R. Missing. | |
| ECLUSE TRENCH | 8 | | In Ecluse Trench. Casualties 3 O.R. Killed, 2.O. R. Wounded. | |
| | 9 | | " " 2 O.R. Killed, 2.O.R. Wounded. | |
| FRONT LINE. | 10 | | Relieved 6th Battalion London Regiment in Front Line. Casualties, 3 O.R. killed, 6 O.R. Wounded. | |
| | 11 | | In Front Line. Casualties, 2 O.R. killed, 17 O.R. wounded. | |
| | 12 | | Relieved by 18th Kings Royal Rifles and moved back to CHIPPEWA CAMP near RENINGHELST. Casualties, 3 O. R. Wounded. | |
| CHIPPEWA CAMP | 13 | | At Chippewa Camp, near Reninghelst. Casualties, 1 O. R. accidentally wounded. | |
| | 14 | | At Chippewa Camp, Casualties, Nil. | |
| CAESTRE | 15 | | Marched to Caestre, Casualties, Nil. | |

T2134. Wt. W708—776. 500000. 4/15. Sir J. C. & S.

# 1/15th BATTALION LONDON REGIMENT.

Record of operations South of YPRES-COMINES CANAL, O 4. d., O. 10. A. and O. 10. B. WHITE CHATEAU - DAMMSTRASSE AREA, 7th June, 1917.

---

**GENERAL.** The 15th Battalion attacked in the second phase of the operations of the 7th June, 1917, on a frontage of about 400 yards, with OBLONG ALLEY as the left boundary, and the right on a line running about 50 yards right of OBLONG AVENUE.
The 7th Battalion attacked on the left and the Royal West Kents (41st Division) on the right of the 15th Battalion.
The 8th Battalion had already taken and were holding their objectives, viz, OAK TRENCH, OAK SUPPORT, and OAK RESERVE.

**PRELIMINARY RECONNAISSANCE.** Prior to the time laid down for the 15th Battalion to advance from their Assembly position, the Battalion scouts, who had gone ahead with the 8th Battalion and reconnoitred the ground, returned to report.
They had thoroughly examined the ground up to and including the stream and series of pools running between the DAMMSTRASSE and the lake behind WHITE CHATEAU and were able to report that this waterway, which up to this time had been considered as a possible serious obstacle, could be traversed without much difficulty. They were also able to inform the Company Commanders of the nature of the ground on the line of the advance.
The information furnished by these scouts proved of immense value, as it obviated the necessity of carrying bridging ladders for the stream; and Company Commanders were enabled to inform every N. C. O. of the actual situation before the Battalion advanced to attack.

**ASSEMBLY.** As the enemy put a very weak barrage on our lines it was possible for the Battalion to move up according to the original scheme of assembly, i. e. by C. Trench from WEST TRENCH area to the OLD BRITISH FRONT and SUPPORT LINES, which had been selected as the "Jumping off" trenches.
The Battalion was in position in these trenches at Zero plus 2 hours 30 minutes.
The situation then was such that it was found possible to line up the various waves on top outside the "Jumping off" trenches and the officers and N. C. O's gave the men the general direction and some information as to the situation at the moment.
Watches were finally synchronised at Zero plus 3 hours.

**ATTACK.** The attack was carried out in four waves.

1st wave ([illegible] platoon of each company with one in rear) (A.C.B.D. Coys)
2nd wave (two platoons) C. D. Coys.
3rd wave (One platoon of each company) A.C.B.D. Coys.
4th wave (One platoon of each company with one extra platoon in rear) A.C.B.D. Coys. A. Coy.

At Zero plus 3 hours 15 minutes the first wave moved off in lines of sections in single file, and passing through the 8th Battalion reached the line OAK RESERVE, held by the 8th Battalion.
The first wave extended after crossing OAK RESERVE and continued to the stream, which was crossed without difficulty. The wave then moved on and closed up

RECORD OF OPERATIONS.

under the barrage which was then on the line OAK CRESCENT (First objective)
At Zero plus three hours 40 minutes the barrage lifted from OAK CRESCENT and the first wave captured the trench with slight opposition. The second wave then moved up and remained in the first objective.
The third wave moved forward following the barrage closely and reached OBLONG TRENCH (2nd objective)
At the same time the platoon of 3. Company which had been detailed to advance in rear of the first wave and deal with a suspected strong point in three ruined cottages between first and second objectives rushed the position and cleared the way for the advance of the third wave.
OBLONG TRENCH was captured immediately the barrage lifted from it, the defenders being overwhelmed at once and 30 prisoners taken and sent back.
The 4th wave immediately moved forward to attack OBLONG RESERVE, supported by the original 1st wave which moved forward from OAK CRESCENT when the 4th wave had passed through.
OBLONG RESERVE was easily rushed by this strong combination as soon as the barrage lifted and a number of prisoners taken and sent back.
In the meantime the platoon of the left Company, which had followed up closely behind the last wave, had crossed OBLONG TRENCH and swung round and occupied a line parallel to OBLONG ALLEY so as to form a defensive flank on the left. The actual line of OBLONG ALLEY could not be held as it was being heavily barraged.
Immediately OBLONG RESERVE had been captured 2/Lt. DAVENPORT who took over command after Capt. BOWERS TAYLOR was killed pushed forward a platoon to reconnoitre and, if possible, capture DELBSKE FARM on the right flank.
This platoon found that the farm was occupied by the enemy but immediately rushed them before any strong resistance could be put up and about 25 prisoners were secured.
Forty men were immediately sent forward by 2/Lt. DAVENPORT from OBLONG RESERVE to re-inforce, and the trench running from DELBSKE FARM to WHITE CHATEAU wood was occupied.
From this trench, the observation of OLIVE TRENCH was very good. It did not appear to be very strongly held, but was under our artillery barrage at the time. When the barrage had lifted the enemy were observed trying to move up to OLIVE TRENCH in small detached parties but were severely dealt with by our forward Lewis Guns and by rifle fire.
Patrols were sent through RAVINE WOOD on the right and WHITE CHATEAU WOOD on the left. The right patrol got in touch with the Royal West Kents who were about 300 yards away in a line with OBLONG RESERVE. The left patrol got in touch with the 8th London Battalion, who were in OPAL RESERVE.
Both of these units stated that they were not holding a line forward of their positions and the DELBSKE FARM line was held as an outpost line with 30 men and 2 Lewis Guns. The remainder of the garrison were withdrawn to assist in the consolidation of OBLONG RESERVE.
The Battalion was then re-organized in depth on a four Company front and consolidation was carried on until the Battalion was relieved by the 2nd Leinsters during the morning of the 8th June, 1917.

All ranks were very keen and kept close up under our Barrage even to the extent of suffering a number of casualties and I am satisfied that they were so quickly into the objective that even had the opposition been much stronger it would easily have been swept aside.
A considerable number of documents ... and bundles of letters were forwarded to Brigade.

A

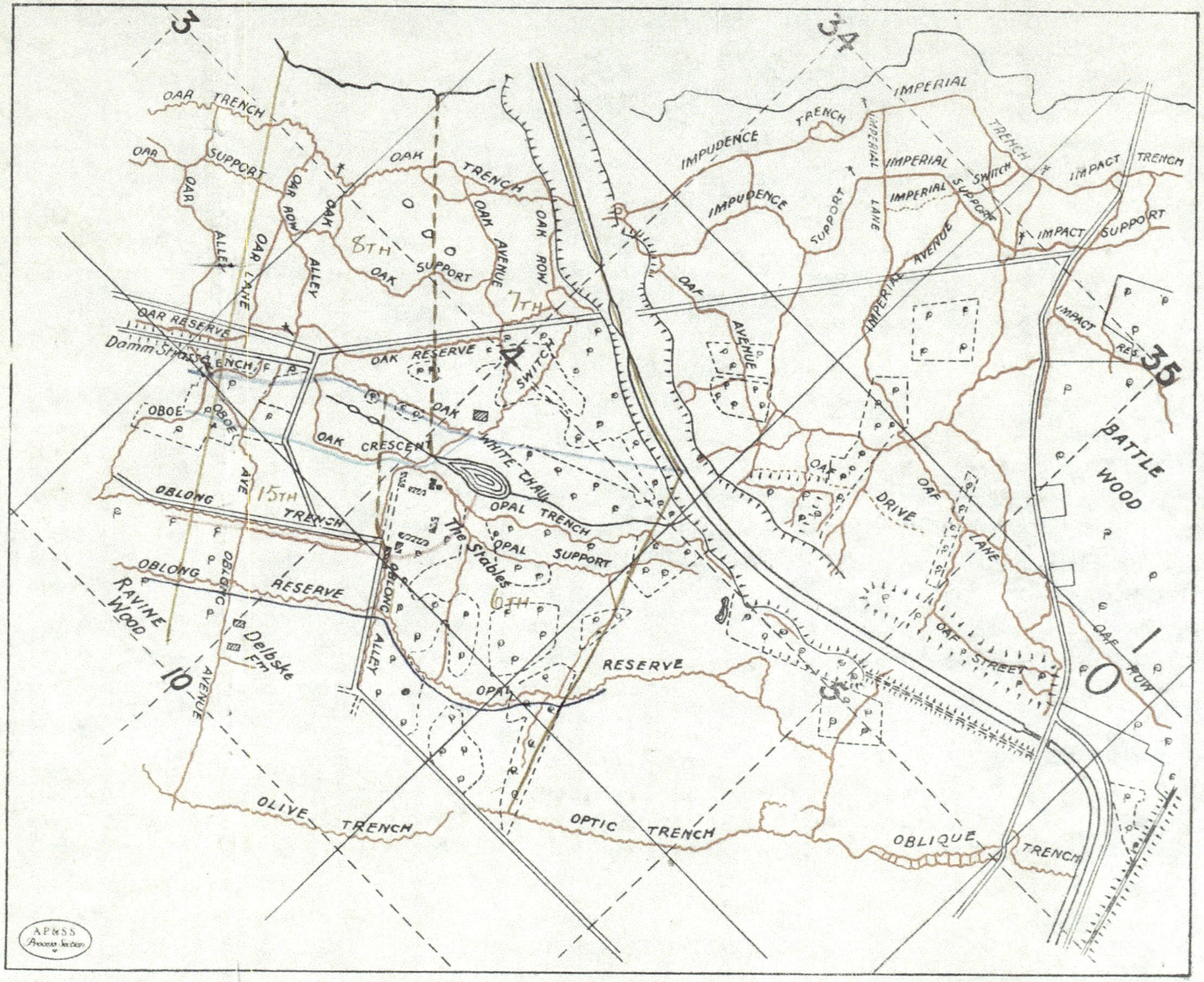
3
34
35
4
5
10
O
I
OAR TRENCH
OAR SUPPORT
OAR ALLEY
OAR LANE
OAR ROW
OAR RESERVE
Damm Strasse
TRENCH
OAK TRENCH
OAK SUPPORT
OAK ALLEY
OAK AVENUE
OAK ROW
OAK RESERVE
OAK CRESCENT
SWITCH
8TH
7TH
6TH
15TH
OBOE
OBOE AVE
OBLONG TRENCH
OBLONG RESERVE
OBLONG ALLEY
OBLONG AVENUE
RAVINE WOOD
Delbske Fm
WHITE CHAU
OPAL TRENCH
OPAL SUPPORT
OPAL RESERVE
The Stables
OLIVE TRENCH
OPTIC TRENCH
OBLIQUE TRENCH
IMPERIAL TRENCH
IMPUDENCE TRENCH
IMPUDENCE SUPPORT
IMPERIAL LANE
IMPERIAL SUPPORT
IMPERIAL SWITCH
IMPERIAL AVENUE
IMPACT TRENCH
IMPACT SUPPORT
IMPACT RES.
OAF AVENUE
OAF DRIVE
OAF LANE
OAF STREET
OAF ROW
BATTLE WOOD
AP&SS Process Section

PRINTED BY No. 3 ADVANCED SECTION A P. & S. S

.......... DIVISION

Map reference or
Mark on MAP on
Back.

1. I am at..........

2. I am at..........and am consolidating

3. I am at..........and have consolidated

4. Am held up by M.G. at....................

5. I need:- Ammunition
   Bombs
   Rifle Grenades
   Water
   Very Lights
   Stokes shells

6. Counter attack forming up at..........

7. I am in touch with..........on RIGHT/LEFT at..........

8. I am not in touch on RIGHT/LEFT

9. Am being shelled from..........

10. I estimate my present strength at..........rifles

11. Hostile {BATTERY / MACHINE GUN / TRENCH MORTAR} active at..........

Time..........m Name..........

Date.......... Platoon..........

Company..........

Battalion..........

Vol 25

1/15th Batt., London Regt..
(Civil Service Rifles)

# War Diary.

## July 1917.

Army Form C. 2118.

Instructions regarding War Diaries and Intelligence Summaries are contained in F. S. Regs., Part II. and the Staff Manual respectively. Title pages will be prepared in manuscript.

# WAR DIARY
*or*
~~INTELLIGENCE SUMMARY.~~
*(Erase heading not required.)*

| Place | Date 1917. | Hour | Summary of Events and Information | Remarks and references to Appendices |
|---|---|---|---|---|
| | July. | | | |
| SPOIL BANK. | 1. | | In Support in O.G.1. Casualties; 1 O.R. Killed, 2 O.R. Wounded. | |
| do. | 2. | | do. do. Casualties; Killed 1 O.R., Wounded 3 Officers, 9 O.R. | |
| do. | 3. | | Relieved by 23rd Battalion London Regt., and moved back to MURRUMBIDGEE CAMP, LA CLYTTE, near Reninghelst. Casualties; Killed 8 O.R., Wounded 14 O.R. | |
| MURRUMBIDGEE CAMP, LA CLYTTE. | 4. | | At Murrumbidgee Camp. Casualties; N I L. | |
| | 5. | | At Murrumbidgee Camp, Casualties; N I L. | |
| | 6. | | do. do. Casualties; N I L. | |
| | 7. | | do. do. Casualties; N I L. | |
| | 8. | | Relieved 24th Batt. London Regt., in Support in BOIS CONFLUENT. Casualties; N I L. | |
| BOIS CONFLUENT | 9. | | In Support. Casualties; Killed 1 O.R., Wounded 1 O.R.. | |
| | 10. | | do. Casualties; N I L. | |
| | 11. | | do. Casualties; N I L. | |
| | 12. | | do. Casualties; N I L. | |
| | 13. | | do. Casualties; N I L. | |
| | 14. | | Relieved 7th Batt. London Regt. in Right Section, Subsector, S. of Canal. Casualties; Killed 2 O.R., Gassed 1 O.R. | |
| FRONT LINE. | 15. | | In Front Line. Casualties; Killed 1 O.R. Wounded 2 O.R. | |
| | 16. | | do. Casualties; N I L. | |

Army Form C. 2118.

Instructions regarding War Diaries and Intelligence Summaries are contained in F. S. Regs., Part II. and the Staff Manual respectively. Title pages will be prepared in manuscript.

# WAR DIARY
*or*
# INTELLIGENCE SUMMARY.
*(Erase heading not required.)*

| Place | Date 1917. | Hour | Summary of Events and Information | Remarks and references to Appendices |
|---|---|---|---|---|
| | July | | | |
| FRONT LINE. | 17 | | In Front Line. Casualties; Wounded 5 O.R.. | |
| | 18 | | do. Casualties; N I L . | |
| | 19 | | do. Casualties; Killed 1 O.R., Wounded 3 O.R.. | |
| | 20 | | do. Casualties; Wounded 1 O.R.. | |
| | 21 | | do. Casualties; Killed 1 O.R., Wounded 2 O.R.. | |
| | 22 | | do. Casualties; Killed 1 O.R., Wounded 8 O.R.. | |
| | 23 | | do. Casualties; Wounded 2 O.R.. | |
| | 24 | | Relieved by 18th K.R.R.C. and moved to CARNARVON CAMP, near WESTOUTRE. Casualties; Killed 3 O.R., Wounded 4 O.R. | |
| CARNARVON CAMP. | 25 | | At Carnarvon Camp. Casualties; Killed 1 O.R., Wounded 1 Officer, 2 O.R.. | |
| | 26 | | do. Casualties; N I L . | |
| | 27 | | do. Casualties; N I L . | |
| | 28 | | do. Casualties; N I L . | |
| | 29 | | do. Casualties; N I L . | |
| | 30 | | Entrained at Wippenhoek Station, detrained at St.Omer, and marched to TATINGHEM. Casualties; N I L . | |
| TATINGHEM. | 31 | | At Tatinghem. Casualties; N I L . | |

J.W. Parish
Lt-Colonel,
Commanding, 1/15th Battalion London Regiment,
(P.W.O. CIVIL SERVICE RIFLES.)

A/53

A5834 Wt. W4973/M687 750,000 8/16 D. D. & L. Ltd. Forms/C.2118/13.

SECRET. Copy No....5....

# 140th INFANTRY BRIGADE.

## Operation Order No. 184.

12th July 1917.

1. The 15th Bn London Regt will relieve the 7th Bn London Regt. and the 6th Bn London Regt. will relieve the 8th Bn London Regt. in the right and left front trenches respectively on the night of the 14th/15th July, under arrangements to be made between Os.C. Battalions.

2. Relieving Units will take over works programmes of units relieved and will be responsible for work on the night of relief.

3. The 8th and 7th Bns London Regt. will on relief withdraw to the positions in support now occupied by the 6th and 15th Bns London Regt. respectively, and will take over the working parties found by the Support Battalions from and including the night of relief.

4. Troops in the GREEN and BLACK LINES can only be relieved after dark. Troops in rear of the BLACK LINE can be relieved by daylight in small parties.

5. Receipts will be given for trench stores taken over, and copies will be forwarded to Brigade Headquarters by 6 pm on the 15th instant.

6. Completion of relief will be at once reported to Brigade Headquarters - Code word NUFFSAID.

ACKNOWLEDGE.

[signature]
Captain,
A/Brigade Major,
140th Infantry Brigade.

Issued to Signals ...7.45pm...

| | |
|---|---|
| Copy No. 1. File. | Copy No. 11. 141st Inf. Bde. |
| " 2. War Diary. | " 12. 58th Inf. Bde. |
| " 3. G.O.C. | " 13. Staff Captain. |
| " 4. 6th Bn London Regt. | " 14. B.T.C. |
| " 5. 7th Bn London Regt. | " 15. Intelligence Offr. |
| " 6. 8th Bn London Regt. | " 16. St. ELOI Group. |
| " 7. 15th Bn London Regt. | " 17. Oosthoek Group. |
| " 8. 140th Machine Gun Coy. | " 18. Battle Wood Group. |
| " 9. 140th Trench Mortar Batty. | " 10. 517th Coy. R.E. |
| " 10. 47th Division. | " 20. 520th Coy. R.E. |

Copy No. 21. 47th Div. Signals.
" 22. Signal Officer.

SECRET. COPY No. 14

## 1/15th Battalion London Regt.

## ORDER No. 71.

Reference Map: WYTSCHAETE 1/10000. *July 17 1/15 London*

1. The Battalion will relieve the 7th Battalion on the night of 14th/15th July in the right front trenches.
2. A Coy will relieve C Coy, 7th Battalion in the Green and Black lines.

| | | | |
|---|---|---|---|
| B | " " " | B " " " | in O.G.1 |
| C | " " " | D " " " | in O.B.1 |
| D | " " " | A " " " | in OAK RESERVE |

3. B, C & D Coys will relieve in daylight, moving in that order by half platoons at 100 yds distance. The leading half platoon of B Coy will move off at 7.0 p.m. Guides will be met at the MOUND CRATER O.2.d.4.6 at 7.15 p.m.
4. A Coy, together with two Lewis Guns of C Coy and one Lewis Gun of B Coy will move off at 9.0 p.m. by ½ platoons at 100 yds distance and will pick up Guides at 7th Battalion H.Q. at 10.0 p.m.

   H.Q. Coy will follow A Coy.
5. One officer and one senior N.C.O. per Coy will go up in advance to take over stores etc.
6. Receipts for trench stores will be forwarded to H.Q. by 9.0 a.m. on the 15th inst.
7. Packs will not be taken into the trenches, but will be stacked with dixies and boxes for the transport limbers at the Ration Dump at 5.0 p.m.
8. Rations for the 15th inst. will be distributed before the Battalion moves.
9. [illegible] will be carried up by hand, and one dixie per Coy will be taken to cook-house in O.B.1, under arrangements to be made by the Sergeant Master Cook.
10. Relief complete will be reported by Second Army Trench Code.

ACKNOWLEDGE.

H. Davenport
2/Lieut. & A/Adjutant.
1/15th Battalion London Regt.

COPY No. 1. Brigade
2. C.O.
3. H.Q. Mess
4. O.C. "A" Coy.
5. " "B" "
6. " "C" "
7. " "D" "
8. " "H.Q." "
9. Lewis Gun Officer
10. Bombing Officer
11. Q.M. & T.O.
12. R.S.M.
13. Sgt. Mr. Cook.
14. 7th Bn. London Regt
15. File.
16. Intelligence Officer

Vol 26

140/47

# WAR DIARY.

1/15th Batt. London Regt
(P.W.O. Civil Service Rifles)

AUGUST, 1917.

H/785.

Army Form C. 2118.

Instructions regarding War Diaries and Intelligence Summaries are contained in F. S. Regs., Part II. and the Staff Manual respectively. Title pages will be prepared in manuscript.

# WAR DIARY
*or*
~~INTELLIGENCE SUMMARY~~.
*(Erase heading not required.)*

| Place | Date 1917. | Hour | Summary of Events and Information | Remarks and references to Appendices |
|---|---|---|---|---|
| | August. | | | |
| TATINGHEM. | 1. | | At Tatinghem. Casualties; Nil. | |
| | 2. | | do. do. | |
| | 3. | | do. do. | |
| | 4. | | do. do. | |
| | 5. | | Battalion carried out Musketry practices on "A" Range, near TILQUES. Casualties; Nil. | |
| | 6. | | Inter-platoon Musketry Competition on "A" Range, near TILQUES. No. 10 Platoon was the winning platoon with average individual score of 66. | |
| | 7. | | At Tatinghem. Casualties; Nil. | |
| | 8. | | do. do. | |
| | 9. | | do. do. | |
| | 10. | | Firing practices carried out on "C" Range, CORMETTE. Casualties; 1 O.R. Accidentally wounded. | |
| MORINGHEM. | 11. | | Marched to Moringhem. Casualties; Nil. | Operation Order No.73 |
| | 12. | | Battalion Church Parade. Casualties; Nil. | |
| | 13. | | Marched past Brigadier General of 142nd Infantry Brigade. Casualties; Nil. | |
| | 14. | | Fired on "A" Range near TILQUES during the morning. Inspected by General Sir H.C.O. PLUMER, G.C.M.G.,G.C.V.O.,K.C.B.,A.D.C., Commanding Second Army. Casualties; Nil. | |

A5834 Wt. W4973/M687 750,000 8/16 D. D. & L. Ltd. Forms/C.2118/13.

Army Form C. 2118.

Instructions regarding War Diaries and Intelligence Summaries are contained in F. S. Regs., Part II. and the Staff Manual respectively. Title pages will be prepared in manuscript.

# WAR DIARY
*or*
# INTELLIGENCE SUMMARY.

*(Erase heading not required.)*

| Place | Date | Hour | Summary of Events and Information | Remarks and references to Appendices |
|---|---|---|---|---|
|  | August. |  |  |  |
| TATINGHEM. | 15. |  | Marched to TATINGHEM and took over old billets. Casualties; Nil. | Operation Order No.74 |
|  | 16. |  | Training at Tatinghem. Casualties; Nil. |  |
|  | 17. |  | do. do. |  |
|  | 18. |  | do. do. |  |
|  | 19. |  | Brigade Church Service at LONGUENESSE. Casualties; Nil. |  |
|  | 20. |  | Battalion inspected by Brigadier General Commanding 140th Infantry Brigade. Casualties; Nil. |  |
|  | 21. |  | Training. Casualties; Nil. |  |
|  | 22. |  | 140th Infantry Brigade inspected by General Sir H.C.O. PLUMER, G.C.M.G.,G.C.V.O.,K.C.B.,A.D.C., Commanding Second Army. Casualties; Nil. |  |
|  | 23. |  | At Tatinghem. Casualties; Nil. |  |
| VANCOUVER CAMP. | 24. |  | Battalion moved by bus to VANCOUVER CAMP, near VLAMERTINGHE. Casualties; Nil. | Operation Order No.75. |
|  | 25 |  | At Vancouver Camp. Casualties; Nil. |  |
|  | 26. |  | do. do. |  |
|  | 27. |  | do. do. |  |
|  | 28. |  | do. do. |  |
|  | 29. |  | do. do. |  |
|  | 30. |  | do. do. |  |
|  | 31. |  | do. do. |  |

Lt-Colonel,
Commanding, 1/10th Battalion London Regiment,
(P.W.O. CIVIL SERVICE RIFLES.)

A5834 Wt. W4973/M687 750,000 8/16 D. D. & L. Ltd. Forms/C.2118/13.

W. Dury

SECRET.                                                  COPY NO. 14..

# CIVIL SERVICE RIFLES.

## OPERATION ORDER NO. [illegible]3.

Reference; HAZEBROUCK 5A. 1/100,000

10th August, 1917.

1. The Battalion will march from its present Billets in Tatinghem via Zudausques to Billets in Meringhem, Petit Difques, and Grand Difques tomorrow, 11th August, 1917.

2. The Battalion will parade in full marching order with helmets on packs on the Transport Field at 2.55 p.m.

3. A Billeting Party of one N. C. O. per Company and one for Battalion Headquarters, will report to 2/Lt. P. Fallon at Battalion Headquarters at 8 30 a.m. The party will proceed to Boisdinghem and report to the Staff Captain of the 142nd Infantry Brigade at 10.0 a.m. at the Area Commandant's Office. Cycles can be obtained from the Signalling Officer.

4. Officers valises will be ready for collection by Transport at 12.0 noon. Cookers and mess boxes, limit two per Company, will be ready to be fetched by the Transport at 1.30 p.m.

(Sd) [illegible] Davenport

2/Lt. and A/Adjutant,
CIVIL SERVICE RIFLES.

Usual Distribution.

S E C R E T.

CIVIL SERVICE RIFLES.

ORDER No. 74.

14th August, 1917.

1. The Battalion will move to TATINGHEM tomorrow. Each Company will occupy its old billets.

2. The Battalion will parade in full marching order on the MORINGHEM - BARSINGHEM road, ready to move off at [illegible] p.m. Head of Battalion will be at Battalion Headquarters. Order of march will be : Band, B. D. A. H.Q. C. Companies.

3. Transport will be formed up in the road ready to follow the Battalion as it passes.

4. All officers' valises and boxes for G.S. Wagons will be ready for collection by the Transport Officer at 12-0 noon. Light mess boxes for the Mess Cart will be ready for collection at 1-0 p.m.

5. Lewis Guns will be loaded on to limbers by 9-0 a.m.

6. Teas will be cooked on the march and will be ready on arrival at TATINGHEM.

[illegible]

2/Lt. & A/Adjutant,
CIVIL SERVICE RIFLES.

Copy No. 1 Brigade.
" 2 C.O.
3 O.C. A Coy.
4 " B "
5 " C "
6 " D "
7 H.Q. Coy.
8 T.O. & Q.M.
9 R. S. M.
10 L. G.O.
11 Bombing Officer.
12 War Diary.
13 File.

SECRET

COPY No.

# CIVIL SERVICE RIFLES.

## ORDER No. 75.

1. Battalion will move by bus this afternoon to HALIFAX CAMP.

2. Battalion will parade in the road outside D Coy. billet facing ST. MARTIN at 12.45 p.m.
Order of march will be:- H.Q. D. B. A. C.

3. Buses, each holding 25 are allotted as follows:

| | | |
|---|---|---|
| Battn. Headquarters | | No. 33 |
| Orderly Room, Police and R.S.M. | – | 34 |
| H.Q. Company | – | 35 – 39 |
| D " | – | 40 – 44 |
| B " | – | 45 – 49 |
| A " | – | 50 – 54 |
| C " | – | 55 – 59 |
| Cooks & ~~[illegible]~~ mess boxes | | 60 |

Officers will distribute themselves among the buses of their Companies.

4. Further orders will be issued for collection of dinners and mess boxes.

Davenport

2/Lt. and A/Adjutant
CIVIL SERVICE RIFLES.

Copy No. 1 A Coy.
2 B "
3 C "
4 D "
5 Coy.
6 File.

140/47

8/55

1/15 Batt. London Regt.-

Vol 27

CIVIL SERVICE RIFLES

WAR DIARY

SEPTEMBER, 1917.-

Army Form C. 2118.

Instructions regarding War Diaries and Intelligence Summaries are contained in F. S. Regs., Part II. and the Staff Manual respectively. Title pages will be prepared in manuscript.

# WAR DIARY
*or*
# INTELLIGENCE SUMMARY.
*(Erase heading not required.)*

| Place | Date | Hour | Summary of Events and Information | Remarks and references to Appendices |
|---|---|---|---|---|
| | September | | | |
| VANCOUVER CAMP | 1 | | At VANCOUVER CAMP Casualties Nil. | |
| " | 2 | | do do do | |
| " | 3 | | do do do | |
| " | 4 | | do do do | |
| " | 5 | | do do do | |
| " | 6 | | do do do. | |
| CHATEAU SEGARD. | 7. | | Moved to CHATEAU SEGARD, relieving 8th Battalion Loyal North Lancs. Casualties Nil - | Order No. 76 att'd |
| " | 8 | | At CHATEAU SEGARD. Casualties, Nil | |
| IN SUPPORT | 9 | | Relieved 2nd South Lancs Battn in SUPPORT. - Casualties 3 O.R wounded. - | Order No 77 att'd |
| " | 10 | | In Support, Casualties, 4 O.R wounded. | |
| " | 11 | | do Casualties, Nil | |
| " | 12 | | do Casualties, 7 O.R wounded. | |
| " | 13 | | do Casualties Nil. | |
| | 14 | | do Casualties { 2/Lt E. G. Mendes (13th LONDON Regt attached) wounded; 2 O.R Killed; 6. O.R wounded. | |
| | 15 | | do Casualties { 2/Lt J. M. NORTHAM Killed, 2/Lt A.W. MELLISS wounded 9 O.R wounded. | |

Instructions regarding War Diaries and Intelligence Summaries are contained in F. S. Regs., Part II. and the Staff Manual respectively. Title pages will be prepared in manuscript.

# WAR DIARY
*or*
# INTELLIGENCE SUMMARY.
*(Erase heading not required.)*

Army Form C. 2118.

| Place | Date | Hour | Summary of Events and Information | Remarks and references to Appendices |
|---|---|---|---|---|
| CHATEAU SEGARD | 16 | | Relieved by 2nd Australian Infantry Battalion and moved to CHATEAU SEGARD Casualties 4. OR. wounded. | Order No. 78 attached |
| " | 17 | | At CHATEAU SEGARD Casualties. Nil | |
| STEENVOORDE | 18 | | Moved to STEENVOORDE Area, Casualties. Nil | |
| " | 19 | | At STEENVOORDE, Casualties Nil | |
| EECKE | 20 | | Moved to EECKE, Casualties Nil | |
| " | 21 | | At EECKE, Casualties. Nil | |
| FREVENT CAPELLE | 22 | | Entrained at CAESTRE. Detrained at AUBIGNY and marched to billets at FREVENT CAPELLE – Casualties. Nil. | |
| | 23. | | At FREVENT CAPELLE – Casualties Nil. | |
| AUBREY CAMP | 24 | | Moved to AUBREY CAMP near ROCLINCOURT, Casualties, Nil | Order No. 79 att |
| FRONT LINE | 25 | | Relieved DRAKE Battalion in front line trenches at GAVRELLE – Casualties Nil. | " 80 " |
| " | 26 | | In Front Line, Casualties Nil | |
| | 27 | | do do | |
| | 28 | | do do | |

Instructions regarding War Diaries and Intelligence Summaries are contained in F. S. Regs., Part II. and the Staff Manual respectively. Title pages will be prepared in manuscript.

# WAR DIARY
*or*
# INTELLIGENCE SUMMARY.
(*Erase heading not required.*)

Army Form C. 2118.

| Place | Date | Hour | Summary of Events and Information | Remarks and references to Appendices |
|---|---|---|---|---|
| FRONT LINE | 29 | | In Front Line, Casualties Nil | |
| | 30 | | do do | |

E Legrave Lt Colonel
Cdg 1/15 Batt London Regiment
(PWO Civil Service Rifles)

T2134. Wt. W708—776. 500000. 4/15. Sir J. C. & S.

SECRET. COPY NO. 10

# CIVIL SERVICE RIFLES.

## ORDER NO.78.

Reference Map
Sheet 28 N.W. 1/20,000.

7th September, 1917.

1. Battalion will relieve 8th Battalion Loyal North Lancs Regt. in CHATEAU SEGARD area tomorrow in accordance with the following time table:-

| | | | | | | | |
|---|---|---|---|---|---|---|---|
| A. Coy | will | move | off | at | | 9.45 | a.m. |
| B. " | " | " | " | " | | 10.45 | " |
| C. " | " | " | " | " | | 11.45 | " |
| D. " | " | " | " | " | | 2.0 | p.m. |
| H.Q. " | " | " | " | " | | 3.0 | " |

2. Companies will move by platoons at 100 yards distance.

3. Officers valises and heavy mess boxes will be dumped in the Guard Room by 10.0 a.m. ready for collection by Transport Officer.

4. Light Mess Boxes and Medical Stores will be dumped at C. Company's cooker ready for collection by the Transport Officer at 11.0 a.m. B. and C. Coy's Cookers and Lewis Gun Limbers will be ready at the same time

5. Packs of N. C. O.s and men will be taken to Q. M. Stores tonight in accordance with verbal instructions given to Company Commanders.

6. Each Company will draw 1 Very Gun 1½" and 2 Very Pistols 1" from R. S. M. tonight.

[signature]

2/Lt. and A/Adjutant,
CIVIL SERVICE RIFLES.

Copy. No. 1 File.
2 O. C. A. Coy.
3 " B. "
4 " C. "
5 " D. "
6 Lewis Gun Officer.
7 Signalling Officer.
8 Transport Officer.
9 Quartermaster.
10 War Diary.
11 140th Infantry Brigade, for information

SECRET. Copy No. 10

# CIVIL SERVICE RIFLES

## ORDER No. 77.

8th Sept 1917.

Reference; Map Sheet 28 1/20,000 or ZILLEBEKE 10,000

1. Battalion will relieve 3 Companies of the 2nd South Lancs Battn in SUPPORT tomorrow, as follows –

A Coy relieves D Coy 2nd S. Lancs
C " " C " " "
D " " B " " "

B Company will occupy trenches in O.B.1 in ZOUAVE WOOD. One platoon of A Company together with the Band and a party of H.Q. Coy already detailed will be accommodated in HALFWAY HOUSE.

2. Companies will move off in the following order, starting at 3-0 p.m.:–

A. H.Q. C. D. B. Party for HALFWAY HOUSE will follow in rear of B Company.

3. All movements by day will be by parties of 10 at 70 yards interval. Route to be followed is via SHRAPNEL CORNER and WARRINGTON ROAD.

4. Guides from the 2nd South Lancs Battn will be at HALFWAY HOUSE at 5-0 p.m.

5. Work policy of 2nd South Lancs will be taken over and continued.

6. Copies of receipts for Trench Stores will be sent to Battn. H.Q. by 9.0 p.m.

7. Mess boxes and Medical Stores will be loaded on to the mess limbers at 3.0 p.m. One servant per Coy may march with the limbers which, with the Lewis Gun limbers, will leave at 4.0 p.m. to join the ration limbers. All limbers will unload at HOOGE Camp at 6.30 p.m. All Coys. will send their own carrying parties to this Camp immediately on arrival in the trenches.

8. Relief complete will be reported by runner.

2/Lt & A/Adjutant.
CIVIL SERVICE RIFLES.

Copy No. 1 A Coy
2 B "
3 C "
4 D "
5 T.O.&Q.M.
6 Signals
7 C.O.
No. 8 140 Inf Bde
9 2nd S. Lancs
10 File
11 War Diary

2

to the ration dump, where they will be collected by the transport at 4.20 p.m. One man per team will be left in charge at the dump and will march with the limbers.

7 Receipts for trench stores, maps etc. will be handed into the Orderly Room on arrival at the next camp. All maps except Sheet 28 N.W. will be handed over.
Petrol cans will be handed over and receipts taken.
O.C. D Coy. will arrange to have the 20 boxes of biscuits (iron rations) taken to the Ration Dump and loaded on limbers by 1.0 p.m.

8 Code word for relief will be Coy. Commanders name.

Copy No. 1. O.C. A Coy. (Sd.) R. Davenport 2/Lt
2 B
3 C
4 D
5 Sigs.
6 T.O. & Q.M.
7 140 Infy Bde
8 File
9 War Diary

a/Adjt

SECRET. CIVIL SERVICE RIFLES. COPY NO. 9.

ORDER. NO. 78.

13th Sept. 1917.

Reference Maps Sheet 28 1/40,000.

1 Bn will be relieved by the 2nd Australian Infy Bn to-morrow.
• 3 Platoons A Coy and 2 Platoons C in IGNORANCE TRENCH will be relieved by
• A Coy and 1 Platoon C Coy.
B Coy will be relieved by B Coy

2 One guide per platoon and one for H.Q. will report to 2/Lt ILLING at B Coy H.Q. in ZOUAVE TRENCH at 12.15 p.m. they will meet incoming platoons at HALFWAY HOUSE at 1-0 p.m.

3 On relief platoons will march to Camp vacated by 2nd Australian Battn in DICKEBUSCH – CHATEAU SEGARD AREA. Guides from Battn. details will meet platoons at CAFE BELGE.

4 Movement will be by parties of 10 at 50 yards distance.

5 Dixies and mess boxes, medical stores, will be ready at the ration dump for collection by transport at 1-0 p.m. One servant per Coy will march with the limbers.

6 On relief, Lewis Guns will be taken

## APPENDIX I

### Action of 6th Battalion London Regt

The 6th Batt London Regiment [illegible] in depth on a frontage of [illegible] on left of 15th Battalion. They were to capture [illegible] [illegible] of [illegible] of [illegible] the [illegible]. The first at the same time as [illegible] the [illegible] first objective [illegible] at the same time as the 15 Batt [illegible] objective.

They were then to capture by [illegible] [illegible] following [illegible] OPAL TRENCH and OPAL SUPPORT [illegible] [illegible] second objective [illegible] OPAL RESERVE [illegible] minutes.

Q.Y. No 13

[illegible] London Regiment

ORDER No 60.

3rd June 1917

[illegible]
[illegible]

1. The [illegible] Division will co-operate on Z day in an attack by Second Army against MESSINES - WYTSCHAETE Ridge.

2. (a) The [illegible] Infantry Brigade will attack immediately South of [illegible] CANAL. Brigade boundaries are shown by continuous brown line on attached map "A".
(b) The [illegible] Brigade will attack on Right.
The [illegible] Division will attack on Right.

3. The [illegible] Brigade attack will be divided into two phases.
(a) 1st Phase
Attacking force :- 7th and 8th Battalions.
Final Objective :- [illegible] LINE on Map "A".
(b) 2nd Phase
Attacking force :- 6th and 15th Battalions.
Final Objective :- BLACK LINE on Map "A".

4. Boundary between 7th and 8th Battalions and 6th and 15th Battalions are shown dotted in brown [illegible] on Map "A".

5. (a) Attack of 7th and 8th Battalions (1st Phase) will be [illegible], and both Battalions will [illegible] BLUE LINE by [illegible] + 60 minutes.
(b) Attack of 6th and 15th Battalions (2nd Phase) will take place [illegible]

6. Objectives of 15th Battalion are shown on attached [illegible]
1st Objective :- Green Line ([illegible])
2nd Objective :- Red Line ([illegible] TRENCH)
[illegible] Objective :- Black Line ([illegible])

7. BARRAGE [illegible] There will be [illegible] barrages, [illegible] and [illegible] of Stationary Barrage.
(a) [illegible]
(b) [illegible]
(c) [illegible]

[illegible]

[illegible] Objective at 1 [illegible] 45 minutes

[illegible] 3 hours 40 minutes to a line [illegible] between 1st and 2nd [illegible]

[illegible] to 2nd Objective

[illegible] 2 hours 44 minutes [illegible] to 3rd Objective

[illegible] 3 hours 52 minutes [illegible] to a line 200

[illegible] hours 5 minutes [illegible]

[illegible] 3rd Objective [illegible] to a line

[illegible] 9 minutes

[illegible] 3rd Objective

[illegible] with the [illegible]

[illegible] will be organised in depth [illegible]

D. B. C. A. Companies

[illegible] be carried out [illegible]

[illegible] The attack [illegible]

[illegible] Platoons of D Coy [illegible] one platoon [illegible]

Platoons of B Coy

[illegible] C

[illegible] A

[illegible] Platoons of D Coy

[illegible] Platoons of [illegible]

[illegible]

3

(contd)

Platoon of D Coy [illegible] through the 1st Objective [illegible] behind the creeping barrage and taking [illegible] of O.K. & 38 [illegible] the barrage [illegible]

[illegible] will account for wave in [illegible] waves and will [illegible] up 1st objective [illegible] will take 2nd objective

[illegible] will take third objective. [illegible] of [illegible] between second and third [illegible] defensive flank [illegible]

[illegible] will follow the wave [illegible] 1st objective and will [illegible]

[illegible] will be [illegible] the [illegible] along the [illegible] of communication [illegible] trenches.

11. (a) Before Zero [illegible] Battalion will be [illegible] WEST TERRACE [illegible] permits [illegible] Zero [illegible] ESTAMINET.

(b) As soon as [illegible] move forward [illegible] will [illegible] British Front Line.

1st and 2nd Waves in British Support Line.

3rd & 4th [illegible] in British [illegible] para. 12

[illegible] shown in [illegible] barrage [illegible] British

(c) Should [illegible] British Front Line [illegible] from any [illegible] of British Front Line [illegible]

[illegible] para. 12.

12. Advance will be carried out as follows:–

| Unit | [illegible] | [illegible] | [illegible] |
|---|---|---|---|
| [illegible] | 4 Waves [illegible] | [illegible] | [illegible] |

[illegible] detailed

0 5

[illegible] flank along OBLONG [illegible]

[illegible] This will be effected [illegible]

[illegible]

by the enemy

[illegible]

[illegible] TRENCH [illegible]

[illegible] WEST TRENCH [illegible]

[illegible] as soon as possible [illegible]

[illegible] RESERVE.

[illegible] TRENCH [illegible]

[illegible]

SECRET.

COPY NO. 1

CIVIL SERVICE RIFLES.

ORDER NO. 79.

23rd September, 1917.

Reference Map:- Sheet 51B N.W.

1. Reveille to-morrow will be at 6.0 a.m. Breakfast 7.0 a.m.

2. The Battalion will relieve 24th Battalion to-morrow in AUBREY CAMP G.4.a. via ACQ - ECOIVRES - ECURIE.

3. The Battalion will parade in column of route in the main road at 8.55 a.m. Head of column to be outside Battalion H.Q. Order of march will be :- Band, H.Q. A. B. C. D.

4. Billeting Parties consisting of C.Q.M.S' will parade in full marching order under 2/Lt. SOUTER at Battalion H. Q. at 8.0 a.m.

5. Valises and all mess boxes will be dumped in the main road opposite Company Headquarters (D. coy. outside Battalion H.Q.) at 8.15 a.m. Cookers will be ready for collection at the same time.

[signature]

2/Lt. and A/Adjutant,
CIVIL SERVICE RIFLES.

Copy No. 1 War Diary.
2 File.
3. C. O.
4 O.C. A Coy.
5. B
6 C
7 D
8 Signals.
9 T. O. & Q.M.
10 L.G.O.

SECRET. COPY NO.....

## CIVIL SERVICE RIFLES.

## ORDER NO. 80.

Reference Map, 51B N.W.
1/20,000

24th September, 1917.

1. The Battalion will relieve DRAKE Battalion tomorrow on the right of XIIIth Corps front. Each Company will relieve same letter company of DRAKE Battalion.

2. Battalion will move off at 8.45 a.m. in following order:-

   D. B. A. C. H. Q. Companies.

   Route will be by cross country track to ROCLINCOURT thence via CHANTECLER to fork roads at H. 1. A. 9. 3. Guides will be met at end of trench board track on railway at H. 1. B. 8. 8. at 10.0 a.m. Movement will be by companies at 200 yards intervals.

3. Fighting Order will be worn with filled water bottles. Packs will be taken to Q. M. Stores by 8.0 a.m.

4. Advance parties of one officer and C. S. M. per company will report to DRAKE Battalion Headquarters at 8.0 a.m. to take over trench stores etc.

5. Copies of receipts for trench stores, maps and aeroplane photographs will be sent to Battalion Headquarters by 8.0 p.m. Dispositions will be reported at the same time.

6. Code word for relief complete will be Company Commanders name.

7. One pair of dirty socks for every N. C. O. and man will be handed to Q. M. at 8.0 a.m. Socks should be made up in bags by platoons and clearly labelled. Numbers handed in will be reported to Battalion Headquarters by 6.0 p.m.

8. All officers valises and heavy mess boxes will be dumped at Q. M. Stores by 8.0 a.m. Light Mess boxes outside Guard Room at same time.

9. Lewis Gun Limbers and Mess Cart will move off at 9.15 a.m. two men per team marching with them. They will be unloaded at the point where trench board track enters trench.

Davenport.
2/Lt. and A/Adjutant,
CIVIL SERVICE RIFLES.

Copy No. 1 War Diary.
2 File.
3 C. O.
4 O. C. A. Coy.
5 " B. "
6 " C. "
7 " D. "
8 Signals
9 T. O. and Q. M.
10 L. G. O.
11 Brigade.
12 DRAKE Battalion.

Missing Oct '17 - Jan '18

CONFIDENTIAL

WAR DIARY

OF

1/15th BATTALION LONDON REGIMENT (P.W.O. CIVIL SERVICE RIFLES.

FEBRUARY 1918.

1.

Instructions regarding War Diaries and Intelligence Summaries are contained in F. S. Regs., Part II. and the Staff Manual respectively. Title pages will be prepared in manuscript.

# WAR DIARY
*or*
# INTELLIGENCE SUMMARY.
*(Erase heading not required.)*

Army Form C. 2118.

| Place | Date | Hour | Summary of Events and Information | Remarks and references to Appendices |
|---|---|---|---|---|
| | 1918. February | | | |
| BERTINCOURT. | 1st | | The right section of the left subsector of the Divisional sector was reconnoitred today preparatory to relieving the 24th Battalion London Regt tomorrow. | |
| | | | Ration strength. 23 Officers. 654 OR's. | EJW. |
| | | | Trench strength. 22 Officers. 536 OR's. | |
| | 2nd | | At 8.45am this morning the Battalion paraded to bid farewell to the remnants of the 6th 7th + 8th Battns who leave the Division today owing to the reduction of the Division from 12 to 9 Battns. | |
| | | | This afternoon the Battn left BERTINCOURT in motor lorries to proceed up the line to relieve the 24th Battalion London Regt in the right Battalion front of the left Brigade. | |
| | | | Right Boundary L.13.c.7.7. Left Boundary K.18.b.5.4 | |
| | | | DISPOSITIONS. A. Coy Right front line | EJW. |
| | | | B. Coy. Left front line | |
| | | | C. Coy Right support. | |
| | | | D. Coy Left support. | |
| | | | Battn H.Q. K.24.b.3.8. | |

A6945 Wt. W11422/M1160 350,000 12/16 D. D. & L. Forms/C./2118/14.

Instructions regarding War Diaries and Intelligence Summaries are contained in F. S. Regs., Par. II. and the Staff Manual respectively. Title pages will be prepared in manuscript.

Army Form C. 2118.

# WAR DIARY
*or*
# INTELLIGENCE SUMMARY.
*(Erase heading not required.)*

| Place | Date | Hour | Summary of Events and Information | Remarks and references to Appendices |
|---|---|---|---|---|
| | 1918. February | | | |
| FLESQUIERES. | 2 | | COMPANY DISPOSITIONS. A Coy. Right front line. | |
| | | | 2 platoons front line 4 Lewis Guns by day. 5 Lewis Guns by night. | |
| | | | 2 platoons. Gunpits L.13.d.4.2. Coy H.Q. L.13.c.2.4. | |
| | | | C. Coy Right support. | |
| | | | 2 platoons. dugouts in sunken road L.13.c.2.4. | |
| | | | 2 platoons in ~~SUPPORT L.19.a.4.7.~~ in houses K.24.b.45.90. Coy H.Q. L.13.c.2.4. | EYW. |
| | | | B. Coy Left front line. | |
| | | | 2 platoons + 4 Lewis Guns front line | |
| | | | 2 platoons. Gunpits K.18.d.8.6 Coy H.Q. house K.18.d.55.30. | |
| | | | D. Coy Left support Coy. | |
| | | | 3 platoons CATACOMBS K.18.c.7.4. | |
| | | | 1 platoon in house K.18.d.4.3. | |
| | | 9 pm | Relief complete. | |
| | 3rd | | A quiet day. This evening we took over from the 19th Battn the line up to STATION AVENUE L.13.d.4.2. The 21st Battn took over our left post & our left boundary is at K.18.b.7.3. | EYW. |

A6945 Wt. W11422/M1160 350,000 12/16 D. D. & L. Forms/C./2118/14.

Instructions regarding War Diaries and Intelligence Summaries are contained in F. S. Regs., Part II. and the Staff Manual respectively. Title Pages will be prepared in manuscript.

# WAR DIARY
*or*
# INTELLIGENCE SUMMARY

*(Erase heading not required.)*

Army Form C. 2118.

| Place | Date | Hour | Summary of Events and Information | Remarks and references to Appendices |
|---|---|---|---|---|
| FLESQUIERES | 1918. February 4th | | A quiet day. Very little artillery activity on our front, but during the night the enemy shelled the village intermittently.<br>Reinforcement 16 ORS. | E.W. |
| | 5th | | Between 4.am. & 7. am the enemy shelled the village & neighbouring trenches and at 6.10am he put down a barrage along ~~along~~ the front line support line & the village. The Barrage was particularly heavy in the neighbourhood of the BEETROOT FACTORY. The barrage line appears to be along front line. & along QUORN STREET, SHERWOOD SWITCH in square L.13.c, and CULL SUPPORT with a switch line between QUORN STREET & BEETROOT FACTORY. All was quiet again by 7.30 am.<br>An inter Company relief took place tonight. C Coy relieved A. D Coy relieved B Coy. On completion of relief B Coy H.Q. moved back to CATACOMBS & 1 platoon to CATACOMBS & 2 platoons moved out of them into dugout under the Church at K.18.c.7.4.<br>The Commanding Officer returned from RFC course tonight and assumed command.<br>Casualties 4. ORs wounded. | E.W. |

2449 Wt. W14957/M90 750,000 1/16 J.B.C. & A. Forms/C.2118/12.

4.

Instructions regarding War Diaries and Intelligence Summaries are contained in F. S. Regs., Part II. and the Staff Manual respectively. Title Pages will be prepared in manuscript.

# WAR DIARY
*or*
# INTELLIGENCE SUMMARY
*(Erase heading not required.)*

Army Form C. 2118.

| Place | Date | Hour | Summary of Events and Information | Remarks and references to Appendices |
|---|---|---|---|---|
| FLESQUIERES | 1918 Feby 6th | | During the day hostile artillery was normal. There was slight shelling in the vicinity of the BEET ROOT FACTORY in the morning. | |
| | | | In the afternoon there was considerable enemy aerial activity | E.J.W. |
| | | | In the evening hostile machine guns were very active on our front chiefly from the direction of ORIVAL WOOD & during the night the enemy fired burst of H.E. in this vicinity | |
| | | | Casualties 3. ORs. wounded. | E.J.W. |
| | | | Honours & Rewards. | |
| | | | His Majesty the King has approved the award of the BELGIAN CROIX DE GUERRE. to the undermentioned soldier:- | E.J.W. |
| | | | No 532585 Lance Corporal S. FLETCHER of the 1/15th London Regt. | |
| | 7th | | A dull day with poor visibility consequently artillery activity was small at 8 pm the enemy shelled the village & roads leading to it in the hope of catching ration limbers. | E.J.W. |
| | | | 2nd Lieut IVEY. rejoined the Battalion today from hospital. | |

2449 Wt. W14957/M90 750,000 1/16 J.B.C. & A. Forms/C.2118/12.

5/

Instructions regarding War Diaries and Intelligence Summaries are contained in F. S. Regs., Part II. and the Staff Manual respectively. Title Pages will be prepared in manuscript.

# WAR DIARY
or
# INTELLIGENCE SUMMARY

(Erase heading not required.)

Army Form C. 2118.

| Place | Date | Hour | Summary of Events and Information | Remarks and references to Appendices |
|---|---|---|---|---|
| FLESQUIERES | 1918. Febry 8th | | A quiet day very little activity of any kind except the 6" Stokes trench mortars who fired on targets during the night. At 7.10 pm the enemy shelled this village heavily for 15 minutes. The neighbourhood of the church receiving most attention. During the night the enemy shelled the village. There was an inter Coy relief tonight A Coy relieved C. B relieved D. Casualty 1 OR wounded | EJW |
| | 9th | | A very clear day with good visibility & the enemy shelled this village intermittently all day especially in the vicinity of the church where he scored a direct hit on one of the entrances beneath it causing the Strombos gas alarm to go off. The Lewis Gun post at L.13.a.50.00. was shelled by an 77m gun during the morning and the BEETROOT FACTORY received considerable attention. At about 9 pm bursts of H.E. were fired on the roads in the village & approaches. | EJW. |
| | 10th | | The enemy's artillery has been particularly active throughout the day. The village has been shelled intermittently. This afternoon our front line was shelled between the two Sunken roads & 3 direct hits were obtained | |

2449 Wt. W14957/M90 750,000 1/16 J.B.C. & A. Forms/C.2118/12.

6

Instructions regarding War Diaries and Intelligence Summaries are contained in F. S. Regs., Part II. and the Staff Manual respectively. Title pages will be prepared in manuscript.

# WAR DIARY
*or*
# INTELLIGENCE SUMMARY.
*(Erase heading not required.)*

Army Form C. 2118.

| Place | Date | Hour | Summary of Events and Information | Remarks and references to Appendices |
|---|---|---|---|---|
| FLESQUIERES | 1918 Feby. | | | |
| | 10th | | At 7.30 pm the enemy heavily shelled the village & all road and tracks leading to it also routes frequented by ration parties. It lasted about 30 minutes. Our ration parties were caught in it & had to scatter for safety. The enemy obtained direct hits on the left front line Coy's H.Q. killing the officers mess cook and on the house occupied by 1 platoon of the left support Coy at K.18.d.4.3. Casualty 1. OR. Killed. | E.W. |
| | 11th | | There was a considerable amount of promiscuous shelling today owing to clear visibility. The sunken road where A & C Coys H.Q are situated (L.13.c.15.25.) was shelled during the morning with 5.9s. There was intermittent shelling of back areas in the afternoon. There was an inter Coy relief tonight C Coy relieved A. D Coy relieved B Coy. Lt Shepherd late of the 1/6th Battn joined the Battalion tonight from leave. At 4.15 pm a British Tank was observed moving E along CAMBRAI ROAD under its own power. It stopped at K.16.b.50.15. | E.W. |

T2134. Wt. W708—776. 500000. 4/15. Sir J. C. & S.

7

Instructions regarding War Diaries and Intelligence Summaries are contained in F. S. Regs., Part II. and the Staff Manual respectively. Title pages will be prepared in manuscript.

# WAR DIARY
*or*
# INTELLIGENCE SUMMARY.
*(Erase heading not required.)*

Army Form C. 2118.

| Place | Date | Hour | Summary of Events and Information | Remarks and references to Appendices |
|---|---|---|---|---|
| | 1918. Febry | | | |
| FLESQUIERES | 12. | | A dull day with bad visibility therefore no artillery activity. For the first time for some days the enemy did not shell the village at night to catch rations coming up | E.K.W. |
| | 13 | | A wet & foggy day no activity during the day of any kind. This evening a party of 30 N.C.Os & men under 2nd Lieut BOYES left our line at 8pm to raid the small bit of trench running from L.13.a.5.6 to L.13.a.2.7. where it was known that the enemy were working with large parties at night. The night was so dark that gaps cut in our wire could not be found & the party had to climb through our wire. The going in no mans land was bad. The men could only just see each other at 2 paces interval. The advance was made in a single line with an N.C.O on either flank & 2 more distributed along the line. 2nd Lt BOYES walked in the right centre. On arrival at the trench it was found that parts of it had a line of low wire entanglement other parts only trip wire & yet other parts with no wire at all. On getting into the trench it was found to be empty with no signs of occupation. The party divided & went right and left. The trench was not continuous, but the dug parts varied in depth from 5ft to 2ft and was traversed. The party remained a quarter of an hour & then returned to our own line. | E.K.W. |

T2134. Wt. W708—776. 500000. 4/15. Sir J. C. & S.

8/

Instructions regarding War Diaries and Intelligence Summaries are contained in F. S. Regs., Part II. and the Staff Manual respectively. Title pages will be prepared in manuscript.

# WAR DIARY
*or*
# INTELLIGENCE SUMMARY.
*(Erase heading not required.)*

Army Form C. 2118.

| Place | Date | Hour | Summary of Events and Information | Remarks and references to Appendices |
|---|---|---|---|---|
| FLESQUIERES | 1918. July | | | |
| | 13. Cont. | | No artillery barrage was used for the raid but arrangements were made with the artillery to deal with certain points if necessary. | EJW. |
| | 14 | | At 5.30 am the enemy shelled the neighbourhood, the front line near the BEETROOT FACTORY receiving a good deal of attention as well as the village itself and all approaches. | |
| | | | This evening the 20th Battn relieved this Battalion, the 20th taking over as follows. | |
| | | | A Coy 20th relieving C Coy 15th in Right front line | |
| | | | D Coy " " D Coy 15th " Left front line | EJW. |
| | | | B Coy " " A Coy 15th " Right support. | |
| | | | C Coy " " B Coy 15th " Left support. | |
| | | | Relief complete at 12 midnight. | |
| | | | On completion of relief the Battalion marched to K.32.b.2.8. where it entrained for BERTINCOURT at 2.10 am. The journey took an abnormal length of time owing to congestion on the Rly and the Battalion eventually arrived in billets very tired and cold at 6.30 am. | |

T2134. Wt. W708—776. 500000. 4/15. Sir J. C. & S.

9.

Instructions regarding War Diaries and Intelligence Summaries are contained in F. S. Regs., Part II. and the Staff Manual respectively. Title pages will be prepared in manuscript.

# WAR DIARY
*or*
# INTELLIGENCE SUMMARY.
*(Erase heading not required.)*

Army Form C. 2118.

| Place | Date | Hour | Summary of Events and Information | Remarks and references to Appendices |
|---|---|---|---|---|
| | 1918. | | The principle features of this tour in the trenches were: | |
| | | | (1.) Every night our artillery harassed the enemy's communications villages + roads which provoked retaliation on the part of the enemy who shelled the roads by which the transport entered the village + the neighbourhood round Battn H.Q. where rations were dumped, as well as the village itself. | |
| | | | (2.) A considerable amount of work was carried out nightly on the front line by the Battalion and a company from the support Battn. The front line was deepened widened + a part trench boarded + when the Battn was relieved the front line was 5 ft deep along the whole length. About 200 yds of double apron fence wire was erected in front of the line where the wire was weakest, besides strengthening the existing wire. | |
| | | | (3.) Patrols were sent out nightly to visit specified localities + to locate the enemy. The patrols consisted of 1 Officer + 8 ORS. | |
| | | | (4.) There was very little activity on the whole with exception of the two enemy shoots in the early morning of the 5th + 14th insts + the shelling of the village at night to catch the rations. | |
| | | | (5.) The Battalion ran a very successful canteen in the line for the benefit of the Brigade | |

T2134. Wt. W708—776. 500000. 4/15. Sir J. C. & S.

10/

Instructions regarding War Diaries and Intelligence Summaries are contained in F. S. Regs., Part II. and the Staff Manual respectively. Title pages will be prepared in manuscript.

# WAR DIARY
*or*
# INTELLIGENCE SUMMARY.
*(Erase heading not required.)*

Army Form C. 2118.

| Place | Date | Hour | Summary of Events and Information | Remarks and references to Appendices |
|---|---|---|---|---|
| | 1918. Febry | | | |
| BERTINCOURT. | 16th. | | Reinforcements 4 officers (2nd Lts L. A. NUTBROWN. L. W. PICKARD. C. A. WILLMOTT. and H. J. GOLBY.) 102 O.R.S. | E.Y.W. |
| | 17th. | | There was an exceedingly successful Battalion concert tonight under the direction of Lieut MATHESON, at which the new Battalion orchestra performed for the first time, in the Follies theatre. This orchestra formed part of the band of the 6th Battalion who came to us when the 6th Battalion was disbanded. | E.Y.W. |
| | 18th. | | The Battalion paraded this morning + went up train to the GRAND RAVINE W^n TRESCAULT to work on the new Corps ~~line~~ Defence line. The work carried out was the erection of wire entanglements. | E.Y.W. |
| | 21st. | | Today the Brigade moved into Corps Reserve in the ETRICOURT area. This Battalion paraded at 11 am + marched to MANANCOURT arriving at 1 pm. The Battalion is billeted in huts which require a great deal of work to improve them. | E.Y.W. |

11/

Instructions regarding War Diaries and Intelligence Summaries are contained in F. S. Regs., Part II. and the Staff Manual respectively. Title pages will be prepared in manuscript.

# WAR DIARY
*or*
# INTELLIGENCE SUMMARY.
*(Erase heading not required.)*

Army Form C. 2118.

| Place | Date | Hour | Summary of Events and Information | Remarks and references to Appendices |
|---|---|---|---|---|
| | 1918. Feby | | | |
| MANANCOURT. | 23. | | Today we started company training after a Battalion parade. | EJW. |
| | 25. | | Company training continued which consisted of close order drill, musketry. physical training + Bayonet fighting<br>This afternoon the Battalion football team played the 2nd Divisional H.Q. team + beat them 5 goals to 4.<br>Lieut SEEBERT of the U.S.M.S. The M.O of this Battn left us and was replaced by Lieut M.W. ROBERTSON. of the U.S.M.S. | EJW. |
| | 26. | | B & C. Coys shot on the range today A & D. Coys carried out Coy training. | EJW. |
| | 27 | | This afternoon 300 men of the Battalion proceeded by train to the forward area for work in the Battle Zone. Half the party detrained at TRESCAULT (Q.10.a.0.4.) while the rest of the men went on to Q21.b.2.8. arriving at 6.30 pm. This party proceeded to the site on which the work was to be carried out which consisted of digging a new fire trench. The first party was sent for to join the latter but on the way the enemy opened a very heavy | EJW. |

T2134. Wt. W708—776. 500000. 4/15. Sir J. C. & S.

Instructions regarding War Diaries and Intelligence Summaries are contained in F. S. Regs., Part II. and the Staff Manual respectively. Title pages will be prepared in manuscript.

# WAR DIARY
*or*
# INTELLIGENCE SUMMARY.
*(Erase heading not required.)*

Army Form C. 2118.

| Place | Date | Hour | Summary of Events and Information | Remarks and references to Appendices |
|---|---|---|---|---|
| | 1918. Febry 27 | | Gas bombardment on the whole area. The party at once put on helmets & took cover in some artillery dugouts. The bombardment lasted for 1¾ hours. Very little work was carried out owing to the shelling & the party entrained at ~~[illegible]~~ 11. pm arriving in billets at 1 am. 28th inst. | |
| | | | Casualties 1. OR. Killed, 2 ORs wounded, 1 OR gassed. | |
| | | | Reinforcements. 1 Officer (2Lt BROAD) & 8 ORs. | |
| | 28 | | On inspection of the men out last night on the working party it was found that 63 men were suffering from the effects of the gas. Coy training & musketry on the range was carried out this morning. | |
| | | | During this period in Corps Reserve training was carried out as follows. | |
| | | | Close order Drill. Musketry. ~~At~~ grouping, application & rapid practices were carried out on the range. Physical training & Bayonet fighting. A special point was the training of specialists viz Lewis Gunners, Signallers & Scouts. | |
| | | | A large amount of work was carried out on improving the camp [illegible] provided for all the men. | |
| | | | In the German cemetery at RUYALCOURT the grave of No 2980 Private [illegible] on the 21.9.16 in German hands has been found. This is of particular intere[st] [illegible] | |

Army Form C. 2118.

Instructions regarding War Diaries and Intelligence Summaries are contained in F. S. Regs., Part II. and the Staff Manual respectively. Title pages will be prepared in manuscript.

# WAR DIARY
*or*
# INTELLIGENCE SUMMARY.
*(Erase heading not required.)*

| Place | Date | Hour | Summary of Events and Information | Remarks and references to Appendices |
|---|---|---|---|---|
| | | | Grave to be discovered of a man of this Regiment who has died as a prisoner. | |
| | | | All references to maps refer to.<br>PREMY. 1/10000 trench map.<br>MOEUVRES 1/20000 do.<br>Sheet 57.C. 1/40000. | |
| | | | Operation orders attached<br>No 101. 102. 103. | |
| | | | [illegible] Lt Col<br>Comd. 1/15 London Regt | |

SECRET.

Copy No 3

# CIVIL SERVICE RIFLES

## ORDER No 101.–

Reference map
Sheet 57c 1/40.000.–

2nd February 1918.

1. 15th Battn. will relieve 24th Battn in the right section. Left Sub sector. tonight. 2/3rd February.

2. Battalion will entrain at P.13 A.7.8. at 3.0 pm and detrain at P10. A.4.4.

3. Battalion will parade in column of fours ready to march off at junction of the BUS Road and CHURCH ST. i.e. rear C. Coy. billet at 2.40 pm.–

4. One guide per platoon and one for Headquarters will be met at the cross roads. TRESCAULT, Q10.a.4.4. at 5.30 pm.–

5. Disposition of Companies:–
A. Coy Right Front Line   B. Left Front Line
C. " Right Support   D. Left Support

6. Transport will take Lewis Guns to H.Q. where Companies will pick them up.–

7. All Trench Stores, aeroplane photographs, Defence Schemes, Work Schemes will be taken over of copies of receipts forwarded to Battalion H.Q. by 12.0 noon on the 3rd.

8. Code word for relief complete "SOCKS".–

A Whiteley Lieut & A/Adjutant
CIVIL SERVICE RIFLES.–

Copy No 1 C.O.
" 2 File
" 3 War Diary
4 O/C A. Coy.
5 " B. "
6 " C. "
7 " D. "
8 Signal
9 L.G.O
10 T.O. & Q.M.
11 140th Infantry Brigade (for information)
12 24th Battalion London Regt.

SECRET.

War diary

# CIVIL SERVICE RIFLES

## ORDER No. 102

13th February, 1917

Reference Map Sheet 57c.

1. 15th Battalion will be relieved to-morrow night 14th/15th Feby. 1918 by the 1/20th Battn. London Regiment, and will move to billets in BERTINCOURT in the area now occupied by the 18th Battalion.

2. Companies of the 15th Battn. will be relieved by Companies of the 20th Battalion as shown in table below:
Order of relief will be as follows: Left Front, Right Front, Left Support, Right Support, Headquarters.
Train arrangements are being made to convey Battalion from TRESCAULT to BERTINCOURT, further instructions later.
Coys. will move independently to entraining point, but at least 100 yards distance will be kept between Companies.

| Coy. 20th Battn. | Relieved by Coy 15th. | Guides. |
|---|---|---|
| A | C | * 1 per Platoon + 2 for H.Q. will be at cross-roads K 32 b 75 · 80 at 6·30 p.m. |
| D | D | |
| B | A | |
| C | B | |

* Guides will report at Battn. H.Q. to-morrow at 9-0 a.m. to reconnoitre the way to the cross roads. They will report to 2/Lt. W. L. IVEY.

3. All work, defence schemes, trench maps, aeroplane photo's etc., will be handed over and copies of receipts forwarded to the Orderly Room by noon, 15th inst.
Mess kits, Lewis Guns, surplus water cans etc., will be carried to the junction of SHERWOOD SWITCH with the FLESQUIERES – RIBECOURT ROAD, K 24 b 95.15. where the Transport will be waiting.
Each Company and H.Q. will hand over 8 water cans. The remainder will be sent down by the Transport.

4. Relief complete will be wired to Battn. H.Q. by the use of the Coy. Commanders name.

Usual distribution. A Whiteley
Lt. & a/Adjutant,
CIVIL SERVICE RIFLES

SECRET

War Diary

B.M. No. 3.

CIVIL SERVICE RIFLES

ORDER No 108.

Reference Map
Sheet 57c 1/20000.

20th February 1916.

1. 15th Battalion London Regiment will leave present billets and move to camp in [illegible] tomorrow. 21st. —

Head of column will pass starting point P.7.c.9.3 at 11.5 am

Route. — BUS — LECHELLE, Road junction at P.32 D.4.9. — Road junction V.8.a.7.6. thence road through V.7.D and V.13.b.

100 yards distance will be maintained between Companies.

2. Companies will parade in full marching order in column of route facing S. on BUS ROAD, head of column opposite end of Church Street ready to move off at 10.55 am.

Order of march

Cyclists, Band, HQ, A, B, C, D, Companies.

Transport will move 100 yards in rear of Battalion

3. Lewis Guns and Panniers will be loaded on limbers under supervision of the M. SOUTER by 10.0 am. Companies will arrange to send guns to Q.M. Stores by 10.30 am.

Cookers will be ready for collection by teams at 10.30 am.

4. Dinners will be cooked on route.

5. Officers Chargers for Bn HQ will be at Bn H.Q. at 10.45 am and for Companies at Coy. H.Q. at 10.30 am.

A. Whitehead
Lieut. & A/Adjt, Civil Service Rifles

Usual Distribution

47th Division

140th Infantry Brigade

Civil Service Rifles.

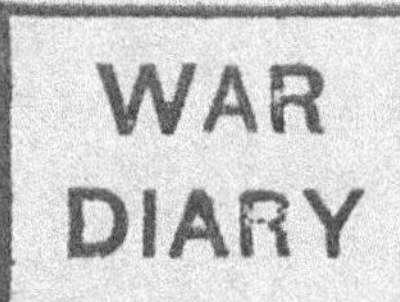


1/15th BATTALION

LONDON REGIMENT

MARCH 1 9 1 8

140/47

1/15 London Regt Vol 33

CIVIL SERVICE RIFLES.

# WAR DIARY.

MARCH, 1918.

Instructions regarding War Diaries and Intelligence Summaries are contained in F. S. Regs., Part II. and the Staff Manual respectively. Title pages will be prepared in manuscript.

# WAR DIARY
*or*
# ~~INTELLIGENCE SUMMARY.~~

(*Erase heading not required.*)

March 1918

Army Form C. 2118.

| Place | Date | Hour | Summary of Events and Information | Remarks and references to Appendices |
|---|---|---|---|---|
| MANANCOURT | 1 | | Battalion in camp. Company training. Brigade Tactical Scheme. Working party of 5 officers and 310 o.r. by night in forward area. | |
| | 2 | | A company on Range. B & C companies training. D company bathing at ETRICOURT. Battalion Concert at 7.30 pm. in Church Army Hut. | |
| | 3. | | Sunday. Usual services. No. 530827 L/Cpl. T. P. GREIG awarded M.M. in connection with the fighting at BOURLON and GRAINCOURT. Lt. C. M. KILNER took over command of B company | |

A5834 Wt. W4973/M687 750,000 8/16 D. D. & L. Ltd. Forms/C.2118/13.

2

Instructions regarding War Diaries and Intelligence Summaries are contained in F. S. Regs., Part II. and the Staff Manual respectively. Title pages will be prepared in manuscript.

# WAR DIARY
*or*
# INTELLIGENCE SUMMARY.
*(Erase heading not required.)*

Army Form C. 2118.

| Place | Date | Hour | Summary of Events and Information | Remarks and references to Appendices |
|---|---|---|---|---|
| | 4. | | Training & Musketry. Football & games | WS |
| | 5. | | Training & Musketry & Bathing. Football & games | WS |
| | 6. | | Training & Musketry. Bathing. Football & games | WS |
| | 7. | | Training & Musketry. Bathing. Football & games | WS |
| | 8. | | Training & Musketry. Bathing. Football & games | WS |
| | 9. | | Brigade Tactical Exercise (Attack). Brigade Gymkhana | WS |
| | 10. | | Sunday. Usual Services | WS |
| | 11. | | Rifle & Bayonet Competition (postponed). Football & games | WS |
| | 12. | | Training & Musketry. Bathing. Football & games<br>Capt. F.D. BALFOUR took over command of B company. | WS |
| | 13. | | Battn. attended Tank demonstration at HARLINCOURT<br>Capt. F.D. BALFOUR, Capt. P. FALLON, 2 Lt. W.E. HOSTE, 2 Lt. A. WILSON } awarded M.C. | WS |

A5834 Wt. W4973/M687 750,000 8/16 D. D. & L. Ltd. Forms/C.2118/13.

3

Instructions regarding War Diaries and Intelligence Summaries are contained in F. S. Regs., Part II. and the Staff Manual respectively. Title pages will be prepared in manuscript.

# WAR DIARY
*or*
# INTELLIGENCE SUMMARY.
*(Erase heading not required.)*

Army Form C. 2118.

| Place | Date | Hour | Summary of Events and Information | Remarks and references to Appendices |
|---|---|---|---|---|
| | 14. | | Divisional Tactical Scheme. | |
| | 15. | | Rifle & Bayonet Competition (postponed from 11th inst.) | |
| | 16. | | Working parties of 492 o.r. in forward area under R.E. | |
| | 17. | Sunday | Working parties of 470 o.r. in forward area under R.E. Evening services. | |
| | | | Anniversary of Battalion landing in France. | |
| | 18. | | Bathing. - Divisional Commander inspected Scouts and Observers at training. | |
| | | | <u>Celebration</u> of <u>Battn.</u> <u>landing</u> in <u>France</u> | |
| | | | Holy Communion 9.0 am | |
| | | | Commemoration Service 10.0 am | |
| | | | Concert & Sports 2.0 pm. | |

A5834 Wt. W4973/M687 750,000 8/16 D. D. & L. Ltd. Forms/C.2118/13.

4.

Army Form C. 2118.

Instructions regarding War Diaries and Intelligence Summaries are contained in F. S. Regs., Part II. and the Staff Manual respectively. Title pages will be prepared in manuscript.

# WAR DIARY
*or*
# ~~INTELLIGENCE SUMMARY.~~
*(Erase heading not required.)*

| Place | Date | Hour | Summary of Events and Information | Remarks and references to Appendices |
|---|---|---|---|---|
| ETRICOURT | 19. | 6.30pm. | Battalion left by train for trenches. | Ref. Maps 57 C |
| | | 8.30pm. | Arrived WINCHESTER VALLEY | |
| BEAUCAMP RIDGE | | | Relieved 1st Berkshire Regt. (2nd Div.) on BEAUCAMP RIDGE (support line) Quiet relief, completed at 11pm. LINCOLN RESERVE, Q18. Bn. H.Q. at Q18 c 5.3. | |
| | 20. | | Quiet day. Very little hostile shelling. 17th & 18th London Regts. in front line. | |
| | 21. | 4.30am | Heavy hostile bombardment, H.E. & gas shells. S.B.R.s worn for 6½ hours. Afternoon quiet. Casualties – 2 o.r. K.I.A. 38 o.r. wounded or gassed. During night 17th & 18th London Regts. fell back, leaving Battn. trench as front line. | |
| | 22. | | Bn. H.Q. moved to Q17 c 7.2 (140th Bde. H.Q.) | |
| | | 2.0am | Quiet morning on immediate front. Orders received to withdraw to DESSART RIDGE SWITCH with left on METZ - FINS road & right on V6 central | |

A5834 Wt. W4973/M687 750,000 8/16 D. D. & L. Ltd. Forms/C.2118/13.

5

Instructions regarding War Diaries and Intelligence Summaries are contained in F. S. Regs., Part II. and the Staff Manual respectively. Title pages will be prepared in manuscript.

# WAR DIARY
*or*
# ~~INTELLIGENCE SUMMARY.~~

(*Erase heading not required.*)

Army Form C. 2118.

| Place | Date | Hour | Summary of Events and Information | Remarks and references to Appendices |
|---|---|---|---|---|
| DESSART RIDGE | 23 | | Withdrawal successfully carried out & completed by dawn. | |
| | | | Disposition - left to right. A. B. C. D. | |
| | | | Bn. H.Q. in shed at bank at Q 31 a | |
| | | | In morning D company were in touch with enemy on their right at V. 6 a (approx.) | |
| | | 7.0am | In touch with enemy all along the line. | |
| | | 8.0am | Enemy made a determined bombing attack on right of D company & established M.G. posts which enfiladed Bn. positions. | |
| | | 9.0am | Large numbers of troops began to retire from (apparently) METZ SWITCH. These were rallied & led forward with H.Q. company of C.S.R. to a position along the ridge at Q 25 d. and Q 31 b. & d., facing East & at right angles to the DESSART SWITCH line. This was done to form a rallying line for retiring troops & a defensive flank to DESSART RIDGE SWITCH. Shortly after this enemy shelled Bn. H.Q. & the ridge behind & established other M.G. posts towards the left (S. & S.E. of METZ) | |
| | | 12.15 pm | Troops on left of this line retired, thus leaving our left flank exposed & necessitating withdrawal of C.S.R. H.Q. company to the VALLULART WOOD line. Remainder of the Bn. which was in the DESSART SWITCH line facing South continued the fight in the same position, forming a flank to the 3rd System which was now occupied by C.S.R. & also other troops. | |
| | | 4.0pm | This 3rd System & DESSART SWITCH were abandoned | |

A5834 Wt. W4973/M687 750,000 8/16 D. D. & L. Ltd. Forms/C.2118/13.

6.

Instructions regarding War Diaries and Intelligence Summaries are contained in F. S. Regs., Part II. and the Staff Manual respectively. Title pages will be prepared in manuscript.

# WAR DIARY
*or*
# INTELLIGENCE SUMMARY.
*(Erase heading not required.)*

Army Form C. 2118.

| Place | Date | Hour | Summary of Events and Information | Remarks and references to Appendices |
|---|---|---|---|---|
| | | | Right Company (D) C.S.R. had apparently been surrounded by the enemy & was never extricated. The reason for this was the fact that this company's right flank was completely en l'air from the time the position was reached. | |
| | | | Bn. H.Q. (less H.Q. company) was in 3rd System till 4.0 pm. & subsequently at ROCQUIGNY | |
| | | 6 pm. | A party of about 50 C.S.R. was collected by C.O. & placed in position on the ridge in P31 b North of FOUR WINDS FARM, from which position they were forced back at dusk. | |
| | | | By this time the remnants of C.S.R. were split up into so many parties whose movements are too complicated to follow. | |
| | | | Casualties. 2 o.r. K.I.A.<br>71 o.r. wounded<br>210 o.r. missing | |
| | | | Major E.J. WOOLLEY, M.C.<br>Capt. M. McDONALD, M.C.<br>Lt. T. WOODS<br>2Lt. L.W. PICKARD<br>W.L. IVEY<br>E.J.V. CAVEY<br>C.A. WILMOTT<br>} Wounded | |
| | | | Capt. F.D. BALFOUR, M.C.<br>R. MIDDLETON, M.C.<br>Lt. W.V.M. BROAD<br>2Lt. H. MATHESON<br>A.G.A. AYLMORE<br>F.A. BRIGHT<br>} Missing | |

A5834 Wt. W4973/M687 750,000 8/16 D. D. & L. Ltd. Forms/C.2118/13.

7.

Instructions regarding War Diaries and Intelligence Summaries are contained in F. S. Regs., Part II. and the Staff Manual respectively. Title pages will be prepared in manuscript.

# WAR DIARY
*or*
# ~~INTELLIGENCE SUMMARY.~~
(*Erase heading not required.*)

Army Form C. 2118.

| Place | Date | Hour | Summary of Events and Information | Remarks and references to Appendices |
|---|---|---|---|---|
| | 24. | 9.0am | Details of CSR numbering about 150, under C.O., were in position in O 32 C, in support of a party of 21st London Regt. holding the higher ground to the East. | |
| | | 12 noon | Another line taken up in N 36 a & c. | |
| | | 3.0pm | Details withdrew & took up a rearguard position east of GUEUDECOURT in N 22 C. | |
| | | 5.30pm | Orders received from Brigade to withdraw to MARTINPUICH, which was done. Bn. H.Q. was with above party till 5.45 pm. & rejoined it at BAZENTIN LE PETIT at 10. pm. | |
| BAZENTIN LE PETIT | | | Here further officers & details rejoined Battn., bringing strength up to 230. An outpost position was taken up along East edge of village, S 8 b & d, Battn. H.Q. in the wood. | |
| | | | Casualties 2 o.r. wounded | Ref. Map |
| | | | Transport retired through COMBLES, LONGUEVAL, CONTALMAISON, ALBERT to BOUZINCOURT. | 57 D |
| | 25 | 10 am | Battn. withdrew to a position along CONTALMAISON RIDGE, X 12 a. Battn. H.Q. in trench X 12 a. This position was held by rifle fire & bayonet fighting until withdrawal. | |
| | | | Casualties. 4 o.r. K.I.A.<br>5 o.r. wounded<br>4 o.r. missing | |

A5834 Wt. W4973/M687 750,000 8/16 D. D. & L. Ltd. Forms/C.2118/13.

8

Instructions regarding War Diaries and Intelligence Summaries are contained in F. S. Regs., Part II. and the Staff Manual respectively. Title pages will be prepared in manuscript.

# WAR DIARY
*or*
# INTELLIGENCE SUMMARY.
*(Erase heading not required.)*

Army Form C. 2118.

| Place | Date | Hour | Summary of Events and Information | Remarks and references to Appendices |
|---|---|---|---|---|
| BOUZINCOURT | 26 | 3 am | Battn. withdrew & marched via CONTALMAISON, LA BOISELLE, across country to AVELUY & BOUZINCOURT where battn. arrived at 8 am. & went into billets. | |
| LOUVENCOURT | | 4 pm | Battn. marched to LOUVENCOURT to billets. | |
| CLAIRFAYE FARM | 27 | 9 am | Battn. marched to CLAIRFAYE FARM | |
| TOUTENCOURT | | 4.30 pm | Battn. marched to TOUTENCOURT to billets | |
| WARLOY | 28 | 12 noon | Battn. marched to WARLOY to billets | |
| | 29 | 6 pm | Battn. marched to front line & relieved 6th Buffs (12th Div.) | |
| MARTINSART | | | 1½ coys. outpost position — AVELUY WOOD<br>2½ coys. & Bn. HQ. — ravine, 800 yards south of MARTINSART<br>21st London Regt. on left with gap of 400 yards. | |
| | 30 | | Fairly quiet day. Casualties — 3 o.r. wounded | |
| | 31 | | Fairly quiet day. Ravine shelled. Casualties. 3 o.r. wounded<br>2 Lt. A.F. BELL wounded. | |

E.Segrave Lt Col.
Comd. 1/Civil Service Rifles

A5834 Wt. W4973/M687 750,000 8/16 D. D. & L. Ltd. Forms/C.2118/13.

140th Brigade.
47th Division.

1/15th BATTALION (Civil Service Rifles)

THE LONDON REGIMENT

APRIL 1 9 1 8

Operation Orders.

1/15 London Regt
Vol 34

# CIVIL SERVICE RIFLES.

# WAR DIARY.

## APRIL. 1918.

1

Instructions regarding War Diaries and Intelligence Summaries are contained in F. S. Regs., Part II. and the Staff Manual respectively. Title pages will be prepared in manuscript.

Army Form C. 2118.

# WAR DIARY
or
# ~~INTELLIGENCE SUMMARY.~~
(Erase heading not required.)

April, 1918.

| Place | Date | Hour | Summary of Events and Information | Remarks and references to Appendices |
|---|---|---|---|---|
| MARTINSART SENLIS | 1 | | Battalion relieved in front line by 25th London Regt. & proceeded to Brigade Reserve. Billets at SENLIS. Transport lines at WARLOY. Casualties. 4 o.r. K.I.A. 4 o.r. wounded. | Ref. Map LENS 11. |
| | | | | |
| | 2 | | In billets. Reorganisation, & bathing. | |
| | 3 | | In billets. Reorganisation, & bathing. | |
| BOUZINCOURT | 4 | 8pm | Battn. relieved 21st London Regt. in front line. Dispositions. A coy on right {W15a 3.3 to W15a 7.3} C coy centre {W15a 7.3 to W9d 4.4} 1 coy 21st London left. (attached) {W9d 4.4 to W9a 8.2} B & D coys. in support. W8a & c. Battn. Hd. in BOUZINCOURT, W7d 6.8. Quiet night. 9th R.F. 36th Inf. Bde, 12th Div. on right. 142nd Inf. Bde on left. Major L. L. PARGITER, Middlesex Regt. joined as 2nd in Command | Ref. Map ALBERT |

A5834 Wt. W4973/M687 750,000 8/16 D. D. & L. Ltd. Forms/C.2118/13.

2.

Instructions regarding War Diaries and Intelligence Summaries are contained in F. S. Regs., Part II. and the Staff Manual respectively. Title pages will be prepared in manuscript.

# WAR DIARY

*or*

~~INTELLIGENCE SUMMARY.~~

*(Erase heading not required.)*

Army Form C. 2118.

| Place | Date | Hour | Summary of Events and Information | Remarks and references to Appendices |
|---|---|---|---|---|
| | 5 | 7 am | Enemy opened heavy bombardment with H.E. & gas shells on our front line & support trenches & on BOUZINCOURT. Except for three short intervals of about half an hour each this bombardment continued until 4.30 pm. – From 1.30 pm to 4.30 pm the bombardment of BOUZINCOURT was particularly intense. – Enemy's machine guns were very active all day on our front line & support trenches with both direct & indirect fire.<br>Before 7 am. enemy were seen on the crest about W15a in twos & threes (total about 150), some carrying timber. Our rifle fire caused these parties to keep down & dispersed them. | |
| | | 10 am | Enemy in twos & threes dribbled over crest (W15a) & made use of cover afforded by huts & sheds to get to the trees & broken ground in W15a and W9c & d (total about 300, with light machine guns.) Rifle and Lewis gun fire was opened on these targets as they appeared. – Enemy's machine guns at W15a 6.6 and about W15a 7.7 (two) & minenwerfer (two) about W15a 8.6 enfiladed our trenches all day. – The enemy in the broken ground pushed forward & in some places were within 100 yards of our front line. These parties showed up several times as if about to rush our trenches, but never succeeded in leaving the broken ground. Our rifle & Lewis gun fire was opened on them whenever they appeared. | |
| | | 11 am | Enemy seen digging in along the crest in W15a as if consolidating a position. | |
| | | 1 pm | No further signs of enemy advancing. Our artillery was sweeping the ground in W9 c & d and the crest in W15a with great effect.<br>Between 7am & 9am. parties of enemy were seen advancing in | |

3.

Instructions regarding War Diaries and Intelligence Summaries are contained in F. S. Regs., Part II. and the Staff Manual respectively. Title pages will be prepared in manuscript.

# WAR DIARY
*or*
# ~~INTELLIGENCE SUMMARY.~~
*(Erase heading not required.)*

Army Form C. 2118.

| Place | Date | Hour | Summary of Events and Information | Remarks and references to Appendices |
|---|---|---|---|---|
| | | | W10 b & d in a north-westerly direction towards the south-west edge of AVELUY WOOD. Lewis gun & rifle fire was opened on them from our front line, at range of about 1800 yards. | |
| | | | Casualties. 2/Lt. S.G. CLARKE & 5 o.r. K.I.A. | |
| | | | 2/Lt. E.S. SHEPHERD } & 37 o.r. wounded. | |
| | | | " L.A. NUTBROWN } | |
| | | | Lt. Col. W.H.E. SEGRAVE, D.S.O. slightly affected by gas & ordered by G.O.C. Division to proceed to Transport lines for a rest | |
| | | 9pm | D coy. relieved No. 2 coy. 21st London (on left front) who proceeded into support. | WF |
| | 6 | 7am | Enemy in twos & threes were walking about open ground in W15a under cover of the mist. Our snipers got many targets & one of above enemy was captured after being wounded. | |
| | | | There was shelling by enemy throughout the day. | |
| | | | Enemy machine gun at W15a 66 was very active. Our artillery was put on to it, & obtained several direct hits on target, which silenced the machine gun. | |
| | | 8pm | Enemy opened heavy bombardment to our right which spread to our front & continued till 10pm gradually dying down. No infantry movement was seen. The remainder of the night was quiet. | |
| | | 11pm. | B coy relieved C coy. (centre front) who proceeded into support. | |
| | | | Casualties. 3 o.r. K.I.A. | |
| | | | 3 o.r. wounded. | WF |

A7092 Wt. W12839/M1293 750,000. 1/17. D. D & L., Ltd. Forms/C2118/14.

4

Instructions regarding War Diaries and Intelligence Summaries are contained in F. S. Regs., Part II. and the Staff Manual respectively. Title pages will be prepared in manuscript.

# WAR DIARY
or
# ~~INTELLIGENCE~~ SUMMARY.
(*Erase heading not required.*)

Army Form C. 2118.

| Place | Date | Hour | Summary of Events and Information | Remarks and references to Appendices |
|---|---|---|---|---|
| | 7 | | Some shelling by enemy. | |
| SENLIS | | 9pm | Battn. relieved by 17th & 21st London Regts. & proceeded to billets at SENLIS. | |
| | | | Casualties. 1 o.r. K.I.A.<br>4 o.r. wounded<br>3 o.r. missing | WP |
| | 8 | | Bathing & cleaning up. Slight gas shelling by enemy. | |
| HEDAUVILLE | | 7pm | Battn. marched to HEDAUVILLE to billets<br>Lt Col. SEGRAVE, D.S.O. rejoined from Transport lines<br>Casualties nil. | WP |
| | 9 | 3pm | Battn. marched to ACHEUX where they embussed & proceeded to billets at GEZAINCOURT, ~~[illegible]~~ settled in at 12 midnight. | Ref. Map LENS 11 |
| GEZAINCOURT | | | Capt. & Adjt. V. DAVENPORT, M.C. rejoined.<br>Draft of 590 o.r. joined. | WP |
| | 10 | | Reorganisation - cleaning up.<br>Capt. G.G. BATES, M.C. took over command of "C" company. | WP |

A5834 Wt. W4973/M687 750,000 8/16 D. D. & L. Ltd. Forms/C.2118/13.

M. 5.

Instructions regarding War Diaries and Intelligence Summaries are contained in F. S. Regs., Part II. and the Staff Manual respectively. Title pages will be prepared in manuscript.

# WAR DIARY
*or*
# ~~INTELLIGENCE~~ SUMMARY.
*(Erase heading not required.)*

Army Form C. 2118.

| Place | Date | Hour | Summary of Events and Information | Remarks and references to Appendices |
|---|---|---|---|---|
| DOMART | 11 | | Battn. marched to DOMART to billets. | |
| | | | | W |
| CANCHY | 12 | | Battn. marched to CANCHY to billets. | Ref. Map. ABBEVILLE - 14 |
| | | | | W |
| | 13 | | Reorganisation - cleaning up. | |
| | | | Capt. G.B. MARTIN to 17th London Regt. for duty. | |
| | | | Capt. C.M. KILNER took over command of B coy. | W |
| | 14 | | Sunday. Church Parade. Divisional Commander attended. | |
| | | | | W |
| | 15 | | Training - bathing - reorganisation. | |
| | | | 29 o.r. joined Battn. | |
| | | | | W |

T2134. Wt. W708-776. 500000. 4/15. Sir J. C. & S.

6

Instructions regarding War Diaries and Intelligence Summaries are contained in F. S. Regs., Part II. and the Staff Manual respectively. Title pages will be prepared in manuscript.

# WAR DIARY
*or*
# ~~INTELLIGENCE SUMMARY.~~
*(Erase heading not required.)*

Army Form C. 2118.

| Place | Date | Hour | Summary of Events and Information | Remarks and references to Appendices |
|---|---|---|---|---|
| | 16 | | B.G.C. inspected Battn & complimented all ranks on the superb fight put up by them since 21st March. | WP |
| | 17 | | Training – musketry – bathing. | WP |
| | 18 | 9.30am | G.O.C. Division inspected training. | |
| | | 11.30am | Battn marched to Brigade parade at FORREST L'ABBAYE, where | |
| | | 12.30pm | G.O.C. Division complimented Brigade on their part in recent operations. | |
| | | | 2/Lt. H.J.C. HARTLEY (from 1/7th London Regt.) joined & posted to B Coy. | |
| | | | 33 OR joined Battn. | WP |
| | 19 & 20 | | Training – musketry – bathing. | WP |
| | | | During afternoon the heats for Divisional Sports were run off. | WP |

T2134. Wt. W708–776. 500000. 4/15. Sir J. C. & S.

7

Instructions regarding War Diaries and Intelligence Summaries are contained in F. S. Regs., Part II. and the Staff Manual respectively. Title pages will be prepared in manuscript.

# WAR DIARY
*or*
# INTELLIGENCE SUMMARY.
*(Erase heading not required.)*

Army Form C. 2118.

| Place | Date | Hour | Summary of Events and Information | Remarks and references to Appendices |
|---|---|---|---|---|
| | 21 | | Sunday Church parade. | |
| | | 2.0pm | Divisional Sports. Battn. won 100 yards. 1st Cpl. CARRINGTON. 2nd L/C SLACK. Second in Cross Country Team Race. First man in was Pte. FEWSTER & third Pte. HOWARD, both of Battn. | WP |
| | 22 | | Training - Musketry. | |
| | | | 2 Lt. F.J. SPENCER joined & posted to D coy. | |
| | | | Draft of 18 o.r. joined. | WP |
| | 23 | | Training & Musketry. - The following officers joined | |
| | | | 2nd Lt. T.J. BOOTH, " R.C. HUGHES, " E.J. ENOCH } posted to A coy. | |
| | | | " M.H. GARRETT, " A.L. VIGAL, " H. KING, " R.L. JONES } posted to B coy. | |
| | | | Capt. A. LEIGHTON, 2nd Lt J.W. HALLIFAX, " E.T. WILTSHIRE, " P.A. BENNETT } posted to C coy. | |
| | | | " G.W. PRYNN, " C.E. BARNETT, " H.C.T. BATTCOCK, " F. BARNES } posted to D coy. | |
| | | | Draft of 5 o.r. joined. | WP |

T2134. Wt. W708–776. 500000. 4/15. Sir J. C. & S.

Instructions regarding War Diaries and Intelligence Summaries are contained in F. S. Regs., Part II. and the Staff Manual respectively. Title pages will be prepared in manuscript.

# WAR DIARY or INTELLIGENCE SUMMARY.

(Erase heading not required.)

Army Form C. 2118.

| Place | Date | Hour | Summary of Events and Information | Remarks and references to Appendices |
|---|---|---|---|---|
| | 24 | | Training & Musketry. | |
| | | 12 noon | Inspection of draft by G.O.C. Division. 100 or. sent to 22nd London Regt. 150 " " 23rd London Regt. | |
| | | 2.30pm | Brigade Transport Show. | WF |
| | 25 | | Battn. exercise in CRECY Forest. | |
| | | | One company at Musketry. 7.0pm. Battn. Concert. | WF |
| | 26 | | Training & Musketry | |
| | | 5.30pm | Rugby football match. | WF |
| | 27 | | Training & Musketry. | |
| | | 3.30pm | Confirmation by D.C.G. - 9 candidates. | |
| | | 5.0pm | Battn. v. Div. Train (holders of Div. Cup.) Battn. won 4-0. | WF |
| | | | Capt. S.T. SMITHER to 17th London Regt. for duty. | |
| | 28. | 10am | Sunday. Transport moved for ST. OUEN. | |
| | | 10.30am | Church parade, & Celebration (120 communicants) | |
| | | 2.0pm | C.O.s treat to village children - Cinema, conjurer, refreshments. | WF |

T2134. Wt. W708–776. 500000. 4/15. Sir J. C. & S.

9

Instructions regarding War Diaries and Intelligence Summaries are contained in F. S. Regs., Part II. and the Staff Manual respectively. Title pages will be prepared in manuscript.

# WAR DIARY
*or*
~~INTELLIGENCE SUMMARY.~~

*(Erase heading not required.)*

Army Form C. 2118.

| Place | Date | Hour | Summary of Events and Information | Remarks and references to Appendices |
|---|---|---|---|---|
| WARLOY | 29 | 9.30am | Brigade entrained at CANCHY & proceeded to billets at WARLOY, arriving at 8 pm. Transport rejoined Battn. — Strength 25 Officers, 690 o.r. Details left at ESTREES-LES-CRECY (map, ABBEVILLE 14), strength, 8 Officers, 240 o.r. | Ref. map LENS, 11. |
| | 30. | 10.30am | Officers proceeded to the line to reconnoitre trenches occupied by 2nd Australian Division. | |

E. Legrave [?] Lt. Col.
Comd. 1/ Civil Service Rifles

A7092. Wt. W12839/M1293 750,000. 1/17. D. D & L., Ltd. Forms/C2118/14.

**Civil Service Rifles** SECRET.

Operation Order No. 1 COPY No 6.
by
Lt Col Segrave DSO Cmdg

In the field. 1st April 1918

**Para I** The Battalion will be relieved by the 20th Bn London Regt tonight (night 1/2nd April).

A Coy will be relieved by B Coy 20th Ldn
C " " " " D " 20th "
B " } " " " C " 20th "
D " }

**Para II** **Guides.**
Guides as below will report to Lieut KILNER at Batt. H.Q. at 8 p.m.
A Coy will send 4 Guides (1 per platoon)
C " " " 2 " (D Coy of 20th having only 2 ptns)
B " " " 2 guides
D " " " 2 " including one for L.G. post at X Roads
HQ " " 2 Guides

**Para III** Lewis Gun & S.A.A. limbers Mess & Medical Cart will be at Batt H.Q at 9.0 p.m.
Stretchers will be loaded on Medical Cart

O. O. 1. Contd

Para IV. Relief complete will be notified to Battn H.Q. by runner.

Para V. On completion of relief Companies will move independently to Billets in SENLIS. Billeting Guides will meet Companies at Road JUNCTION at V. 17 a Central (entrance to SENLIS)

Para VI. Tools and S.O.S. will be handed over and receipts obtained & forwarded to Battn H.Q. by 10. 30 a.m. 2nd April 18.

Receipts are not required for Water Cans.

Reserve Ammunition in FRONT LINE will be handed over to Relieving Coy.

Para 7. Reveille tomorrow will be at 8 A.M. & Breakfast at 9. A.M.

Coys will be at the disposal of Coy Commanders for Cleaning clothing arms & equipment.

Copy No 1 A Coy
2 B "
3 C "
4 D "
5 File
6 O.C. H.Q. Coy

[illegible]
Capt & Adjt

SECRET

COPY No. 2

## CIVIL SERVICE RIFLES

## ORDER No 104

Reference Map
Sheet 57c [illegible]

[illegible] March 1918.

1. Battalion will relieve [illegible] in Support [illegible] Brigade [illegible].

2. Battalion will [illegible] at [illegible] [illegible] of March [illegible]
"C B A HQ D"
Entraining Point. [illegible] ( [illegible] B [illegible] ) —
Detraining Point. [illegible] ( [illegible] B [illegible] ). —
From Detraining Point Platoons will move at 200 [illegible] interval.
Guides will be met at Detraining Point at 8.0 p.m. 1 per platoon and 2 for H.Q.

[illegible] Dress Full Marching Order. [illegible] at the [illegible].

3. [illegible] per [illegible] will be [illegible] by [illegible]. Remainder will be sent up with [illegible] tonight.

4. Heavy [illegible] Boxes [illegible] will be sent to the [illegible] by 2.30 p.m.

5. Dixies will be [illegible] with [illegible] Company [illegible].

6. [illegible] must be taken [illegible] and [illegible] billets [illegible] and [illegible] will be forwarded to Battalion H.Q. by 9 a.m. tomorrow.

7. Lists of Trench Stores [illegible] to be taken over will be sent to Battalion H.Q. by [illegible] tomorrow.

8. Code word for relief complete [illegible]

9. ACKNOWLEDGE.

[illegible]
Capt & Adjutant
Civil Service Rifles

[illegible] Distribution

CIVIL SERVICE RIFLES

P.A.

SECRE[T]

ORDER No. 106

In the Field 4th April 191[illegible]

Reference Map 57D 1/40000

1.- The 1/15th Bn London Regt will relieve the 21st London in the RIGHT Front Brigade Sub-Sector tonight 4/5 April

| | | | |
|---|---|---|---|
| A Coy will be in | RIGHT | Front line |
| C | do | LEFT | " |
| B | do | RIGHT | SUPPORT |
| D | do | LEFT | SUPPORT |

2. Coys will move off independently as below & pass the starting point at Cross Roads in V.12.c where guides will be met

| | | |
|---|---|---|
| A Coy will pass starting point at | | 9.0 pm |
| C | do | 9.5 " |
| D | do | 9.10 " |
| B | do | 9.15 " |
| HQ | do | 9.20 " |

3. Lewis Guns & Magazines will be loaded on limbers opposite Bn HQ. by 8.25 pm. & will proceed to a point 100 yards W of BOUZINCOURT

on the ~~HENDECOURT~~ HEDAUVILLE - BOUZINCOURT Rd. One man from each L.G. team will accompany the limbers. Lewis Guns will be dumped at above point where they will be picked up by Coys as they pass. The leading platoon of each of the Front Line Coys will take up 2 Lewis Guns & an extra Lewis Gun team.

4. Ration Dump is situated at W.8.a 3.1. Ration parties should be ordered to report at this point at a time which will be notified later.

5. All packs & valises to go to Transport Lines will be dumped in a house near Bn. H.Q by 6.0 pm. A guide will be at Bn. H.Q to point out this dump. The mess cart will be outside B Coy billet at 8 pm. to convey mess goods to Transport Lines.

6. Hot suppers will be given to the men before leaving at 7.30 pm.

-3-

7. Mess goods for the line will be dumped in the Orderly Room by 8 pm

8. Copies of receipts for stores taken over will be sent to Bn. H.Q. by 9 pm. 5th inst

9. Relief complete will be notified in writing to Bn. H.Q. by the use of the Coy Commanders name

10. Fighting order with greatcoats on will be worn (packs being left behind) Waterproof sheets strapped on the waist belt.

A. Whiteley
Lieut & A/Adjutant
Cape Town Rifles.

SECRET

Copy No.

[illegible] CIVIL SERVICE RIFLES

ORDER No. 108

Reference map
LENS 1/100,000

11th April 1918.

1. Battalion will move by route march today to billets in DOMART area: Route via CANDAS. FIENVILLERS BERNEUIL. –

2. Packs and blankets will be carried on lorries. – They should be stacked by Companies at Q.M. Stores by 11.30. a.m.

3. Battalion will parade in column of route in the main Road facing S.E. ready to move at 1.15 p.m. – Head of column to be at Cross Roads by QM. Stores.

Dress. – Fighting Order :– Haversacks to be carried on the back, steel helmets strapped to haversacks and groundsheets rolled and strapped on their belts. –

Order of march will be Band. A. B. H.Q. C. D. Transport. – 200 Yards interval will be maintained between Companies during the march. –

4. Dinners will be at 12.45 p.m and cookers will be ready for collection by Transport by 1.45 p.m.

5. Officers valises will be collected from their billets by Transport and should be ready by 11.0 a.m. Mess Boxes will be ready for collection by 1.0 p.m.

6. Certificates to the effect that billets have been left clean will be handed in on parade.

-Sgd- P. DAVENPORT

Capt & Adjutant
Civil Service Rifles

Copy No. 1 C.O.
2 War Diary
3 File
4 O/C A Coy.
5 " B "
6 " C "
7 " D "
8 Intelligence Officer
9 T.O.
10 Q.M.
140 Infantry Brigade

SECRET

Copy No 2

[illegible]

109

1. Battalion [illegible] march today to CANCHY leaving present billets at 9.30 am.

Dress Fighting order.

Order of march will be Band. D. HQ. C. A. B Transport. Companies will pass starting point (Cross Roads E. of the U in DOMART-EN-PONTHIEU) at one minute intervals commencing with Band and D Coy at 9.35 Am.

2. Route will be via GORENFLOS – St RIQUIER – NEUILLY L'HOPITAL – CANCHY.

3. Packs and Blankets are to be dumped at QM. Stores by 8.30 Am. MO. will detail men to report to QM. for loading lorries

4. Officers valises and mess boxes will be ready for collection by Mess Cart by 8.45 Am.

5. There will be a 2 hours halt for dinners between 1 & 3 pm.

6. Certificates that Billets have been left clean will be handed in on parade with parade state.

Davenport

Capt & Adjutant

Civil Service Rifles

Usual Distribution

Instructions regarding War Diaries and Intelligence Summaries are contained in F. S. Regs., Part II. and the Staff Manual respectively. Title pages will be prepared in manuscript.

WD/1

# WAR DIARY
*or*
~~INTELLIGENCE SUMMARY.~~
*(Erase heading not required.)*

Army Form C. 2118.

1/15 London Regt

May, 1918.

Vol 35

| Place | Date | Hour | Summary of Events and Information | Remarks and references to Appendices |
|---|---|---|---|---|
| WARLOY | 1/5/18 | | Battn relieved 21st Australian Battn. on night 1/2 May on the right of Divl front. The Battn was astride the AMIENS - ALBERT road with Battn. Hdqrs at D.12.d.6.8 (ref map 62D NE) It was a very quiet relief which passed off without any incident. There were no casualties. Battn H.Q. was a new dugout under the AMIENS - ALBERT road which was still under construction. A Coy was in reserve in a trench known as DIRTY TRENCH. C Coy was on the left with one platoon in outpost line in front holding four posts. One platoon and Coy H.Q. in a trench behind them and two platoons in PIONEER SUPPORT which was connected to DIRTY TRENCH by DIGGER AVENUE. B Coy was in the centre with Coy H.Q and 2 platoons in PIONEER SUPPORT and 2 platoons holding five posts in front, the right of the Coy on the ALBERT road. D Coy was on the right (which was also the right of the Division) on the S. side of the ALBERT road with 2 platoons holding outpost positions in front, one platoon in EMMA TRENCH and Coy HQ with one platoon in between. Lt. A. WHITELEY was in command of A Coy. Capt. C.M. KILNER, B Coy. Capt. G.G. BATES C Coy. and Lt. C.S. STEVENSON, D. Coy. | |
| LINE | 2/5/18 | | The day was very quiet on our front. By order of Divl. Comdr. Battn Comdrs in Bde. went back to Tpt. lines, leaving Major L.L. PARGITER to command the Battn in the line. All Coys were employed on digging new trenches to connect up outpost positions at night and making communication trenches forward from PIONEER SUPPORT and EMMA TRENCH. There were no casualties on this day. In the evening warning was received that enemy attack was likely to develop on our front in near future. | |
| " | 3/5/18 | | The day passed very quietly, without any incident of note. All Coys were working all night digging trenches to connect up the outposts lines with each other and digging C.T.s forward. We had our first casualty No. 393565 Pte. F.R.K. FATHING of C Coy. who was wounded in the outpost line early in the morning by shell fire. A start was made on digging a new R.A.P. under the ALBERT road near Bn. H.Q. | |

A7092 Wt. W12539/M1293 750,000. 1/17. D. D. & L. Ltd. Forms/C2118/14.

Instructions regarding War Diaries and Intelligence Summaries are contained in F. S. Regs., Part II. and the Staff Manual respectively. Title pages will be prepared in manuscript.

# WAR DIARY
*or*
~~INTELLIGENCE SUMMARY.~~
*(Erase heading not required.)*

Army Form C. 2118.

May, 1918.

| Place | Date | Hour | Summary of Events and Information | Remarks and references to Appendices |
|---|---|---|---|---|
| LINE | 4/5/18 | | Early in morning patrols of B. C & D. Coys. all reported that at 2 a.m. a noise resembling that of steam tractors was heard on or near the railway S of ALBERT Rd. As a result the R.A.F. carried out a special reconnaissance during the day and found four enemy tanks at E.3.d.15.65. In forwarding this information to the C.O. the Brig. Genl expressed his appreciation of good work of our patrols. ~~The~~<br>The day was not so quiet as the days previous had been, and we had three men of B. Coy. (Ptes O.C. WRIGHT, J.R. FOULDS and F.J.G. MOIST) killed by a shell which hit their trench.<br>The ration parties at night were also shelled and L/Cpls. F.T. DODGE and W.M. COOPER of A Coy. and Sgt. S. FELL of D Coy. were slightly wounded but remained at duty. Pte T. HONES of D Coy. however was more seriously wounded. His life was saved by his steel helmet.<br>The 21st Bn sent a party of men to work permanently on new R.A.P.<br>No. 531599 L/Cpl. R. SHIRLEY awarded Bar to Military Medal. No. 531510 Cpl. H.G. KNIGHT and No. 532890 Pte H.L. ARMFIELD and No. 320873 L/Sgt. F.A. GORING, No. 533625 Pte G.E. KNOTT, No. 492245 Pte. H.F. MAUNDER, No. 495703 Pte. S. WOLVIN, No. 471810 Pte. C.B. PHILLIPS, No. 532275 Pte G.E. ASHDOWN, No. 531348 L/Cpl. C.E. WEARN, No. 531349 Pte. E. STRUGNELL, No. 531664 L/Cpl. H.E. HICKS and No. 322802 Pte F.H. COOLEY awarded the Military Medal. | |
| | 5/5/18 | | Ptes WRIGHT, FOULDS and MOIST were buried side by side near Bn. Hdqrs at D.12.d.50.80. The chaplain Rev. E.H. BEATTIE came up from WARLOY to read the burial service.<br>The day was quiet and uneventful, but the weather was bad, and life in the outpost line was not pleasant. Casualties - 1. O.R. wounded. O.O. 112 issued | App I |

A7092 Wt. W12839/M1293 750,000. 1/17. D. D & L., Ltd. Forms/C2118/14.

Instructions regarding War Diaries and Intelligence Summaries are contained in F. S. Regs., Part II. and the Staff Manual respectively. Title pages will be prepared in manuscript.

# WAR DIARY

*or*

~~INTELLIGENCE SUMMARY.~~

*(Erase heading not required.)*

Army Form C. 2118.

May 1918.

| Place | Date | Hour | Summary of Events and Information | Remarks and references to Appendices |
|---|---|---|---|---|
| LINE | 6/5/18 | | After a quiet day, there was a somewhat complicated relief due to a reshuffle of Bdes on the Corps front, on night of 6/7th. First of all A Coy took over a piece of line from the Right Coy of 17th Bn. on our left. The Coys on the N. side of the ALBERT ROAD were then relieved by the 11th Royal Fusiliers and D Coy. S. of the road was relieved by a Coy. of the 6th Northants Regt. The weather during the relief could scarcely have been worse. The night was as dark as it could be and the rain poured down in torrents the whole night long. It was not surprising therefore that the relief took a long time and it was 3.40 am before the relief was complete. The Bde. frontage had now moved slightly N. and the Bn. came into Bde. support with one Coy (A) in WALLABY TRENCH E of MILLENCOURT, one Coy (D) in COPSE TRENCH between HENENCOURT and MILLENCOURT and 2 Coys (B and C) in a trench immediately E of HENENCOURT. Casualties 1 OR wounded. | |
| IN SUPPORT. | 7/5/18 | | Trenches taken over were nothing more than scratches in the ground and only D Coy had any shelter at all. A.B.C Coys were accordingly put into cellars, the former in MILLENCOURT and the two latter in HENENCOURT. It was daylight before all the men were under cover, and during the day D Coy moved back into a barn in the Chateau Stables yard. H.Q was at the Grand Caporal Estaminet, HENENCOURT – a "house" that had been a favourite resort of our signallers when we were in this district in September 1916. At night each Coy went to work on the trenches to make them into suitable battle positions. News was received today that the Commanding Officer had been awarded a second bar to his D.S.O. for his work during the recent withdrawal. | |

A7092. Wt. W12839/M1293 750,000. 1/17. D. D & L. Ltd. Forms/C2118/14.

Army Form C. 2118.

Instructions regarding War Diaries and Intelligence Summaries are contained in F. S. Regs., Part II. and the Staff Manual respectively. Title pages will be prepared in manuscript.

# WAR DIARY
*or*
# INTELLIGENCE SUMMARY.
*(Erase heading not required.)*

| Place | Date | Hour | Summary of Events and Information | Remarks and references to Appendices |
|---|---|---|---|---|
| IN SUPPORT | 8/5/18 | | A search was made throughout the village for tubs and a bath house was started in the Chateau yard. All the men in HENENCOURT had baths and clean clothes. | |
| | 9/5/18 | | In the early morning enemy shelled HENENCOURT but we had no casualties. A. Coy in MILLENCOURT however had 14 men gassed by one shell which burst outside one of their cellars and filled it immediately with gas. At night C. Coy moved forward and occupied the Northern end of MELBOURNE TRENCH E of MILLENCOURT and E of A. Coy's battle trench. They had one casualty (532244 Cpl. H.C. CLARIDGE) caused by shell fire upon arriving at the position. | |
| | 10/5/18 | | A. Coy had two casualties from shell fire in the early morning while at work on their battle positions. otherwise we spent a quiet day. At night we relieved the 17th Battn. on the right of the Bde. front. H.Q was in a cellar in MILLENCOURT. A and D Coys were in the front line in BRISBANE TRENCH astride the MILLENCOURT-ALBERT Road, A on the right and D on the left. C Coy was in support in a trench called KING STREET running due N from the MILLENCOURT-ALBERT road and B Coy was in reserve in QUEEN STREET parallel to and behind KING STREET. The relief was a pleasant contrast to our last one. The weather was fine, the situation very quiet and the relief was complete by 12.30 a.m. (O.O.113) The chief difficulty here was cooking. None whatever could be done in the trenches and all the food had to be cooked at WARLOY and brought up at night. The men in consequence only got one hot meal a day. This arrived about 11 pm daily. The tea was sent up in petrol cans carried in packs filled with hay and this method appeared to be very satisfactory. | App II |

A7092 Wt W12839/M1293 750,000. 1/17. D. D & L., Ltd. Forms/C2118/14.

Army Form C. 2118.

Instructions regarding War Diaries and Intelligence Summaries are contained in F. S. Regs., Part II. and the Staff Manual respectively. Title pages will be prepared in manuscript.

# WAR DIARY
*or*
# INTELLIGENCE SUMMARY.

(*Erase heading not required.*)

| Place | Date | Hour | Summary of Events and Information | Remarks and references to Appendices |
|---|---|---|---|---|
| LINE | 11/5/18 | | The day was quiet and uneventful except for a little shelling of MILLENCOURT at night. C. Coy went up to dig a new front line in front of the existing out-post positions, and B. Coy after carrying rations to A and D Coys. put up wire in front of the new front line. In the evening No. 530956 Pte R. WALLIS was wounded by shell fire at Bn. H.Q. He had been H.Q. Mess Wanter since the Battn. came to France and had never been away sick or wounded during that time. | |
| | 12/5/18 | | Quiet and uneventful. Digging new trench and wiring in front of it continued. | |
| | 13/5/18 14/5/18 | | The 13th was wet. On the night of the 14th C Coy started digging the new trench Northwards from our Battalion boundary and joined it with BRISBANE trench (21st Bn front line.) There was now a new front line straightening out the re-entrant which existed in the old front line BRISBANE trench. This had been wired with double apron wire by B. Coy. (O.O. 114 issued 14.5.18) | App III |
| | 15/5/18 | | On the night of the 15/16th we were relieved by 6th Bn. 58th Div. and battalion moved out into billets at WARLOY | |
| WARLOY | 16/5/18 | | Battalion bathed in WARLOY. Division now became Corps Reserve. | |
| | 17/5/18 | | Ordered to move into tented camp in Bois le Haut, N. of BAZIEUX. accommodation very poor. Most of the men slept in the open. C.O. took over command of 141st Inf Bde. Major L.L. Pargiter took over command of the Battalion. | |

A7092. Wt. W12839/M1293 750,000. 1/17. D. D & L., Ltd. Forms/C2118/14.

Army Form C. 2118.

Instructions regarding War Diaries and Intelligence Summaries are contained in F. S. Regs., Part II. and the Staff Manual respectively. Title pages will be prepared in manuscript.

# WAR DIARY
*or*
# ~~INTELLIGENCE SUMMARY.~~

(*Erase heading not required.*)

May 1918.

| Place | Date | Hour | Summary of Events and Information | Remarks and references to Appendices |
|---|---|---|---|---|
| BOIS la HAUT | 18/5/18 | | All officers reconnoitred positions of assembly. Brigade was under orders to move to as soon as enemy's expected attack started. Orders for counter attacking at various points of Corps front prepared, and it was announced that the attack would be launched on the 20th. During the night 18/19th an intense bombardment was heard. Our sentries passed on an alarm which was heard in the next wood, and the Battalion at once stood-to, but our services were not required. The next day we learnt that the bombardment had been covering a successful Australian raid in AVELUY WOOD. | |
| | 19/5/18 | | Voluntary services were held during the day in the wood. | |
| | 20/5/18 | | Whit Monday, which at home would have been spent as a bank holiday, was spent by the whole battalion burying cable near HENENCOURT WOOD. There was again a big bombardment at night, but profiting by our experience, we did not stand to. | |
| | 21/5/18 | | Qualifying competitions of the Rifle and Bayonet competition under Army Rifle assoc. rules were held on the ranges in the field S. of the camp. | |
| | 22/5/18 | | The four leading platoons competed in the final competition with the following result — No. 9 platoon 1st No 11 platoon 2nd No 3 platoon 3rd No 6 platoon 4th. In the early morning of this day, the camp was shelled with the result that 2 horses were killed and 2 wounded. Cpl. Banks of the Transport Section was very severely wounded. He was taken to No 4 C.C.S. where he died during the morning. Cpl. Banks had been a member of the C.S.R's for some years before the war and had been with the transport section since mobilization without missing a day. He was an exceedingly popular member of the Transport Section, was well known throughout the Battalion and his loss was keenly felt by all who knew him. | |

Instructions regarding War Diaries and Intelligence Summaries are contained in F. S. Regs., Part II. and the Staff Manual respectively. Title pages will be prepared in manuscript.

# WAR DIARY
or
~~INTELLIGENCE SUMMARY.~~
(Erase heading not required.)

Army Form C. 2118.

May 1918

| Place | Date | Hour | Summary of Events and Information | Remarks and references to Appendices |
|---|---|---|---|---|
| BOIS la HAUT. | 23/5/18 | | The whole Battalion worked on cable burying and in the evening experiments were carried out by the Adjutant and all N.C.O's with the No. 36 Rifle Grenade. Unfortunately, after firing one box, the party was warned off the range by an irate Major of the 18th Division who was unable to sleep in his camp owing to the noise of the explosions. It was thought the No 36 seemed to be the best we had used so far | |
| | 24/5/18 | | The Division relieved the 18th Division on the right of the Corps front the Brigade being in Divisional Reserve. (O.O. 115 issued) Battalion turned out for cable burying and this day had to work in pouring rain. C.E. 47th Div Sig. Coy expressed his appreciation of the digging done by the C.S.R.'s and said the Battalion had undoubtedly worked better than any other Battalion in the Division. In the evening we relieved the 8th E. Surrey Rgt. in the quarry near the Franvillers–Albert road. Hdqrs were surrounded by guns and howitzers of all calibres, and in many cases men were bivouacked round the muzzles of guns. It was a very wet night, so no-one was particularly comfortable. The only good thing we got out of this move was a draft of 18 N.C.O's of this Battn who had been wounded on the Somme in 1916 and who by some whim of the D.A.G. had since been sent to another Battalion. | App IV |
| BAIZIEUX | 25/5/18 | | We moved to better if not safer billets in BAIZIEUX and were very comfortable. H.Q Mess was in the room where the Div. Comdr. had his last Christmas dinner. It had however been considerably knocked about since then. | |

A7092. Wt. W123/9/M1293 750,000. 1/17. D. D & L., Ltd. Forms/C2118/14.

Instructions regarding War Diaries and Intelligence Summaries are contained in F. S. Regs., Part II. and the Staff Manual respectively. Title pages will be prepared in manuscript.

# WAR DIARY
*or*
# ~~INTELLIGENCE~~ SUMMARY.
*(Erase heading not required.)*

Army Form C. 2118.

May 1918

| Place | Date | Hour | Summary of Events and Information | Remarks and references to Appendices |
|---|---|---|---|---|
| LAVIEVILLE DEFENCES | 26/5/18 | | We relieved 4th R.W.F. in the Lavieville defences. Coys were all in trenches and all ranks were much more comfortable than they had been while in Corps Reserve. (O.O. 116) | App V |
| | 27/5/18 | | Battalion again on cable burying near Battn H.Q. Men worked well but there were three cases of accidental injury through excessive zeal in the use of the pick. | |
| | 28/5/18 | | Battalion engaged upon cable burying. | |
| | 29/5/18 | | Battalion engaged upon cable burying. O.C. 47th Div Sigs. again informed us that C.S.R. worked better than any other Battn. (O.O 117 issued) On the night of the 29th we were relieved by 21st Battn. Battn moved to tents and bivouacs in valley near BAIZIEUX where we arrived at 2 a.m. Battn fairly comfortable. | App VI |
| | 30/5/18 | | Battn moved to a point N. of FRANVILLERS-BEHENCOURT road in the rear defences of LAHOUSSOYE system, where we made a camp. Men were accommodated in tents and bivouacs and whole Battn was very comfortable. (O.O 118) | App VII |
| | 31/5/18 | | Was spent in refitting and bathing at the Prisoner of War cage BAIZIEUX. O.O. 119 issued. | App VIII |

[illegible signature]
Major,
Comdg 1/Civil Service Rifles
(1/15th Bn. Lon Regt)

SECRET. COPY No. 2

App. I

War Diary

# CIVIL SERVICE RIFLES.

## ORDER No. 112

5th May, 1918.

Reference Maps 62D N.E. and 57D S.E. 1/20,000.

1. Brigade will side step to the North by one battalion frontage on night 6/7th May, 1918.

2. A. Company will take over from the 17th Battalion during the day of the 6th on the frontage from the present left boundary of C Company to the new Southern Brigade Boundary (a line E and W through E.2.a.0.0.)

3. A. B. and C Companies will be relieved on the night 6/7th by 3 Companies of the 11th Royal Fusiliers, the 4th Company of the Fusiliers being accommodated in DIRTY TRENCH. D Company will be relieved by a Company of the 6th Northants Regiment.

4. One guide per platoon and one for each Company H.Q. will report to Battalion H.Q. at 7.0 p.m. to proceed to HENENCOURT where they will meet the incoming platoons. 2/Lt. H. KING. will be in charge of these guides.

5. On relief Companies will move to trenches as follows:-

A Company. Trenches about V.30.c.
D " " " D.4.b and V.28.d.
C} " " running N-S through V.28.central
B} and D.4.a central with C Coy. at N. end.

Battalion H.Q. will be in HENENCOURT.

6. Billeting parties of 1 Officer per Coy. and 1 N.C.O. per platoon will go to new trenches on morning of 6th. and will meet their Companies on relief at their present ration dumps and guide them to new trenches.

7. Dixies, food containers and water cans will be collected by transport from Ration Dumps at 10.0 p.m. and taken back to WARLOY.

8. Lewis Guns and Mess Boxes will be carried by Coy. to their new trenches.

9. All secret trench maps, aeroplane photos and works schemes will be handed over with trench stores and receipts obtained. These will be forwarded to Battalion H.Q. by 9.0 a.m. on the 7th.

10. Relief complete will be wired by Coy Commanders name and reported by runner on arrival at new trenches.

[signature]
Capt and Adjutant,
CIVIL SERVICE RIFLES.

Copy No. 1 C.O.
2 War Diary
3 File.
4 140 Infy Bde.
5 O.C. A Coy.
6 " B "
7 " C "
8 " D "
9 T.O.
10 Q.M.
11 – I.O.
12 – Signals
13 – R.S.M.
14 11th Fusiliers
15 6th Northants Regt.

SECRET. COPY No. 3.

App. II

CIVIL SERVICE RIFLES

ORDER No. 113

10th May. 1918.

Reference Maps 57D S.E. 1/20,000 and 62D N.E. 1/20,000.

1. Battalion will relieve 17th Battalion in the front line on the night 10/11 May as follows:-
A. Company Civil Service Rifles relieves D. Coy. 17th Right Front.
D. " " " " C " 17th Left Front.
C. " " " " A " 17th Support.
B " " " " B " 17th Reserve.

2 Guides from 17th Bn. will meet Companies as follows:- C Company in MELBOURNE TRENCH at 9.30 p.m. ~~B & D~~ B & D Companies outside 17th Battalion H.Q. at MILLENCOURT at 9.30 p.m. and A. Company in their billets in MILLENCOURT at 10.30 p.m.

3. A. B. and D Companies will have a hot meal in their billets before moving, the former at 9.30 p.m. and the two latter at 8.0 p.m. C Company's hot meal will reach the Ration Dump where the road crosses MELBOURNE TRENCH at 10.0 p.m. Empty dixies from this morning's meal and water cans must be at the dump with socks in time to go back by the 10.0 p.m. limber.
Breakfasts for all Companies will reach the Ration Dump at 3.0 a.m. The limbers will take back empties from C Coy's evening meal and will pick up A. Coy's empties at Battalion H.Q. (the N.W. corner of MILLENCOURT).
B Company will carry rations and meals to A. and D. Companies daily and C Coy. will carry their own.

4. Companies will send to Headquarters by first run 11th a sketch map showing their dispositions and also location of their S.A.A. Grenade etc. dumps with quantities in each. Lewis Gun arcs of fire should also be shown.

5 Copies of receipts for trench stores taken over and receipts for trench stores handed over to 17th Battalion in Support trenches will be sent to H.Q. by first run on the 11th.

6. Times for reports to reach Battalion H.Q. will be the same as when the Battalion was last in front line.

7. All ranks are to be again warned that water from shell holes is not to be used for any purpose whatever owing to danger of gas.

8. A.B. C and H.Q. Coys. will take over S.O.S. bugles from the 17th Bn. All picks and shovels now in possession will be taken into the line.

9. Code word for relief complete will be Company Commander's name.

Davenport
Capt. and Adjutant
CIVIL SERVICE RIFLES.

Copy No. 1 C.O.
2 File
3 War Diary
4 140 Infy. Bde.
5/8 A.B.C.D. Coy.
9 R.S.M. and Sig. Sgt.
10 Q.M.
11 T.O.
12 Int. Off.
13 17th Battalion.

SECRET. COPY No. 3

App. III

## CIVIL SERVICE RIFLES.

## ORDER No. 114.

14th May 1918.

Reference Maps: 57D 1/40,000
62D 1/40,000.

1. Battalion will be relieved on the night 15/16 May by 6th London Regiment as follows:-

| | | |
|---|---|---|
| A Coy. Civil Service Rifles | will be relieved by | C Coy. 6th. |
| D " " " | " " " | D " " |
| C " " " | " " " | A " " |
| B " " " | " " " | B " " |

2. One guide per platoon and one for Coy. H.Q. will parade under 2/Lt. H. KING at Battalion H.Q. at 9.0 p.m. They will meet incoming platoons at HENENCOURT CHATEAU gates at 9.20 p.m.
B. and C Companies should send their guides down before daylight on the 15th.

3. The Battalion will move on relief to billets in WARLOY.

4. Route to be followed on coming out will be via MILLENCOURT – ALBERT ROAD. Platoons will keep a distance of 100 yards all the way. Companies will each send out one N.C.O. per platoon to report to 2/Lt. F.J. EASTON at Battalion Headquarters at 9.0 a.m for billeting.

5. Empty tins, water cans, ice boxes etc. will be sent to Ration Dump at 10.0 p.m. where they will be picked up by Transport. Lewis Gun limbers will be at Ration Dump at midnight. Companies passing there before that time will dump their guns and magazines there leaving sufficient men to load them under the N.C.O. in charge of each team.

6. All picks and shovels will be carried out by the men except the few which were taken over from the 19th Battalion.

7. All work in hand will be explained and handed over and trench stores, aeroplane photos and Defence Schemes etc will also be handed over and receipts forwarded to Battalion H.Q. on arrival in billets. [illegible] will not be handed over.

8. Code word for relief complete will be Company Commanders name.

Davenport
Capt. and Adjutant
CIVIL SERVICE RIFLES.

Copy No. 1 C.O.
2 File
3 War Diary
4 140 Infy. Bde.
5/8 A.B.C.D. Coys.
9 R.S.M. and Sigs. Sgt.
10 Q.M.
11 T.O.
12 Int. Officer.
13 6th Bn. London Regt.

SECRET. COPY No. 3.

App IV

# CIVIL SERVICE RIFLES

## ORDER No 115.

24th May, 1918.

Reference Maps 57D 1/40,000
62D 1/40,000

1. The Battalion will move today to Camp at present occupied by 8th East Surrey Regt at D. 13. c.

2. Billeting parties consisting of one Officer per Coy and one N.C.O. and one man per platoon, and one N.C.O. for H.Q. Coy will parade outside H.Q. at 2.15 pm. and proceed to take over these new areas. 2/Lt HALLIFAX will be in charge of the party, and will allot the tents, shelters, etc to Companies.

3. Immediately the billeting parties have taken over their new areas the men will return to Camp to act as Guides for their platoons. The Officers and N.C.O's. will remain in the new camp.

4. Officers valises will be loaded on to the Baggage wagon at 4.15 p.m. Mess boxes and Orderly Room boxes will be loaded on to the Mess Cart at 5.0 pm.
All furniture, tables, forms, wire beds, etc will be stacked beside the water carts at 5.0 pm.

5. The Battalion will move off in full marching order by platoons at 100 yds distance in the following order:–

A Coy at 5.0 pm
C " " 5.10 "
B " " 5.20 "
D " " 5.30 "
HQ " " 5.35 "

6. Cookers, Water Carts, Baggage wagon & mess cart will follow the Battalion under the direction of the T.O.
Lewis Gun Limbers will be loaded by 4.0 pm. and will go with leading Company.

7. All Sanitary men will parade outside the Medical Room at 5.0 pm. and will work as detailed by the M.O.

8. All tents, bivouacs, trench stores, maps, Defence Schemes Reserve Rations & Water and S.O.S. Rockets will be taken over, and copies of receipts will be forwarded to the Orderly Room on arrival in Camp.

9. Dispositions and Orders issued to Coys of the 8th East Surreys will be taken over and complied with.

No 1 C.O.
2 File
3 War Diary
4 140 Infy Bde
5/8 A B C D Coys.
9 R.S.M. & Signal Sgt.
10 Q.M.
11 T.O.
12 Intelligence Officer
13 8th East Surrey Regt.

[signature] Davenport
Capt. & Adjutant
of Civil Service Rifles

SECRET

COPY No 3

App. V

# CIVIL SERVICE RIFLES

## ORDER No 116

Reference maps 62 D NW
62 D NE

26th May. 1918

1. The Battalion will relieve 4th Bn. Royal Welsh Fusiliers, and one Company of 17th Bn. London Regiment on the night 26/27 May, as follows :—

A Company Civil Service Rifles relieves C. Coy R.W.F.
B " " " " " B " "
C " " " " " A " "
D " " " " " D " 17th Bn. London Regt

2. D. Coy will move off at 8.45 pm by Platoons at 100 yards distance and will meet guides as already arranged between O/C Coys concerned. L.G. Limber will go with leading Platoon

3. Remaining Companies will move in the order C. B. A. HQ, first Platoon passing Chateau Gates at 8.30 p.m. Platoons will move at 100 yards distance. Route will be via the BAIZIEUX - HENENCOURT Road, and D track. Guides will be met at 9.30 p.m. at Junction of C and D tracks near the Cemetery at D.2.d.7.3

4. Each Company will take up four Lewis Guns. The fifth Gun will be dumped at H.Q at 8.0 p.m.

Anti aircraft positions will be taken over, but there will be no anti aircraft firing at night. By day only low flying hostile aircraft will be fired on.

5. Lewis Gun limbers for the line will be loaded at 8.0 pm at Battalion H.Q as follows:-
- Two limbers for A.B. & C Coys
- One " " D Coy. (which will report at D.Coy. HQ 8.0 pm)
- B C and D mess boxes will go with their L.G. limbers

A Coy. and H.Q mess boxes will go on the mess Cart which will be loaded at 8.0 pm at Battalion H.Q.

6. Cookers will return to Transport Lines tonight with one Cook per Company. Two Cooks per Company will come into the Trenches. Dixies and Camp Kettles will be dumped at Bn. H.Q at 8.0 p.m. and will be taken by limber to the Cookhouse near the new Bn. H.Q. Cooks will march with the limbers

7. Water Carts will accompany the dixie limber and will remain at the Cookhouse. They will refill each night

8. Copies of receipts for trench stores will be sent to Bn. H.Q by 8.0 a.m. 27th May.

9. Code word for relief complete will be Company Commanders name

J Davenport
Captain & Adjutant
1/ Civil Service Rifles.

No. 1. C.O.
2. File
3. War Diary
4. 140 Inf Bde
5/8 A B C D Coys
9 RSM & Cigs Sgt.
10 QM
11 T.O
12 Intelligence Officer
13. 4th Bn. Royal Welsh Fusiliers
14 17th " London Regt.

Vol 36

June 1918

WAR. DIARY.

15th Battn. London Regt.
(P.W.O. Civil Service Rifles.)

Army Form C. 2118.

# WAR DIARY
*or*
# ~~INTELLIGENCE SUMMARY.~~
(*Erase heading not required.*) June '18

Instructions regarding War Diaries and Intelligence Summaries are contained in F. S. Regs., Part II. and the Staff Manual respectively. Title pages will be prepared in manuscript.

| Place | Date | Hour | Summary of Events and Information | Remarks and references to Appendices |
|---|---|---|---|---|
| FRANVILLERS | 1.6.18 | | The Battalion left the tented camp at FRANVILLERS to relieve the 24th London Regt in the Div'l front opposite DARNANCOURT. The relief took a rather long time, not being completed until 1.50 am 2nd inst. Two companies went into the front line, EMU TRENCH, C Company on the right and B on the left. D Company went into support in DINGO TRENCH and A into reserve in DINGO SUPPORT. Capt. Rathbone was in command of A Coy, Lt C. P. Stevenson B Coy, Lt Gibson C Coy and Capt L. D. Eccles D Coy. | |
| LINE | 2.6.18 | | In the early part of the morning a few gas shells were fired on and around the Bn area. Otherwise the day was uneventful. At night, however, there was a certain amount of rifle & M.G. fire during which Pte J. D. Smith was unfortunate enough to get hit while unloading a limber at Bn H.Q. by the enemy. Death occurred on the following day (3rd) at 41 C.C.S. He was an old member of the Transport very popular with all his comrades & the loss of him was keenly felt. | |

D. D. & L., London, E.C. (A8004) Wt. W1771/M2-31 750,000 5/17 Sch. 52 Forms/C2118/14

Army Form C. 2118.

# WAR DIARY
*or*
# ~~INTELLIGENCE~~ SUMMARY.

*(Erase heading not required.)*

Instructions regarding War Diaries and Intelligence Summaries are contained in F. S. Regs., Part II. and the Staff Manual respectively. Title pages will be prepared in manuscript.

| Place | Date | Hour | Summary of Events and Information | Remarks and references to Appendices |
| --- | --- | --- | --- | --- |
| LINE | 3.6.18 4 " 5 " | | Ordinary trench routine was carried out. The situation remained quiet and nothing unusual occurred. Patrols went out nightly from each Coys front, but found little of interest. The one which went out on the 4th bombed a hostile M.G. Whilst withdrawing the party suffered a casualty, 2/Lt A.L. Vigar the leader, being wounded by a piece of a grenade. Both front line Companies started a new belt of wire in front of the old one. | |
| " | 6.6.18 | | On the night of the 6/7 the Battn was relieved by the 17th London Regt and moved into Brigade Support in DARLING & DARWIN RESERVE, (on either side of the AMIENS Rd) where the accommodation was far from good. Bn H.Qs were in a deep dugout near a bank south of the ALBERT Rd - D17a 7.2. Move order No 120 attached. | |
| IN SUPPORT | 7.6.18 | | In the early morning the enemy artillery was somewhat active, but no damage of consequence was inflicted on the Bns area. With the evening came a casualty, Cpl L.P.T. Pumper, who was killed by a piece of a stray shell near DARWIN RESERVE. The loss of this Cpl was very much regretted. | |

D. D. & L., London, E.C. (A8004) Wt. W1771/M2 31 750,000 5/17 Sch. 52 Forms/C2118/14

Instructions regarding War Diaries and Intelligence Summaries are contained in F. S. Regs., Part II. and the Staff Manual respectively. Title pages will be prepared in manuscript.

# WAR DIARY
*or*
# ~~INTELLIGENCE SUMMARY.~~
*(Erase heading not required.)*

Army Form C. 2118.

| Place | Date | Hour | Summary of Events and Information | Remarks and references to Appendices |
|---|---|---|---|---|
| IN SUPPORT | 8/6/18 | | Small working parties were found for tunnelling at Bde. H.Q. The new open air bath on the AMIENS Rd, near Brigade H.Q., having now in working order all the men were sent down in small parties to bathe & change into clean underclothes. | |
| " | 9/6/18 | | During the night of the 9/10 the Battn relieved the 21st London on the left of the Brigade front with two companies in the front line in ETHEL TRENCH, A on the right & D on the left, with C in support in ECHUCA ALLEY & B in reserve in NINE ELMS TRENCH. The relief was quite quiet and passed off without incident of note. A party of Officers & NCOs of the American Army was attached to the Bn for the purpose of learning trench routine. Move order No 121 attached. | |
| LINE | 10/6/18 | | The day passed quietly without any event of importance except an attack by the Australian Division on our right. | |
| " | 11/6/18 | | All personnel of the Battn who had been sent to the Divl Reception Camp returned, & a new party went down under Lt C. D. Stevenson. | |

D. D. & L., London, E.C.
(A8004) Wt. W1771/M231 750,000 5/17 Sch. 52 Forms/C2118/14

Instructions regarding War Diaries and Intelligence Summaries are contained in F. S. Regs., Part II. and the Staff Manual respectively. Title pages will be prepared in manuscript.

# WAR DIARY
*or*
# ~~INTELLIGENCE SUMMARY.~~
*(Erase heading not required.)*

Army Form C. 2118.

| Place | Date | Hour | Summary of Events and Information | Remarks and references to Appendices |
|---|---|---|---|---|
| LINE | 12.6.18 | | While out wiring in front of our own front line on the night of the 12/13 2/Lt B.J. Wiltshire and Pte A.G. Hurst, both of D Coy were hit by M.G. bullets, the latter being unfortunately killed. The body was taken down to the Transport lines on the following night and buried in CONTAY CEMETERY on the 14th | |
| " | 13.6.18 | | No event of importance occurred. | |
| " | 14.6.18 | | The Battn was relieved by the 17th London Regt on the night of the 14/15 & moved back again into support, the Companies occupying the same positions as on the 6th inst. On the same night 2/Lt Lloyd Jones & 5 O.R. of B Coy attempted a silent raid on the enemy trenches opposite the Right Bn but owing to artillery activity on both sides found the enemy too alert. The same party repeated the attempt on the following night but were again unsuccessful. Move order No 122 attached. | |

D. D. & L., London, E.C.
(A8004) Wt. W1771/M2-31 750,000 5/17 Sch. 52 Forms/C2118/14

Instructions regarding War Diaries and Intelligence Summaries are contained in F. S. Regs., Part II. and the Staff Manual respectively. Title pages will be prepared in manuscript.

# WAR DIARY
*or*
# INTELLIGENCE SUMMARY.
*(Erase heading not required.)*

Army Form C. 2118.

| Place | Date | Hour | Summary of Events and Information | Remarks and references to Appendices |
|---|---|---|---|---|
| IN SUPPORT | 15.6.18 | | On the afternoon of the 15th A & D Companies went to dig a new Support line in the Left Bn area. On commencing the work they were shelled with 5.9s somewhat heavily & had 10 wounded, after which the Companies were withdrawn by order of the Brigade Commander. | |
| | 16.6.18 | | The Bn again bathed in the open air baths on the AMIENS Rd. The baths were found to have been improved a good deal since the last visit. At night the Bn had to move up to relieve the 21st London Regt on the Right of the B'de front. The Companies occupied the same positions as those occupied by them when in this sub sector previously. Move order No 123 attached | |
| LINE | 17.6.18 | | The day was uneventful except for a small raid by the 142 Bde on our left. Retaliation took place, trench mortars as well as shells being fired on our line. One of the former unfortunately struck a dug out in the front line in which C.S.M. E.A. Kingham & Pte F.C. Mill (Stowman) were dividing | |

Instructions regarding War Diaries and Intelligence Summaries are contained in F. S. Regs., Part II. and the Staff Manual respectively. Title pages will be prepared in manuscript.

# WAR DIARY
*or*
# ~~INTELLIGENCE SUMMARY.~~
*(Erase heading not required.)*

Army Form C. 2118.

| Place | Date | Hour | Summary of Events and Information | Remarks and references to Appendices |
|---|---|---|---|---|
| | | | out rations. The C.S.M. was killed outright; the storeman was badly wounded & died the following day at No. 41 C.C.S. The former was buried on the 19th inst at D17 a 7.2, the officiating Chaplain being Rev. Capt. A.C. James. ~~and the latter~~ | |
| | | | The loss of C.S.M. Kingham was keenly felt. He had only recently been promoted C.S.M. but had always been conscientious at his work & had made a good name for himself. Pte Mill had been with C Coy for nearly 3½ yrs & had during that time done valuable work for his Coy. His death was a great loss not only to his Coy but to his Bn. | |
| LINE | 18.6.18 | | An uneventful day | |
| " | 19.6.18 | | In the early hours of the morning the Bn was relieved by the 6th London Regt of the 58th Div, which had been occupying the LAVIEVILLE LINE. The relief was late in arriving & also took a long time to get into position (till 3 am) principally on account of the presence of only one good C.T. to the front line. Hostile artillery was | |

D. D. & L., London, E.C.
(A10266) Wt W5300/P713 750,000 2/18 Sch. 52 Forms/C2118/16.

Army Form C. 2118.

Instructions regarding War Diaries and Intelligence Summaries are contained in F. S. Regs., Part II. and the Staff Manual respectively. Title pages will be prepared in manuscript.

# WAR DIARY
*or*
# ~~INTELLIGENCE~~ SUMMARY.

(*Erase heading not required.*)

| Place | Date | Hour | Summary of Events and Information | Remarks and references to Appendices |
|---|---|---|---|---|
| | | | somewhat active during the change over & 3 O.R. of this Bn & 2 O.R. of the 6th London were wounded | |
| | | | The Bn by platoons, marched in pouring rain back to BEHENCOURT, reaching that village at 5 am. After resting till the afternoon it moved to a tented camp at MOLLIENS au BOIS, 3¾ h, arriving in the evening & taking over from the Q.V. Rifles. The camp in good weather would doubtless be a pleasant one, but in the weather such as the Bn experienced at this time it was far from nice & in places was like a quagmire. Move orders Nos 124 & 125 attached | |
| MOLLIEN au BOIS | 20.6.18 | | at MOLLIEN au BOIS. The day was spent in cleaning up. The band of our neighbours in the camp, the 17th Londons, provided music throughout the day | |
| GUIGNEMICOURT | 21.6.18 | | The camp was taken over by a Bde of the American E.F. & the Bn moved by busses along a circuitous route through AMIENS to FERRIERES, from which place it marched to GUIGNEMICOURT. | |

D. D. & L., London, E.C.
(A10266) Wt.W5300/P713 750,000 2/18 Sch. 52 Forms/C2118/16.

Instructions regarding War Diaries and Intelligence Summaries are contained in F. S. Regs., Part II. and the Staff Manual respectively. Title pages will be prepared in manuscript.

Army Form C. 2118.

# WAR DIARY
*or*
# INTELLIGENCE SUMMARY.
*(Erase heading not required.)*

| Place | Date | Hour | Summary of Events and Information | Remarks and references to Appendices |
|---|---|---|---|---|
| | | | accompanied by the 2AND just returned from G.H.Q. Move order No 126. | |
| | | | A copy of the letter from II H.Q. complimenting the guard which had done duty there very satisfactorily for some weeks was issued. | |
| | | | H.Q. were at the chateau & the companies were billetted in barns along the main road. The accommodation generally was good. | |
| GUIGNEMICOURT | 22.6.18 | | Actually the longest day but in the eyes of the troops one of the shortest for the weather was superb & the day simply devoted to cleaning up. | |
| " | 23.6.18 | | Church Parade in the Chateau grounds at which the new padre the Revd E. Farebrother officiated. Several officers reconnoitred the area east of BOVES, which the French occupied. | |
| | 24.6.18 | | Bn parade in the morning followed by Coy training. Football matches, six a side, were played by all during the afternoon. | |

D. D. & L., London, E.C.
(A10266) Wt W5300/P713 750,000 2/18 Sch. 52 Forms/C2118/16.

Army Form C. 2118.

Instructions regarding War Diaries and Intelligence Summaries are contained in F. S. Regs., Part II. and the Staff Manual respectively. Title pages will be prepared in manuscript.

# WAR DIARY
*or*
# ~~INTELLIGENCE SUMMARY~~.
*(Erase heading not required.)*

| Place | Date | Hour | Summary of Events and Information | Remarks and references to Appendices |
|---|---|---|---|---|
| GUIGNEMICOURT | 25.6.18 | | Bn parade in the morning followed by Coy training. Similar football matches to yesterday were played during the afternoon. While the games were in progress the III Corps Commander, the Divl General & the Brigadier visited the grounds & watched the play. The band was with the Bn both in the morning and afternoon. | |
| GUIGNEMICOURT | 26.6.18 | | Battalion and Company training during the morning. Inter platoon six a side football matches in the afternoon. | |
| — do — | 27.6.18 | | Training as on 26th. Battalion football match against 24th Bn resulted in a draw | |
| — do — | 28.6.18 | | Training as on 27th. | |
| — do. — | 29.6.18 | | All Coys assembled during morning training to witness demonstration of ranging by observation of fire of Lewis Guns, and fire effect of six Lewis Guns concentrated on a Strong Point. Two officers attended Brigade tactical exercise without troops. Bn football match v. 17th Bn Lost 0-3. | |
| — do — | 30.6.18 | | Church parade in Chateau grounds by Rev. C. Brown Wilkinson C.F. 2/Lts H.H. TAYLOR and R.E.W. SCOTT 22nd London joined the Bn | |

W. [illegible] Major
Cdg 1/Civil Service Rifles

D. D. & L., London, E.C.
(A10266) Wt W5300/P713 750,000 2/18 Sch. 52 Forms/C2118/16.

June 21st 1918 Copy No. 2

## CIVIL SERVICE RIFLES

## OPERATION ORDER No. 123

Ref. map [illegible] AMIENS 17.

1. Battalion will move by bus to [illegible] to-day embussing at 100 yds. N. of crossroads at [illegible].
2. Capt. A. LEIGHTON will be embussing officer and will report to Capt. R.H. SOMM at embussing point at 10 a.m. taking with him embussing strength.
3. All camp kettles and mess boxes to be taken by bus will be carried to embussing point by 10.0 a.m. Capt. A. LEIGHTON will allot Company dumps for these.
4. The Orderly officer will take charge of the dump at the debussing point and will not leave until it is cleared.
5. Battalion will move to embussing point in full marching order at 10.15 a.m.
6. Order of march – H.Q. Coy & H.Q. Staff, A, B, C, D. 50 yds. distance to be maintained between Companies.
7. Transport will move by RAINNEVILLE – COISY – BERTANGLES – ST. SAUVEUR, thence by any route at 12 noon. They are not to [illegible] the AMIENS – VILLERS BOCAGE Rd. before 1 p.m.

Copy No. 1 – File
" 2 – War Diary
" 3 – [illegible]
" 4 – [illegible]
5 to 9 A, B, C, D, H.Q.
10 – [illegible]

[illegible signature]
Lieut. and Adjt.
Civil Service Rifles

SECRET  COPY No. 3

# CIVIL SERVICE RIFLES

## ORDER No. 120.

6th June 1916

Reference map SENLIS 1/20,000

1. Bn will be relieved by 17th Bn on the night 6/7 June as follows:–
   A Coy 17th relieves C Coy Civil Service
   B " " " B
   C " " " D
   D " " " A
2. One guide per platoon will report [illegible] Bn. H.Q. at 7.30 pm and will go to the 17th Bn [illegible] support after leading in the incoming [illegible]. These guides will take out their own platoons to the positions vacated by 17th Bn.
3. The two S.O.S. [illegible] of A Coy [illegible] Trench will not be relieved. [illegible] be sent up with those of the 17th Bn.
4. Each Coy will send one officer [illegible] to the 17th Bn this afternoon to take over [illegible]
5. Rations and water tonight will come up [illegible]
   for H.Q. B & C Coys at new Bn. H.Q.
   " A & D Coys at the junction of [illegible] Avenue and ORCHARD [illegible]
6. Transport will call at present Bn H.Q. [illegible] to take back [illegible] the [illegible] cans. One water cart will [illegible] H.Q. to fill water bottles.
7. Receipts for trench stores handed over [illegible] receipts for [illegible] stores taken over [illegible] by [illegible] [illegible] will be replaced [illegible] handed over.
8. Code word for relief complete [illegible]

Copy No. 1. C.O.
2. File
3. War Diary
4. [illegible]
5. [illegible]
6. [illegible]
8. [illegible]
9. [illegible]
12. [illegible] Officer
13. 17th Bn.
14. 47th M.G. Bn.

[illegible]
Captain & Adjutant
[illegible]

SECRET

COPY No. 3

# CIVIL SERVICE RIFLES

## ORDER NO. 121

9th June 1918.

Reference map 140 Bde. SECRET F.G.12.

1. Battalion will relieve 21st Bn. Lon. Regt on left of Bde. front to-night as follows:—

| | | | | | |
|---|---|---|---|---|---|
| A | Coy. Civil Service | relieves | D | Coy. 21st | (Right) |
| B | " " | " | B | " " | (Reserve) |
| C | " " | " | C | " " | (Support) |
| D | " " | " | A | " " | (Left) |

Each Coy. will take in 5 L.G's and from these B & C Coys. will each find two guns for a battery of 4 S.O.S. guns in EMMA TRENCH. These 4 Guns will report to Bn. H.Q. at 9.30 p.m. to-night ready to move to their new positions.

2. One guide per platoon will report to Coy Commdrs. at 9.45 p.m. and one for Battery of L.G's at Bn.H.Q. at 9.30 p.m.

3. Coys. will move off by Platoons at 100 yds distance at following times:—

| | | |
|---|---|---|
| 4 L.G's from H.Q. | at | 9.45 p.m. |
| A Coy. | — | 10.0 p.m. |
| D " | — | 10.10 p.m. |
| C " | — | 10.20 p.m. |
| B " | — | 10.30 p.m. |
| H.Q. " | — | 10.40 p.m. |

4. Advance parties of 1 officer & 1 Senior N.C.O. per Coy. will report to Coys of 21st Bn. at 6 p.m. to take over trench stores. Similar parties from 21st Bn. will report to Coys. here at the same time.

5. Receipts for stores handed over & copies of receipts for stores taken over, will be sent in by first run to-morrow 10th inst.

6. All defence schemes & works programmes will be taken over & continued.

7. Code word for relief complete will be Coy. Comdrs name.

8. Acknowledge.

[illegible signature]

Captain & Adjutant
Civil Service Rifles

Copy No. 1 C.O.
2 File
3 War Diary
4 140 Inf. Bde.
5-8 [illegible]
9 [illegible]
10 [illegible]
11 [illegible]
12 [illegible] Officer
13 21st Lon. Regt.

SECRET.

War Diary

1/CIVIL SERVICE RIFLES

ORDER No. 123

16th June 1918

1. Bn. will relieve 1/21st Bn. London Regt tonight on right of Bde. front. Coys. will be disposed as follows:–

| | |
|---|---|
| C Coy | RIGHT FRONT |
| B " | LEFT " |
| D " | SUPPORT |
| A " | RESERVE |

2. Coys will be ready to move at 9.45 p.m and one guide per platoon will report to them at that time. C Coy will move at 10.0 p.m. by platoons at 100 yards distance; B Coy at 10.10 p.m D Coy 10.15 p.m.; A Coy 10.20 p.m.; H.Q. Coy 10.30 p.m.

3 Receipts for trench stores will be handed in to first runner tomorrow morning.

Davenport

Capt & Adjt
1/Civil Service Rifles

SECRET.

# CIVIL SERVICE RIFLES

COPY No. 3

## ORDER No 129

14th June, 1918

Reference Map SENLIS 1/20000

1. Battalion will be relieved by the Poplar and Stepney Rifles today as follows:-

| | | | | |
|---|---|---|---|---|
| A Coy | CIVIL SERVICE | relieved by | D Coy | POPLAR & STEPNEYS |
| D " | ——— | do. ——— | C | ——— do. ——— |
| C " | ——— | do. ——— | A | ——— do. ——— |
| B " | ——— | do. ——— | B | ——— do. ——— |

2. C and B Coys will be relieved at about 5.30 p.m and 6.30 p.m. respectively. On relief these Coys will do 4 hours digging on the new Support Line. Details of this work will be sent to Coy. Commanders. No guides will be required for these Coys. but A and D Coys. will send one guide per Platoon to report to Poplar and Stepney Bn. H.Q. at 9.0 p.m

3. On relief Bn. will move into Support and Coys will occupy same positions as before.

4. One officer and a senior N.C.O. per Coy. will go to new positions at 4.0 p.m to take over trench stores. Receipts for trench stores handed over and copies of receipts for those taken over will be sent in by first run tomorrow.

5. Work in progress will be fully explained to incoming Coys, and all working parties handed over.

6. All empty water cans will be returned to R.S.M. at H.Q. Coy. cookhouse by 6.30 p.m

7. Each Coy will bring out 25 picks and 40 shovels and all targets.

8. Rations will arrive at new positions at midnight.

9. Code word for relief complete will be Coy. Commanders name.

Copy No. 1. C.O.
" 2. File
" 3. War Diary
" 4. 140th Inf. Bde
5–8. A B C & D Coys
9. R.S.M. & Sigs Sgt.
10. Q.M. & T.O.
11. Int. Offr
12. Poplar & Stepney Rifles

Davenport
Capt. & Adjutant,
1/CIVIL SERVICE RIFLES

SECRET.

War Diary

11th CIVIL SERVICE RIFLES
OPERATION ORDER No. 124.

Copy No. 3

13th June 1918.

Reference Maps:
SENLIS 1/40000
AMIENS 1/40000

1. Battalion will be relieved on the night 18th/19th instant by the 6th Bn London Regt. Details of Coy reliefs will be issued later.

2. One guide per platoon will report to 2/Lt Gray at Bn. H.Q. at 8.0 p.m. These will report to the H.Q. of the 6th London Regt. at D.9.C.6.7 (LAVIEVILLE [illegible]) at 9.0 p.m.

3. Trench Stores, message carrying [illegible], defence schemes, aeroplane photographs, and S.O.S. [illegible] will be handed over. Receipts for trench stores will be forwarded to Bn. H.Q. on arrival at new billets.

4. Code word for relief complete will be Coy Commanders name.

5. On relief, Coys will march to the Embussing Point on the CONTAY–FRANVILLERS Road. The head of the column will be behind Brigade H.Q. and T.M.B., facing South, at Cross Roads 1½ miles S.W. of BAIZIEUX. Bn. will embus at 4.0 a.m. and will debus on the BRIQUEMESNIL–FERRIERES Road [head of column facing East at Eastern end of FERRIERES] and will march to the village of BOUGAINVILLE. Capt. A. LEIGHTON will act as Embussing Officer and will report to Capt. [illegible] at Embussing Point at 3.0 a.m. Instructions are being sent to him separately.

6. Dixies, mess boxes and all empty water cans will be dumped at Bn. H.Q. at 8.0 p.m. on the 18th. [illegible] will be taken by the Transport to the Embussing Point. [illegible] and at least one representative from each [illegible] will [illegible] with the limbers.

7. Transport and Q.M. Stores will move under orders issued to them direct by Brigade.

8. Billeting party under 2/Lt SPENCER will go by [illegible] at [illegible] on the 19th. Orders have been issued to [illegible]

[illegible] O.C. | S.Y. [illegible]
[illegible] | Q. R.S.M. [illegible]
[illegible] | [illegible]
[illegible]

War Diary

[illegible] Bn [illegible] SERVICE RIFLES [illegible] 2

ORDER No 125

[illegible] June 17

Ref Map 62D 1/40000

1. The Battalion will move this evening to camp at present occupied by [illegible] in MOLLIENS WOOD B 8 c.

2. Coys will move independently and will pass the starting point (Road junction B 10 [illegible]) in the following order:-

C Coy 8.15 pm
HQ " 8.20 "
A " 8.25 "
B " 8.30 "
D " 8.35 "

Coys in full marching order.
Route will be via BEAUCOURT and turning [illegible] at B11 c 6.2 and along the road through B9 and B10.

3. All valises and mess boxes will be dumped at Bn HQ at 5.30 pm.
Transport Officer will arrange to convey them to the new camp.

4. Transport Officer will arrange for horses of mounted officers to be at Bn HQ at 8.0 pm.

Davenport
Capt & Adjt
[illegible] Service Rifles

SECRET.

COPY No. 3

App VI

CIVIL SERVICE RIFLES

ORDER No 117

29th May, 1918.

Reference Map SENLIS 1/20.000.

1. Battalion will be relieved by 21st Battalion to-night as follows:-

| | | | |
|---|---|---|---|
| B Coy. | (Left) will be relieved by | A Coy. | 21st |
| C " | (Centre) | C " | |
| D | (Right) | D | |
| A | (Reserve) | B | |

2. One guide per platoon will report to 2/Lt HARTLEY at Bn. H.Q. at 9.0 p.m. They will meet incoming platoons in the Square at BRESLE D 15 a 55.70 at 9.45 p.m.

3. Lewis Gun limbers for B. C. and D Coys. will arrive at their Ration Dump at 10.30 p.m. and will wait there for mess boxes and Lewis Guns. A Coys L.G. limber will be at Bn. H.Q. from 8.30 p.m. onwards. Limbers for dixies, water cans, tools etc. and mess cart will report to cookhouse at 8.30 p.m.

4. On relief Coys. will move via BRESLE to camp now occupied by 21st Battalion.

5. Code word for relief complete will be Company Commanders name.

6. Receipts for trench stores etc. will be handed in to Orderly Room on arrival at Camp.

Davenport

Capt. and Adjutant.
CIVIL SERVICE RIFLES.

Copy No. 1 C.O.
2 File
3 War Diary
4 140 Infy. Bde.
5/8 A.B.C.D. Coys.
9 R.S.M. and Sigs. Sgt.
10 Q.M.
11 T.O.
12 Intelligence Officer
13 21st Bn. London Regt.

App VIII

War Diary Copy

[illegible] 118

[illegible]

[illegible]

Kits will be [illegible] [illegible]

ANVILLERS - [illegible] RD.

[illegible]

[illegible] Sgt HARTLEY in full marching order at 2.15 pm and will proceed to [illegible] [illegible] will be allotted [illegible].

[illegible] will [illegible] [illegible] [illegible] [illegible] [illegible] [illegible] will be [illegible] at 4.30 pm [illegible] [illegible] He will [illegible] [illegible] [illegible] breakfast and march off [illegible] [illegible] [illegible] [illegible] will [illegible] [illegible] will be [illegible] [illegible] at 10 pm.

Mar 16

[illegible] Capt [illegible]

[illegible] Regt

Draw 16 tents
Give up 19 bivvies.

| | | | |
|---|---|---|---|
| A | 4 | | -5 |
| B | 4 | 15 | -5 |
| C | 1.3 | 18 | -4 |
| D | 1.3 | | -4 |
| HQ | 2.2 | | -1 |

SECRET.

COPY No 3

# CIVIL SERVICE RIFLES

## ORDER No. 119.

App VIII

31st May 1918.

Reference map Senlis $\frac{1}{20.000}$.

1 Battalion will relieve 24th Bn. London Regt on the night of 1st/2nd June as follows:-

| | | | |
|---|---|---|---|
| A Company C.S.R. relieves | D. Coy. 24th Bn. | in reserve |
| B " " " | A " " " | left front |
| C " " " | D " " " | right front |
| D " " " | C " " " | in support. |

2. Battalion will leave at 8.15 p.m. in the order:- C. B. D. A HQ. Movement will be by platoons at 100 yards distance. The route will be via FRANVILLERS and the ALBERT ROAD. Dress fighting order..

3 Guides will be met at 9.30 p.m. at the Cross roads D. 21. a. 6. 7.

4 L. GUNS. B. Coy will take in 6 Lewis Guns
C " " " " 5 " "
D " " " " 3 " "
A " " " " 4 " "

Lewis Gun limbers will go with leading platoon of each Coy. and will carry Coy. Mess boxes as well as the guns. Cooking will be done at Cook Houses at D 18. d 5 3 near Bn HQ

5. Advance parties consisting of 1 Officer per Coy, 1 N.C.O. per platoon and 1 N.C.O. for Bn. HQ will parade at 1.0 p.m. outside Orderly Room in readiness to go up the line to take over trench stores and remain until their Coys come in. Four H.Q. Runners will accompany this party.

Receipts for trench stores will be forwarded to H.Q by 8.0 a.m. on 2nd June.

Code word for relief complete will be Coy Commanders name.

Davenport
Captain & Adjutant
// Civil Service Rifles.

Copy No 1. C.O
2. File
3. War Diary
4. 140 Inf Bde
5/8. ABCD Coys.
9. R.S.M. and Sig. Sgt
10. QM
11. T.O.
12. Intelligence Officer
13. 3rd Lon. Regt

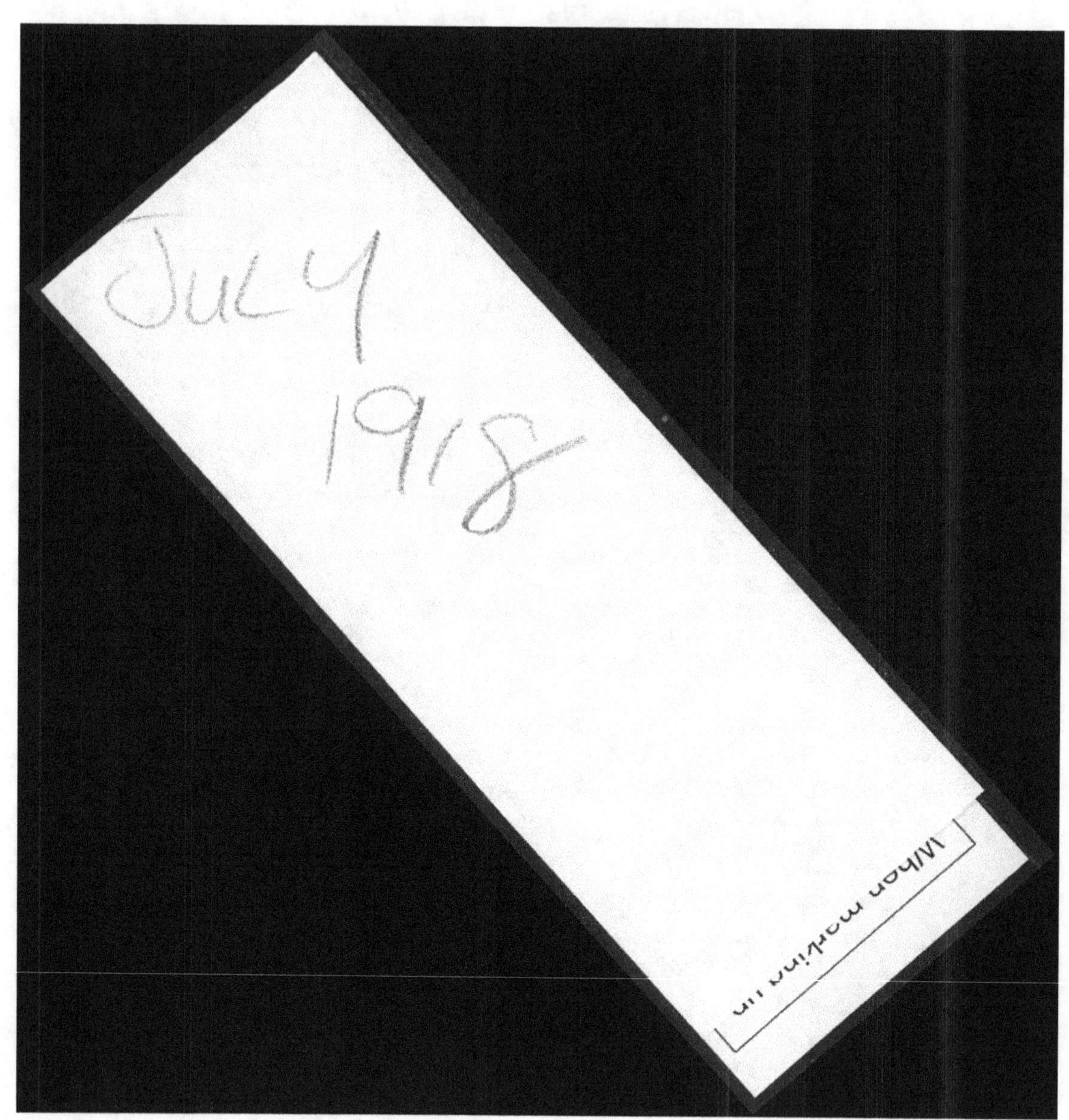
July
1918
When marking in

# WAR DIARY
*or*
# INTELLIGENCE SUMMARY.
*(Erase heading not required.)*

Instructions regarding War Diaries and Intelligence Summaries are contained in F. S. Regs., Part II. and the Staff Manual respectively. Title pages will be prepared in manuscript.

Army Form C. 2118.

1/15 London Rgt  140/47

WO 37

| Place | Date | Hour | Summary of Events and Information | Remarks and references to Appendices |
|---|---|---|---|---|
| [illegible] | 1/7/18 | | Battalion and Company training carried on during the morning and one Company (A) fired on a new Range N.E. of PISSY. Finals of six a side football matches was played in the evening resulting in a win for a B Coy team. There was afterwards an exhibition game of Pullocks which was introduced to the Battalion by Major [illegible] — a game that at once became very popular in the Battalion and each Company was equipped with a set of gear by the pioneers. 2/Lt W.T. BIRCHETT joined the Battalion. | [initialled] |
| —do— | 2/7/18 | | Four Lewis Guns sections, with two guns each, under 2/Lt SOUTER and four snipers per Coy under Sergt Thomas carried out range practices [illegible] on an old French range on the western outskirts of AMIENS. B Coy fired on the range near PISSY and remaining Coys [illegible]. In the afternoon officers and NCOs attended a demonstration by Stokes Mortars in the training area N.E. of BOUGUES. The Divisional Follies gave a performance for the Battalion in the [illegible] grounds. Lt Col. W.H.G. Segrave and Capt W.L. RATHBONE A.C.O. returned from leave. | [initialled] |
| —do.— | 3/7/18 | | The day was a holiday to allow all ranks to attend the Divl. Water Carnival at PICQUIGNY. Lorries and G.S. wagons were used to take down competitors and spectators. The events were mostly decided in PICQUIGNY LOCK on the R. Somme. The Bn. was successful in the inter Battalion water polo with the following team C/Sergt Watts W.S. (B Coy) Cpl. Wraight O.S. B Coy, Cpl. S. BYRON B Coy, L/Cpl. H.G. Terry A Coy, Ptes T. N Smale B Coy, S. Paisley and R. Bull Tpt. The R.Q.M.S. repeated his last year's success in the Odd craft race, but this year he entered two boats which he had built — the KAPIV and the COTAM, which finished first and second respectively. Pte E.G. MANFIELD won third prize in the back stroke race and the following team got a place in the Divl. Relay Race. Cpl. O.S. Wraight B Coy, Ptes Bull (Tpt.) F.T. Garnham B Coy and R.A. Pooley D Coy. | [initialled] |

(A10266) W. W5300/P713 750,000 5/18 Sch. 52 Forms/C2118/14. D. D. & L., London, E.C.

Army Form C. 2118.

Instructions regarding War Diaries and Intelligence Summaries are contained in F. S. Regs., Part II. and the Staff Manual respectively. Title pages will be prepared in manuscript.

# WAR DIARY
*or*
# INTELLIGENCE SUMMARY.

*(Erase heading not required.)*

| Place | Date | Hour | Summary of Events and Information | Remarks and references to Appendices |
|---|---|---|---|---|
| GUIGNEMICOURT | 4/7/18 | | At Battalion parade the Major General G.F. Goring K.C.B. K.C.M.G. D.S.O. presented Bars and ribbons to the following officers NCO's and men who were awarded the honours shown for work during the operations of March last:- Capt S.T. Smither (now with 17th Bn) Bar to M.C. Capt. G.B. Martin (now with 17th Bn) M.C. Cpl. Amsden C.S. D.C.M. Sergt. Knight H.G. M.M. and bar. Cpl. Shirley R. M.M. bar to M.M. Sergt. Goring F.A. M.M. Cpl. Wean C.E. M.M. Ptes. Stringnell C. Ashdown G.G. and Maunder L.F. all received M.M. The usual training was carried on afterwards and in the evening the Battalion football team was beaten 0-2 by the 4th R.W.F. The following represented the Battalion:- Pte. W.T. Whenman (Tpt.) Goal. Pte. J.M. Thomson (Tpt.) and Sergt. P. Hague (D Coy) backs. Sergt. M.E. Bradford (C Coy) Pte. N.W. Woodford (Capt.) Tpt. and Pte. T.H. Harris Tpt. Halves. L/Cpl. Terry (A Coy) Pte. A. Ryall (A Coy) C.S.M. O.H. Levey (C Coy) Sergt. F. Harris (H.Q.) and Pte. J.E. Postle (Tpt.) forwards. | [initials] |
| | | | 2/Lts. R. Upton, E.R. LASCELLES and 2/LT. P. Ewan (25th Cyclists) and LIEUT. S. HASLETT (11th Lond.) joined the Bn. | |
| -do.- | 5/7/18 | | Brig. Genl. H.B. Kennedy C.M.G. D.S.O. came to see the Battalion training. In the evening the Bn football team went to PISSY and drew 2-2 with the 24th Bn. Following represented the Bn:- Pte. W.T. Whenman (Tpt.) Goal. Sergts. P. Hague (D Coy) and A.G. Taylor (B Coy) backs. Sergts. W.C. Lehan (H.Q.) and M.E. Bradford (C Coy) and Pte. L. Alsing (A Coy) halves. Pte. J.E. Postle (Capt.) Tpt. L/Cpl. B.F. Houlahan (B Coy) C.S.M. O.L.H. Levey (C Coy) Pte. A. Ryall (A Coy) and L/Cpl. H. Terry (A Coy) forwards. | [initials] |
| -do.- | 6/7/18 | | The morning was spent in kit inspections and in the afternoon the Bn. was photographed by photographers from the French Flying Corps. In the evening the Warrant Officers and Sergeants of the Bn held a dinner in the village estaminet, and the following team went to SAISSEVAL and beat the 17th Bn at football by 2 goals to 1:- Pte. Whenman W.T. Goal. Ptes. Alsing L. and Edwards W. (A Coy) backs. Sergt. Chubb W. (B Coy) Pte. Woodford N.W. (Tpt.) (Capt.) and Sergt. M.E. Bradford (C Coy) halves. Pte. Postle J.E. (Tpt.) L/Cpl. Houlahan B.F. (B Coy) Pte. Perry R.A. (A Coy) C.S.M. Levey O.L.H. (C Coy) and L/Cpl. H. Terry A Coy forwards. | [initials] |
| | | | There was a very welcome reduction in the number of cases of Influenza, and the Bn. hospital which had been instituted for the treatment of these cases, was at last empty. During the past month nearly 100 members of the Bn. had suffered from this epidemic which was prevalent throughout the whole Army, and which we hope was also prevalent in the German Army. | |

D. D. & L., London, E.C. (A7786) Wt W5300/P713 750,000 2/18 Sch. 52 Forms/C2118/16.

Instructions regarding War Diaries and Intelligence Summaries are contained in F. S. Regs., Part II. and the Staff Manual respectively. Title pages will be prepared in manuscript.

# WAR DIARY
*or*
# INTELLIGENCE SUMMARY.
*(Erase heading not required.)*

Army Form C. 2118.

| Place | Date | Hour | Summary of Events and Information | Remarks and references to Appendices |
|---|---|---|---|---|
| GUIGNEMICOURT | 7/7/18 | | Rev. S. Farebrother took the Church Parade and in Chateau Grounds. In the early morning a lorry left Bde. H.Q. at BOVELLES to convey officers for a joy ride to LE TREPORT. The following football team representing the Battalion beat the 18th Bn (London Irish) on our ground by 2 goals to 1. L/Cpl. Haynes F.J. (C Coy) goal: Ptes Alsing L (A Coy) and Edwards W (A Coy) backs: Sergt. Bradford M.E (C Coy) Pte. Woodford N.W (Tpt.) capt. and Sergt. L Chubb (B Coy) halves: L/Cpl. H. Terry (A Coy) Pte. A. Ryall (A Coy) C.S.M. Levey O.L.H. (C Coy) and Ptes. Perry R.A. and Postle S.E (Tpt.) forwards. A photographer from the French Aerodrome came to photograph our horses. | |
| – do. – | 8/7/18 | | The training programme was varied from the previous week by the introduction of simple Company tactical exercises and also by the addition of wiring instruction and bombing instruction. Basket ball was introduced into the afternoon recreational training and to encourage indifferent shots to enter for the evening sweepstake shoots the whole battalion was classified into six shooting classes and a handicap framed accordingly. In the evening a Battalion Concert was given in the chateau grounds and in spite of the doubtful weather it was well attended. With the exception of Major Porteous, Cpl. Hart and Pte. Jones of the Divisional Signals Co. the whole of the artistes came from the Battalion. In addition to the Regimental Band the following contributed to a very successful programme:– Lt. A. Knox (M.O.R.C. U.S.A.) 2/LTS BOOTH and Jones, C.S.M. Grosvenor, Ptes Crawley (A Coy) Perrin (Band) Scripe (D Coy) and Linfield (A Coy). The "star spangled banner" was played for the first time in the Regiment. | |
| – do. – | 9/7/18 | | Major General Gorringe visited the Battalion training in the morning and in the afternoon all officers attended a most interesting lecture by Capt. A. Wilson (Intelligence G.H.Q) on the military situation. The Battalion beat the 18th (London Irish) at PICQUIGNY by 2 to 1 with the following team:– Pte W.T. Whenman (T) Sgt P. Hague (D) Pte. W.E. Edwards (A) Sgt. M.E. Bradford (C) Pte N.W. Woodford (Capt.) (T) Sgt. E.A. Merchant (A) L/Cpl H. Terry (A) Pte A. Ryall (A) C.S.M. O.L.H Levey C. Pte R.A. Perry (T) Pte. Postle (T). Major L.L. Pargiter (Middlesex Regt.) who had been with us since 4 Apl. as 2nd in command, left to command the 22nd Bn. | |

D. D. & L., London, E.C.
(A12266) Wt W5300/P713 750,000 2/18 Sch. 52 Forms/C2118/16.

Army Form C. 2118.

Instructions regarding War Diaries and Intelligence Summaries are contained in F. S. Regs., Part II. and the Staff Manual respectively. Title pages will be prepared in manuscript.

# WAR DIARY
or
# INTELLIGENCE SUMMARY.
*(Erase heading not required.)*

| Place | Date | Hour | Summary of Events and Information | Remarks and references to Appendices |
|---|---|---|---|---|
| GUIGNEMICOURT | 10/7/18 | | The Battalion ~~route~~ marched to OISSY and bathed in the lake there. Dinners were cooked on the march and after dinner at OISSY the Bn returned to billets. The Regimental Band went to ST. PIERRE A GOUY to play at the XXII Corps Race Meeting. It is interesting to note that the Band was described on the Race Card as the Band of the 47th Division. Capt. G.G. Bates M.C. came to HQ. to act as 2nd in command and Capt. A. Whiteley took over command of C Coy. Lieut. W. EDMED 25th (Cyclist Bn) London Regt. joined the Battalion. | |
| ditto | 11/7/18 | | The usual training was carried out in the morning, except that the L.G. Sections paraded under the L.G.O. for range practice. At 12.45 pm. a Voluntary memorial Service for Civil Servants who had fallen in the war was conducted by the Revd. FAREBROTHER; the band rendered Chopin's "Funeral March". About 400 attended. At the same time, a service at which Their Maj. The King & Queen were present, was being held in WESTMINSTER ABBEY with the same intention. The afternoon was devoted to Sports, - the following being a list of events & prizewinners:- | |

1. High Jump (1) Sgt LEHAN – H.Q. (2) Pte RING – B (3) Pte BIRMINGHAM – Trans.
2. Officers Relay (1) D (2) A.
3. Putting Shot (1) Cpl PATTISON – TRANS. (2) C.S.M. Turner – B (3) Lt. KNOX – H.Q.
4. Obstacle (1) " " " (2) Pte. LEIGH – B (3) Cpl. STRONG – C.
5. 100 (1) Lcpl SLACK – ~~B~~ C (2) C.S.M. TURNER – B (3) Pte. EDWARDS – A.
6. HURDLES (1) Sgt. LEHAN – H.Q. (2) Cpl. PATTISON – T (3) Pte. England – C.
7. Long Jump (1) Lieut. KNOX – H.Q. (2) C.S.M. TURNER – B (3) Sgt. LEHAN – H.Q.
8. 220 (1) Pte. POSTLE – T (2) Pte EDWARDS – A (3) Pte. MUMMERY – A.
9. 3 Legged (1) B (2) D (3) Transport
10. 440 (1) Pte. FEWSTER – D (2) Pte. WILLIAMS – T (3) Pte HOWARD – D
11. Relay (O.R.) (1) D (2) Transport (3) B
12. Veterans (1) C.S.M. TURNER – B (2) Capt RATHBONE M.C. – A (3) 2/Lt BOOTH – A

**Championship Marks**

1. D Coy 49
2. B – 29
3. A – 21
4. C – 7

(HQ. & Transport ineligible).

— PRIZES —

360 francs from C.O's fund was allocated to prizes which were distributed later on account of rain.

The success of Lieut KNOX, attached to us from the American Army, in Events 3 & 7 is noteworthy.
-Billeting party from 11/ R. Fus. arrived in the evening to take over billets.

| Place | Date | Hour | Summary of Events and Information | Remarks and references to Appendices |
|---|---|---|---|---|
| WARLOY | 12/7/18 | | The battalion embussed at FERRIERES & passing through AMIENS reached WARLOY in the early afternoon, relieving the 2nd BEDFORDS. The fifth platoons in each Coy debussed at MOLLIENS – au – BOIS for special training while the Battn was forward. | Vide 140 O.O. No 251 of 11th July attached; also Battn O.O. No 127. |
| ditto. | 13/7/18 | | Baths were started under battalion arrangements & clean clothing issued. Kit inspections were held - otherwise the day was one of rest. | |

D. D. & L., London, E.C.
(A10266) Wt W5300/P713 750,000 2/18 Sch. 52 Forms/C2118/16.

# WAR DIARY
or
# INTELLIGENCE SUMMARY.
(*Erase heading not required.*)

Instructions regarding War Diaries and Intelligence Summaries are contained in F. S. Regs., Part II. and the Staff Manual respectively. Title pages will be prepared in manuscript.

Army Form C. 2118.

| Place | Date | Hour | Summary of Events and Information | Remarks and references to Appendices |
|---|---|---|---|---|
| SENLIS — HENENCOURT ROAD | 17/7/18. | | Cash drawn from Field Cashier at MOULLIENS-au-BOIS & men paid.<br>Commanding Officer reconnoitred positions held by 1/24 in Support.<br>Coys. carried out the same working parties & routine as yesterday.<br>Capt. Grimsdale rejoined the battalion and was posted to 'B' Coy.<br>2 Lt. Gray (Intelligence Officer) left for 4 days' attachment to the Div<sup></sup>l 4.5 Howitzers | R. |
| — ditto. — | 18/7/18. | | Same routine & working parties as yesterday.<br>At 10 p.m. Battn relieved 1/24 in Support.<br>2 Lt. Stevenson ('D' Coy) left for GRANTHAM on transfer to M.G.C.<br>News received of successful French Counter attack in SOISSONS region. | vide C.S.R. order No. 129 of 18-7-18 attached. R. |
| SENLIS — MILLENCOURT ROAD | 19/7/18. | | Work programme started, including linking up 'C' Coy's trench in V 23 d. with HAM REDOUBT, construction of Cookhouse near Battn & Coy H.Q., improvement of latrines & cutting of clover to provide green food for horses.<br>The Brigade Commander took lunch at Battn H.Q. Capt [illegible] rejoined from MOULLIENS-AU-BOIS | R. |
| ditto | 20/7/18. | | Same routine & working parties as yesterday<br>2nd Lt Gray returned to the Bn after his attachment to the 4.5 Howitzers,<br>at night the Bn relieved the 17th London in SWAN TRENCH, on the right of the left Brigade front. D Coy was on the right front, A Coy left front, with C & B in support & reserve respectively.<br>The relief was a quiet one but took a long while to perform.<br>Various detachments of the 131st American Regt joined the Bn for tuition purposes. | vide C.O.'s order No [illegible] attached. |

D. D. & L., London, E.C.
(A10266) Wt W5300/P713 750,000 2/18 Sch. 52 Forms/C2118/16.

Instructions regarding War Diaries and Intelligence Summaries are contained in F. S. Regs., Part II. and the Staff Manual respectively. Title pages will be prepared in manuscript.

# WAR DIARY
*or*
# INTELLIGENCE SUMMARY.
*(Erase heading not required.)*

Army Form C. 2118

| Place | Date | Hour | Summary of Events and Information | Remarks and references to Appendices |
|---|---|---|---|---|
| LINE | 21.7.18 | | The usual trench routine was carried out. Working parties improved the accommodation in the lines & assisted the R.E.s in the digging of a water well in the valley N. of MELBOURNE TRENCH. Situation quite quiet. | |
| " | 22.7.18 | | The same routine and working parties as yesterday. At night the Americans with the Bn were relieved by Americans of L Coy 131st Regt 33rd U.S.A. Div. | |
| " | 23.7.18 | | The day was a very quiet one. Same routine & working parties as yesterday. An "A" Coy night patrol found a L.G., several magazines & rifles at a suspected enemy post & brought them back to our line. | |
| " | 24.7.18 | | A raiding party of the 22nd London came into our line and carried out a raid opposite our front. Two prisoners were taken, & despite the artillery, T.M. and drum fire directed on the enemy front no retaliation took place on our lines. At night the Bn was relieved by the 1st Bn 131st American Regt. The relief was performed expeditiously, notwithstanding the march | |

D. D. & L., London, E.C.
(A10266) Wt W5300/P713 750,000 2/18 Sch. 52 Forms/C2118/16.

Instructions regarding War Diaries and Intelligence Summaries are contained in F. S. Regs., Part II. and the Staff Manual respectively. Title pages will be prepared in manuscript.

# WAR DIARY
*or*
# INTELLIGENCE SUMMARY.
*(Erase heading not required.)*

Army Form C. 2118.

| Place | Date | Hour | Summary of Events and Information | Remarks and references to Appendices |
|---|---|---|---|---|
| WARLOY | 14/7/18 | | The Divisional Baths were allotted to the Battn; about half the men bathed.<br>A Voluntary Church Service was held in the School at 12.15 pm. & over 400 attended.<br>The Commanding Officer reconnoitred the Reserve position occupied by 1/21st.<br>2/Lt. A.E. CLARKE (wounded at LOOS when with our 'B' Coy.) joined the battn from 1/17th and was posted to 'B' Coy. | [illegible] |
| WARLOY | 15/7/18 | | The battalion carried out training during the morning under Coy. arrangements.<br>After dinners advance parties left to take over Stores &c. from 1/21st.<br>Battle Surplus left for MOULLIENS-AU-BOIS. 'The Dollies' were engaged for the battalion in the theatre, which accommodated 350, and provided a new & excellent programme, during the afternoon.<br>In the evening the battalion relieved the 1/21st in COURT SUPPORT & CAVALRY TRENCH about the SENLIS-HENENCOURT Road.<br>R.E. Working parties for mineshafts were provided during the night. | [illegible]<br>vide C.S.R. order No 128 of 15/7/18. |
| SENLIS-HENENCOURT Road | 16/7/18 | | R.E. parties continued. The canteen was moved up from the Depot.<br>The Commanding Officer attended a Brigade Conference at WARLOY.<br>The draw for the Lottery arranged by the Battn for W. Savings Certs. took place at B. H.Q. About 680 tickets were sold thus enabling nearly 90 W.S. Certs to be purchased. The prizes were 1 of 10 Certs, 2 of 4, 5 of 3, 12 of 2 & 30 of 1; the small balance of about £3 being allocated to the C.S.R. Prisoners of War Fund. | [illegible] |

D. D. & L., London, E.C.
(A10266) Wt W5300/P713 750,000 2/18 Sch. 52 Forms/C2118/16.

# WAR DIARY
*or*
# INTELLIGENCE SUMMARY.
*(Erase heading not required.)*

Instructions regarding War Diaries and Intelligence Summaries are contained in F. S. Regs., Part II. and the Staff Manual respectively. Title pages will be prepared in manuscript.

| Place | Date | Hour | Summary of Events and Information | Remarks and references to Appendices |
|---|---|---|---|---|
| LINE | 24.7.18 | | greater strength of the american platoons, & the Bn, less the C.O., Adjutant, 4 Coy Commanders & some senior NCOs & specialists (who remained to assist the new garrisons) moved by platoons to CONTAY, which place the last platoon reached at 6 am 25th. | |
| CONTAY | 25.7.18 | | The day was spent in cleaning up & bathing at VADENCOURT. Capt. Kilner returned from the line to go to the Reception Camp at MOLLIENS au BOIS & Capt. Whiteley to proceed to the III Army Coy Commanders school for a course. Capt. Bates was in command of the Battalion. | |
| " | 26.7.18 | | Training under Coy arrangements. The C.O. Adjutant, & other personnel who assisted the Americans returned from the line. Capt. Bates went into line to replace C.O. | |
| " | 27.7.18 | | Heavy falls of rain interfered with training. In the afternoon officers & N.C.Os attended a lecture on Contact Aeroplanes given in the MAISON HUT CONTAY. | |
| " | 28.7.18 | | Church Parade attended by the Major General. At the conclusion the American Battle hymn was sung. On the night 28/29 the Bn relieved the 1/7th London in support. C Coy went into MELBOURNE TRENCH, B into M..ARAY TRENCH, A into POSSUM TRENCH & D into CARSON TRENCH. | Vide [illegible] order 41 dated [illegible] |

D. D. & L., London, E.C.
(A10266) Wt W5300/P713 750,000 2/18 Sch. 52 Forms/C2118/16.

Instructions regarding War Diaries and Intelligence Summaries are contained in F. S. Regs., Part II. and the Staff Manual respectively. Title pages will be prepared in manuscript.

# WAR DIARY
*or*
# INTELLIGENCE SUMMARY.
(*Erase heading not required.*)

Army Form C. 2118.

| Place | Date | Hour | Summary of Events and Information | Remarks and references to Appendices |
|---|---|---|---|---|
| IN SUPPORT | 29.7.18 | | Coys carried out the usual trench routine & worked on improving the accommodation in the line. Capt. Bates (2nd in command) returned to the Bn after assisting the 131st American Regt. for 3 days. | |
| ditto | 30.7.18 | | Coys. carried out the usual trench routine. Battn. relieved at night by 1/19th & moved into Forward position of reserve Bde, vacated by 1/18th. | Vide C.S.R. O.B. No 133 G.B. |
| HENENCOURT – SENLIS RD (Forward Reserve Bde). | 31.7.18 | | Coys. worked with Tunnelling Unit removing spoil and also improved their own Areas. The Band played at Brigade HQ during the afternoon. | G.B. |
| ditto | 1/8 | | | |

G. Gordon Bates Capt.
for Lt. COL.
Comndg. 1/CIVIL SERVICE RIFLES.
1/8/18.

D. D. & L., London, E.C. (A10266) Wt W4000/P713 750,000 2/18 Sch. 52 Forms/C2118/16.

SECRET. CIVIL SERVICE RIFLES Copy No. 2

ORDER No. [illegible] [illegible] July 1918.

Ref map. SENLIS SHEET.

1. The Battalion will be relieved tonight by the 1st. Battn. 131 American Regt. each Company being relieved by the same letter Company.
2. One guide per platoon and one for Battn. H.Q. will report to 2/Lt. GREY at Battn. H.Q. at 7.0 p.m. and will meet the incoming platoons at Brigade H.Q. V.20.d 4.4 at 8.30 p.m.
3. On relief Companies will march to billets in CONTAY, a distance of 100 yds. being kept between platoons.
4. The following will remain behind to assist the American Battn. for 24 hours.

Bn. H.Q.

C.O. and Adjt.
R.S.M.
Sigs. Sergt.
2 Signallers
2 Runners

Each Company

Company Commander and 1 Subaltern.
4 Platoon Sergts.
No. 1 of all L. G. Guns.
x 6 Signallers and Runners.

x As B and C Coys. have only one signal station they will leave 6 Sigs. and Runners for the two Companies.

Following will be attached to American Battn. for 48 hours:

R.Q.M.S.
2 Transport N.C.O's or Senior men.
4 Coy. Qr. Mr. Sergts.

5. Details of all working parties and work in progress will be handed over to American Coys, as will also programme of trench routine and lists of reports due.
6. All trench stores S.O.S. grenades etc. will be handed over and receipts sent to Orderly Room on arrival at Contay.

2

7. Limbers for Lewis Guns, mess things etc will report to Coy. ration dumps at 12.30 a.m. Any Lewis Gun teams relieved before that time will dump their guns at that place and leave one representative in charge.
Mess Cart will be at H.Q. ration dump at 10.30 p. to take back H.Q. mess things. Companies may send their mess things in this cart if they prefer it, but must send a servant to march with the cart.

8. Q.M. will arrange for cooker with hot tea to be on the track at V.20 d. 6 8 (N of HENENCOURT WOOD) at 1.30 a.m.
Route to be followed going out is via Cross country tracks to Cross roads V 22.c.8.8 thence via track to WARLOY.

9. Code word for relief complete will be Company Commanders name.

10. On completion of relief Capt. Grimsdale will be in command of the Battalion during the absence of the C.O. and 2nd in command.

Davenport
Capt. and Adjt.
1/Civil Service Rifles.

Copy No. 1. File
2. War Diary
3. C.O.
4–7. A, B, C & D Coys.
8. R.S.M. & Sigs.
9. T.O. & Q.M.
10. M.O.
11. 140 Bde.
12. 131 U.S. Inf/Cy.

will be sent to Orderly Room by 1st run, 31st

6. Disposition sketches in new positions will also be forwarded by 1st run.

7. Q.M. will arrange for cooks and dixies to be at Coy. cookhouses in the new area before the Bn arrives there. Water tanks will be filled there and rations delivered to the new positions.

8. All empty water cans will be sent to Bn H.Q. by 7.0 p.m today. Letters for post and socks will be sent down at the same time and the whole delivered to Sgt. PINDER

9. Lewis Guns will be carried to new positions by Coys and each Coy. will bring out 12 picks and 25 shovels. Mess things will be carried out

10. T.O. will have three limbers at Bn H.Q. at 10.0 p.m to take back stores, kits, etc. to depot and to new area

11. Code word for relief complete will be Coy Commander's name.

[illegible]

Capt & Adjt.
Civil Service Rifles.

1 File
2 War Diary
3 C.O.
4/7 A B C D Coys
8 L.G.O.
9 M.O. & I.O.
10. R.S.M. & Sigs
11 T.O. & Q.M.
12 140th Infy Bde
13 [illegible]

SECRET. 1/CIVIL SERVICE RIFLES. COPY No. 2

ORDER No. 127. 11th. July 1918.

Reference maps:-
AMIENS - Sheet 17. $\frac{1}{100,000}$
SENLIS - $\frac{1}{20,000}$

1. Battalion will embus to-morrow for WARLOY on the BRIQUEMESNIL – FERRIERES road at 8.0 a.m.
Companies etc. will pass starting point, D Company Cooker billet, as follows:-

| | |
|---|---|
| Band and D Company | 7.30 a.m. |
| A " | 7.31 " |
| B " | 7.32 " |
| C " | 7.33 " |
| H.Q. Company which will include Q.M. Stores personnel | 7.34 " |

2. Capt. G.G. BATES. M.C. will act as Battalion Embussing officer. He will report with 2 runners to Capt. R.H. CARTER at 7.0 a.m. at the cross roads, 600 yds. South of the third R in FERRIERES on the BRIQUEMESNIL – SAVEUSE road.
3. Each Company will detail one Officer to act as embussing officer. He will report to Capt. G.G. BATES. M.C at the Chateau gates at 6.30 a.m. and will bring with him the embussing strength of his Company.
2/Lt. A. SOUTER will represent H.Q. Company.
4. Before leaving this area Company Commanders will themselves inspect their area and ensure that it is left in a clean and sanitary condition, and that no stores of any kind including ammunition or empty S.A.A. boxes are left behind. A certificate to the effect that this has been done will be handed to the adjutant at the starting point to-morrow.
5. One platoon of each Company will debus at MOLLIENS – AU – BOIS and go to the training camp of the 2nd. Bedfords. These platoons will all embus in the rear of the Battalion. The strength of the platoon and the name of the Officer in charge will be reported to the Q.M. at 4.45 a.m. to-morrow so that he can arrange to deliver kits, cooking utensils &c. for this party at MOLLIENS Camp.

Copy No. 1. C.O.
2. File
3. War diary
4. Bde.
5-8 A, B, C, D Coys.
9 R.S.M. & Sigs.
10 T.O. & Q.M.

Davenport
Capt. and Adjt.
1/CIVIL SERVICE RIFLES.

SECRET CIVIL SERVICE RIFLES COPY No. 2

ORDER No. 128. JULY 15th 1918.

Ref. map SENLIS 1/20,000

1. Battalion will relieve First Surrey Rifles this afternoon in the forward area in COURT SUPPORT and CAVALRY TRENCH as follows:- Each Company will relieve the corresponding letter Company of the First Surrey Rifles.

2. Companies will be in readiness to move immediately after tea and on the order to move will march off by platoons at 100 yards distance in the following order D, C, B, A Companies. Route to be followed will be via the main WARLOY - SENLIS road.

3. Rations and dixies will be loaded onto limbers at 4.0 p.m. & will go up with the valise wagon. Coy. cooks will go with this limber and at least one servant per Company will go with the valise wagon. Two Lewis Gun limbers containing the Lewis Guns of all Companies will go with the leading platoon. Lewis Guns and magazines will be loaded at 4.0 p.m. at Transport lines, and one representative from each team will march with the limbers.

4. All water bottles will be filled before leaving and there will be no more drinking water available until 3.0 p.m. to-morrow.

5. Receipts for Trench Stores will be sent to Battalion H.Q. at V 22 b 3.7 (near the ruined mill) by last run to-night.

6. A Company will take over all working parties at 8.0 p.m. to-night and these will be taken over by B, C, and D Companies after each 24 hours. Schedule of working parties will be published to all Companies this evening.

7. Code word for relief complete will be Company Commanders name.

Distribution

Copy No. 1 - File
" 2 - War Diary
" 3 - C.O.
" 4-7 - A, B, C, D Coys.
" 8 - R.S.M. & Sigs.
9 - T.O. & Q.M.
10 - L.G.O.
11 - M.O.
12 - 140 Bde.
13 - F.S.R's.

V. Davenport

Capt. & Adjutant
1/CIVIL SERVICE RIFLES.

SECRET. CIVIL SERVICE RIFLES Copy No. 2

ORDER No. 132

Ref. map SENLIS SHEET $\frac{1}{20,000}$

1. The Battn. will relieve the 17th. Battn. in support to-night. Companies of the CIVIL SERVICE RIFLES will occupy the same positions as when the Battn. was last in Support except C Company who will be in MELBOURNE TRENCH.
2. Advance parties consisting of one officer per Coy., one Senior N.C.O. per platoon, and one N.C.O for Battn. H.Q. will report to 2/Lt. GRAY at the Orderly Room at 2.30 p.m. and will then go up to take over trench stores which will be carefully checked.
3. Packs will be dumped by Coys. at the Canteen Stores as follows:-

| | | |
|---|---|---|
| H.Q. Coy. | at | 3. 0 p.m. |
| A " | " | 3.10 " |
| B " | " | 3.20 " |
| C " | " | 3.30 " |
| D " | " | 3.40 " |

S.D. caps will on no account be taken into the trenches.
4. Companies will be ready to move off at 7.30 p.m. Order of march will be C.B.A.D.HQ. On receipt of orders to move Coys. will move off independently, a distance of 100x being kept between platoons and at least 100x between Coys.
5. Guides from the 17th. Battn. for C Coy. will be at cross roads X.22.C.8.8 at 10.0 p.m. The advance parties of A.B.D and H.Q. Coys. will be at the same place at 10.0 p.m. and will act as guides for their Coys.
6. Lewis Guns will be dumped at Canteen Stores at 6.0 p.m., each team leaving one man for loading. Limbers will collect from that place and will go, one with leading platoon of C Coy. and one with leading platoon of A Coy.. Loading parties will march behind their own limber.
7. Mess boxes will be dumped at Canteen Stores at 8.30 p.m. Coys. may each leave 2 servants behind with these. They will march up with the Mess Cart.

8. Officers valises and boxes for Q.M. Stores will be dumped at Canteen Stores by 6.0 p.m.
9. Companies will have a combined tea and supper at 5.45 p.m.
10. Company Commanders will send in to H.Q. by first run to-morrow a certificate to the effect that they have inspected their area on leaving CONTAY and that it was left clean and sanitary, and that no stores were left behind.
Copies of receipts for trench stores will be forwarded by first run to-morrow.
11. Code word for relief complete will be Company Commander's name

Davenport

28th. July '18.

Capt. and Adjt.
1/Civil SERVICE RIFLES.

No. 1. - File.
" 2. - War Diary
" 3. - C.O.
" 4-7 - A, B, C, D Coys.
" 8 - Int. Offr. & L.G.O.
" 9 - R.S.M. & Sigs.
" 10 - M.O.
" 11 - 17th. Bn.
" 12 - T.O & Q.M.
" 13 - 140 Inf. Bde.

SECRET.    CIVIL SERVICE RIFLES.    COPY No. 2

ORDER No. 129.    18 JULY 1918.

Ref. map SENLIS 1/20,000

1. Battn. will relieve 24th. London Regt. to-night: each Company relieving same letter Company in 24th.

2. Companies will move off by platoons at 100 yds distance in following order:–

B, A, C, D, H.Q.

Leading platoon of B Company will pass starting point (Cross Roads V.22.c.8.8.) at 10.0 p.m.
Guides will be met at Cross Roads V.23.d.15.40. at 10.15 p.m.

3. Lewis Guns and mess things will be carried up with Companies.

Suppers will be at 8.0 p.m.
All dixies and officers valises and any surplus mess boxes will be dumped at H.Q. Coy. cookhouse at 9.0 p.m., and all cooks will remain with them as a guard. These will be collected by Transport after delivering rations to-night.
Transport will deliver rations at Coy. dumps at 11.30 pm

4. Each Company will take with it 12 picks and 25 shovels.

5. Advance parties of 1 officer per Coy., 1 N.C.O. per platoon and 1 from H.Q. Coy. will leave Orderly Room at 5.0 p.m. and go up to the new positions to take over stores which must be very carefully checked.

6. Men will fill their water bottles at usual time to-day, and will be warned that no further drinking water will be available until to-morrow night. Every water can in the Battn. area will be delivered to R.S.M. at 7.0 p.m. and these will be taken back by Transport.

7. Code word for relief complete will be Company Commanders name.

Copy no. 1. File
2. War Diary
3. C.O.
4-7. A, B, C & D Coys.
8. R.S.M. & Sigs.
9. 140 Bde.
10. 24 L. Bn.
11. M.O.

Davenport.

Capt. and Adjt.
1/Civil Service Rifles.

SECRET

# CIVIL SERVICE RIFLES.

Copy No. 2

## ORDER No. 130.

JULY 20th. 1918.

Ref. map SENLIS sheet $\frac{1}{20,000}$

1. The Battalion will relieve the Poplar & Stepney Rifles on the night 20/21st. inst. as detailed in Warning Order issued this morning.
2. Guides will be met at B Coy. H.Q. at 12.15 a.m. for B Coy. and where trench crosses track at V.30.a.9.9 for A, C, & D Coys. at midnight.
   Companies will pass this point in following order, 1st platoon passing at 12.0 midnight – A. D. C.
   B Coy. will move off with their guides at 12.15 am.
3. All empty water cans will be handed over by Coy.
4. Each platoon will carry with it 2 Lewis Guns.
5. Parties going to WARLOY will march off at 11.0 p.m., each Coy. taking with it one Lewis Gun. Companies will each send out an advance party of 1 N.C.O. and 1 man to Q.M. Stores to take over billets. They will meet their platoons at WARLOY church at 12.0 mid-night and guide them to their billets.
6. Hot meals will arrive at Company ration dumps to-night at 10.0 p.m. and Transport will take back the dixies.
7. Rations will arrive at 1.30 a.m. as follows:- A and D Coys. at W.20.d.0.6, B, C. & H.Q. Coys. at W.25.b.3.7. Companies will have parties there to meet Transport.
8. Receipts for trench stores handed over and copies of receipts for stores taken over will be sent to Orderly Room by 1st. run 21st.
9. Code word for relief complete will be Company Commanders name.

Copy No. 1. – File
" 2. – War Diary
" 3. – C.O.
" 4–7 – A, B, C, D Coys.
" 8 – R.S.M. & Sigs.
" 9 – T.O. & Q.M.
" 10 – 140 Bde.
" 11 – M.O.
" 12. – P.S.R's.

[signature] Davenport for
Capt. and Adjt.
1/CIVIL SERVICE RIFLES.

WARNING ORDER. Spare Copy.

Battalion will relieve Poplar and Stepney Rifles on right of Bde. front to-night.

A Coy. Civil Service Rifles will relieve A Coy. P. S. R. on left.
D " " " " " B " " right.
C " " " " " C " " in support.
B " " " " " D " " in reserve.

Coy. Commanders will go up to reconnoitre this morning, taking with them one runner, and reporting at P. S. R. - H.Q. in MELBOURNE TRENCH at W.25.b.05.75 at 10.0 a.m.

Sgt. MOORE, Sgt. THOMAS, Cpl. SHIRLEY and 2 Battn. H.Q. runners will go up this morning.

Advance parties of 1 officer per Coy. and 1 N.C.O per platoon, and 1 fo H.Q. Coy. will leave their Coy. H.Q. at 2.0 p.m. and go up to new positions to check & take over stores.

About 50 U.S.A. soldiers of all ranks will be attached to each Coy. in the new area to be instructed in trench duties.

These will be distributed equally throughout the Coy. and each American will be "paired" with a C.S. Rifleman of similar rank, who will do his utmost to give him the benefit of his knowledge and experience. The Americans will be treated in every way like the members of platoons to which they are attached, and their rations will come up with the platoon rations.

In order to make room for the above, each Coy. will send its strongest platoon to billets in WARLOY, and in addition any "light duty" or surplus men from other platoons or Coy. H.Q.; making a total for the Coy. of one Officer & 35 O.R. The number and strength of the platoon going down, together with nominal roll of the extra men, will be wired to Adjutant before 10.0 a.m.

20.7.18.

Capt. & Adjt.
1/CIVIL SERVICE RIFLES.

War Diary

# CIVIL SERVICE RIFLES
## ORDER No 133

COPY No 2

Refer Map
SENLIS Sheet 1/20000

20th July 1917

1/ The Bn will be relieved tonight by the 19th Bn as follows:-

| | | | |
|---|---|---|---|
| A Coy CIVIL SERVICE relieved by | B | Coy | 19th |
| B " " " " | D | " | 19th |
| C " " " " | C | " | 19th |
| D " " " " | A | " | 19th |

2/ One guide per platoon and one for H.Q. Coy will report to 2/Lt GRAY at HQ at 9 30 p.m. and will meet incoming platoons at 10.0 p.m at the end of AUSTRALIA ST V.29 c.5.7

3/ On relief Bn will move to the forward position of the Support Brigade and Coys will occupy the same trenches as when the Bn was last there

4/ Advance parties consisting of one officer per Coy and one NCO per platoon will go to the new positions at 4.0 p.m. to check and take over trench stores

5/ Receipts for trench stores handed over and copies of receipts for trench stores taken over

140th Bde.
47th Div.

15th BATTALION,

LONDON REGIMENT,

AUGUST 1918.

140 Infantry Brigade,

Herewith WAR DIARY

for the month of July last.

4/38
2.8.'18

[signature]
Capt.
for Lt. Col.
Cdg 1/Civil Service Rifles.

E 26/101

140 Inf Bde.

Herewith War Diary for month of August last

[illegible]

Lt Col.

Cdg. 1/Civil Service Rifles (15th Lond Rgt).

18/9/1918.

15 London Regt

Vol 38

Army Form C. 2118.

Instructions regarding War Diaries and Intelligence Summaries are contained in F. S. Regs., Part II. and the Staff Manual respectively. Title pages will be prepared in manuscript.

# WAR DIARY

*or*

# INTELLIGENCE SUMMARY.

*(Erase heading not required.)*

| Place | Date | Hour | Summary of Events and Information | Remarks and references to Appendices |
|---|---|---|---|---|
| IN SUPPORT | 1/8/18 | | The usual trench routine was carried out and working parties provided to perform tunnelling & digging in the area. Each Coy sent men to bathe at HENENCOURT CHATEAU | [illegible] |
| | 2.8.18 | | Trench routine as usual. The day was very wet and digging was almost impossible. Further parties bathed at HENENCOURT. The Transport Section took part in the Brigade competition & was given 2nd place the 21st Bn being given 1st place. | [illegible] |
| | 3.8.18 | | Lt Col Segrave left the Bn to take command of the 140 Brigade during the General's absence on leave. Major Gordon Bates MC took command of the Bn. During the morning the Bn was relieved by the 2/10th London and moved to billets at WARLOY, just prior to moving the Bn heard of the enemy's withdrawal from around ALBERT. The remainder of the morning & the afternoon were spent in bathing and cleaning up. | [illegible] Vide C.S.R order No 1314 |
| WARLOY | 4.8.18 | | Church parade. In the afternoon the C.O., Asst Adjt & 4 O.Cs reconnoitred the line S.W. of ALBERT. | [illegible] |

D. D. & L., London, E.C. (A10266) Wt W5300/P713 750,000 2/18 Sch. 52 Forms/C2118/16.

Instructions regarding War Diaries and Intelligence Summaries are contained in F. S. Regs., Part II. and the Staff Manual respectively. Title pages will be prepared in manuscript.

# WAR DIARY
*or*
~~INTELLIGENCE SUMMARY~~.
*(Erase heading not required.)*

Army Form C. 2118.

| Place | Date | Hour | Summary of Events and Information | Remarks and references to Appendices |
|---|---|---|---|---|
| WARLOY | 5-8-16 | | On the night 5/6th the Bn relieved the 24th London on the right of the Right Brigade front. B company occupied O.G. 1 & 2, recently vacated by the enemy, & placed three sentry groups alongside the WEST of the railway embankment overlooking the ANCRE and BELLEVUE FARM. A & C Coys went into O.G. 1, YARRA & PIONEER TRENCHES & D into SUPPORT in DIRTY TRENCH. The night was a very wet one & in consequence of the outpost Coy having to journey nearly a mile from our front line & go over a somewhat difficult route the relief was not complete until late. No casualties occurred during the relief. | Bde Op. order No 135 dated 5th Aug. 16 [illegible] |
| LINE | 6-8-16 | | The usual trench routine was carried out & parties worked on effecting improvements in their line. Care was taken by the garrison in the O.G. trenches to avoid [illegible] booby traps left by the enemy. Lt Col. [illegible] DSO, was promoted to Brigadier General & left the Bn to take command of the 152nd Brigade in the 51st Division | [illegible] |

D. D. & L., London, E.C.
(A10266) Wt W5300/P713 750,000 2/18 Sch. 52 Forms/C2118/16.

Instructions regarding War Diaries and Intelligence Summaries are contained in F. S. Regs., Part II. and the Staff Manual respectively. Title pages will be prepared in manuscript.

# WAR DIARY
*or*
~~INTELLIGENCE SUMMARY~~.

*(Erase heading not required.)*

Army Form C. 2118.

| Place | Date | Hour | Summary of Events and Information | Remarks and references to Appendices |
|---|---|---|---|---|
| | 6.8.18 (continued) | | 2/Lt Mills & 2/Lt Spencer, Quartermaster & Asst Adj respectively were both wounded by a bomb dropped on their billet at WARLOY. | |
| LINE | 7.8.18 | | A very quiet day. Trench routine was carried out & work done to improve the area. | [illegible] |
| | 8.8.18 | | The Major General inspected the Bn's area with Major Bates M.C., in command, and expressed his appreciation of the work recently performed by the Bn. Early in the morning (4 am) a big attack by the allies commenced, & the guns in our locality were busy all day. Cpl Shirley MM whilst accompanying the Adjutant round the line was wounded by a bomb dropped by an aeroplane. | [illegible] |
| | 9.8.18 | | The usual trench routine was carried out. On our right the allies attack recommenced at 5.30 pm. The Bn was relieved during the night by the 21st London & went into support in DARLING RESERVE, HILL ROW, DODO & MILLIE TRENCHES. Capt. Gompery, MC. rejoined the Bn to act as | [illegible] Vide C.S.R. Order No 131 dated 9th Aug 18 |

D. D. & L., London, E.C.
(A10266) Wt W5300/P713 750,000 2/18 Sch. 52 Forms/C2118/16.

Army Form C. 2118.

Instructions regarding War Diaries and Intelligence Summaries are contained in F. S. Regs., Part II. and the Staff Manual respectively. Title pages will be prepared in manuscript.

# WAR DIARY
*or*
# ~~INTELLIGENCE SUMMARY.~~
*(Erase heading not required.)*

| Place | Date | Hour | Summary of Events and Information | Remarks and references to Appendices |
|---|---|---|---|---|
| | 9-8-18 Continued | | M.O. in place of Lt A. KNOX who went on leave. | AW. |
| In Support | 10-8-18 | | The day was quiet and was spent in cleaning. Several working parties were provided. A draft of 20 O.R joined the Bn | AW. |
| | 11-8-18 | | The Battalion was relieved by the 7th Bn Royal West Kents and moved back into billets in BAIZIEUX. 12 O.R joined Bn. | AW. Vide O.O 137 dated 11th Aug 18 |
| In BAIZIEUX | 12-8-18 | | A warning was received from Brigade that the Bn would probably move at very short notice. The C.O and asst adjt reconnoitred the position held by the 22nd Bn LONDON Regt in K13 | AW. |
| | 13-8-18 | | Voluntary Communion Services were held and Inspections carried out during the day. At night the Bn relieved the "A" Bn of the 175th Brigade in the forward position of the Support Brigade. The Depot moved to BONNAY. The position taken up by the Bn was in the Old British System WEST of MORLANCOURT in K13. | Vide O.O 138 dated 13th Aug 18. |
| Old British Line | 14-8-18 | | The Bn remained in the above mentioned position. The day was spent in collecting salvage. | |
| | 15-8-18 | | In position as stated for the 13th inst, the day was again spent in collecting salvage. The C.O + Adjt reconnoitred the position held by the 22nd LONDON Regt in the Right Sector of the Front Line. | |
| | 16-8-18 | | In the above mentioned position during the day. Relieved the 22nd Bn London Regt at night in the Right Front Line BOIS des TAILLES. A + D Coys in Front Line, B Coy in Support and C Coy in Reserve. | Vide O.O. 139 dated 16-8-18. |
| FRONT LINE | 17-8-18 | | The Bn area was fairly heavily shelled during the day. At night the two front line Coys endeavoured to establish two advanced posts each on the ETINEHEM – MEAULTE Rd. Owing to hostile M.G. only one – under 2nd Lt BARNETT – was established. Casualties were sustained as follows – 2nd Lt R.C. HUGHES + 1 O.R killed 10 O.R wounded and 4 O.R missing, the bodies of the last named being recovered later. | Vide O.O. 140 dated 17-8-18 |
| | 18-8-18 | | At night two further posts were established on the ETINEHEM – MEAULTE Rd. by parties under Lt UPTON and 2nd Lt BATTCOCK. The sector was very heavily shelled during the day – total casualties being 9 O.R killed + 32 O.R. wounded. | |

D. D. & L., London, E.C.
(A10256) Wt W5300/P713 750,000 2/18 Sch. 52 Forms/C2118/16.

Instructions regarding War Diaries and Intelligence Summaries are contained in F. S. Regs., Part II. and the Staff Manual respectively. Title pages will be prepared in manuscript.

# WAR DIARY

or

~~INTELLIGENCE SUMMARY.~~

(*Erase heading not required.*)

Army Form C. 2118.

| Place | Date | Hour | Summary of Events and Information | Remarks and references to Appendices |
|---|---|---|---|---|
| FRONT LINE | 19-8-18 | | An attempt was made to establish a fourth post WEST of the ETINEHEM – MEAULTE Rd but failed owing to hostile M.G fire. Casualties:– 2nd Lt R.J. ENOCK wounded, 2 O.R. killed, 10 O.R. wounded and 4 missing.) Lt COL R.C. FEILDING D.S.O. arrived at Brigade H.Q and took over Command of the 1/C.S.R on the 21st inst. 20 O.R. also joined the Bn. | aw. |
| | 20-8-18 | | The Bn was relieved by the 20th Bn LONDON Regt at Midnight and proceeded to area previously occupied by the 23rd Bn L.R in J17. 1 O.R was killed & 14 O.R wounded during the day. 12 O.R joined the Bn. | vide O.O 143 dated 20-8-18 aw. |
| In Reserve | 21-8-18 | | The day was spent in cleaning and inspections. 20 O.R joined the Bn. | aw. |
| | 22-8-18 to 31-8-18 | | } For report dealing with the operations between these dates see narrative appended. | aw. |

R C Feilding
Lt Col

Cmdg 1/CIVIL SERVICE RIFLES

D. D. & L., London, E.C.
(A10266) Wt W5300/P713 750,000 2/18 Sch. 52 Forms/C2118/16.

War Diary.

Reference Sheet 62D.NE.
" " 62C.NW.
" " 62C.NE.

140th. Infantry Bde.

I beg to submit the following report, dealing with the operations in which the Battalion under my command took part between 22/8/18 and 6/9/18, both dates inclusive.

22/8/18.

The orders were that at 4.40 a.m. the 47th. Division, in conjunction with the 12th. Division on the left and the Australians on the right, should take part in the Fourth Army offensive, to be resumed this day. The 141 Infantry Bde. was to leave the RED Line (K.5.central: K.6.d.0.0: K.7.c.0.5: K.7.c.5.4: K.19.b.3.0.) at zero, and to capture and consolidate the BROWN Line (F.19 central: F.26.central: F.26.d.5.0: L.2.central: L.8.central:). The 142 Infantry Bde. was to pass through the 141 Infantry Bde. at zero plus 10 minutes, and to capture and consolidate the GREEN Line (F.13.central: F.20.central: F.27.b.3.0: F.27.d.4.0: L.3.d.3.0: L.9.d.3.8: thence West of the Crucifix - L.15.c.2.7). The programme was that Corps Cavalry (consisting of 200 Yeomen) and twelve Whippet Tanks should then pass through the 141 and 142 Infantry Brigades and capture the BLUE Line (F.9.central: F.16.central: F.23.central: thence round GREAT BEAR in F.23.c. to Railway at F.23.c.2.0), the 140 Infantry Bde. remaining in Divisional Reserve, ready to move forward and consolidate the BLUE Line when captured.

At 6.10.a.m. the Battalion under my command marched forward, by Companies at intervals of 100 yards, from the trenches near MARETT WOOD (J.11) where they had rested for the night. By 7.50.a.m. the Battalion was in position at the rendezvous - the vicinity of the sunken road in K.10.d., where we found a squadron of Cavalry - about 80 strong - waiting its turn to go forward. At 7.55 a.m. this squadron advanced to the attack, accompanied by Tanks, but both came dribbling back, about an hour later, having met with serious opposition.

At 3.45 p.m. I received orders from Brigadier General KENNEDY as to the part to be played by the 1/Civil Service Rifles in an attack to be delivered by the 140 Infantry Bde. at 4.45 a.m. the following morning upon the BLUE Line. These, however, were subsequently cancelled owing to the withdrawal of the 142 Infantry Bde. from the GREEN Line under pressure from the enemy, and the reoccupation by the latter of HAPPY VALLEY (F.26 and 27: L.2 and 3).

Upon receipt of the above news the 1/Civil Service Rifles were at 7.0.p.m. ordered up to fill the gap between the right flank of the 141 Infantry Bde. and the left flank of the Australians, and I sent two Companies to the bank in L.8.a. and two Companies to the ETINEHAM - MEAULT road to support them. I established my H.Q. temporarily in the old front line N.E. of the BOIS DES TAILLES (K.12.b).

KEP.

By order of the Brigadier I went, at 11.0.p.m., to see Lt. Colonel FERGUSSON (commanding 19th. London Regt.) - who had command of the front line - at his H.Q. on the Railway (K.6.b.3.2). Here I received instructions as to the line to be held, and I also met Lt.Colonel BERRY (commanding 20th. London Regt.), with whom I visited this line.

I then moved two companies forward to conform with the 20th. London Regt., linking up with the latter's right. These Companies dug in during the remainder of the night on the reverse slope of the ridge. I found the Australian left to be at the CHALK PIT (L.3.d.5.8), leaving a long gap between themselves and my right, and as they stated that they had no troops available to cover this gap I placed a Company at their disposal for the night. A short time later, however, the Australians pushed ~~themselves~~ forward and established a screen of troops along the BRAY-ALBERT road, and the Company I had lent them then occupied the ridge at L.1.d.9.7 in their support. The remaining Company I kept in reserve at the foot of the bank (L.8.a), to which position I also removed my H.Q. at 2.30 a.m. on the morning of 23/8/18.

23/8/18.
At 4.30 a.m. the Battalion stood-to till daylight.

At 10.15 a.m. a rocket signal was picked up, apparently sent back by an Australian Officer from the BRAY-ALBERT road. It stated that the enemy was concentrating behind the railway on his front. Nothing of interest developed, however, from the direction indicated.

During the day the position occupied by the Battalion was subjected to considerable shelling from the enemy, mostly ineffective.

Orders were received for an attack to be made during the night on the GREEN Line and HAPPY VALLEY, in which the 1/Civil Service Rifles were detailed to act as "moppers up".

The orders stated that the attack was to be made by the 140 Infantry Bde. on the left and the 175 Infantry Bde. on the right. The 21st. Battalion was to be on the left of the 140 Infantry Bde; the 17th. Battalion on the right; and the 1/Civil Service Rifles in support. The boundary on the left to be from F.25.a.0.0. to F.20.a.4.2. On the right from F.26.c.0.0. to F.21.d.0.0. The dividing line - STRAGGLY TREE to F.20.d.4.3. The 12th. Division were to co-operate on our left.

24/8/18.
At 12.30 o'clock, during the night (23-24), I moved my H.Q. to K.6.a.9.1.

At 12.55 a.m. the Battalion assembled in the Chalk Quarry (L.2.c).

Soon after 1.0.a.m.(the zero hour), each Company having previously been allotted an area for the mopping up of which it was ~~they were~~ to be held responsible, the Battalion moved forward under Major G.G.BATES,M.C., and by 2.0.a.m. parties of prisoners began to reach my H.Q. The operation had been entirely successful, the Battalion having captured some 300 prisoners in HAPPY VALLEY, as well as a considerable number of machine guns and some Trench Mortars.

KGD.

At 4.45 a.m. I went forward to the BRAY-MEAULT road, where Major Bates had established his H.Q. The Division on our left had apparently been held up, and a dangerous gap existed between their right and the left of the 21st. Battalion. For some hours the position at this point was precarious and, several times, enemy counter attacks were threatened: in fact, as I crossed the open to reach my Companies an S.O.S. Rocket signal was fired from our outpost line. The enemy shell fire was considerable at the time, and the ground was freely swept by his machine gun fire. The S.O.S. was repeated at 8.15 a.m., but my Adjutant - Capt. PAUL DAVENPORT, M.C., - whom I had sent forward to re-arrange the Companies with a view to assisting the 21st. Battalion to secure their exposed left flank, shortly returned to my H.Q. and reported the situation as well in hand. The disposition of the Companies was now as follows :- "A" Co. were forming a defensive flank from the cross-roads in F.25.b. to the Copse in F.26.a. "B" Co. extended from the Copse about 200 yds. towards the railway. "C" and "D" Companies occupied the railway cutting near F.26.central.

At 12.30 p.m. I received orders from Brigadier General KENNEDY concerning an advance to be made during the coming night in conjunction with the 175 Infantry Bde. on the right. The Brigade objective was to be the Line F.17.d.3.3: F.24.c.1.7: F.24.c.2.0: The 21st. Battalion was to advance on the left; the 17th. Battalion in the centre; and the Battalion under my command on the right of the Brigade. The objective of the last named Battalion was to be the line F.24.c.1.7 - F.24.c.2.0, in front of BILLON COPSE. Zero hour was to be 2.30.a.m.

<u>25/8/18</u>.
The Battalion advanced to the attack behind a creeping barrage at 2.30 a.m. and reached the neighbourhood of the objective - some 2500 yds. in front of the starting line - practically without opposition. The casualties incurred, some thirty-five in number, were caused almost, if not entirely, by our own barrage.

At 4.30 a.m. I left my H.Q. in HAPPY VALLEY and joined the Battalion. A thick fog had settled down, and considerable difficulty was experienced in finding even so prominent a landmark as BRONFAY FARM. However, in due course, the objective was reached and manned by "A" and "C" Companies, while "B" and "D" Companies remained in the railway loop behind, in support.

During the day I had opportunity to take a walk round the HAPPY VALLEY, in the course of which I actually counted twenty-one enemy machine guns, which had covered this small valley; and there were probably more. There were also several Minenwerfers. The German dead, at a moderate estimate, must have exceeded 100. There were also a considerable number of German wounded, whom, after their wounds had been dressed, we evacuated.

At 5.0.p.m. an order was received to withdraw the Battalion to the GREEN Line for the night, and the following day (26/8/18) it marched back to the trenches near MARETT WOOD (J.11), taking with it one captured minenwerfer, and four heavy and ten light enemy machine guns.

Major DESMOND YOUNG, M.C., joined the Battalion as Second-in-Command on the evening of 25/8/18.

-----<u>27/8/18</u>.
At 3.30.p.m. Lt.General Sir A.J.GODLEY, K.C.B., K.C.M.G., commanding III Corps, interviewed the Battalion Commanders of the Brigade, and congratulated them on the fine work done by their Battalions.

KD

28/8/18.

At 11.45.a.m. Brig. General H.B.KENNEDY, C.M.G., D.S.O., inspected and addressed the Battalion, congratulating all ranks on the part played by the Battalion in the recent fighting.

At 3.0.p.m. Major General Sir F.G.GORRINGE, K.C.B., K.C.M.G., D.S.O., commanding 47th. Division, met the Officers of the Battalion, and added his congratulations.

29/8/18.

At 2.0.p.m. the Battalion marched. I established my H.Q. for the night at CARNOY CRATERS. The Companies took up a line in front of the BRIQUETERIE (A.4.b.).

30/8/18.

At 7.0.a.m. the Battalion marched to MAUREPAS RAVINE, where the day was spent. Considerable shelling from the enemy's heavy artillery was experienced during the day.. At 3.15 p.m. the Adjutant (Capt. PAUL DAVENPORT, M.C.) was wounded by a shell which fell about 1000 yards away from him. This point is of interest as evidence of the great spread caused by the instaneous fuse, now almost universally employed by the enemy.

A draft of 100 men joined the Battalion this day.

31/8/18.

The Battalion rested the day at MAUREPAS RAVINE.

At 3.0.p.m. I received orders from Brig.General Kennedy for an attack to be made by the 140 Infantry Bde. on the following morning.

The 140 Infantry Bde. in conjunction with the 141 Infantry Bde. on the right, and the 18th. Division (55th. Infantry Bde.) on the left, was to advance and capture the line of trench following the S.W.edge of the St.PIERRE VAAST WOOD, the Brigade Boundary being C.3.d.3.5. on the right, and U.26.d.2.5. on the left. The 21st. Batt. London Regt. was to be on the right, the 1/Civil Service Rifles on the left, and the 17th. Battn. London Regt. to be responsible for mopping up the trenches in B.6.c. and d. and C.1.c., as well as the village of RANCOURT.

The right boundary of the 1/Civil Service Rifles to be C.3.a.3.2.

The positions of assembly were to be a line running from the road C.7.a.5.0. to C.7.a.0.7.

I immediately sent Major YOUNG, 2nd. in Command, with the Company Commanders, to reconnoitre the assembly positions

Casualties 22/8/18 - 31/8/18 :-

OFFICERS

| Killed. | Died of Wounds. | Wounded. | Missing. |
|---|---|---|---|
| - | 1 | 2 | - |

OTHER RANKS

| Killed. | Died of Wounds. | Wounded. | Missing. |
|---|---|---|---|
| 7 | 1 | 48 | 1 |

R. Fielding Lt Col.
Comdg 1/Civil Service Rifles
(1/15 Lond Regt)

War Diary

1/9/18.

At 2.45.a.m. the Battalion moved up to its assembly positions.

The first wave was to consist of C. and D. Coys., D. Co. being on the right, with its right on the sunken road in C.7.c., with A. and B. Coys. in support. Battalion H.Q. were established at the cross roads N.E. of LE FOREST in B.11.c.9.2. with advanced H.Q. in a shell hole near the assembly positions.

A certain amount of shelling was encountered on the way up, and one shell which burst in the mouth of the new Battalion H.Q. unfortunately killed three, including Sergt. Moore the Signalling Sergeant, and wounding others.

Zero was fixed for 5.30 a.m. After a five minutes "crash", the Battalion was to move forward behind a creeping barrage - C. and D. Coys. to the final objective, A. and B. Coys. to a position in support in ALERT and ABSINTHE TRENCHES.

The Battalion was in the assembly position shortly after 5.0.a.m.

Some anxiety was felt when the 21st. Battalion had not arrived on our right at 5.27 a.m. but, thanks to 2/Lt. F.GRAY, Intelligence Officer to the 1/Civil Service Rifles, touch was established with them before Zero.

The attack was completely successful, prisoners beginning to come down within five to ten minutes of Zero.

Lt. E.R.LASCELLES, commanding C.Co., and 2/Lt. R.L.KIRK, whose first day in action in France it was, were killed early in the advance, but otherwise losses were slight, and by 7.30.a.m. all objectives had been reached, and were being consolidated.

The trench on the edge of the wood was found to be overgrown and with no field of fire, and C. and D.Coys therefore took up a position in shell holes about fifty yards in rear.

Touch was obtained with the East Surreys (55th. Infantry Bde.) on the left, but there was a gap on the right, the 21st. Battn. not having advanced as far as their final objective.

Large numbers of prisoners and machine guns were captured - the Battalion's share amounting to about 150 - 200 men and some 10 Machine Guns.

During the process of consolidation, B. and D.Coys. were subjected to heavy shelling from a German Field Gun Battery, which remained in action in the open, firing over open sights from about 1000 yards range.

Advanced Battn. H.Q. were established in ABOVE LANE at C.2.c.4.7. and Battn. H.Q. about C.1.c.5.3.

An attempt by the enemy at infiltration through the gap on our right was prevented by Lewis Gun fire from developing.

At 6.5.p.m. a warning order was received to the effect that the 1/15th. Battn. would be relieved during the night, and would take part in an operation the following morning, in conjunction with the 74th. Division.

At about 11.30.p.m. the Battn. was relieved by the London Irish (18th. London Regt.) and marched to a position of assembly on the RANCOURT - PERONNE road, just S.W. of BOUCHAVESNES, and 300 yds. N. of the old Quarry (C.20.central).

The plan was that the 74th. Division should attack from Trenches immediately S. of the 141st. Infantry Bde. boundary (C.10.c.7.9.), their final objective being NURLU. The 74th. Division was also to be responsible for the capture and "mopping up" of MOISLAINS. The 140 Infantry Bde. was to follow them closely, the 1/15th. Battn. on the left, the 1/17th. Battn. on the right and the 1/21st. Battn. in support. After crossing the CANAL du NORD (E. of MOISLAINS) the 140 Infantry Bde. was to wheel left, forming a defensive flank on the high ground to the N. of MONASTIR trench, where they were to join up with the 142 Infantry Bde. who were to capture this trench. Order from left to right on defensive flank;- 21st. London, 1/Civil Service Rifles, 17th. London. The 140th. Infantry Bde. was to follow the 229 Infantry Bde., who would also prolong the defensive flank, facing N. as far as NURLU.

~~From the outset the Brigade came under heavy shell and M.G.fire, and, as it moved down the slopes to the S.W. of MOISLAINS, under still heavier M.G.fire directed from the village and from both~~

Zero hour was to be 5.30 a.m., but the 140th. Infantry Bde. was to move at 5.0.a.m. in order to get well up behind the 229 Infantry Bde. The Battn. was in position at the place of assembly at about 3.0a.m; A. and B. Coys. leading (A.Co. on left); C. and D. ... Battn. H.Q. bringing up

The 140 Infantry Brigade was to pass MOISLAINS on the South, and the formation of the defensive flank therefore presupposed the capture by the 74th Division of the village.

In spite of ... the Battn. succeeded in establishing itself in MOISLAINS TRENCH, with details of the 21st. Battn. on the left, the 17th. Battn. on the right, and an Officer and about 15/20 O.R. of the North Devon Yeomanry.

The enemy were found to be occupying both MOISLAINS TRENCH to our left, and QUARRY TRENCH to our left rear, while they could clearly be seen moving in MOISLAINS, and assembling in the village and in the huts immediately to the S. of it.

Simultaneous counter-attacks were, in fact, developed on our left rear, and our right front, while the enemy at the same time attempted to bomb up the trench on our left.

Both the parados and parapet were manned, and the attacks across the open were beaten off, but the bombing attacks continued all day, and, owing to scarcity of bombs, were with difficulty held up.

It was at once obvious that there were no British troops to our front, though elements of the 74th Division could be seen in the distance on the right, on a level with MOISLAINS TRENCH. In the face of the very heavy flank and frontal M.G.fire, of the heavy casualties incurred, and of the fact of one flank at least being in the air, it did not appear pacticable either to me or to Lt.Colonel DAWES, commanding 21st. Battn., for our Battalions to assume the roles allotted to the 74th. Division, and to attempt, without a barrage, to capture the village, which, as a result of the failure, or absence of that Division, was still firmly held by the enemy.

A small local attack by about two Companies was actually delivered by the 74th. Division on our right, but though it made some little progress, and at one point, crossed the Canal, it hardly did more than establish our right flank.

With this exception, there was no indication of any attack having been delivered by the 74th. Division in the vicinity of MOISLAINS.

A German Field Gun Battery was, in fact, in action for some four hours in the open, immediately S. of the Village, and less than 1000 yards E. of the CANAL, and firing over open sights on our trench.

The above facts were confirmed by a very careful examination by myself of the battlefield, made afterwards. I saw no British dead either in MOISLAINS or to the E. of MOISLAINS TRENCH in C.17.b. The only dead in rear of MOISLAINS TRENCH in C.17.a. and b. were those of the 140th. Infantry Bde., and of Germans killed in the counter-attack on our left rear. In this area 25 men of this Battn. alone were found and buried in an hour, and many others of the Brigade still lay there.

The only dead of the 74th. Division whom I personally saw in the section of ground with which my Battn. was concerned, were lying about 300 yds. from our starting point, - the RANCOURT-PERONNE road. Since these dead were not there when we originally advanced, I can only come to the conclusion, which is shared by all who were with me on the battlefield during the action and after, that here, at least, the 140th. Infantry Bde., instead of being in support, found itself with its flanks unsecured, and with the barrage so far ahead as to be useless, carrying out the main attack on a strong enemy position, and that the 74th. Division, so far from being in front of us, was behind us.

Having failed to establish communication with the Brigade I left the front trench at 1.0.p.m., and went to the Quarry (C.20.central)

Zero hour was to be 5.30 a.m., but the 140th. Infantry Bde. was to move at 5.0.a.m. in order to get well up behind the 229 Infantry Bde. The Battn. was in position at the place of assembly at about 3.0a.m; A. and B. Coys. leading (A.Co. on left); C. and D. Coys. in support (C.Co. on left); with Battn. H.Q. bringing up the rear. ← Insert A

From the outset the Brigade came under heavy shell and M.G.fire, and, as it moved down the slopes to the S.W. of MOISLAINS, under still heavier M.G.fire directed from the village and from both flanks.

In spite of casualties amounting to over half its strength the Battn. succeeded in establishing itself in MOISLAINS TRENCH, with details of the 21st. Battn. on the left, the 17th. Battn. on the right, and an Officer and about 15/20 O.R. of the North Devon Yeomanry.

The enemy were found to be occupying both MOISLAINS TRENCH to our left, and QUARRY TRENCH to our left rear, while they could clearly be seen moving in MOISLAINS, and assembling in the village and in the huts immediately to the S. of it.

Simultaneous counter-attacks were, in fact, developed on our left rear, and our right front, while the enemy at the same time attempted to bomb up the trench on our left.

Both the parados and parapet were manned, and the attacks across the open were beaten off, but the bombing attacks continued all day, and, owing to scarcity of bombs, were with difficulty held up.

It was at once obvious that there were no British troops to our front, though elements of the 74th. Division could be seen in the distance on the right, on a level with MOISLAINS TRENCH. In the face of the very heavy flank and frontal M.G.fire, of the heavy casualties incurred, and of the fact of one flank at least being in the air, it did not appear practicable either to me or to Lt.Colonel DAWES, commanding 21st. Battn., for our Battalions to assume the roles allotted to the 74th. Division, and to attempt, without a barrage, to capture the village, which, as a result of the failure, or absence of that Division, was still firmly held by the enemy.

A small local attack by about two Companies was actually delivered by the 74th. Division on our right, but though it made some little progress, and at one point, crossed the Canal, it hardly did more than establish our right flank.

With this exception, there was no indication of any attack having been delivered by the 74th. Division in the vicinity of MOISLAINS.

A German Field Gun Battery was, in fact, in action for some four hours in the open, immediately S. of the Village, and at less than 1000 yards E. of the CANAL, and firing over open sights on our trench.

The above facts were confirmed by a very careful examination by myself of the battlefield, made afterwards. I saw no British dead either in MOISLAINS or to the E. of MOISLAINS TRENCH in C.17.b. The only dead in rear of MOISLAINS TRENCH in C.17.a. and b. were those of the 140th. Infantry Bde., and of Germans killed in the counter-attack on our left rear. In this area 25 men of this Battn. alone were found and buried in an hour, and many others of the Brigade still lay there.

The only dead of the 74th. Division whom I personally saw in the section of ground with which my Battn. was concerned, were lying about 300 yds. from our starting point, - the RANCOURT-PERONNE road. Since these dead were not there when we originally advanced, I can only come to the conclusion, which is shared by all who were with me on the battlefield during the action and after, that here, at least, the 140th. Infantry Bde., instead of being in support, found itself with its flanks unsecured, and with the barrage so far ahead as to be useless, carrying out the main attack on a strong enemy position, and that the 74th. Division, so far from being in front of us, was behind us.

Having failed to establish communication with the Brigade I left the front trench at 1.0.p.m., and went to the Quarry (C.20.central)

where a telephone had been installed. Here, I received orders from Brig. General KENNEDY to withdraw the Battn. at 10.30.p.m. and to rest the men in the trenches in C.2.central, establishing my H.Q. at B.11.c.9.2.

3/9/18.

The Battalion rested.

4/9/18.

The Battalion rested. Owing to its heavy losses, the Battn. was re-organized on a two Company basis, each of two Platoons.

5/9/18.

At 5.30.a.m. the 141 Infantry Bde. passed through the 142 Infantry Bde. At 8.0.a.m. the 140th. Infantry Bde. followed the 141 Infantry Bde., the 17th. London in front, the 1/Civil Service Rifles plus one Company 21st. London (which was attached to the Battalion for duty) in support.

The position of assembly for the 1/Civil Service Rifles was PALLAS TRENCH (C.10.c.), where also I established my H.Q.

At 12.0.noon Battn H.Q. was moved forward to the SUNKEN road (C.11.b.2.5.), at which time the disposition of the Companies was as follows :- AB. and CD. Coys. in SORROWITZ TRENCH (C.11.b.), and the 21st. Battn. Co. in the SUNKEN road.

At 12.30.p.m., under orders from the Brig. General I sent AB. Co. under Lieut. R, UPTON to the CANAL bank (C.12.ad), CD. Co. under Capt L.D.ECCLES to form a defensive flank in the trench in D.13.a. and D.14.c. The remaining Co. was retained in reserve, half in SORROWITZ TRENCH and half in the SUNKEN ROAD. During the afternoon, Lt. R.UPTON, commanding AB. Co., was wounded, and 2/Lt. T.J.BOOTH assumed command of the Co.

At 7.0.p.m., considerable opposition having been met with from the enemy, an organized attack was made on the big QUARRY (C.14.b.) and the PERONNE-NERLU road by the 17th. London Regt. in conjunction with the 141 Infantry Bde. and the 12th. Division on the left. The right was protected by Capt. L.D.ECCLES' Coy. (1/Civil Service Rifles) as above described. The operation was entirely successful.

6/9/18.

At 6.0.a.m. the 19th. and 20th. Battalions of the 141 Brigade, and the 17th. Battn. of the 140th. Infantry Bde. established themselves on a line about D.10.central - D.16.central.

At 8.0.a.m. the 18th. London and 1/Civil Service Rifles, who had formed up behind the new front line in conjunction with the 12th. Division on the left, and 74th. Division on the right, moved forward, their objective being a N. and S. line about E.13.central, on the right of LIERAMONT.

H.Q. At 8.15.a.m. I moved forward and established advanced Battn. H.Q. in the big QUARRY (D.14.b.). Later, I went forward, accompanied by the Brigade Major - Capt. L.M.GIBBS, M.C., - reaching the objective about noon, just as the Battn. was reaching it. The 18th. London on the left had not yet arrived and heavy enemy M.G. fire was raking our men from that direction, as well as rapid fire from his Field Artillery, as they appeared over the crest.

The men behaved with the greatest steadiness, falling back slowly to the reverse slope, where they immediately turned and dug in.

During the night the Battn. was relieved by the 9th. London (58th. Division) and moved to the Valley in D.13.c. which they reached about 3.0. a.m. in the morning of 7/9/18, and where they bivouaced.

The casualties sustained by this Battalion during the fighting was as follows:-

| | | Officers | N.C.Os. & men. |
|---|---|---|---|
| Aug. 22 - 30 | Killed in action | - | 7 |
| | Died of wounds | 1 | 1 |
| | Wounded | 2 | 48 |
| | Missing | - | 1 |

....

| | | Officers. | N.C.O. & men. |
|---|---|---|---|
| Aug. 31 to Sept.6. | Killed in action | 4 | 35 |
| | Died of wounds | - | 4 |
| | Wounded | 6 | 241 |
| | Missing | 1 | 38 |

Total:- 389.

7/9/18.
In the morning the bodies of those killed on 2/9/18, near MOISLAINS, were buried.

I have already forwarded the names of those Officers and men whom I wish to bring to the Brigadier-General's notice for special gallantry.

R C Feilding
Lt Col
Comdg 1/Civil Service Rifles

140/47

Army Form C. 2118.

# WAR DIARY

~~or INTELLIGENCE SUMMARY~~

(Erase heading not required.)

Instructions regarding War Diaries and Intelligence Summaries are contained in F. S. Regs., Part II. and the Staff Manual respectively. Title pages will be prepared in manuscript.

1/15 London Reg

39

| Place | Date | Hour | Summary of Events and Information | Remarks and references to Appendices |
|---|---|---|---|---|
| | 1-9-18 to 6-9-18 | Inclusive | For report dealing with the operations between these dates see narrative appended.* | * Sent on with August W.D. A.W. |
| | 7-9-18 | | The Bn. was ready to embus at 7-30 A.M. but the busses did not arrive until about Noon. During the morning the C.O., 2nd in Command, Chaplin and the M.O. with a party of Pioneers visited the Battle field of 2nd Sept and found a number of bodies of NCOs and men of the Bn. which they buried. The Bn. embussed about Noon and arrived in billets in HEILLY at 4-0 P.M. A considerable number of Officers and O.R. immediately took advantage of the nice day and went to the river for a bathe. Hot baths were also allotted to the Bn.. 7 O.R. joined the Bn.. | A.W. |
| HEILLY | 8-9-18 | | Voluntary Church services were held in the morning and evening. The remainder of the day was spent in bathing and cleaning Arms, clothing and equipment. An advanced party under 2nd Lt GOLBY was sent on to billet the Bn. in CHOCQUES. Capt + Q.M. J. FARNSWORTH joined the Bn. and took over the duties of Q.M., 3 O.R. also joined. | A.W. |
| " | 9-9-18 | | The Brigade Group entrained at HEILLY for CHOCQUES. The C.S.R entrained at 2-45 PM and arrived in billets in CHOCQUES at 3-0 AM on the 10th inst, it was raining heavily. A hot meal prepared by the advanced party was ready for the men on arrival. Only a very few civilians were living in the town. 5 O.R. joined the Bn.. | vide C.S.R. O.O. 156 dated 8-9-18. A.W. |
| CHOCQUES | 10-9-18 | | The day was spent in cleaning. A Ceremonial Guard Mounting was held in the evening. | A.W. |

D. D. & L., London, E.C.
(A10266) Wt.W5300/P713 750,000 2/18 Sch. 52 Forms/C2118/16.

Instructions regarding War Diaries and Intelligence Summaries are contained in F. S. Regs., Part II. and the Staff Manual respectively. Title pages will be prepared in manuscript.

# WAR DIARY

~~or INTELLIGENCE SUMMARY.~~

(Erase heading not required.)

Army Form C. 2118.

| Place | Date | Hour | Summary of Events and Information | Remarks and references to Appendices |
|---|---|---|---|---|
| CHOCQUES | 11-9-18 | | The day was again devoted to the cleaning of Arms, Clothing and Equipment. All Lewis Guns and L.G equipment were inspected and kit inspection held. A letter – from the G.O.C. III Corps – of appreciation and thanks for work done by the Division was read to all ranks. An advanced party under 2nd Lt GOLBY left for AUCHEL to billet the Bn. 9 O.R. joined the Bn. | A.W. |
| " | 12-9-18 | | The 140th Bde marched to the AUCHEL area. The C.S.R moved off at 11-0AM and marched via LAPUGNOY and MARLES-LES-MINES to AUCHEL, arriving at the latter place at 1-0PM. A hot meal was cooked en route and was served immediately the Bn arrived in billets. 2nd Lt P.H. SMALL (11th Bn LONDON Regt) reported for duty with this Bn. | vide C.S.R. O.O. 157 dated 11-9-18 A.W. |
| AUCHEL | 13-9-18 | | Companies turned out at 7-30AM for ¼ hours run. The morning was spent in Drill under the supervision of Company Commanders. The C.O visited the men at work and inspected billets during the morning. 11. O.R. joined the Bn. | A.W. |
| " | 14-9-18 | | The morning was again devoted to drill under Company arrangements. Training was carried out on the AERODROME DRILL GROUND. At Noon the M.O. inspected Companies in billets. The Band played in the market square during the evening. 2nd Lt SIMPSON 21st Bn LON. Regt reported for duty as Signal Officer until the return of ~~[illegible]~~ Lt EMED from the 4th Army Signal School. 2nd Lt L.L.E. BARRETT and 2nd Lt H.E.J. CHARTER (11th Bn LON. Regt) reported for duty. | A.W. |
| " | 15-9-18 | | A Brigade Church Parade service was held at 10-30 AM on the AERODROME Ground. The Army Commander Gen. Sir W.R. BIRDWOOD, KCB., KCSI, KCMG, CIE, DSO. attended the service and addressed the troops. | A.W. |

D. D. & L., London, E.C.
(A10266) Wt W5300/P713 750,000 2/18 Sch. 52 Forms/C2118/16.

Instructions regarding War Diaries and Intelligence Summaries are contained in F. S. Regs., Part II. and the Staff Manual respectively. Title pages will be prepared in manuscript.

# WAR DIARY
~~or~~
# INTELLIGENCE ~~SUMMARY~~.

(Erase heading not required.)

Army Form C. 2118.

| Place | Date | Hour | Summary of Events and Information | Remarks and references to Appendices |
|---|---|---|---|---|
| | 15-9-18 Contd. | | During the course of the address the Army Commander extended a warm welcome to the Brigade and the Division on their return to the Army under his command. | |
| | | | Non-Conformist and R.C. services were held in the town. Cinema entertainments were given in the WHITE STAR Cinema RUE de TEMPLE in the afternoon and evening. The C.S.R. band again played in the Square. | AW. |
| AUCHEL | 16-9-18 | | The Bn. paraded on the AERODROME Ground at 9-0AM for inspection and drill by the C.O after which training was carried out in accordance with the programme issued to Company Commanders. Capt G.C. GRIMSDALE was appointed Bn. Musketry and Sports Officer. arrangements were made to serve hot soup daily on the training area at 10-30AM. A Recreation Room in RUE de TEMPLE was opened for NCOs and men of the Bn. An Assocn. Football Competition was arranged, the 1st round of which took place in the afternoon, H.Q.Coy. V. Depôt : D,Coy V. B,Coy : A,and C, Coys being given byes. The Depôt won by 2 goals to 1 and B,Coy won by 3 goals to 2. The "ARCHIES" gave an entertainment in the evening in the Cinema. A sports programme was arranged including a Flat Race 80 yards for the AUCHEL children, but this was subsequently cancelled owing to the proposed move to ITALY. | AW. |
| " | 17-9-18 | | The C.S.R took part in a tactical exercise in conjunction with the 47th M.G.Bn. The object of the scheme was to locate and outflank M.G. nests. In the afternoon L.G. NCOs were given instruction in the handling of German M.Gs. LESLIE HENSON'S concert party gave an entertainment in the evening in the WHITE STAR Cinema. | AW. |

D. D. & L., London, E.C.
(A10266) Wt W5300/P713 750,000 2/18 Sch. 52 Forms/C2118/16.

Instructions regarding War Diaries and Intelligence Summaries are contained in F. S. Regs., Part II. and the Staff Manual respectively. Title pages will be prepared in manuscript.

# WAR DIARY

or

~~INTELLIGENCE SUMMARY~~.

(Erase heading not required.)

Army Form C. 2118.

| Place | Date | Hour | Summary of Events and Information | Remarks and references to Appendices |
|---|---|---|---|---|
| AUCHEL | 18-9-18 | | Training was carried out on the AERODROME ground. After the inspection and drill by the C.O. specialist training was continued according to programme. In the afternoon the Semi-Finals of the Football Competition were played off A, Coy V B, Coy and C, Coy V Depôt; the result was a victory for A, Coy by 2 goals to 1 and for the Depôt by 4 goals to NIL. A concert was given in the evening by members of the Bn in the Theatre RUE HOUDAIN, LESLIE HENSON'S party gave a second show in the Cinema. | AW. |
| " | 19-9-18 | | The C.O. inspected the Bn on the MARKET SQUARE at 9-0AM after which the specialists were marched to the AERODROME ground for training under the specialist officers. The remainder of the Bn carried out drill on the Square until 10-45AM when they were also marched to the AERODROME ground, for musketry. The final of the Football Competition was played in the afternoon, A, Coy V Depôt, A, Coy won by 4 goals to 1. A Cinema entertainment was given in the evening in the Cinema Hall. Orders and particulars of entrainment for ITALY were received from Brigade and issued to Companies. | AW. Vide C.S.R. O.O.158 dated 19-9-18 AW. |
| " | 20-9-18 | | The Lewis Gun classes paraded from 8-30AM to 11-30AM for instruction. The Bn was bathed during the morning in the baths at FOSSE.3. Preparations for entrainment were carried on and a certain amount of stores were sent to the station but these had to be brought back owing at a wire being received to the effect that the move was ~~indefinitely~~ postponed. An entertainment was given in the evening by the "YELLERS" in the Cinema. "The YELLERS" being a concert party composed of a number of picked turns from the Brigade and the "ARCHIES". | AW. |
| " | 21-9-18 | | The following Officers joined the Bn today;- Lt W.E. HOSTE, 2nd Lt T.N. BATCHELOR, 2nd Lt J.J. TITCOMBE, 2nd Lt P.E. BEDDOW, 2nd Lt J.H. FRENCH, 2nd Lt H.W. GEORGE. | |

D. D. & L., London, E.C.
(A10266) Wt W5300/P713 750,000 2/18 Sch. 52 Forms/C2118/16.

Instructions regarding War Diaries and Intelligence Summaries are contained in F. S. Regs., Part II. and the Staff Manual respectively. Title pages will be prepared in manuscript.

# WAR DIARY

~~or~~

~~INTELLIGENCE SUMMARY.~~

(Erase heading not required.)

Army Form C. 2118.

| Place | Date | Hour | Summary of Events and Information | Remarks and references to Appendices |
|---|---|---|---|---|
| AUCHEL | 21-9-18 | | Owing to wet weather the usual parades could not take place. Companies carried on with L.G training and musketry in billets. At 11-30AM the rain cleared, Companies were ordered to parade on the Market Square, they were inspected by the 2nd in Command. The "YELLERS" and the Cinema gave a combined show in the evening. All monies taken at the door were devoted to the purchase of War Bonds and these were split up into 12 prizes. Each person received a numbered ticket at the door duplicates of which were put into a bag. The 1st twelve numbers to be drawn out were the winners, the draw took place on the stage during the show. The C.S.R won 9 out of the 12 prizes. | AW. |
| " | 22-9-18 | | Church of England service was held in the Cinema at 10-30AM, the C.S.R. band provided the music. The Non-Conformist service was held in the Eglise Evangelique and the R.C. in the Parish Church. Voluntary services were also held in the evening. A Rugby football match arranged between the C.S.R and the 142nd Squadron R.A.F resulted in a ~~victory~~ for the C.S.R. 6 Points to NIL. | AW. |
| " | 23-9-18 | | The morning was spent in the usual way, Drill & specialists training. A Football match was arranged between the Officers + Sgts of the Bn, the Sgts won by 2 goals to NIL. The following NCOs and men were awarded the Military Medal:- A.Coy: 537095 Pte V.L.DAWSON: 394730 Pte H.O.TWITCHEM: 530354 Pte J.S.ARMSTRONG; B.Coy: 531585 Pte H.J.HOCKLEY: 531321 Sgt H.T.COX: C.Coy: 530209 Sgt (A/CSM) C.IBBETT: 548034 Pte G.A.BOTT: 474283 Pte F.G.WELLS: D.Coy: 394649 Pte A.L.FEWSTER (K.I.A) 531040 L/Cpl G.W.NELSON: 531706 Sgt P.S.HAGUE: H.Q.Coy. 548058 L/Cpl R.L.ANGEL: 391349 Pte C.J.LEWINGTON: | AW. |

D. D. & L., London, E.C.
(A10266) Wt W5300/P713 750,000 2/18 Sch. 52 Forms/C2118/16.

Instructions regarding War Diaries and Intelligence Summaries are contained in F. S. Regs., Part II. and the Staff Manual respectively. Title pages will be prepared in manuscript.

# WAR DIARY

~~or~~

~~INTELLIGENCE SUMMARY~~

(Erase heading not required.)

Army Form C. 2118.

| Place | Date | Hour | Summary of Events and Information | Remarks and references to Appendices |
|---|---|---|---|---|
| AUCHEL | 24-9-18 | | The Bn moved off at 8-30AM and marched to the Range at ALLOUAGNE for firing practice. A lecture on Gas was given at 2-0PM in the Cinema by the Divisional Gas Officer to Officers and NCOs. Boxing Contests were arranged for the evening and took place in the Cinema. A draft of 90 O.R. joined the Bn. Orders were again issued for entrainment to ITALY, entrainment to take place on the 26th inst. | A.W. Vide O.O.159. dated 24-9-18 |
| " | 25-9-18 | | The orders for entrainment were again postponed. Training was carried out in billets owing to wet weather. A Rugby football match took place between the 14E Night Bombing Squadron R.A.F. and the C.S.R near PERNES, the R.A.F won by 5 points to 4. A Cinema entertainment was given in the evening. | A.W. |
| " | 26-9-18 | | The usual daily training was carried out. A Cinema entertainment was given in the evening, after which a dance took place, to ~~which~~ civilians were invited. | A.W. |
| " | 27-9-18 | | The Brigade marched to the St. POL area, the C.S.R being billeted in FOUFFLIN-RICAMETZ. The Bn left billets in AUCHEL at 8-30AM and arrived in the new area at 4-30PM, a hot meal was provided en-route. | Vide C.S.R. O.O. No160 dated 26-9-18 A.W. |
| FOUFFLIN-RICAMETZ | 28-9-18 | | Companies carried out training in billets owing to bad weather. | A.W. |
| " | 29-9-18 | | Baths were allotted to the Bn at St MICHEL from 9-0AM to 3-0PM. Voluntary C of E. and Non Conformists services were held in the school, the R.C service being held in the Parish Church. The school-room was also opened as a recreation room. 2nd Lt H. KING rejoined from hospital and ~~Lieut~~ R.W. FORD (1/14 LONDON Regt) reported for duty. | A.W. |
| " | 30-9-18 | | Outdoor training was again cancelled owing to bad weather. A Coy moved to billets in ROELLECOURT owing to the poor accommodation in FOUFFLIN-RICAMETZ. | A.W. |

R. Fielding
Lt Colonel
Cmdg 1/CIVIL SERVICE RIFLES.

D. D. & L., London, E.C.
(A10266) Wt W5300/P713 750,000 2/18 Sch. 52 Forms/C2118/16.

Vol 40

CONFIDENTIAL

WAR DIARY.

of

1/15th Battalion London Regiment (P.W.O. CIVIL SERVICE RIFLES.

from 1st October, 1918 to 31st October, 1918.

---

Army Form C. 2118.

Instructions regarding War Diaries and Intelligence Summaries are contained in F. S. Regs., Part II. and the Staff Manual respectively. Title pages will be prepared in manuscript.

# WAR DIARY
or
# INTELLIGENCE SUMMARY.
(Erase heading not required.)

| Place | Date | Hour | Summary of Events and Information | Remarks and references to Appendices |
|---|---|---|---|---|
| FOUFFLIN-RICAMETZ | 1/10/18 | | Bn carried out training under the supervision of Coy Commanders. Lewis Gun classes were held under 2nd Lt C.E. BARNETT. 2nd Lt P. EWEN rejoined for duty from hospital. Orders were issued at 2200 that Bn would move to the 5th Army area the following day. | [illegible] |
| | 2/10/18 | | Bn stood by ready to move. No training was carried out during the day. 2nd Lt A.E.J. CHARTER left at 1630 to make arrangements for entraining at ST POL. 2nd Lt BARNETT L.L.E with one N.C.O. from each Coy went to LESTREM to arrange billets for Bn. The Bn left FOUFFLIN-RICAMETZ at 1700, and entrained at ST POL at 20.15. Capt W.L. RATHBONE M.C. to hospital. | [illegible] |
| LESTREM | 3/10/18 | | Bn arrived at MERVILLE at 03.40 and marched to LESTREM arriving at 04.50. Bn bivouacked at R15 a7.4. (Sheet 36A). Bn stood by ready to move. Orders were issued at 14.05 to parade at 14.25 to march to FAUQUISSART. Bn arrived at 18.30 and stayed the night in dug-outs off RUE TILLELOY. Orders were issued at 20.30 to move next morning. Capt GRIMSDALE detached as Town Major of LESTREM. | [illegible] |
| IN RESERVE | 4/10/18 | | Bn left FAUQUISSART at 06.15. Bn reached reserve trenches - NEAR AVENUE | [illegible] |

D. D. & L., London, E.C.
(A10266) Wt W5300/P713 750,000 2/18 Sch. 52 Forms/C2118/16.

Army Form C. 2118.

# WAR DIARY
or
# INTELLIGENCE SUMMARY.
(Erase heading not required.)

Instructions regarding War Diaries and Intelligence Summaries are contained in F. S. Regs., Part II. and the Staff Manual respectively. Title pages will be prepared in manuscript.

| Place | Date | Hour | Summary of Events and Information | Remarks and references to Appendices |
|---|---|---|---|---|
| IN RESERVE | 4/10/18 | | N.l.d. to O7a. Sheet 36SW and 36SW2 RADINGHEM. Bn H.Q. at O7a 5.2. O.O. No 101 issued. Bn in position at 10.30. Transport at HAYEM O10d. Patrols sent out from each Coy to reconnoitre. A Coy report:- "Encountered slight machine gun fire along SCREENS road in O2d, O3c, O3b which was under observation. 19th Bn on left held up by enemy along railway cutting O4a, and O4c. Slight shelling of road O9b 2.8 to O9b 8.5." C+D Coys submitted same report:- "Cross roads at LE BAS HAU under direct observation from railway embankment." B Coy report:- "Patrol sniped at along SCREENS road. Enemy appeared to be holding railway embankment & high ground in O4a, O4c and O4b. M.G. believed to be in houses about O4b 6.8." Nothing further was done during the day. | Vide O.O. No 101 4/10/18 |
| | 5/10/18 | | Orders issued during the morning that the Bn would relieve the 18th Bn. London Regt at 2030. Cpl DOUGLAS and 4 others went out to reconnoitre, they reported:- No enemy movement or machine guns in ground in front of railway embankment. Companies moved off - order B.C.D.A - at 2030 at 200x interval to relieve the 18th Bn in support to the 17th Bn. Bn H.Q. remained in its present position. Hot suppers served to men on arrival in new positions. | Vide O.O. No 102 5/10/18 |

D. D. & L., London, E.C.
(A10266) Wt W5300/P713 750,000 2/18 Sch. 52 Forms/C2118/16.

* Instructions regarding War Diaries and Intelligence Summaries are contained in F. S. Regs., Part II. and the Staff Manual respectively. Title pages will be prepared in manuscript.

# WAR DIARY

or

~~INTELLIGENCE SUMMARY.~~

*(Erase heading not required.)*

Army Form C. 2118.

| Place | Date | Hour | Summary of Events and Information | Remarks and references to Appendices |
|---|---|---|---|---|
| IN RESERVE | 5/10/18 | | Rations dumped by Transport at Oc19 at 2200 for B. Coy. Rations dumped at O2a7.4 at 22.00 for A. D. & C. Coys. Bn in position in OIL AVENUE and OIL STREET from O2a to O8c, A Coy on left B Coy on right. | [illegible] |
| IN SUPPORT | 6/10/18 | | Situation reports received from Coys at 0330. Cpl DOUGLAS and 3 observers sent out to reconnoitre. The following report sent to Bde HQ at 11.30:- "Situation normal. Wind S.S.W. Cross roads at O3 b 5.8 under machine gun fire from a gun apparently situated in O10 d 1.0. Small party of enemy (2 or 3) seen this morning in houses about 400 yds EAST of embankment O4 b 5.5. Crows nest in trees about same position occupied this morning between 0700 and 0800." | [illegible] |
| | 7/10/18 | | Cpl DOUGLAS & 3 observers sent out at 0730 to reconnoitre. Intelligence report sent to Bde HQ at 1120:- "Bombs dropped by enemy aircraft about O2a. At 0515 shelling was experienced by one howitzer – probably 5.9 – firing from extreme range. Situation quiet. Wind SSW mild. Railway embankment from O4a 30.10 to O4c 8.7 reported clear of enemy at 1000. Enemy machine gun post established at O4c 8.4 during the night 6/7. T.M. emplacement believed to be at O4b 65.25." Draft of 70 O.R. arrived at 18.00. Attached | [illegible] |

D. D. & L., London, E.C.
(A10266) Wt W5300/P713 750,000 2/18 Sch. 52 Forms/C2118/16.

119

Army Form C. 2118.

Instructions regarding War Diaries and Intelligence Summaries are contained in F. S. Regs., Part II. and the Staff Manual respectively. Title pages will be prepared in manuscript.

# WAR DIARY
*or*
# ~~INTELLIGENCE SUMMARY.~~

*(Erase heading not required.)*

| Place | Date | Hour | Summary of Events and Information | Remarks and references to Appendices |
|---|---|---|---|---|
| IN SUPPORT | 7/10/18 | | to H.Q. for rations and training. Two OR wounded during the night in A Coy. (4.2 guns) | |
| | 8/10/18 | | Cpl DOUGLAS and 2 observers sent out to reconnoitre. The following Intelligence report sent to Bde H.Q. at 11.30:- "Occasional shelling during the night on O2C and O2d — 4.2 guns. Situation quiet. Wind S.W. One of our patrols headed by Cpl DOUGLAS walked right into an enemy post at O4C 8.5 at 1000. T.M. position believed to be at O4d 45.90." Draft carry out training:- Drill under R.S.M., Musketry under Sgt BOWMAN, P.T. under Sgt LEHAN. | |
| | 9/10/18 | | Cpl DOUGLAS and 2 observers sent out to reconnoitre. Nothing of importance to report. Orders issued that Bn will be relieved by 19th London Regt and go in reserve, taking over from 18th London Regt. Draft carry out training as on 8/10/18. The following officer awarded the Military Cross:- 2nd Lt C.E. BARNETT. The following N.C.Os & men awarded the Distinguished Conduct Medal:- Sgt JONES T.W. | Vide O.O. No 103 9/10/18 |

D. D. & L., London, E.C.
(A10266) Wt W5300/P713 750,000 2/18 Sch. 52 Forms/C2118/16.

Instructions regarding War Diaries and Intelligence Summaries are contained in F. S. Regs., Part II. and the Staff Manual respectively. Title pages will be prepared in manuscript.

# WAR DIARY
or
~~INTELLIGENCE~~ SUMMARY.
(Erase heading not required.)

Army Form C. 2118.

| Place | Date | Hour | Summary of Events and Information | Remarks and references to Appendices |
|---|---|---|---|---|
| IN SUPPORT | 9/10/18 | | Sgt NEILL T.J. MM L/Cpl POOLE J.E.S. The following W.O. N.C.O's and men awarded the Military Medal:- C.S.M. TURNER C.E.T., Sgt PINDER H.F., L/Cpl BARNES R.J., Pte BRADLEY, A.F., Pte SURRIDGE A.J., Sgt BROWN A.J., L/Cpl DARMODY J.F. L/Cpl UNDERWOOD G. Capt L.D. ECCLES returned to duty from leave. | |
| IN RESERVE | 10/10/18 | | Bn back in positions originally occupied 4/10/18 with the exception of H.Q. Draft carry out training as on 7/10/18. Orderly Room, Band, Shoemakers, Tailors now with H.Q. Musketry & Lewis gun classes carried out under company arrangements. The following Officer and N.C.Os detached to 5th Army School Musketry Course:- 2nd Lt T.J. BOOTH, L/Cpl JOHNSON, L/Cpl FLOYD. | |
| | 11/10/18 | | The Bn carried out Musketry training under Coy arrangements. The draft carried out training as on 10/10/18. The following N.C.Os detached to the 5th Army School, S.O.S course at PREUVRES:- | [initials] |

D. D. & L., London, E.C.
(A10266) Wt W5300/P713 750,000 2/18 Sch. 52 Forms/C2118/16.

Instructions regarding War Diaries and Intelligence Summaries are contained in F. S. Regs., Part II. and the Staff Manual respectively. Title pages will be prepared in manuscript.

# WAR DIARY
*or*
# ~~INTELLIGENCE~~ SUMMARY.
(*Erase heading not required.*)

Army Form C. 2118.

| Place | Date | Hour | Summary of Events and Information | Remarks and references to Appendices |
|---|---|---|---|---|
| IN RESERVE | 11/10/18 | | Cpl HOULAHAN and L/Cpl SMITH R.W. Pte PALMER transferred to 1/22 London Regt. Cpl SHIPTON. A proceeded on leave to ENGLAND. Sgt GORING and Cpl BARNETT proceeded to ENGLAND to take up commissions. | |
| | | | Cpl MOUNTFORD and Pte AMBROSE (RAMC) detached to the 5th Field Ambulance | |
| | | | Major D.S. YOUNG rejoined for duty from 1/21 London. Major D.S. YOUNG proceeded on leave to Paris. The Band played selections of music in D Coy's area. Shelling around Bn H.Q. by 5.9's from 1800 to 1815. Capt J.C. FARNSWORTH struck off strength on being posted to the 15/17 West Yorks. 2nd Lt T. FRENCH takes over duties as Q.M. The Bn bathed at FROMELLES during the day. | |
| | 12/10/18 | | Companies under Coy arrangements carry out training during the morning as on previous days. A football match (Association) was played between the Bn and the 235 Bde R.F.A. The Bn won by 2 goals to 0. The Band played to B Coy in Coy area. | |
| | 13/10/18 | | Orders issued that the 140 Bde would not relieve the 141 Bde. 2nd Lt H.E.J. CHARTER with one N.C.O from each Coy left as advance billeting party. | |
| | | | Church services were held:- Holy Communion in Band billet at 1000 and Evening Service (C. of E.) at 18.00. 2nd Lt J. HALLIFAX left with advance billeting party consisting of one N.C.O. from each Coy for ST VENANT. | |

D. D. & L., London, E.C.
(A10266) Wt W5300/P713 750,000 2/18 Sch. 52 Forms/C2118/16.

WAR DIARY

~~or~~

~~INTELLIGENCE SUMMARY.~~

*(Erase heading not required.)*

Army Form C. 2118.

Instructions regarding War Diaries and Intelligence Summaries are contained in F. S. Regs., Part II. and the Staff Manual respectively. Title pages will be prepared in manuscript.

| Place | Date | Hour | Summary of Events and Information | Remarks and references to Appendices |
|---|---|---|---|---|
| IN RESERVE | 14/10/18 | | The Bn was relieved by the 1st Royal Munster Fusiliers of the 172 Bde at 10.30 and marched to ESTAIRES arriving at 21.30. 2nd Lt [illegible] WILLIAMS joined for duty as Q.M. 2nd Lt J. WALKER joined for duty. | Vide O.O. No 164 13/10/18. |
| ESTAIRES | 15/10/18 | | The Bn left ESTAIRES at 09.20 and marched to ST VENANT arriving at 13.45. Nothing further was done during the day. | Vide O.O. No 165 14/10/18. |
| ST VENANT | 16/10/18 | | The day was spent in cleaning billets, the vicinity of same, clothing & equipment. Lt W. EDMED rejoined for duty as Signalling Officer from course. 2nd Lt S.A. SILLITOE joined for duty. A football match was played between the Bn H.Q and Bde H.Q at 14.30. The Bn H.Q won by 6 goals to 2. A Rugby match was played between the Bn and 148 Squadron R.A.F. The Bn lost by 6 points to 3. Winter clothing [illegible] to [illegible]. | |
| FONTES | 17/10/18 | | The Bn left ST VENANT at 08.45 and marched to FONTES arriving at 12.15. 2nd Lt H.E.J. CHARTER with one N.C.O. from each Coy left for FONTES as advance billeting party. 2nd Lt C.E. BARTETT M.C. proceeded on leave to ENGLAND. Capt. P. [illegible] rejoined for duty from hospital. Capt. [illegible] rejoined for duty and [illegible] the duties of Town Major of ESTRÉEM. Nothing further was done during the day. | Vide O.O. No 166 16/10/18. |
| FONTES | 17/10/18 | | After the Commanding Officer's inspection the Bn carried out training under company arrangements. | |

D. D. & L., London, E.C.
(A10266) Wt W5300/P713 750,000 8/18 Sch. 52 Forms/C2118/16.

Instructions regarding War Diaries and Intelligence Summaries are contained in F. S. Regs., Part II. and the Staff Manual respectively. Title pages will be prepared in manuscript.

# WAR DIARY
or
# INTELLIGENCE SUMMARY.
(Erase heading not required.)

Army Form C. 2118.

| Place | Date | Hour | Summary of Events and Information | Remarks and references to Appendices |
|---|---|---|---|---|
| FONTES | 18/10/18 | | 2nd Lt F. S. EASTON proceeded on leave to ENGLAND. CAPT. G. GRIMSDALE detached to Div H.Q. | |
| | 19/10/18 | | The Bn carried out training at the Chateau training grounds. A football match was played between the Bn and the 517 Field Coy R.Es. The Bn won by 1 goal to 0. Baths for A.Q. Coy at LA GOULEE. | |
| | 20/10/18 | | Bde Church Service at ST HILAIRE cancelled on arrival owing to inclement weather. The Military Medal was presented to 15 N.C.O.s and men of the Bn by the G.O.C. Div. Service for Nonconformists at the School at 10.15 and for Roman Catholics at NORRES-FONTES at 10.15. Evening service in the school at 17.30. Holy Communion in the school at 07.30 and 18.30. 7 O.R. joined for duty from the base. | |
| | 21/10/18 | | The Bn carried out musketry training and L.G. classes in billets till 09.45 owing to bad weather, and then carried out training in the Chateau training grounds. Baths at LA GOULEE for A+B Coys. | |
| | 22/10/18 | | The Bn marched to the Rifle Range at T.15.b.55 (Sheet 36 A). All ranks fired the following practices:- At 100 yds 5 rounds grouping; at 200 yards 5 rounds application and one minute rapid. Lewis Gunners fired L.G. practices. Baths at LA GOULEE for 18 O.R. H.Q. Coy. One platoon of D Coy | [initials] |

D. D. & L., London, E.C.
(A10266) Wt W5300/P713 750,000 2/18 Sch. 52 Forms/C2118/16.

Army Form C. 2118.

Instructions regarding War Diaries and Intelligence Summaries are contained in F. S. Regs., Part II. and the Staff Manual respectively. Title pages will be prepared in manuscript.

# WAR DIARY
*or*
# INTELLIGENCE SUMMARY.
*(Erase heading not required.)*

| Place | Date | Hour | Summary of Events and Information | Remarks and references to Appendices |
|---|---|---|---|---|
| FONTES | 22/10/18 | | gave a demonstration in the training of a platoon and one officer from I.G. training in the Chateau training grounds at 14.30 | |
| | 23/10/18 | | The Bn carried out a tactical scheme in conjunction with one section [illegible] plus one section of A Coy M.G. Bn and one section of 140 T.M. Battery. The Div Staff and the officers of 140 Bde were present. In the afternoon the following football matches were played:- A Coy beat D Coy by 1-0; Depot beat B Coy by 2-1. | [illegible] 01 22/10/18 |
| | 24/10/18 | | The Bn carried out training in the Chateau training grounds. In the afternoon the following football matches were played:- H.Q. Coy drew with Depot 1-1 after extra time; C Coy beat A Coy by 1-0; Bn team [illegible] lost to the [illegible] R.E. Signals by 2-1. Billets at LA BOISSEE for Transport and Band. 2nd Lt P.A. BENNETT proceeded on leave to ENGLAND. | |
| | 25/10/18 | | The Bn carried out tactical schemes under Company arrangements in the FONTES training area. The Transport left for LOMME area at 08.35. 2nd Lt A.E.S. CHARTER with the Q.M.S. left for LOMME area at 08.30 as advance billeting party. | [illegible] 2+10/18 |

D. D. & L., London, E.C.
(A10266) Wt W5300/P713 750,000 2/18 Sch. 52 Forms/C2118/16.

Army Form C. 2118.

Instructions regarding War Diaries and Intelligence Summaries are contained in F. S. Regs., Part II. and the Staff Manual respectively. Title pages will be prepared in manuscript.

# WAR DIARY
or
~~INTELLIGENCE SUMMARY~~.
(Erase heading not required.)

| Place | Date | Hour | Summary of Events and Information | Remarks and references to Appendices |
|---|---|---|---|---|
| FONTES | 26/10/18 | | The Bn left FONTES at 13.00, entrained at BERGUETTE 15.15, detrained at PERENCHIES 17.45 and marched to LOMME, arriving at 18.45. | |
| LOMME | 27/10/18 | | The day was spent in cleaning up clothing and equipment. Officers, W.Os, and N.C.Os were allowed on pass to LILLE. Voluntary Services were held as follows:- C of E. in Factory at 18.00, followed by Holy Communion. Mass for Roman Catholics at LAMBERSART ~~at 09.30~~. | |
| | 28/10/18 | | The Bn took part in the march of the 47th Div through LILLE on the occasion of the official entry of the Fifth Army Commander into the city. C. Coy formed a cordon round the GRAND PLACE. The Bn, less C Coy, paraded at 10.45, and arrived at HELLEMMES at 13.30. Nothing further was done during the day. CAPT F. S. FAREBROTHER proceeded on leave to ENGLAND. | |
| HELLEMMES | 29/10/18 | | No parade was held during the day to enable all ranks to visit LILLE. 2nd Lt G.W. PRYNNE proceeded on leave to ENGLAND. 5 O.R. returned from Div. Rest Camp. | |
| | 30/10/18 | | 2nd Lt H.E.J. CHARTER and C.Q.M.S. left at 07.00 as advance billeting party. Bn left HELLEMMES at 11.30 arriving at CHÉRENG 13.30. The C.O. ADJT, Signalling Officer, and Coy Commanders reconnoitred front line. | Vide O.O. No 168 29/10/18 |
| CHÉRENG | 31/10/18 | | Baths were allotted to all Coys at the rate of 60 per hour under Bn arrangements. 4 Cpl McDOWELL detached to S.O.&S. course 5th Army School at PREURES. The Bn relieved the 2/4 S. Lancs in the front line. A Coy on the right, C Coy on the left, B Coy in support and D Coy in reserve. Patrols sent out from A. B. & C Coys. Casualties NIL. 2 O.R. proceeded on leave to ENGLAND. | Vide O.O. No [illegible] 30/10/18 |

[signature]
Lt. Colonel, [illegible]

D. D. & L., London, E.C.
(A10266) Wt W5300/P713 750,000 2/18 Sch. 52 Forms/C2118/16.

SECRET. 1/CIVIL SERVICE RIFLES. COPY NO. 3

ORDER NO.164.

13th October, 1918.

Reference Maps -
36 1/40,000
36A do.

1. The 140th Infantry Brigade will be relieved by the 172nd Infantry Brigade of the 57th Division tomorrow, 14th October, and will march to the ESTAIRES Area.

2. The Brigade Group will be prepared to continue the march on the 15th October, to the CALONNE Area at about 09.30.

3. S.O.S. Rockets, Tents, Trench Shelters and Pack Saddlery surplus to establishment will be handed over to the incoming Brigade and receipts obtained and forwarded to the Orderly Room immediately on arrival in the new area.

4. Particulars of relief will be notified later. The time will be about 14.00.

5. Transport, less cookers etc. with Battalion, will march under the B.T.O. at 10.00.

6. Brigade Headquarters will close at M.17.c at 14.00 on 14th inst., and reopen at the Convent, ST.VENANT, on arrival.

7. Officers' valises, mess boxes, and Orderly Room boxes will be collected as follows at 10.00 :- Coy. valises and mess boxes will be collected from A. Coy. H.Q.; Bn. H.Q. valises, mess boxes and Orderly Room boxes from Bn. H.Q..

8. All Lewis Guns and Lewis Gun stuff will be loaded on to L.G. Limbers during the morning under the supervision of Cpl. STRINGER.

9. The packs and music of the Band will be dumped with H.Q. valises and loaded on to G.S. wagon.

10. Transport Officer will arrange for one G.S. wagon, and one limber for Lewis Guns to report at Bn. H.Q. at 09.30. Officers' Chargers with grooms must report by 12.00.

WS
for

2/Lt. & A/Adjutant,
1/CIVIL SERVICE RIFLES.

Distribution :-
Copy No. 1 C.O.
2 File.
3 War Diary.
4 A. Coy.
5 B. Coy.
6 C. Coy.
7 D. Coy.
8. Intelligence Offr.
9 T.O. & Q.M.
10 L.G.O.
11 R.S.M.

"A" Form

Army Form C. 2121
(in pads of 100)

**MESSAGES AND SIGNALS.**

No of Message...........

| Prefix........Code........m | Words | Charge | This message is on a/c of: | Recd. at........m |
|---|---|---|---|---|
| Office of Origin and Service Instructions. | | | ..................Service | Date.............. |
| War Diary | Sent | | | From.............. |
| | At............m. | | | |
| | To.............. | | | |
| | By.............. | | (Signature of "Franking Officer") | By.............. |

TO { Operation Orders No [illegible]
Refer map. 36 A [illegible] Oct 14/1916

| Sender's Number | Day of Month | In reply to Number | AAA |
|---|---|---|---|
| * | | | |

| | | | |
|---|---|---|---|
| Reveille | 7.00 | Suppers | 8.00 |
| Breakfast | 8.00 | Roll Call | 9 pm |
| Dinners | en route | Lights low | 9.15 |
| Teas on arrival at destination. | | Lights out | 9.30 |

The Battalion will continue the march tomorrow proceeding to ST. VENANT via LA GORGUE. – BEAUPRE – K. 35. b. 4. 3 – Q. 5. b. 6. 4. CALONNE-CORNET MALO.

The Battn. will parade ready to move off at the Bridge in 29. d 9 2. at 9. 20. Order of march HQ. Band. D C B A. Tpt.

Officers Valises, and mess boxes will be collected from Coy. and HQ messes at 8. 30 [illegible]

| From | | |
|---|---|---|
| Place | | |
| Time | | |

*The above may be forwarded as now corrected* (Z)

..................... Censor

[illegible signature]

Signature of Addressor or person authorised to telegraph in his name

* This line should be erased if not required [illegible]

(7700.) Wt. W492/M1647 110,000 Pads 5/17 C & R Ltd. (E. 1187.)

War Diary

SECRET. CIVIL SERVICE RIFLES. COPY NO. 8 +3

ORDER NO.186.

16.10.18.

Refce. Map: 36A. 1/40,000

1. The 140th Brigade Group will march to the ST. HILAIRE area tomorrow.

2. The 1/15th Bn. London Regt. will march to FONTES and LIETTRES. The Battalion will parade in the Market Square at 08.30 in quarter column, B. Coy. leading.

3. All Transport will accompany the Battalion. They will be in Rue de Paris near Bn. H.Q. ready to move off at 08.30.

4. Blankets, rolled in bundles of ten, and men's packs will be dumped at the Q.M. Stores by 07.30. Officers' valises, mess boxes and Orderly Room boxes will be collected from Bn. and Coy. messes at 07.30.

5. Billeting party consisting of C.Q.M.S. of each Coy. including H.Q. Coy. and a representative from the Q.M. Stores and Transport sections will report at cross roads FONTES (K.29.a.5.2) at 10.30 to meet Lt. Chambers of Brigade H.Q. Six bicycles will be available for this party at the Orderly Room at 08.30.

6. Two lorries will be available for the 15th Bn. as extra transport and will be at Brigade H.Q. at 08.30. Q.M. will send a guide to conduct the lorries to the Battalion area.

Dominic Foster

2/Lt. & A/Adjt.,
1/CIVIL SERVICE RIFLES.

Distribution:-
Copy No. 1 C.O.
2 File.
3 War Diary.
4 A. Coy.
5 B. "
6 C. "
7 D. "
8. Int. Offr.
9 T.O. & Q.M.
10 R.S.M.

War Diary

SECRET. 1/CIVIL SERVICE RIFLES. COPY NO. 3.

ORDER NO. 167.

Reference Maps :-
36.A and 36 1/40,000.

24th October, 1918.

1. The Battalion will move by train to the LOMME area (West of LILLE) on the 25th October. Time of parade and entrainment will be notified later. Companies will report by Sgts-in-Waiting tonight what their entraining strength will be.

2. Transport will move by road, starting on the 25th October, under 2/Lt. A.J.COLEY, and will pass the starting point (cross roads T.6.c.1.1.) at 08.45. The route for tomorrow will be LILLERS - BUSNES - ROBECQ - CALONNE. No vehicles or horses will be allowed to proceed by train.

3. Officers' valises and heavy mess boxes will be delivered to the Q.M. Stores for loading on to the wagons by 21.00 today. Sufficient cooking utensils will be retained by Companies and Company cookers will be ready for the T.O. by 07.00 tomorrow.

4. All Lewis Gun limbers will be loaded this afternoon and Sgt. GOULDING will march with the limbers tomorrow.

V. Davenport.
Capt. & Adjt.
1/CIVIL SERVICE RIFLES.

Distribution:-
Copy No. 1 C.O.
2 File.
3 War Diary.
4 O.C. A.Coy.
5 " B. "
6 " C. "
7 " D. "
8 Sigs. and Intelligence Offrs.
9 T.O. & Q.M.
10 Lewis Gun Offr.
11 R.S.M.

War Diary

SECRET. 1/CIVIL SERVICE RIFLES. COPY NO. 3

Order No. 168. 29th October, 1918.

Reference Maps:
38A and 37, 1/40,000

1. The Battalion will march tomorrow, 30th October, to billets in CHERENG.

2. 2/Lt. A.E.J.CHARTERS and all C.Q.M.Ss. will parade at the Orderly room at 07.00 and cycle to CHERENG to billet the Battalion. Billeting N.C.O. from the Transport Section will accompany them. Lieut. F.E. KEMPD will arrange for necessary bicycles to be ready at the Orderly Room at that time.

3. The Battalion will parade in full marching order in column of route in the main road facing east, ready to move off at 11.30. Order of march will be:- H.Q. Coy., Band, B., C., D., A. Coys.

4. All billets will be left in a clean and sanitary condition and Coy. Commanders will inspect them personally before parade.

5. Dinners will be cooked on the march so as to be ready on arrival at CHERENG.

6. Lieut. H.H.FORD, one N.C.O. from D. Coy. and a sanitary man from each Coy. will remain behind. Lieut. FORD will report to the Sub-Area Commandant to investigate any claims and to obtain a certificate that the billets have been left clean and sanitary.

Davenport.

Capt. & Adjutant,
1/CIVIL SERVICE RIFLES.

Distribution:-
Copy No. 1 C.O.
2 File.
3 War Diary.
4 O/C A. Coy.
5 B.
6 C.
7 D.
8 Sigs. & Int. Offrs.
9 T.O. & Q.M.
10 R.S.M.

war diary

SECRET. 1/CIVIL SERVICE RIFLES. Copy No. 3

Order No. 169. 30th October, 1918.

Reference Map:- 37 S.W., 1/20,000.

1. The Battalion will relieve the 2/4th South Lancs. Bn. tomorrow, 31st inst., in the front line, each Coy. relieving the same letter Coy.

2. Order of march will be as follows:- D. Coy. will pass starting point, cross-roads N.21.b.5.0 at 13.30, A. Coy. will pass starting point at 13.45, B. Coy. at 14.10, C. Coy. at 14.25, H.Q. Coy. at 14.40. Coys. will march by platoons at 100 yards distance.

3. Lewis Gun limber with A. and D. Coys. guns will accompany leading platoon of D. Coy. Limber with B. and C. Coys. Lewis Guns will accompany B. Coys. leading platoon. One member of each gun team will march behind the limber. Signalling equipment will be carried on the L.G. Limbers.

4. Route will be via BAISIEUX - cross roads in N.21.d. to junction of road and railway in N.16.a.8.4, thence along the railway to O.7.a.9.4, thence to cross-roads O.7.c.9.9, where guides will meet the leading Coy. at 16.30. Lewis Guns will be unloaded 200 yards short of the road junction at N.16.a.8.1. The road between the destroyed bridge at N.12.b.9.0 and the cross-roads at O.7.c.9.9 is out of bounds. Guides for the different posts will be met at Coy. H.Q.

5. Defence schemes, instmuctions for the advance, etc., will be taken over, and copies of receipts sent to the Orderly Room by first run, 1st Nov.

6. One water duty man will go with each Coy. All water must be chlorinated before use.

7. The S.O.S. in force on the Divisional front is a rifle grenade bursting into three lights, green over green over green.

8. B. and D. Coys. cookers will be sent up to their Coy. H.Q. at dusk tomorrow and at the same time the Transport Officer will deliver to Coys., blankets, officers' mess boxes, ammunition, and, in the case of A. and C. Coys., dixies.

9. Code word for relief complete will be Coy. Commanders' name.

10. Time table of reports due and programme of routine will be circulated to Coys. during the morning.

Davenport

Capt. & Adjutant,
1/CIVIL SERVICE RIFLES.

P.T.O.

Distribution:-

| | | |
|---|---|---|
| Copy No. | 1 | C.O. |
| | 2 | File. |
| | 3 | War Diary. |
| | 4 | O/C A. Coy. |
| | 5 | B. |
| | 6 | C. |
| | 7 | D. |
| | 8 | Sigs. & Scout Offrs. |
| | 9 | L.G.O. |
| | 10 | T.O. & Q.M. |
| | 11 | R.S.M. |
| | 12 | M.O. |
| | 13 | 340th Inf. Bde. |
| | 14 | 2/4th South Lancs. Bn. |

CONFIDENTIAL



1/15th Battn. London Regt.
(P.W.O. Civil Service Rifles.)

WAR DIARY

NOVEMBER, 1918

Instructions regarding War Diaries and Intelligence Summaries are contained in F. S. Regs., Part II. and the Staff Manual respectively. Title pages will be prepared in manuscript.

# WAR DIARY
or
~~INTELLIGENCE SUMMARY.~~
*(Erase heading not required.)*

Army Form C. 2118.

| Place | Date | Hour | Summary of Events and Information | Remarks and references to Appendices |
|---|---|---|---|---|
| FRONT LINE | 1/11/18 | | The Bn occupied the front line in houses in a state of defence. At night posts were pushed forward and patrols sent out from A. B. & C. Coys. Draft of 11 O.R. joined for duty. 2nd Lt T. J. BOOTH rejoined the Bn from 5th Army School PREURES. Casualties:- WOUNDED – [illegible] 2 O.R. 2 O.R. proceeded on leave to England. | [initials] |
| | 2/11/18 | | Intelligence Report, Patrol Report, Proposed Patrol Report and Map showing dispositions sent to Bde. The G.O.C. the Div. visited the Bn. Patrols sent out from A, B, & C Coys. Two of A Coy posts pushed forward some 60–70 [illegible]. Working parties improved & strengthened forward posts. Cpl HOULAHAN & L/Cpl SMITH returned from [illegible] course 5th Army School PREURES. 6 O.R. proceeded on leave to ENGLAND. Casualties:- KILLED: 1 O.R.; WOUNDED, 1 officer & 3 O.R. | [initials] |
| | 3/11/18 | | Intelligence report, Patrol report, Proposed Patrol report and Work report sent to Bde. Posts in houses strengthened and sandbagged for defence. Patrols sent out from A, B, & C Coys. Working parties wired forward posts. 6 O.R. proceeded on leave to ENGLAND. Casualties:- WOUNDED 3 O.R. Civilians evacuated from FROYENNES. The Bn was relieved by the 47th Londons. Coys [illegible] to CORNET. Total casualties while in front line: Killed 1 O.R. Wounded 1 officer 10 O.R. | [initials] [initials] Vide O.O. No 170 3/11/18 |
| RESERVE | 5/11/18 | | The day was spent in cleaning [illegible] equipment. Kit inspections were held. Casualties:- NIL. | [initials] |

D. D. & L., London, E.C.
(A10266) Wt W5300/P713 750,000 2/18 Sch. 52 Forms/C2118/16.

Instructions regarding War Diaries and Intelligence Summaries are contained in F. S. Regs., Part II. and the Staff Manual respectively. Title pages will be prepared in manuscript.

# WAR DIARY

*or*

# ~~INTELLIGENCE~~ ~~SUMMARY~~.

*(Erase heading not required.)*

Army Form C. 2118.

| Place | Date | Hour | Summary of Events and Information | Remarks and references to Appendices |
|---|---|---|---|---|
| RESERVE | 6/11/18 | | Platoon training was carried out under the supervision of Coy Commanders. Not much further was done during the day owing to inclement weather. 11 O.R. proceeded on leave to ENGLAND. Casualties Nil. | |
| | 7/11/18 | | Platoon training was carried out under the supervision of Coy Commanders. Baths were allotted under Bn arrangements:- 07.00 to 09.00 C Coy, 09.00 to 11.00 B Coy, 11.00 to 13.00 A Coy, 14.00 to 16.00 D Coy, 50 men per Coy, and 16.00 to 17.00 HQ Coy 40 men. Casualties NIL. 7 O.R. proceeded on leave to ENGLAND. | |
| | 8/11/18 | | Companies were at the disposal of Coy Commanders. Baths were allotted:- 07.00 to 08.00 HQ Coy, 08.00 to 09.00 D Coy, 09.00 to 10.00 A Coy, 10.00 to 11.00 B Coy, 11.00 to 12.00 C Coy, 40 men per Coy. 2nd Lt KING and 6 O.R. proceeded on leave to ENGLAND | |
| | 9/11/18. | | The enemy having withdrawn on this front the Bn moved to HONNEVAIN by Coys at 10.15, being still in reserve to the 21st Bn. On arrival, orders were issued to proceed to FROYENNES to positions originally occupied by the Bn when in the front line 1–4 Nov 1918. Bn arrived at 13.00. The rest of the day was spent in cleaning billets which had been left in a very bad condition. 3 O.R. proceeded on leave to ENGLAND. Maj A.F. YENCKEN M.C. R.F.A. attached to the Bn. | |

Army Form C. 2118.

Instructions regarding War Diaries and Intelligence Summaries are contained in F. S. Regs., Part II. and the Staff Manual respectively. Title pages will be prepared in manuscript.

# WAR DIARY
or
INTELLIGENCE ~~SUMMARY.~~

(Erase heading not required.)

| Place | Date | Hour | Summary of Events and Information | Remarks and references to Appendices |
|---|---|---|---|---|
| FROVENNES | 10/11/18 | | The Bn left FROVENNES at 07·30 and marched to BARBERIE arriving at 15·30. 2nd Lt CLARKE and 4 O.R. proceeded on leave to ENGLAND. | |
| BARBERIE | 11/11/18 | | The Bn should have left BARBERIE at 07·30 as advance guard to the Bde. Orders issued cancelling O.O. No 171 at 01.00. The Bn left BARBERIE at 10·20 and marched to TOURNAI, arriving on the outskirts at 14·45 where the Bn remained billeted. 2nd Lt H.E.J. CHARTER left at 09.00 with Coy Q.M.Ss as advance billeting party. COL. FEILDING D.S.O. evacuated to LILLE with P.U.O. During the march back news was received at 11.00. of the signing of the Armistice. | Vide O.O. No 171 10/11/18. Vide O.O. No 172. 11/11/18. |
| TOURNAI | 12/11/18. | | The day was spent in cleaning area, billets etc. In the afternoon a football match was played between the Bn and 47th M.G.C. The Bn lost by 4–0. A concert was given by the Bn in the convent at 18.00. Lt J.K. WENHAM joined the Bn for duty.. 2 O.R. proceeded on leave to ENGLAND. | |
| | 13/11/18 | | The Bn left TOURNAI at 09·00 and marched to PIPAIX to mend the TOURNAI–LEUZE railway, arriving at 13·30. Lt HOEST and Coy Q.M.Ss left at 06·30 as advance billeting party. 3 O.R. proceeded on leave to ENGLAND. | Vide O.O. No 173 12/11/18 |
| PIPAIX | 14/11/18 | | D Coy & half of A Coy reported to the 520th Field Coy R.E. from 08·00 to 12·00 and B Coy and half of A Coy from 12·00 to 16·00 for work on the railway. The rest of the Bn cleaned billets etc. CAPT F.S. FAREBROTHER returned to the Bn from leave | |

Army Form C. 2118.

Instructions regarding War Diaries and Intelligence Summaries are contained in F. S. Regs., Part II. and the Staff Manual respectively. Title pages will be prepared in manuscript.

# WAR DIARY

or

~~INTELLIGENCE SUMMARY~~.

*(Erase heading not required.)*

| Place | Date | Hour | Summary of Events and Information | Remarks and references to Appendices |
|---|---|---|---|---|
| PIPAIX | 14/11/18 | | Lt S.T. MILLS awarded the CROIX DE GUERRE. 3 O.R. proceeded on leave to ENGLAND. | |
| | 15/11/18 | | B and C Coys [illegible] from 08.00 to 12.00 and A and D Coys from 12.00 to 16.00. [illegible] from 09.00 to 15.30. 1 O.R. proceeded on leave to ENGLAND | [initials] |
| | 16/11/18 | | A and D Coys [illegible] from 08.00 to 12.00 and B and C Coys from 12.00 to 16.00. [illegible] from 09.00 to 16.30. In the afternoon [illegible] 55th [illegible] 6 O.R. [illegible] to ENGLAND. Col FEILDING D.S.O. returned to the Bn from hospital. | [initials] |
| | 17/11/18 | | [illegible] 12.00 [illegible] in Q.M. Stores at 18.00. Holy Communion in the Q.M. Stores at 10.00 and 18.30. 2nd Lt SCOTT and 5 O.R. proceeded on leave to ENGLAND. | [initials] |
| | 18/11/18 | | The Bn left PIPAIX at 09.00 and marched to TOURNAI, arriving at 13.00 and being billeted on the outskirts of TOURNAI. 4 O.R. proceeded on leave to ENGLAND. | Vide O.O. No 17 17/11/18. |
| TOURNAI | 19/11/18 | | The Bn left TOURNAI at 09.00 and marched to WILLEMS arriving at 13.00. 3 O.R. proceeded on leave to ENGLAND. 7 O.R. rejoined the Bn from hospital. 2nd Lieuts P.A. BENNETT, J.H. HALLIFAX and G.W. FRYNN returned from leave | Vide O.O. No 15 18/11/18. |
| WILLEMS | 20/11/18 | | The day was spent in the thorough cleaning of arms, Clothing & Equipment. | [initials] |

D. D. & L., London, E.C.
(A10266) Wt W5300/P713 750,000 2/18 Sch. 52 Forms/C2118/16.

Instructions regarding War Diaries and Intelligence Summaries are contained in F. S. Regs., Part II. and the Staff Manual respectively. Title pages will be prepared in manuscript.

# WAR DIARY
or
~~INTELLIGENCE SUMMARY.~~
*(Erase heading not required.)*

Army Form C. 2118.

| Place | Date | Hour | Summary of Events and Information | Remarks and references to Appendices |
|---|---|---|---|---|
| WILLEMS | 20/4/18 | | 4. O.R. proceeded on leave to ENGLAND. LIEUTS W.H. CRAIG, and H.A. APPLETON rejoined the Bn from the base. | |
| | 21/4/18 | | The Bn paraded at 09.30 for a route march of about 5½ miles. Baths were allotted to all Coys under Bn arrangements. 6 O.R. proceeded on leave to ENGLAND | |
| " | 22/4/18 | | The Bn paraded at 09.30 for a route march of about 6 miles. Baths were allotted to all Coys in the afternoon under Bn arrangements. In the afternoon a football match was played between the right and left half Bn. Lt S.[illegible]BERTS and Capt + Q.M. J.P. FRASER joined the Bn for duty from base. 5 O.R. proceeded on leave. | |
| " | 23/4/18 | | The Coys were at the disposal of Coy Commanders, the route march being cancelled owing to the non-arrival of bread for the Bn till 08.30. In the afternoon the Bn played the 1/17th London and lost by 5 goals to 2. 5 O.R. proceeded on leave to ENGLAND 1 O.R. transferred to home establishment | |
| " | 24/4/18 | | Bde Church Service on the Bde parade ground at 11.30. Voluntary services:- Holy Communion at 08.00 and 12.00. Mass for Roman Catholics at 09.15 and Benediction at 17.00 in the Parish Church. In the afternoon the officers of the Bn played the Officers of the 17th London & won by 1 goal to 0. LT G.M. WILLIAMS returned to the Bn from leave. 2 O.R. transferred to home establishment. | |
| | 25/4/18 | | Coys were at the disposal of Coy Commanders. CAPT R.W. FORD [illegible] left at 17.30 | |

D. D. & L., London, E.C.
(A10266) Wt W5300/P713 750,000 2/18 Sch. 52 Forms/C2118/16.

Instructions regarding War Diaries and Intelligence Summaries are contained in F. S. Regs., Part II. and the Staff Manual respectively. Title pages will be prepared in manuscript.

# WAR DIARY
*or*
# ~~INTELLIGENCE SUMMARY.~~

(*Erase heading not required.*)

Army Form C. 2118.

| Place | Date | Hour | Summary of Events and Information | Remarks and references to Appendices |
|---|---|---|---|---|
| WILLEMS | 25/11/18 | | as advance billeting party to HABOURDIN. A football match was played between the officers and sergeants of the Bn. The sergeants won by 3 goals to 1. | MK |
| | 26/11/18 | | The Bn left WILLEMS at 08.00 and marched to HABOURDIN arriving at 14.30 | Vide OO No 176 25/11/18 MK |
| HABOURDIN | 27/11/18 | | The Bn left HABOURDIN at 23.30 and marched to BETHUNE arriving at 10.45. The original order to proceed via CHOCQUES and pass the starting point at 10.00 was cancelled at 21.30 by Bde | Vide OO No 177 26/11/18 MK |
| BETHUNE | 28/11/18 | | The Bn left BETHUNE at 10.00 and marched to FERFAY arriving at 14.15. | Vide OO No 178 27/11/18 MK |
| FERFAY | 29/11/18 | | The day was spent in cleaning arms, equipment, clothing. Kit inspections were held. | |
| " | 30/11/18 | | Coys were at the disposal of Coy Commanders. A concert was given by the Bn in the theatre at 18.00. | MK |

[signature] Lt Col
Comdg 1st C.S.R.

D. D. & L., London, E.C.
(A10266) Wt W5300/P713 750,000 2/18 Sch. 52 Forms/C2118/16.

**SECRET.** 1/CIVIL SERVICE RIFLES. Copy No 2.

Order No. 170. 3rd Nov. 1918.

Reference Map :- 37 S.W., 1/20,000

1. The Battalion will be relieved by the 17th. Bn. London Regt., tomorrow as follows:-

| | | | |
|---|---|---|---|
| C. Coy. | 17th. Bn. relieves | A. Coy. | Civil Service Rifles |
| D | " " | C. | " " |
| A. | " " | B | " " |
| B. | " " | D. | " " |

2. One guide per platoon will be at cross roads at O 7 Central at 16.30.

3. The Company of the 17th. Bn. which relieves A Coy. C.S.R. will only have 4 Platoons, and the Coy. of the 17th. Bn. which relieves D. Coy. will have its full strength of 4 Platoons. O/C. D Coy will therefore send 4 guides to the cross roads.

4. Cookers will be collected by the Transport Officer immediately after dusk. One limber will proceed to each Coy. for Lewis Guns, dixies, mess-boxes, petrol cans and signallers' equipment as follows:-

D. Coy. 17.30 : B Coy 18.30 : A and C Companies 19.30 : HQ. Coy 20.00

A G.S. wagon will visit each Coy. H.Q. to collect blankets as follows:-

B; A; H.Q; C and D, starting with B. Coy at 17.30.

5. On relief the Bn. will move into Reserve at village of CORNET, and will occupy billets now occupied by 21st. Bn. London Regt.

2/Lt. J.H. FRENCH and all C.Q.M.Ss will go there early tomorrow morning to billet the Battalion.

6. Coys. will march to CORNET independently via :- railway to BLAINDAIN Stn. – LES EMPIRES – CORNET.

7. 2/Lt. FRENCH will have guides awaiting Coys at AU POTEAU CABARET – Map ref: N 8 d. 5.5.

8. Trench Stores, maps, Defence schemes, and Instructions for Advance, will be handed over and receipts sent to Orderly Room on arrival at CORNET.

9. The code word for relief complete will be Coy. Commander's name.

Distribution

Copy No 1. C.O.
2. Files
3. War Diary
4. A Coy
5. B "
6. C "
7. D "
8. Sigs. and Scouts Officer
9. L.G.O.
10. T.O. & Q.M.
11. R.S.M.
12. M.O.
13. 140 Infantry Brigade
14. 17th Bn. London Regt.

[signature]

Capt. and Adjt.
1/15th. Bn. London Regt.,
(P.W.O.) CIVIL SERVICE RIFLES.

Secret.

1/ Civil Service Rifles. No. 90.

10/11/1918.

Order No. 171.

Ref. Maps No. 37 & 38 1/40,000.

1. 140th Infantry Brigade will march as an Advanced Guard tomorrow, 11th inst, on the general line of the R DENDRE. The objective being the Bridges over the DENDRE CANAL.

2. Boundaries will be: N. Grid line running through ... G. H. & I central. S. Grid line running through M 1.2.3.4.5 to M 1.8 at central.

3. The Civil Service Rifles will form the vanguard and will be preceded by the 19th Hussars.

4. The Civil Service Rifles will form up in the MAIDVAIN Road at 07.30 and will advance by Companies at 100 distance in the order D.B.C.A.H.Q. Co. Scouts, Messengers & M[illegible]

5. After the first halt the advance will be by Co[mpanies] platoons at 70x distance and each Co. will have [illegible] its L.G. limber with the leading platoon.

6. The advance will be along the road through G. 27 a.4, G.28 c.2, G.29 G 19 central, G.20 central, G.36 a.6 and H 31 a.4.

7. RSM will distribute bombs equally among Limbers except Smoke bombs and S.O.S. grenades will all go to D. Co.

8. Each Company will detail 2 scouts to 2/Lieut SMALL at Battalion HQ at 06.45 together with 3 Signallers will go in advance of the Battalion and keep touch with the Cavalry screen.

9. Transport (except cookers, L.G. limbers, Mess carts, medical cart) will move (under orders of B.T.O.) in order of march passing starting point (Bois Le Sens cross roads) at 09.30.

No. 1 File
2 War Diary
3 C.O.
4/7 H/D Coy.
8 Scout Officer
9 T.O. - Q.M.
10 M.O.
11 RSM & Sig. Sgt
12 140 Inf Brigade.

Davenport

Captain & Adjutant
1/ Civil Service Rifles

SECRET

1/Civil Service Rifles
Order No 172

Copy No 8

11th November 1918

Ref Sheet 37 1/40000

1. Order No 171 is cancelled and the Bn will march to billets in LA TOMBE today and will pass starting point (cross roads K29 c 9 5) at 10.40. Route will be reverse of yesterdays march

2. Usual billeting parties will leave Orderly Room by cycle at 09.00. 2/Lt H E J CHARTER will be in charge and will report to Staff Capt at Church O 11 central at 12.00

3. Transport Officer will collect blankets and Bandsmen's packs, L G limbers and cookers from Coys at 09.00. Coy mess boxes will be carried on these L G limbers

4. Bn will form up in column of route with head of column outside HQ Coy billet facing W. ready to move at 10.20. Order of march HQ, Band, B, C, D, A, Transport and QM Staff. Head of C Coy may remain at road junction K 26 a 55 65 and C and A Coys will then take their places in the column as it passes

5. Dress full marching order. S.D. Caps may be worn

6. A Coy will detail 2 parties of 1 Offr + 20 OR each to fill in 2 road craters between DIRE and LA TOMBE. They will carry tools and will report to an officer of 517 Field Coy RE who will be marching behind the Bn.

Distribution

Copy No 1 File
2 War Diary
3 CO
4/7 A/D Coys
8 Senl Offr
9 TO + QM
10 MO
11 RSM Clrk
12 140th Inf Bde
13 Band

Davenport

Capt + Adjt
1 Civil Service Rifles

PA 8 14/11

**1/ CIVIL SERVICE RIFLES.** Copy No. 3

**ORDER NO. 173.** 12th November, 1918.

Reference Map: 57 1/40,000

1. The Battalion will march to the area R.31.d (PIPAIX) tomorrow.

2. Billeting party consisting of each Coy. Q.M.S. and one N.C.O. for Transport and Q.M.'s Staff will leave at 06.30 under Lt. W.E.HOSTE, M.C. Cycles will be drawn from the runners' billet. These must be cleaned and returned to Sgt. LEHAN tomorrow night.

3. Reveille will be at 07.00, breakfast at 07.30, Sick Parade at 08.00. Dinners will be cooked on the march.

4. The Battalion will parade in column of route in the road outside the Convent, facing South, ready to move off at 08.55. Order of march will be H.Q. Coy., Band, C., D., A., B., Transport and Q.M.Staff. Head of column will be outside Orderly Room.

5. Dress - Full marching order. S.D. caps will be worn. No jerkins will be worn on the march.

6. Transport Officer will collect valises and mess boxes from Coy. H.Q. starting with C. Coy. at 07.45. Blankets will be delivered to Q.M. Stores at 08.00

Davenport

Capt. & Adjutant,
1/CIVIL SERVICE RIFLES.

Distribution:-
Copy No. 1 File.
2 War Diary.
3 C.O.
4 A. Coy.
5 B. "
6 C. "
7 D. "
8 H.Q.Coy. & Sigs.
9 Scout Officer.
10 M.O.
11 T.O. & Q.M.
12 140th Inf. Bde.

1/[illegible] SERVICE [illegible]

2

Order No.174. 17th November, 1918.

Reference Map:- 57, 1/40,000

1. The Battalion will leave [illegible] the [illegible] the night at the Convent, [illegible], [illegible] their former billets there.

2. [illegible] billeting N.C.Os. under [illegible], will leave the Orderly Room at 07.00. Bicycles will not be taken.

3. Transport Officer will collect blankets, officers' valises and mess boxes from Coys., starting with [illegible] at 08.00.

4. [illegible] now in possession of [illegible], must be returned to the [illegible] present.

5. The Battalion will parade in full marching order ready to move at 09.00. Head of column will be outside [illegible]. Order of march will be H.Q.Coy., [illegible], [illegible], Transport and Q.M. Stores.

6. All billets will be inspected by [illegible] before leaving and a certificate to the effect that they have been left clean will be handed in on parade.

Davenport

[illegible] & Adjutant,
1/[illegible] SERVICE [illegible].

Distribution:-
Copy No. 1 File
2 War Diary.
3 C.O.
4 O/C. [illegible] Coy.
5 " [illegible] "
6 " C. "
7 " D. "
8 [illegible]
9 [illegible]
10 [illegible]
11 T.O. & Q.M.
12 140th Infantry Brigade.

1/Civil Service Rifles

Order No 175

2

18th November, 1918

Reference: [illegible] Sheet 37 1/40,000

The Battalion will march tomorrow to WILLEMS.

Billeting parties under Capt R.W. FORD will leave [illegible] at [illegible] and will report to the Area Commandant, WILLEMS at 10:00. They will take with them the proper billet [illegible]. Bicycles will not be taken.

[illegible] in bundles of ten will be delivered [illegible] Q.M. by Coys. at 0?00. The Transport Officer will [illegible] valises and mess boxes from Coys, starting with D Coy at [illegible].

The Battalion will parade in column of route [illegible] ready to move at 09:00. Head of column will be outside Orderly Room. Order of march:- HQ, Band, A, B, C, D.

Route will be:- MALAKOFF CABARET, Pontoon Bridge at O.10.c.[illegible], FROYENNES, BLANDAIN, WILLEMS.

Coy Commanders will inspect their billets before [illegible] and hand in usual certificates on parade.

[illegible signature]

Capt. & Adjt.
1/Civil Service Rifles.

Distribution:-

Copy No. 1 File
2 War Diary
3 C.O.
4/7 A, B, C, D Coys
8 Scout Offr.
9 [illegible] & R.S.M. [illegible]
10 M.O.
11 T.O. & Q.M.
12 140th Inf. Bde.

Copy No. 2

## 1st CIVIL SERVICE RIFLES.

**Order No. 176.** 25th November, 1918.

Refce. Maps: 37 1/40,000 and HAZEBROUCK 5.A.

1. The Battalion will march to HAUBOURDIN tomorrow and will parade in the main road outside the Orderly Room in column of route ready to move at 08.00. Order of march will be H.Q., Band, B, C, D, A, Transport and Q.M. Staff. Head of column will be at cross-roads M.11.c.7.7 facing S.W. Dress: Fighting Order; S.D. caps will be worn, steel helmets carried on the haversacks.

2. The following minimum distances will be observed on the march:-
   Between Coys ......................100 yards.
   Between A. Coy. and Transport....100 yards.

3. Packs of A. Coy. and the Band will be taken to the Transport Lines by 07.00 and will be carried on limbers. Packs of H.Q., B, C, and D Coys., all blankets and valises, and heavy mess boxes will be stacked at the various Coy. H.Q., where they will be collected by the Q.M. They must be ready for collection by 07.30. Light mess boxes for lunch must be delivered to the Q.M. Stores at the same time.

4. Dinners will be cooked on the march so as to be ready by 12.50.

5. Three lorries will be available for the Q.M.. One will be sent direct to FREFAY and the Q.M. will arrange for this lorry to rejoin the Battalion at HAUBOURDIN on the morning of the 27th at 08.00.

6. Coy. Commanders will personally inspect their billets before leaving and will furnish the usual certificates that they have been left clean when the Battalion moves off.

Davenport
Capt. and Adjutant,
1st CIVIL SERVICE RIFLES.

Distribution:-

Copy No. 1 File.
2 War Diary.
3 C.O.
4 O/C. A. Coy.
5 " B. "
6 " C. "
7 " D. "
8 Intelligence Offr.
9 M.O.
10 T.O. & Q.M.
11 R.S.M.
12 140th Infantry Brigade.

Copy No. 2

# 1st CIVIL SERVICE RIFLES.

## ORDER NO. 177 26th November, 1918

Reference Map:- HAZEBROUCK 5A.

1 The Battalion will march to BETHUNE tomorrow and will parade in column of route in the RUE SADI ready to move at 09.00. Order of march will be H.Q., C, D, A, B and Transport. Cookers will march behind their Coys. Usual distances will be maintained between Coys. Head of column will be outside Orderly Room (No. 182). Dress:- Fighting Order. Route will be via main FOURNES-BETHUNE Road. The Battalion will halt from 12.30 to 14.00 for dinners.

2 Packs and blankets will be delivered to the Q.M. Stores at 08.00. Valises and heavy mess boxes will be dumped at Coy. H.Q. ready for collection by Q.M. at the same time. Light mess boxes for lunch will be carried on Coy cookers.

3 Billeting returns will reach Orderly Room by 1700 today.

4 Coy Commanders will inspect billets before leaving and will furnish the usual certificates on parade.

Davenport

Capt & Adjt
1st Civil Service Rifles

Distribution:-

Copy No. 1 File
2 War Diary
3 C.O.
4 A Coy
5 B "
6 C "
7 D "
8 Int. Off.
9 M.O.
10 TO & Q.M.
11 R.S.M.
12 140th Infy Bde.

320

1st CIVIL SERVICE RIFLES. Copy No. 2

ORDER No. 178

27th November 1918

Reference Map :- HAZEBROUCK 5A.

1. Battalion will march to FERFAY tomorrow and will parade on the road outside the Factory in column of route ready to move at 09.40. Head of column will be outside Bn. H.Q. Mess

2. Order of march will be H.Q., D.A.B.C., T.O. & Q.M. Staff. Coy. Cookers will be behind their Coys and usual distances will be maintained. Light Mess boxes will be carried on cookers

3. Route will be via CHOCQUES – MARLES-LES-MINES. Battalion will halt for dinners from 12.50 to 14.00

4. Battalion Guard will march in rear of Transport and will collect any stragglers who will report to M.O. at FERFAY at 18.30.

5. Reveille will be at 07.00, Breakfast 07.30 Sick Parade 0800

6. Blankets and packs will be delivered to Q.M. at 0800. Valises and heavy mess boxes will be dumped at Coy. H.Q. ready for collection by Q.M. at 08.30. G.S. Wagons and Q.M. Staff will parade with Transport Section.

7. Coy. Commanders will inspect billets before leaving and will furnish the usual certificates on parade.

Davenport

Capt & Adjt,
1/Civil Service Rifles

Distribution :-

Copy No. 1 File
2 War Diary
3 C.O.
4 O/C A Coy
5 " B "
6 " C "
7 " D "
8 Int. Off.
9 M.O. ~~[illegible]~~
10 T.O. & Q.M.
11 R.S.M.
12 140th Inf. Bde.

CONFIDENTIAL.

War Diary

of

1/15th Battalion, London Regiment (P.W.O. CIVIL SERVICE RIFLES.)

from 1/12/18 to 31/12/18.

---

Instructions regarding War Diaries and Intelligence Summaries are contained in F. S. Regs., Part II. and the Staff Manual respectively. Title pages will be prepared in manuscript.

# WAR DIARY
or
# INTELLIGENCE SUMMARY.
(Erase heading not required.)

Army Form C. 2118.

| Place | Date | Hour | Summary of Events and Information | Remarks and references to Appendices |
|---|---|---|---|---|
| FERFAY | 1/12/18. | | Church Parade in the Theatre at 10·30. Services for Nonconformists in the Chateau Chapel at 10·15. Mass for Roman Catholics in parish Church at . Draft of 121 O.R joined the Bn from the Base. | |
| | 2/12/18 | | Coys at work clearing Chateau grounds & improving billets. | |
| | 3/12/18 | | Coys at work clearing & improving billets. Baths for all Coys. | |
| | 4/12/18 | | Coys at disposal of Coy Commanders for drill & work on billets & billet area. B Coy clearing Chateau grounds. Baths were allotted to all Coys. Rugby match between right & left half Bn. Educational training started under Lt WENHAM. CAPT. GOSNEY takes over duties of LT. A. KNOX (PARIS leave) | |
| | 5/12/18 | | After C.O.s inspection Coys carried out training under the supervision of Coy Commanders. LT H.A.BERRY and 2nd LT H.E.BROOKS joined the Bn from the Base. Educational training carried out in the theatre. In the afternoon the Bn beat the 5th Field Ambulance by 8 goals to 3. Baths allotted to all Coys. | |
| | 6/12/18 | | After C.Os inspection Coys carried out training under supervision of Coy Commanders. Educational training — Shorthand, Book-keeping, & Electricity – carried out in the theatre at 10·45. Baths allotted to all Coys. | |
| | 7/12/18 | | Same as on 6/12/18. Football:- depot drew with C Coy 2-2. | |

D. D. & L., London, E.C.
(A10266) Wt W5300/P713 750,000 2/18 Sch. 52 Forms/C2118/16.

Instructions regarding War Diaries and Intelligence Summaries are contained in F. S. Regs., Part II. and the Staff Manual respectively. Title pages will be prepared in manuscript.

# WAR DIARY
*or*
~~INTELLIGENCE SUMMARY.~~
*(Erase heading not required.)*

Army Form C. 2118.

| Place | Date | Hour | Summary of Events and Information | Remarks and references to Appendices |
|---|---|---|---|---|
| FERFAY | 8/12/18. | | Church Parade in the theatre at 10.00. Service for Nonconformists in the church in the Chateau grounds. Mass for Roman Catholics in parish church. Evening service in the church in the chateau grounds at 18·00 followed by Holy Communion. Football:- The Bn beat the 21st Bn by 6 pts - 3 (Rugby). Band Concert in the theatre at 18·00 | PMH |
| | 9/12/18 | | After the Commanding Officer's inspection the Bn went for a route march of about 7 miles. Educational training carried on in the theatre and chateau under the supervision of LT WENHAM. Football:- Depot beat with H.Q. Coy 5 - 1. | PMH |
| | 10/12/18 | | After the Commanding Officer's inspection Coys were at the disposal of Coy Commanders. Educational training carried on as on previous day. Band Concert in the theatre at 8·00. | PMH |
| | 11/12/18 | | Bn parade cancelled owing to bad weather. Coys at the disposal of Coy Commanders. Educational training as before. Football:- D Coy drew with B. Coy. 5 - 5. Band concert in the Divisional Recreation Room. | PMH |
| | 12/12/18 | | Bn parade cancelled owing to bad weather. Educational training as before. Football:- The Bn beat the 517 Field Coy R.Es by 8 goals to 0. Bn Orchestra played at Bde H.Q. at 20·00 | PMH |
| | 13/12/18 | | After the Commanding Officer's inspection Coys carried out training till 10.30. Educational training as before. The Band gave a concert in the theatre at 18·00 | PMH |

D. D. & L., London, E.C.
(A10266) Wt W5300/P713 750,000 2/18 Sch. 52 Forms/C2118/16.

Instructions regarding War Diaries and Intelligence Summaries are contained in F. S. Regs., Part II. and the Staff Manual respectively. Title pages will be prepared in manuscript.

# WAR DIARY
*or*
~~INTELLIGENCE~~ SUMMARY.
*(Erase heading not required.)*

Army Form C. 2118.

| Place | Date | Hour | Summary of Events and Information | Remarks and references to Appendices |
|---|---|---|---|---|
| FERFAY | 14/12/18 | | After the Commanding Officers inspection Educational training was carried out as usual. 17 officers and 100 O.R. of the 2nd Bn came over from BOESEGHEM. In the afternoon the 1st Bn beat the 2nd Bn. by 4-3. A concert was given in the theatre at 18.00. The 2nd Bn returned at 21.15. | MH |
| | 15/12/18 | | Church parade in the theatre at 10.00. Services for Nonconformists in the church in the Chateau grounds and for Roman Catholics in the parish church. Voluntary services in the Chateau church at 18.00. Holy Communion at 08.00 & 18.30. Football:- Bde Cup Competition, C Coy beat A Coy 7-1, 21st Bn C Coy beat 15th Bn B Coy 3-2 after extra time. Band concert in the theatre at 19.00. Lt. A. WILSON M.C. rejoined the Bn. | MH |
| | 16/12/18 | | Bn Officers Mess commenced at the Chateau. After the Commanding Officers Inspection, Education training was carried out as usual. Football:- Bde Cup Competition, 21st Bn H.Q. beat 15th Bn D Coy 2-1. | MH |
| | 17/12/18 | | After the Commanding Officers Inspection Educational training was carried out as usual. Football:- Bde Cup Competition 15th Depot beat 17th Bn C Coy by 8-0. Bn Orchestra played at Bde H.Q at 20.00. | MH |
| | 18/12/18 | | Bn Parade cancelled owing to bad weather. Educational training carried out as usual. 9 officers & 80 O.R. attended a lecture at 11.30 at AUCHEL. Football:- The Bn beat the 1/17th London 12 goals to 0. | MH |

D. D. & L., London, E.C.
(A10266) Wt W5300/P713 750,000 2/18 Sch. 52 Forms/C2118/16.

Army Form C. 2118.

# WAR DIARY
*or*
# ~~INTELLIGENCE SUMMARY.~~

*(Erase heading not required.)*

Instructions regarding War Diaries and Intelligence Summaries are contained in F. S. Regs., Part II. and the Staff Manual respectively. Title pages will be prepared in manuscript.

| Place | Date | Hour | Summary of Events and Information | Remarks and references to Appendices |
|---|---|---|---|---|
| FERFAY. | 19/12/18 | | After the Commanding Officers Inspection Educational training was carried out as usual. Football:- Bde Cup Competition:- 1st H.Q. Coy beat 21st D Coy by 3-1. | MS |
| | 20/12/18 | | Route march by Coys from 09.30 to 10.30, after which Educational training was carried out as usual. Football:- Rugby, The Bn beat 148 Squadron R.A.F. by 21 pts to 5. | MS |
| | 21/12/18 | | Bn route march from 09.30 to 10.30 after which Educational training was carried out. Football:- The Bn beat the 1/18 London by 3-0. | MS |
| | 22/12/18 | | Church Services the same as last Sunday. Football:- The Bn beat the 151 Squadron R.A.F. by 4-0. Band concert in the theatre at 19.00. | MS |
| | 23/12/18 | | Route march from 09.30 to 10.30 after which Educational training was carried out as usual. | MS |
| | 24/12/18 | | Route march from 09.30 to 10.30. Football:- Bn Platoon Competition, H.Q. 'A' team beat No 9 Platoon 3-1. No 5 Platoon beat No 10 Platoon - . Bn Concert in the theatre at 18.00 | MS |
| | 25/12/18 | | Parade Services:- C of E. in the Theatre at 11.30. Roman Catholics in the Parish Church at 11.15. Noncomformists in the Protestant Church AUCHEL at 10.45. Football:- Bn Platoon Competition:- Depot A team beat 3 Pln. 3-0. | MS |

D. D. & L., London, E.C.
(A10266) Wt.W5300/P713 750,000 2/18 Sch. 52 Forms/C2118/16.

Instructions regarding War Diaries and Intelligence Summaries are contained in F. S. Regs., Part II. and the Staff Manual respectively. Title pages will be prepared in manuscript.

# WAR DIARY
*or*
# INTELLIGENCE ~~SUMMARY~~.
*(Erase heading not required.)*

Army Form C. 2118.

| Place | Date | Hour | Summary of Events and Information | Remarks and references to Appendices |
|---|---|---|---|---|
| FERFAY | 26/11/18 | | A holiday for all ranks. Football:- The Bn beat the 4th Royal Welsh Fusiliers 13-0. | MS |
| | 27/11/18 | | Route march cancelled owing to bad weather. Educational training as usual. | MS |
| | 28/11/18 | | Route march cancelled owing to bad weather. Educational training as usual. | MS |
| | 29/11/18 | | Church Parade in the theatre at 09·30. Service for Nonconformists in the Church in the Chateau grounds at 11·15 and for Roman Catholics in the parish church at 11·15 Voluntary services:- Holy Communion at 0800 and after Evening Service at 18·00. Band concert in the theatre from 19·00 to 20·30. | MS |
| | 30/11/18 | | Route march from 09·30 to 10·30. Educational training as usual. Football:- Bde Cup Competition:- 21st Bn B Coy beat 15th Bn H.Q. Coy by 1-0 after extra time. | MS |
| | 31/11/18 | | Bn parade cancelled owing to bad weather. Coys at disposal of Coy Commanders. ~~Football~~ Educational training as usual. | MS |

D. Jones
Major.

D. D. & L., London, E.C.
(A10266) Wt W5300/P713 750,000 2/18 Sch. 52 Forms/C2118/16.

47



Army Form C. 2118.

Instructions regarding War Diaries and Intelligence Summaries are contained in F. S. Regs., Part II. and the Staff Manual respectively. Title pages will be prepared in manuscript.

# WAR DIARY

~~or~~

## ~~INTELLIGENCE SUMMARY.~~

*(Erase heading not required.)*

Vol 43

| Place | Date | Hour | Summary of Events and Information | Remarks and references to Appendices |
|---|---|---|---|---|
| FERFAY Pas-de-Calais. | 31/1/19. | | During the whole of January, the Battalion has been billetted at FERFAY and programmes of training in drills and education have been carried out. | |

[illegible signature]





D. D. & L., London, E.C.
(A10216) W1 W5300/P713 750,000 2/18 Sch. 52 Forms/C2118/16

1/15 London R.

44

Army Form C. 2118.

Instructions regarding War Diaries and Intelligence Summaries are contained in F. S. Regs., Part II. and the Staff Manual respectively. Title pages will be prepared in manuscript.

# WAR DIARY

~~or~~

~~INTELLIGENCE SUMMARY.~~

(*Erase heading not required.*)

| Place | Date | Hour | Summary of Events and Information | Remarks and references to Appendices |
|---|---|---|---|---|
| Ferfay. Pas-de-Calais. | 28/2/19. | | Five Officers and 123 Other Ranks left Battalion on 4th February to join the 2/15th Battalion for service with the Armies of Occupation.<br>The Battalion was further reduced by a large number being demobilised.<br>The Cadres of the 1/14th and 1/21st Battalions concentrated at Ferfay on the 18th and 19th respectively and Headquarters of the three Batt's. were established in the Chateau.<br>A scheme of drills and recreational training carried out during the month. | |

Lt.-Colonel,
Cdg. 1st Civil Service Rifles.

D. D. & L., London, E.C.
(A10266) Wt W5300/P713 750,000 2/18 Sch. 52 Forms/C2118/16.

Instructions regarding War Diaries and Intelligence Summaries are contained in F. S. Regs., Part II. and the Staff Manual respectively. Title pages will be prepared in manuscript.

# WAR DIARY 1/15th Bn. London Regt.

or

~~INTELLIGENCE SUMMARY.~~

(Erase heading not required.)

Army Form C. 2118.

45

| Place | Date | Hour | Summary of Events and Information | Remarks and references to Appendices |
|---|---|---|---|---|
| Ferfay, Pas-de-Calais. | 31/3/19 | | During ~~the month~~ the whole of March the Battalion has been billetted at Ferfay and programmes of drills and recreational training have been carried out.<br>Brigadier-General H. B. P. L. Kennedy, C. M. G., D. S. O., said farewell to the Brigade at the final performance of the Divisional "Follies" on Friday evening, 21st.<br>Major-General Sir G. F. Gorringe, K. C. B., K. C. M. G., D. S. O., said farewell to the Brigade on Friday afternoon, 28th.<br>Brigade Headquarters moved to Ferfay on Wednesday, 26th, making the concentration of the 140th Infantry Brigade Group of Cadres at Ferfay complete.<br>Brigadier-General W. F. Mildren, C. B., C. M. G., D. S. O., assumed command of the "47th Brigade Group of Cadres" as from 12.00 hours 24th.<br>Lieutenant-Colonel H. S. Kaye, D. S. O., M. C. (14th Battalion) assumed command of the "140th Brigade Group of Cadres" as from 12.00 hours, 28th.<br>All remaining animals on charge to the Battalion were disposed of during the month. | |

[signature]

Lt. Colonel,
Cdg. 1/15th Battn. London Regt
(P. W. O. Civil Service Rifles.)

Instructions regarding War Diaries and Intelligence Summaries are contained in F. S. Regs., Part II. and the Staff Manual respectively. Title pages will be prepared in manuscript.

Army Form C. 2118.

# WAR DIARY
*or*
~~INTELLIGENCE SUMMARY.~~

*(Erase heading not required.)*

| Place | Date | Hour | Summary of Events and Information | Remarks and references to Appendices |
|---|---|---|---|---|
| PERFAY. | 1919 May 5 | | The Cadre of Battalion entrained at PERNES at 1800 hours and proceeded to HAVRE, arriving at HAVRE at hours on . | |
| | | | Embarked for SOUTHAMPTON. | |
| | | | Left SOUTHAMPTON for FELIXSTOWE. | |

Lt-Colonel,
Cdg., 1st CIVIL SERVICE RIFLES.

D. D. & L., London, E.C. (A10276) Wt W5300/P713 750,000 2/18 Sch. 52 Forms/C2118/16.

www.ingramcontent.com/pod-product-compliance
Lightning Source LLC
Chambersburg PA
CBHW080817010526
44111CB00015B/2571
* 9 7 8 1 4 7 4 5 2 6 3 1 9 *